JOHNSON & REICHARD

P. O. Box 5277
Portland, Oregon 97208-5277

First Printing
ISBN 1-55828-029-4

Printed in the United States of America

Trademarks

AIX and PS/2 are registered trademarks of IBM
A/UX is a trademark of Apple Computer, Inc.
Amiga and AmigaDOS are trademarks of Commodore Business Machines, Inc.
Aviion is a trademark of Data General, Inc.
Cray Y-MP is a trademark of Cray Research, Inc.
DECnet and VMS are trademarks of Digital Equipment Corporation
Esix is a trademark of Everex
Gumby is a registered trademark of Lakeside Games, Inc.
HP-UX is a trademark of Hewlett-Packard, Inc.
Macintosh is a registered trademark of McIntosh Laboratory, licensed to Apple Computer, Inc.
Motif is a trademark of the Open Software Foundation
Open Desktop and SCO Xenix are trademarks of the Santa Cruz Operation, Inc.
Open Look and Unix are trademarks of AT&T
Postscript is a registered trademark of Adobe Systems, Inc.
SPARCstation, SunOS, 386i, and NeWS are registered trademarks of Sun Microsystems, Inc.
386/ix is a trademark of Interactive Systems, Inc.
The X Window System is a registered trademark of the Massachussetts Institute of Technology

Acknowledgments

This book is dedicated to all those who insist on promulgating that terrible acronym GUI (for Graphical User Interface). Not only do acronyms like this inhibit communication, but whenever we see GUI, all we can think about is the old Fig Newtons ad that went: Oooey GUI Rich and Chewy.

This book, like our previous X Window Applications Programming, is dedicated at shedding some light on how to program the very excellent X Window System. We've had a lot of fun with X and hope this book helps you to as well.

So eat a Fig Newton and turn the page already.

Contents

Introduction

This is a sequel to our first book, *X Window Applications Programming,* which covered the basics of the X Window System.

This book goes a step beyond the basics and focuses on some issues that can prove troublesome for even the most advanced X programmer—selections and the infamous ICCCM. This stuff isn't simple, but it must be mastered for sophisticated X library (Xlib) programming.

This book reflects our basic attitude toward programming: when teaching, it's best to use as many examples as possible. We don't expect you to program in exactly the same manner we do, but by using scads of examples we can show you what works well in our experience. We tried to test these programs on many different machines and architectures—including CISC and RISC machines, and monochrome and color monitors—using X Releases 2, 3, and 4. The primary development was completed using an Apple Macintosh IIx running A/UX 1 .1 beta 3 (Apple X11 R2 mono), and a Sun SPARCStation-1 running SunOS 4.0.3c (MIT X11 R3, R4 8-bit color). Further testing was completed on a Sun SPARCStation-1 running SunOS 4.0.3c (Sun OpenWindows 1.0, X11/NeWS 8-bit color), a Hewlett-Packard 9000/370 running HP -UX 6.5 (HP X11 R2 8-bit color), a Sun 386i running SunOS 4.0.1 (MIT X11 R3 8-bit color), and a 386 AT clone running Interactive 386 /ix (ISC X11 R3 4-bit color).

This is not a reference book covering every aspect of X. There are other sources for that—notably the Digital Press and O'Reilly books—that serve as fine references. Instead, we focus on creating professional-quality applications using Xlib. This means slogging through the basics of Xlib and attempting to grasp the complexity of the X Window System.

Make no doubt about it: X is an extremely complex system. Much of that complexity comes because X must deal with a wide assortment of hardware and software configurations—virtually every type of computer graphics display available. There are X implementations running on everything from a PC, Macintosh, and Amiga to a Cray supercomputer, and everything in between.

X serves as an elegant and powerful link between these disparate systems, serving as a common interface across many different computers running a number of operating systems (DOS, AmigaDOS, Unix, and VMS) with a number of different displays. Cray supercomputers can display output on an Apollo workstation or an Amiga. Almost every major computer vendor—including Apple, Xerox, IBM, Hewlett-Packard, Sun—offers and promotes X products.

THE HISTORY OF X

In 1984, Massachusetts Institute of Technology (MIT) officials were faced with a problem common to the business and academic computing worlds: they were the proud owners of a motley set of incompatible workstations acquired through donation and purchase. The goal was to build a network of graphical workstations that could be used as teaching aids. Faced with a crazy quilt of operating systems and hardware vendors, MIT officials decided to form Project Athena, an MIT development team working in association with DEC and IBM.

Project Athena's solution was to design a network-based windowing system that was roughly based on a Stanford University software environment called W. This system could run local applications while being able to call on remote sources. By linking these workstations together through a graphical networking environment, the designers created the first operating environment that was truly hardware and vendor independent: the X Window System.

As Jim Gettys, Robert Scheifler, and Ron Newman wrote in their book *X Window Systems: C Library and Protocol Reference* (Digital Press, 1988), the development team had the following goals:

- Do not add new functionality unless an implementation cannot complete a real application without it.
- It is as important to decide what a system is not as to decide what it is. Do not serve all the world's needs, but make the system extensible so that additional needs can be met in an upwardly compatible fashion.
- If a problem is not completely understood, it is probably best to provide no solution at all.

- If you get 90 percent of the desired effect for 10 percent of the work required to get 100 percent, use the simpler solution.
- Isolate complexity as much as possible.
- Provide mechanism rather than policy. In particular, place user-interface policy in the client's hands.

Of these guidelines, the "mechanism not policy" credo is the most important when discussing X. It's a theory that we'll refer to frequently in the course of this book.

The X Window System was a success. By 1986, the outside world was clamoring for access. In March 1988, MIT released Version 11, Release 2. Later that year Release 3 was introduced. In January 1990 Release 4 was unleashed on the world. Because many vendors still support Releases 2 and 3, we've tried to make the code as portable as possible.

WHY X?

There are several reasons why X has gained momentum in the workplace. For starters, it's an open environment; MIT holds the rights to X, but gives it away. Thus, the X developer isn't tied to a single developer (like Microsoft/IBM and DOS), and companies who release X products aren't beholden to the whims of a single corporation.

Also, the X Window System is a graphical windowing system at a time when the computer industry is besotted with graphical user interfaces (or GUIs, a term that does not trip lightly across our tongues). Studies clearly indicate that graphical interfaces make computing easier.

X has also piggybacked on the growing interest in Unix. While the X Window System wasn't designed specifically for Unix, it has seen its greatest acceptance as a windowing system for the unfriendly (at least perceived as such) Unix. There are other Unix windowing systems, such as NeWS from Sun and the Next interface, but these require licensing fees. Since the computing world often votes with pocketbooks, it's easy to see why X is the most popular of the three.

In an era where linking types of all computers is a paramount concern for software designers, broad-based acceptance for a windowing system is of paramount importance for cross-vendor development. With X, by separating the window manager and the window server (covered later in this introduction), it's possible to link disparate makes of hardware without costly emulation cards and exotic networking schemes. Because the user interface is only making X calls, there's no reliance on any one operating system.

Also, X provides a number of neat features, including:

Portability

X runs on just about every computer. You will find X on PCs, Macintoshes, Hewlett-Packards, PS/2s, Suns, Data Generals, DECs, Amigas, Crays and most everything else. Barring a few minor differences, the C language interface is the same across all these platforms. This is a major benefit of X over most other graphics systems.

Network Transparency

An X program, if written correctly, can run on one machine and display its output on another machine. X, by being operating-system independent, encourages the portability of software. The standard X C library routines are the same on every machine running X, which means your interface code ports directly from one machine to the other.

Backing from Major Computer Vendors

X runs on just about every Unix workstation available today. Digital Equipment, Hewlett-Packard, IBM, and Apple all offer their own versions of X. Other vendors offer the generic X from MIT with their workstations, such as Data General's slick Aviion series. Others have offered merged X servers by combining X with proprietary windowing systems (for example, Sun Microsystems has merged with NeWS) and offer merged X servers.

Inexpensive Licensing

You can get the X sources (written in C) for free. If you cannot find X on your own, you can order X, usually for the price of a tape and a small handling fee, from one of the vendors listed in the appendices. You do not need to pay licensing fees if you release X -based applications.

Shared Resources

The X Window System allows devices such as mice, keyboards, and graphics displays to be shared by several programs at the same time. Actually, as far as X is concerned, your entire workstation is a display, consisting of a keyboard, a pointing device (usually a mouse) and one or more monitor screens. Multiple screens can work together, linked by the keyboard and the pointing device.

WHAT IS X?

As mentioned before, X is an operating system and vendor-independent graphical networking windowing system and environment. That's a mouthful; to discuss it, we'll break up X into logical parts.

A Client/Server Axis

The X Window System divides computing into two parts, based on a client/server relationship. The display server is the program that controls and draws all output to the display monitors, tracks client input, and updates windows accordingly. A Client is an application program that performs a specific task. (Throughout this book, we use "client" and "application" interchangeably.) Because X is a networked environment, unlike most systems the client and server don't necessarily compute on the same system (although they certainly can and do in a number of situations). Instead, X allows distributed processing. For example, a Macintosh running A/UX as an X server can call upon the processing power of a Cray supercomputer within the network, displaying the results of the Cray's computations on the Mac's monitor.

This isn't the only time that X deviates from accepted computer-science terminology. In the micro and mini worlds, a server is the hardware device running at the center of a network, distributing data and processing power to networked workstations and terminals. With X, a server is a local software program that controls the display hardware. Because other systems on the network have access to your display, the X server cannot be thought of the same way file servers are viewed in local-area networks (LANs).

In X, a display is a keyboard, pointing device (usually a mouse), and one or more screens. The display server tracks multiple input, allows users to run several clients (such as a database manager, word processor and graphics application). A display can power multiple screens linked by a keyboard and mouse.

The server acts as a traffic cop between programs (called clients or applications) running on local or remote systems and the power of the local system. The server:

- allows access to a display by a client;
- sends network messages;
- intercepts other network messages from other clients;
- performs two-dimensional drawing, freeing the client from processing-intensive graphics;
- tracks resources (such as windows, cursors, fonts and graphics contexts) that are shared between clients;
- allows distributed processing, as mentioned above;
- allows multitasking, if X is used in conjunction with a multitasking operating system (such as Unix).

Most importantly, the server tracks input from the display and informs the clients. In X, such inputs are called events. When you press down on a key, that's a event; when you let it back up, that's another event. Similarly, moving a cursor with a mouse is an event. These events are delivered to applications through an event queue.

THE SUM OF ITS PARTS

The generic X Window System as shipped by MIT consists of the Xlib graphics subroutine library, the X network protocol, an X toolkit and several window managers (such as `uwm`). The application programmer links the client program though Xlib.

Xlib contains about 300 routines that map to X Protocol requests or provide utility functions. Xlib converts C language function calls to the X protocol request that actually implements the given function, such as `XDrawLine()` to draw a line. These functions include creating, destroying, moving, and sizing windows; drawing lines and polygons; setting background patterns; and tracking the mouse. Xlib allows you to access windows in a variety of ways, including overlapping and simultaneous output to multiple windows. It supports multiple fonts, raster operations, line drawing, and both color and monochrome applications.

X toolkits are program subroutines that can make programming easier. They are prewritten graphics routines; you can put together different parts to form a program. Toolkits are under constant revision from different vendors. We purposely avoid toolkits here (there simply isn't enough space in one book to cover Xlib and any of the many toolkits. In addition, aside from the Xt Intrinsics, most toolkits are tied to specific vendors, such as the Open Software Foundation's Motif. In any case, even if you try to program exclusively with toolkits, you'll find that you really need a firm grounding in the Xlib to write serious X applications to do something the toolkit wasn't meant to do.

The X network protocol defines data structures used to transmit requests between clients and servers. Technically speaking, instead of being based on procedure calls or a kernel-call interface, the X network protocol is an asynchronous stream-based interprocess communication.

The protocol specification is supplied by the X Consortium on tape (see appendix B) and defined in *X Window System Protocol, Version 11,* by Robert Scheifler, which is contained as part of the distribution tape. It can be found on Unix systems under TOP-LEVEL/mit/doc/Protocol/spec (where TOP-LEVEL is the base of your X directory tree).

THIS BOOK'S APPROACH TO X

This book is divided into 22 chapters. The first nine chapters serve as an introduction to X programming; they review concepts first introduced in our previous book, *X Window Applications Programming*. The second section jumps into the meat of advanced programming, as we cover information gleaned from the X server and how to interact with more advanced areas of X. Section 3 travels into one of the most difficult areas of X: making X applications communicate with each other. Application interoperability is a big, hot issue, and X provides many features to help make your programs talk to one another. Section IV covers the programs that connect to multiple X servers and the issues you face when communicating this way. If you stay within the boundaries of good manners, you'll be rewarded with well-behaved programs and won't face fatal X errors. Section V covers the latest release of X from the MIT X Consortium, Release 4. Even though Release 4 is the most professional X release to date, it will probably take a year before most vendors have migrated to R4.

TYPOGRAPHICAL CONVENTIONS

In this book, the following typographical conventions have been used:

C program code references (such as function names and file names) within a text paragraph will appear in a Courier 11-point typeface, as in the following:

`XSendEvent()` sends an event packet to the given `send_to_window`. It is up to you to choose the event type and fill in the `XEvent` structure.

Actual program examples and listings will appear in the following 9-point Courier typeface:

```
/*
* gumby.c
*
* Sets the Root window cursor to a gumby
* shape--what fun.
*
*/
```

After reading this book, you should be able to create much more efficient programs than the code examples we've provided. We've concentrated on designing programs that help explain the text, rather than creating the most efficient code possible. Above all else, have fun. We've thoroughly enjoyed using X for a number of years and hope you have as much fun as we do.

Section I

Introducing X

Section I introduces the X Window System from a moderate-to-advanced C programmer's point of view. This section quickly covers the basics of X11 and its C language interface—Xlib.

Each chapter in section I covers a specific area of X—for example, events or windows—and provides C source code examples to further explain how everything works. In Section I, we build a set of functions to help writing Xlib-based applications (these functions will be used throughout the rest of the book). We end Section I with an an application program that displays bitmap files called Bitview. We also describe how to impress your friends by being hip with X terminology.

After reading section I, you should be aware of the basic X11 concepts of:

Displays
Display connections
Screens
Windows
Events
Bitmaps
Pixmaps
Icons
The Graphics Context
Cursors
Text and Text Fonts

Chapter 1

Defining X

The X Window System can be confusing to those unacquainted with clients and servers, networking, display connections, and the like. It doesn't have to be intimidating, however. If you're unfamiliar with the X Window System, you can initially think of it as a C-language graphics library, containing routines that display lines, text, and shapes. In addition, X reads input from a mouse or other pointing device and provides the means to display the output of multiple graphics programs in many windows at the same time.

Of course, X isn't that simple or that limited, or there wouldn't be a need for X Window programming books. For now, the above definition will suffice; we'll build upon it in subsequent chapters.

THE XLIB C LIBRARY

The programmer's main interface to X is through the X library, or Xlib. Xlib is a low-level library providing access to X graphics and interface functions.

Xlib bindings exist for C and Lisp, and bindings for Ada and other languages are promised. In this book, though, we will concentrate on the C-language version of Xlib.

Xlib provides functions and macros for drawing lines, creating windows, displaying text, and defining colors. Xlib hides most of the gory details about making a connection with an X server (see chapter 2), maintaining network links, and the actual format of X fonts. This is good for the programmer, since it helps make programs portable. That is, your program should work the same on a Sun workstation as it does on a IBM PS/2 running SCO Unix.

Above Xlib sit many X toolkits, like Motif and Open Look, as shown in figure 1-1.

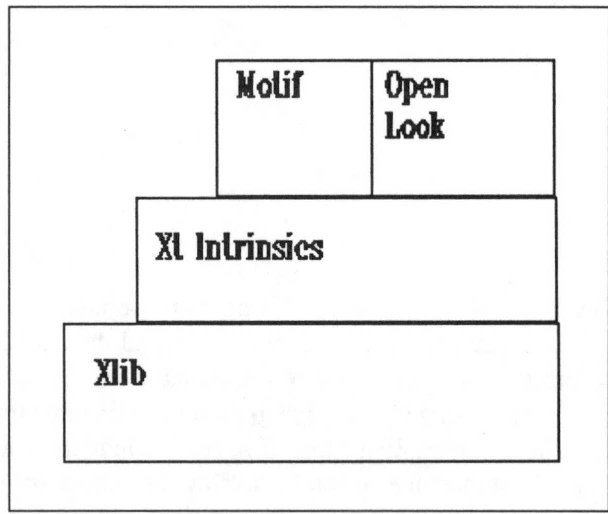

Figure 1-1. X Toolkit Layers

These toolkits (after a steep initial learning curve) can speed the creation of X applications. Even if you plan on using toolkits exclusively, you will still need a thorough grounding in Xlib operations in order to create quality, commercial-grade X applications.

The best way to learn X programming is to do it, so we've provided many example programs and functions to help you. The next step is to jump right in and program.

A QUICK X PROGRAM

Our first program illustrates some Xlib concepts further explained in following chapters. The `gumby` program:

- Establishes a connection to the default X server (see chapter 2);
- Finds the root window, the background window of a screen (see chapter 3);
- Creates a cursor in the shape of the Gumby cartoon character (see chapter 7);
- Sets the root window's cursor to be the Gumby cursor;
- Closes the display connection with the X server.

It shouldn't take more than a few minutes to type in this program. Compile, link, and then run it. Watch how the default cursor (displayed on the root, or background, window) is no longer the default X shape, but a Gumby shape.

The contents of `gumby.c` are as follows:

gumby.c:

```
/*
 *      gumby.c
 *
 *      Sets the Root window cursor to a gumby
 *      shape--what fun.
 *
 *      This program uses the default display and screen
 *      for your system.  Gumby is a very simple program,
 *      used to get going with X11.
 *
 *      Compile and link with the Xlib library, e.g., on UNIX:
 *
 *      cc -o gumby gumby.c -lX11
```

```
 *
 *      On Interactive 386/ix UNIX for PC's, you may need to link in the
 *      inet library, too (see your Interactive manuals):
 *
 *      cc -o gumby gumby.c -lX11 -linet
 *
 *
 *      Written for Advanced X Window Applications Programming
 *
 */

#include  <stdio.h>
#include  <X11/Xlib.h>
#include  <X11/Xutil.h>
#include  <X11/cursorfont.h>

main()

{       /* -- function main */
        Display *display;
        int     screen;
        Window  rootwindow;
        Cursor  cursor;

        /*
         *      Use the default display
         *      (the name is stored in the
         *      DISPLAY environment
         *      variable).
         *
         */
        display     = XOpenDisplay( (char *)NULL );

        if ( display = = (Display *) NULL )
                {
                (void) fprintf( stderr,
                        "Error: Could not open X display connection\n" );
                exit( 1 );
                }

        screen      = DefaultScreen( display );
        rootwindow = RootWindow( display, screen );

        cursor      = XCreateFontCursor( display, XC_gumby );

        /*
```

```
         *       Now, make the root
         *       window have a gumby cursor
         *       (instead of the normal X).
         *
         */
        if ( cursor != (Cursor) None )
                {
                XDefineCursor( display, rootwindow, cursor );

                XFreeCursor( display, cursor );
                }

        XCloseDisplay( display );

        exit( 0 );

}       /* -- function main */

/*
 *      end of file.
 */
```

COMPILING gumby.c

On a Unix system, you can compile and link `gumby.c` with something like the following command:

```
cc -o gumby gumby.c -lX11
```

(Since this book is intended for advanced X window users, compiling X programs should be old hat by now.)

The `-lX11` links the Xlib library. You may have to set the library path (with something like the `-L` option) if you have not installed X in the usual place. (All of the example programs in this book require only the standard C library and the Xlib library; we're not using any X toolkits for the examples.)

If you are running Interactive's 386/ix on a PC clone, however, you may need to also link in their `inet` library:

```
cc -o gumby gumby.c -lX11 -linet
```

(See your vendor-supplied X manuals for more information.)

If you are using the `Makefile` as shown in appendix C, you can simply type:

```
make gumby
```

or,

```
make all
```

and be done with it.

BEING HIP WITH X

When the X Consortium people refer to X, they call it the "X Window System," "X Window," "X11" or just plain "X." People in the know never, never call it "X Windows" (with an "s"); that's a no-no that reveals your ignorance. So, when sales critters refer to "X Windows" you know beyond a doubt their place on the food chain.

There are also various releases of X (always with a capital R, named after Joe Release), including Releases 2, 3, and 4. The newest is Release 4, but as of this writing, few vendor-supported X products employ Release 4. Most people running X11 R4 are using the sources from the MIT X Consortium.

In the chapters that follow, we will delve more fully into the basic concepts of X, starting with displays and screens.

SUMMARY

- On its most simple level, the X Window System simply is a C graphics library, containing routines that display lines, text, and shapes. X also reads input from a mouse or other pointing device, displaying the output of multiple graphics programs in many windows at the same time.
- Low-level programs in X are built around the X Library, or Xlib. The first program you created, `gumby.c`, uses Xlib functions to establish a connection to an X server, substitutes a Gumby cursor, and closes the connection.

Chapter 2

Displays and Screens

You need to make a connection to an X server to do just about anything in X. This chapter covers displays, setting up display connections, closing down display connections, X errors, and X error handlers.

THE X SERVER

X is a network-oriented window system with two parts: a server that controls a display screen, and client application programs, such as text editors, spreadsheets, and clock displays.

The server owns the screens, the keyboard, and the mouse. Your X programs (clients) ask the server to do things like create a window for your application, and draw lines and text. Remember, asking nicely always helps. (This usage of client and server is reversed from the traditional PC local-area network terminology where the host is the server and the clients usually sit at the terminal. In X, the server sits locally with you and the clients are often on other, more powerful, machines.)

In addition, with X a display is not merely the physical monitor connected to your CPU. Rather, an X display is the full set of things controlled by an X server: a mouse, a keyboard and one or more screens. Basically, if you sit down somewhere to run X programs, you're sitting down at a display, be it an X terminal, a Unix workstation, or a PC clone running X server software. Note that even though an X server can support multiple screens (usually separate physical monitors, but sometimes overlay planes on the same monitor), most people running X just have one screen.

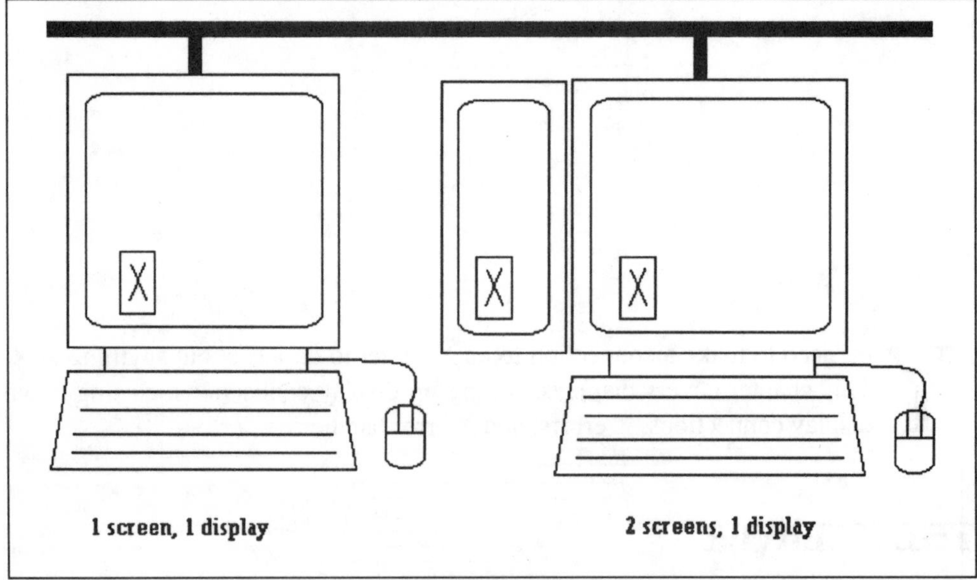

Figure 2-1. X Displays

Clients communicate to the server through a display connection. This connection can be done locally (through a shared memory link) or via a network (usually TCP/IP or

DECnet). Since X is network-oriented, the clients and the server can all be running on different computers. For example, you could run a nuclear power-plant simulation on a Cray Y-MP and display the output on your Sun SPARCStation-1. Don't have a Cray? You can use a 386 PC (under Unix) to run X client programs as well.

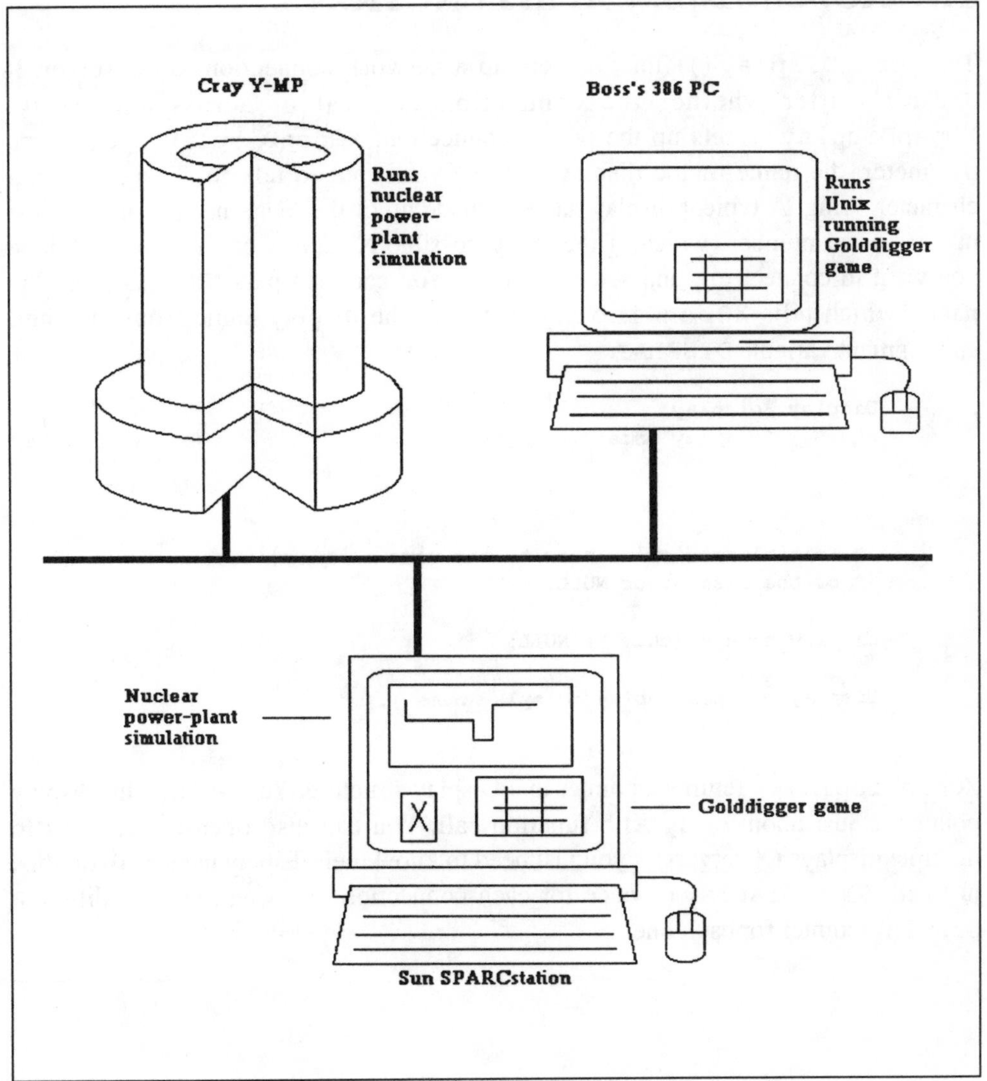

Figure 2-2. X Applications spread over multiple computers

To do almost anything in X, you need to first establish a connection to an X server. To do this, use XOpenDisplay().

THE XOpenDisplay XLIB FUNCTION

The XOpenDisplay() function sets up a network connection to the server. It doesn't matter whether the connection is local or across a network, XOpenDisplay() sets up the proper connection. XOpenDisplay() takes one parameter, the name of the display (server) you want to talk to. This name is a character string. A typical display name is made up of the local machine name (host name), server number (which of the many possible X servers on the given machine you want to connect to), and screen number. You can also pass NULL as a display name, which tells XOpenDisplay() to get the display name from the shell environment variable DISPLAY:

```
Display *display;
char    *display_name;


/*
 * Initialize display_name to the name
 * of the display or NULL.
 */
display_name = (char *) NULL;

display = XOpenDisplay( display_name );
```

XOpenDisplay() returns a pointer to a Display structure. You will use this display pointer in just about every Xlib function call. You can also open connections to multiple displays (X servers)—you just need to know their display names. To do this, just call XOpenDisplay() once for each connection you want, using a different Display pointer for each one.

DISPLAY NAMES

X display names are usually built from three parts: a machine name, a display number (which server), and a screen number (which screen do you want to use as the default screen for the application). For the numbers, zero (0) is the default. The default display name for a Unix workstation named `attila` would be:

```
attila:0.0
```

This is usually the system console. Under normal circumstances, you should set up the `DISPLAY` environment variable to name the default X display you want to use. In the `C shell (csh)`, you can, for example, use:

```
setenv DISPLAY attila:0.0
```

PASSING THE DISPLAY NAME AS A COMMAND LINE PARAMETER

Since X allows applications to connect to any X server on the network (there is some access control in X—see the `xhost` program for more information), friendly X applications allow users to specify the display for connection. Usually, you specify this on the Unix command line:

```
programname -display display_name
```

For the X11 `xclock` program (which should come with your X distribution), a command line could be:

```
xclock -display attila:0.0
```

This command line tells `xclock` to connect the display named `attila:0.0`.

Below, we've set up a simple function to check for a display name on a command-line parameter, `CheckDisplayName()`. `CheckDisplayName()` is passed to the C command-line parameters, `argc` (the number of parameters) and `argv` (a list of parameter strings), and fills in a `display_name` string.

```
CheckDisplayName( argc, argv, display_name )

int     argc;
char    *argv[];
char    display_name[];

{       /* -- function CheckDisplayName */
        int     counter;

        display_name[ 0 ] = '\0';
        counter           = 1;

        while( counter < argc )
                {
                if ( strncmp( argv[ counter ], "-display", 8 ) = = 0 )
                        {
                        counter++;
                        if ( counter < argc )
                                {
                                (void) strcpy( display_name, argv[ counter ] );
                                }
                        else
                                {
                                (void) fprintf( stderr,
                                  "Error: usage is -display DisplayName\n" );
                                }
                        }

                counter++;
                }

}       /* -- function CheckDisplayName */
```

If `CheckDisplayName()` finds no display name in the command-line parameters, it sets the variable `display_name` to a `NULL` string. In either case, you can pass the `display_name` variable to `XOpenDisplay()`, as the `NULL` tells `XOpenDisplay()` to use the `DISPLAY` environment variable to find the name.

WHAT CAN GO WRONG WHEN OPENING DISPLAY CONNECTIONS

Trying to open a display connection may fail. If this happens, XOpenDisplay() will return a NULL pointer. If a program cannot establish a connection to an X server, it is in trouble. Most programs, including the examples in this book (with one exception), normally terminate if the call to XOpenDisplay() fails.

If you have persistent problems with this, check to see if:

1) you are using the correct name for the server.

2) the given X server is really running.

3) you can run any "standard" X client programs; that is, programs that came with the X server software (often things like xclock and xterm).

SCREENS

Each X server may control a number of screens. A screen is usually a physical CRT, but two screens may share one CRT (one screen may be an overlay plane). Some screens may support many colors, others just black and white. The importance of screens here is that each window is created on one screen.

Screens in X are numbered, with screen 0 normally the default screen for a given display (the screen number is passed as part of the display name, so you may have specified a screen number other than 0).

To get the screen number that is the default for your X display connection, use the DefaultScreen() macro:

```
Display *display;
int     screen;

screen = DefaultScreen( display );
```

The next section shows a few utility functions we've created to aid in setting up a display connection, checking for errors, and closing the connection when done.

FUNCTIONS TO AID OPENING DISPLAY CONNECTIONS

OpenDisplay(), developed below, takes a display name and opens a connection to an X server. If successful, OpenDisplay() gets the default screen number. OpenDisplay() returns the display pointer.

```
Display *OpenDisplay( display_name, screen )

char    display_name[];
int     *screen;
{       /* -- function OpenDisplay */
        Display *display;

        display = XOpenDisplay( display_name );

        if ( display != (Display *)NULL )
                {
                *screen = DefaultScreen( display );
                }

        return( display );

}       /* -- function OpenDisplay */
```

OpenDisplay() is not all that interesting, as it is mainly intended as a low-level routine to be called from other functions. One thing to note, though, is that OpenDisplay() does not exit the program if an error occurs.

SetUpDisplay() does exit if an error occurs, and SetUpDisplay() checks the command-line parameters for a display name.

```
Display *SetUpDisplay( argc, argv, screen )

int     argc;
char    *argv[];
int     *screen;

{       /* -- function SetUpDisplay */
        char    display_name[ 120 ];
        Display *display;
```

```
        CheckDisplayName( argc, argv,
                display_name );

        display = OpenDisplay( display_name,
                        screen );

        if ( display == (Display *) NULL )
                {
                (void) fprintf( stderr,
                        "Error could not open X display to %s.\n",
                        XDisplayName( display_name ) );
                exit( 1 );
                }

        return( display );

}       /* -- function SetUpDisplay */
```

Most of the example programs created in this book call `SetUpDisplay()` to handle the details of setting up a display connection. A sample call looks like the following:

```
main( argc, argv )

int     argc;
char    *argv[];

{       /* -- main */
        Display *display;
        int     screen;

        display = SetUpDisplay( argc, argv, &screen );

        ...

}       /* -- main */
```

CLOSING THE DISPLAY CONNECTION

When you are all done with an X connection, call XCloseDisplay(). Usually applications call XCloseDisplay() just before the program exits.

```
Display *display;


XCloseDisplay( display );
```

The Unix operating system automatically breaks all connections when a program terminates, so in theory this call is not necessary if you're writing Unix-only applications. However, we'd advise you to use the XCloseDisplay() call; not using it would eliminate one of X's greatest strengths, its portability. Besides, well-behaved X applications always call XCloseDisplay() before exiting.

TERMINATING ON ERRORS

Sometimes a fatal problem occurs, such as a failure to create an application's main window. In those cases, call QuitX(), a routine that prints out an error message (to stderr) and then calls XCloseDisplay(). QuitX() finally calls exit() to terminate the program.

```
QuitX( display, error_message, error_file )

Display *display;
char    error_message[], error_file[];

{       /* -- function QuitX */

        (void) fprintf( stderr, "ERROR: %s%s\n",
                error_message,
                error_file );

        XCloseDisplay( display );

        exit( 1 );

}       /* -- function QuitX */
```

Most of the calls to QuitX() in the example sources involve a failure to load a font or create a window. QuitX() takes three parameters: a display pointer, an error message string, and a file name or other string that helps explain the error. For example, if the program fails to load a font named "variable,"the program can call QuitX() with:

```
Display *display;

QuitX( display,
        "Error: Could not load font ",
        "variable" );
```

CLOSING THE DISPLAY AND FREEING RESOURCES

The CloseDisplay() function was created to free up common resources and close the display connection. CloseDisplay() is usually called when a program is just about to exit. Since most application programs open a main window and draw in that window, CloseDisplay() frees some X resources as well: a window and a graphics context (GC).

CloseDisplay() merges common clean-up calls into one function: all subwindows of the main application window are destroyed; the window itself is destroyed; the graphics context, gc, is freed; and the connection to the X server (display) is closed. Be careful not to use the variable display as a display pointer after calling CloseDisplay().

```
CloseDisplay( display, window, gc )

Display *display;
Window  window;
GC      gc;

{       /* -- function CloseDisplay */

        XFreeGC( display, gc );

        XDestroySubwindows( display, window );

        XDestroyWindow( display, window );
```

```
        XFlush( display );

        XCloseDisplay( display );

}       /* -- function CloseDisplay */
```

Before closing the display connection, `CloseDisplay()` calls `XFlush()` to flush out any buffered requests to the X server. You should already know about `XFlush()`, of course.

```
        Display *display;

        XFlush( display );
```

Chapters 3 and 4 will cover more on windows and graphics contexts.

SOURCE CODE FOR display.c

All of the routines in this chapter are collected into `display.c`:

```
/*
 *      display.c
 *      X11 C routines for opening and closing display
 *      connections.
 *
 *      Routines:
 *      Display *SetUpDisplay( argc, argv, &screen )
 *      Display *OpenDisplay( display_name, &screen )
 *      CheckDisplayName( argc, argv, display_name )
 *      CloseDisplay( disp, window, gc )
 *      QuitX( display, error_message, error_file )
 *
 *      Written for Advanced X Window Applications Programming
 *
 */

#include  "xbook.h"

Display *SetUpDisplay( argc, argv, screen )

int     argc;
char    *argv[];
```

```
int     *screen;

/*
 *      SetUpDisplay() checks the command-line
 *      parameters for a display name, and then
 *      calls OpenDisplay() to establish a connection
 *      to an X server.
 *
 *      If no connection can be established, the
 *      program will be terminated by a call to
 *      exit().
 *
 */

{       /* -- function SetUpDisplay */
        char    display_name[ 120 ];
        Display *display;


        CheckDisplayName( argc, argv,
                display_name );

        display = OpenDisplay( display_name,
                                screen );

        if ( display = = (Display *) NULL )
                {
                (void) fprintf( stderr,
                                "Error could not open X display to %s.\n",
                                XDisplayName( display_name ) );
                exit( 1 );
                }

        return( display );

}       /* -- function SetUpDisplay */

Display *OpenDisplay( display_name, screen )

char    display_name[];
int     *screen;

/*
 *      OpenDisplay() tries to establish a connection to
 *      an X server.  If successful, it then gets the
 *      number of the default screen (used in many
```

```
 *      other X calls).  OpenDisplay() returns NULL
 *      on an error, so if you want to recover from
 *      a bad display name or errors in making
 *      the connection, use OpenDisplay(), rather
 *      than SetUpDisplay().  (For most X applications,
 *      failure to make a display connection is fatal.)
 *
 */

{       /* -- function OpenDisplay */
        Display *display;

        display = XOpenDisplay( display_name );

        if ( display != (Display *)NULL )
                {
                *screen = DefaultScreen( display );
                }

        return( display );

}       /* -- function OpenDisplay */

CheckDisplayName( argc, argv, display_name )

int     argc;
char    *argv[];
char    display_name[];

/*
 *      CheckDisplayName() checks the command-line arguments
 *      for a display name specification. It initializes display_name
 *      to NULL, if no -display command-line argument is found.
 *
 */

{       /* -- function CheckDisplayName */
        int     counter;

        display_name[ 0 ] = '\0';
        counter           = 1;

        while( counter < argc )
                {
                if ( strncmp( argv[ counter ], "-display", 8 ) = = 0 )
                        {
```

```
                    counter++;
                    if ( counter < argc )
                            {
                            (void) strcpy( display_name, argv[ counter ] );
                            }
                    else
                            {
                            (void) fprintf( stderr,
                              "Error: usage is -display DisplayName\n" );
                            }
                    }

            counter++;
            }

}       /* -- function CheckDisplayName */

CloseDisplay( display, window, gc )

Display *display;
Window  window;
GC      gc;

/*
 *      CloseDisplay() collects a common set of routines
 *      executed together for programs that set up windows.
 *
 */

{       /* -- function CloseDisplay */

        XFreeGC( display, gc );

        XDestroySubwindows( display, window );

        XDestroyWindow( display, window );

        XFlush( display );

        XCloseDisplay( display );

}       /* -- function CloseDisplay */

QuitX( display, error_message, error_file )

Display *display;
char    error_message[], error_file[];
```

```
/*
 *      QuitX() is called to terminate a program, by calling exit().
 *      QuitX() also prints out an error message to stderr.
 */

{       /* -- function QuitX */

        (void) fprintf( stderr, "ERROR: %s%s\n",
                error_message,
                error_file );

        XCloseDisplay( display );

        exit( 1 );

}       /* -- function QuitX */


/*
 *      end of file.
 */
```

A COMMON APPLICATION HEADER FILE

You'll notice that `display.c` includes a file called `xbook.h`. In `xbook.h`, we've collected a number of definitions and included the necessary X11 header files. All of the rest of the example sources will include `xbook.h` to take care of these tasks.

You'll find `xbook.h` in chapter 9, where we develop the first real example application in this book.

FUNCTIONS DEVELOPED IN THIS CHAPTER

```
CheckDisplayName
CloseDisplay
OpenDisplay
QuitX
SetUpDisplay
```

XLIB FUNCTIONS AND MACROS INTRODUCED IN THIS CHAPTER

```
DefaultScreen
XCloseDisplay
XFlush
XOpenDisplay
```

SUMMARY

- X is a network-oriented window system with two parts: a server that controls a display screen and client application programs, such as text editors, spreadsheets, and clock displays. The server owns the screens, the keyboard, and the mouse. Your X programs (clients) ask the server to do things, like creating a window for your application, drawing lines and text, and so on.
- A display is not merely the physical monitor connected to your CPU. Rather, an X display is the full set of things controlled by an X server; that is, a mouse, keyboard and one or more screens. Basically, if you sit down somewhere to run X programs, you're sitting down at a display, be it an X terminal, a Unix workstation or a PC clone running X server software.
- The `XOpenDisplay()` function sets up a network connection to the server. It doesn't matter whether the connection is local or across a network—`XOpenDisplay()` sets up the proper connection. `XOpenDisplay()` takes one parameter, the name of the display (server) you want to talk to. This name is a character string.
- Each X server may control a number of screens. A screen is usually a physical CRT, but two screens may share one CRT (one screen may be an overlay plane). Some screens may support many colors, others just black and white. The importance of screens is that each window is created on a certain screen.
- When you are all done with an X connection, call `XCloseDisplay()`. The Unix operating system automatically breaks all connections when a program terminates, so in theory this call is not necessary if you're writing Unix-only applications, but it is strongly recommended.

- The `CloseDisplay()` function was created to free up common resources and close the display connection. `CloseDisplay()` is usually called when a program is just about to exit. `CloseDisplay()` merges common clean-up calls into one function: all subwindows of the main application window are destroyed; the window itself is destroyed; the graphics context, `gc`, is freed; and the connection to the X server (display) is closed.

Chapter 3

Windows

Since the X Window System is a windowing system, it's obviously important that a programmer grasp the basics of displaying and manipulating windows. In this chapter we explain how X treats all aspects of windows—creating, maintaining, and interacting with various window managers.

Also, this is the first chapter in which the differences in X11 Release 4 have a major impact on X Window application development. For your convenience, we've marked X11 R4-specific passages with a graphic symbol:

WHAT IS A WINDOW?

Windows are rectangles on the screen that can be drawn, can overlap, and can be stacked on top of one another.

The X Window System is first and foremost a graphical windowing system. Obviously, then, knowledge of opening and manipulating windows is key to any application work.

Be warned, however, that we are covering windows here in a cursory fashion. If you want more information on windows, check our earlier *X Window Applications Programming* (also MIS: Press). Nothing with X is particularly simple, and since windows are really at the core of X, it is important that you understand them well. If you feel comfortable with windows, then review this material; if not, then refer to the previous book.

If you have Release 4, windows no longer have to be rectangular, but most windows will be rectangles anyway. You'll find that oval-shaped windows, in particular, swamp most CPUs.

After opening a connection to the display (as outlined in chapter 2) your next step is opening a main application window on the display. Most X applications open one large window for the application. They may also have a number of subwindows inside the main application window.

TOP-LEVEL WINDOWS

The main, or top-level window is very important in X. Window managers often place a title bar or other decorations around top-level windows (most window managers stretch the meaning of the word decoration here). To properly interact with window managers, you need to send information to the window manager about your application and its top-level window. Since the window manager is free to ignore anything you tell it, you're sending hints to the window manager. A well-behaved window manager and well-behaved applications can work together in ways that make the user's tasks much easier. We cannot stress enough the importance of writing well-behaved X applications (see chapter 15 on the infamous ICCCM for more on this topic).

Creating windows, especially top-level windows, is rather complicated—X provides mechanism, not policy, especially relating to user-interface issues. To open up a window, you're faced with a dizzying array of choices, ranging from the thickness of the border to the window's location. In addition, most of your choices can be ignored by whatever window manager you're running.

Window managers are allowed a great deal of control over the look and feel of application top-level windows, including where windows appear, if they can overlap, and if there is a title bar.

As a programmer, you must take into account many possible window managers. Since X does not provide mechanism, the policy of most vendors is to include one or more window managers. X11 comes with a number of window managers, but the main one is `twm` (formerly Tom's window manager—named after Tom LaStrange—and now called the `"Tab"` window manager). Other common window managers are `mwm` for Motif and `olwm` for Open Look. Following a few simple rules should make your applications well-behaved and work with just about every window manager.

CREATING WINDOWS

Two main Xlib calls create windows: `XCreateSimpleWindow()` and `XCreateWindow()`.

```
Display         *display;
Window          window, parent;
int             x, y;
unsigned int    width, height;
unsigned int    border_width;
unsigned long   border_pixel, background_pixel;

window = XCreateSimpleWindow( display,
                        parent,
                        x, y, width, height,
                        border_width,
                        border_pixel,
                        background_pixel );

int                     depth;
unsigned int            class;
```

```
Visual                    *visual;
unsigned long             attributes_mask,
XSetWindowAttributes      attributes;

window = XCreateWindow( display,
                          parent,
                          x, y, width, height,
                          border_width,
                          depth,
                          class,
                          visual,
                          attributes_mask,
                          &attributes );
```

XCreateSimpleWindow() inherits most values from the parent window. XCreateWindow() allows you to set these values, providing more control over the creation of windows. Below, we'll explain the parameters in more depth.

PARENTHOOD

Every window in X has a parent, except for one magic window, the root window. The root window is essentially the background of a screen. Most application top-level windows use the root window as their parent. The macro RootWindow() returns the given screen's root window.

```
Display *display;
int      screen;
Window   parent;

parent = RootWindow( display, screen );
```

This is one reason that our OpenDisplay() and SetUpDisplay() functions (from chapter 2) return the screen number.

The x and y location passed to XCreateWindow() and XCreateSimpleWindow() are in relation to the parent. If the parent is the root window, the coordinates are global. When you create subwindows of your top-level window, the x, y location is in coordinates local to your top-level window.

BIG WINDOWS

The width and height of a window are specified as unsigned integers. Just a word of warning: don't set the width or height greater than 32767. Many X toolkit routines have problems with really big windows.

BLACK AND WHITE

The background_pixel and border_pixel are colors. Typically, you can use black for the border and white for the background of the window—your application will work on both monochrome and color systems (see chapter 14 on color). To get the default black and white values (and not mess with colormaps), use the macros BlackPixel() and WhitePixel():

```
Display         *display;
int             screen;
unsigned long   black, white;

black = BlackPixel( display, screen );
white = WhitePixel( display, screen );
```

DEPTH

Some parameters really beg for defaults. The depth parameter is one of them. You may specify the depth (how many color-planes) for the window—but you may be in trouble if the depth you want isn't one of the supported depths on the given X server you are running. Unless you are writing an image-processing application, use the default CopyFromParent.

You can also use CopyFromParent for the class parameter. The class can be InputOutput, InputOnly or CopyFromParent (normally InputOutput).

The visual parameter will be covered more in chapter 14. For now, also use CopyFromParent. For color-intensive applications, you may want to search for the best visual for your task. Most applications, though, will work just fine with the default visual.

THE XSetWindowAttributes STRUCTURE

The `XSetWindowAttributes` structure allows you to specify more than you ever wanted about your window. Like many X structures, you can fill in what you want and leave the rest blank. However, you must tell the Xlib which fields you filled in. This is done through the `attribute_mask`, a bit mask that contains 1 bit for each field you fill in.

The `XSetWindowAttributes` structure looks like:

```
typedef struct
        {
        Pixmap          background_pixmap;
        unsigned long   background_pixel;
        Pixmap          border_pixmap;
        unsigned long   border_pixel;
        int             bit_gravity;
        int             win_gravity;
        int             backing_store;
        unsigned long   backing_planes;
        unsigned long   backing_pixel;
        Bool            save_under;
        long            event_mask;
        long            do_not_propagate_mask;
        Bool            override_redirect;
        Colormap        colormap;
        Cursor          cursor;
        } XSetWindowAttributes;
```

Use an `OR` these constants to tell Xlib the fields you fill in:

```
CWBackPixmap            (for the background_pixmap
                         field)
CWBackPixel             (background_pixel)
CWBorderPixmap          (border_pixmap)
CWBorderPixel           (border_pixel)
CWBitGravity            (bit_gravity)
CWWinGravity            (win_gravity)
CWBackingStore          (backing_store)
CWBackingPlanes         (backing_planes)
CWBackingPixel          (backing_pixel)
```

```
CWOverrideRedirect          (override_redirect)
CWSaveUnder                 (save_under)
CWEventMask                 (event_mask)
CWDontPropagate             (do_not_propagate_mask)
CWColormap                  (colormap)
CWCursor                    (cursor)
```

Much of this structure was covered in *X Window Applications Programming*, so we won't go into too much detail here.

For example, if you filled in the `background_pixel`, `border_pixel` and `event_mask` fields, you could set the mask as follows:

```
unsigned long   attribute_mask;

attribute_mask = CWBackPixel | CWBorderPixel | CWEventMask;
```

HELPING CREATE WINDOWS

Putting all this together to create a window and get it to appear on the screen can be one of the most daunting tasks in X. The `CreateWindow()` function helps that process:

```
Window
CreateWindow(display,parent,x,y,width,height,border,fore,back,events)

Display         *display;
Window          parent;
int             x, y, width, height, border;
unsigned long   fore, back;
long            events;

{       /* -- function CreateWindow */
        Window                  window;
        XSetWindowAttributes    attributes;
        unsigned long           attribute_mask;
        Visual                  *visual = CopyFromParent;
```

```
        /*
         *      Set up window attributes
         */
        attributes.background_pixel = back;
        attributes.border_pixel     = fore;
        attributes.event_mask       = events;

        attribute_mask              = CWBackPixel | CWBorderPixel |
                                      CWEventMask;

        /*
         *      Create the window
         */
        window = XCreateWindow( display,
                        parent,
                        x, y, width, height,    /* -- location, size */
                        border,
                        CopyFromParent,         /* -- Depth */
                        InputOutput,            /* -- window class */
                        visual,
                        attribute_mask,
                        &attributes );

        if ( window = = (Window) None )
                {
                QuitX( display, "",
                        "Error: Could not open window." );
                }

        return( window );

}       /* -- function CreateWindow */
```

If the call to `XCreateWindow()` fails (it returns `None`), we handle the error by quitting the application, with a call to `QuitX()`. This is not the best method for handling errors, but in general, if you cannot create a window (especially the top-level window), your X application cannot do anything anyway.

If you use the function `CreateWindow()`, you won't ever have to worry about the `XSetWindowAttributes` structure again.

SPECIFYING A WINDOW'S SIZE AND LOCATION

Much like the display names described in chapter 2, X has a convention for specifying where a user wants a particular window to go. The geometry specification, or geometry string, tells a program where to put its top-level window. The assumption is most X programs have only one top-level window–an assumption that may be false.

The geometry specification looks something like:

```
width x height + x + y
```

On the command line, for example, a top-level window to appear at location 10 (x), 200 (y) with a size of 100 pixels across (width) and 125 pixels high (height) has a geometric specification of:

```
-geometry 100x125+10+200
```

Note that in the X Window System, location 0, 0 is at the top left corner. You can also, through a bit of trickery, specify coordinates in relation to other sides of the screen. An x value of -0 means the right edge, a +0 means the left edge. A y value of -0 means the bottom of the screen.

```
+0+0    is the upper left corner
-0-0    is the lower right corner
-0+0    is the upper right corner
+0-0    is the lower left corner
```

`XParseGeometry()` takes a geometry specification, usually from the command line, and sets the values given in the geometry specification.

```
char    *geometry_specification;
int     x, y, width, height, status;

status = XParseGeometry( geometry_specification,
                &x, &y, &width, &height );
```

The return value, status, will contain a number of bit-flags OR'ed together: XValue, YValue, WidthValue, HeightValue, XNegative, and YNegative. The XNegative and YNegative handle the special cases mentioned above.

The function CheckGeometry(), developed below, searches through the command-line parameters (argc, argv) for a geometry specification and then sets x, y, (width and height) accordingly. You will want to place default values in x, y, width and height since CheckGeometry() won't write over a value unless it was set in a geometry specification.

```
CheckGeometry( argc, argv, screen_width, screen_height, x, y, width, height )

int     argc;
char    *argv[];
int     screen_width, screen_height;
int     *x, *y, *width, *height;

{       /* -- function CheckGeometry */
        int     status;
        int     x1, y1, width1, height1;
        int     counter;

        counter  = 1;
        while( counter < argc )
                {
                if ( strncmp( argv[ counter ], "-geom", 5 ) = = 0 )
                        {
                        counter++;
                        if ( counter < argc )
                                {
                                status =
                                        XParseGeometry( argv[ counter ],
                                                &x1, &y1, &width1, &height1 );

                                if ( status & XValue )
                                        *x = x1;
                                if ( status & YValue )
                                        *y = y1;
                                if ( status & WidthValue )
                                        *width = width1;
                                if ( status & HeightValue )
                                        *height = height1;
                                if ( status & XNegative )
                                        *x = screen_width - *width + *x;
                                if ( status & YNegative )
```

```
                                        *y = screen_height - *height + *y;
                                }
                        }

                counter++;
                }

}       /* -- function CheckGeometry */
```

To handle the negative locations, you need to pass the screen's full width and height to `CheckGeometry()`. You can get these values with the following macros:

```
Display *display;
int     screen;
int     screen_width, screen_height;

screen_width    = DisplayWidth(  display, screen );
screen_height   = DisplayHeight( display, screen );
```

SENDING HINTS TO THE WINDOW MANAGER ABOUT TOP-LEVEL WINDOWS

After creating a window, you must send hints to the window manager (even if a window manager is not running). The hints can be something as basic as the position and size of the new window. Of course, the window manager can pick a different position and size, so you're just hinting where you prefer the window to be located.

You need to do an awful lot of hinting. We'll cover the basic hints here and the more advanced ones in chapter 15.

`XSetWMHints()` sends an `XWMHints` structure to the window manager by writing a `WM_HINTS` property on your top-level window. This stuff has changed in Release 4, so watch out.

The `XMWHints` structure appears as follows:

```
typedef struct
        {
        long            flags;
```

```
Bool            input;
int             initial_state;
Pixmap          icon_pixmap;
Window          icon_window;
int             icon_x, icon_y;
Pixmap          icon_mask;
XID             window_group;
} XWMHints;
```

The flags field is filled with a bit mask (OR'ing constants). The bit mask specifies the filled fields. You can OR together the relevant constants shown in the following table:

```
InputHint               (for the input field)
StateHint               (initial_state)
IconPixmapHint          (icon_pixmap)
IconWindowHint          (icon_window)
IconPositionHint        (icon_x, icon_y)
IconMaskHint            (icon_mask)
WindowGroupHint         (window_group)
AllHints                (everything)
```

In general, avoid using All-anything with X, since things are changing. So, skip AllHints and set each flag for each field that you fill in.

THE INPUT FLAG

If your X applications worked under X11 Release 2 (under the uwm window manager) and no longer gets keyboard input under different window managers, listen up.

Set the input field to True (be sure to OR in the InputHint in the flags field, too). This tells the window manager you want the keyboard input.

```
XWMHints        *wmhints;

/* -- Allocate memory for wmhints ... */

...

wmhints->input  = True;
wmhints->flags  |=  InputHint;
```

The initial_state field may be NormalState, IconicState, or WithdrawnState. You will almost always use NormalState.

You set the XWMHints with the XSetWMHints() function. That is, XSetWMHints() sets your XWMHints in a place the window manager will recognize and pick up.

```
Display          *display;
Window           window;
XWMHints         *wmhints;

XSetWMHints( display, window, wmhints );
```

New in Release 4

THE XAllocWMHints( ) FUNCTION

Between X11 Releases 3 and 4, much work was done on the way X applications communicate with each other, including the hints sent to the window manager. Many of the hint structures (like XSizeHints) grew between R3 and R4. They will probably grow in the future, making the hinting process even more complex and difficult. Because these structures may grow, you need to dynamically allocate the memory for the structures. In Release 3, you didn't have to do this. Someday most X users will be running Release 4 systems, but most workstation vendors aren't anywhere near upgrading to Release 4 at the time of this writing.

In Release 4, you use the function XAllocWMHints() to dynamically allocate an XWMHints structure. This function does not exist in the R3 or R2 Xlib.

```
XWMHints         *wmhints;

wmhints = XAllocWMHints();
```

Use XFree() to free the memory when you are done:

```
char    *data;

XFree( data );
```

Or, in this case

```
        XFree( wmhints );
```

Many workstations won't have a Release 4 Xlib library (nor a Release 4 server). But, to accommodate those who do, it's best to write as portable a code as possible.

We built the function `SetWMHints()` because of this incompatibility between X11 Release 4 and previous releases. This function depends on the symbol X11R4. If you define X11R4 (either `#define X11R4` or `-DX11R4` on the `cc` command line), you will compile in Release 4 specific code . Otherwise, the older code will be used.

`SetWMHints()` takes a display, a window and a pixmap to be used as an icon (see chapter 6 for more on icons for now, you can pass `None`). The contents of `SetWMHints()` are as follows:

```
SetWMHints( display, window, icon )
Display *display;
Window  window;
Pixmap  icon;

{       /* -- function SetWMHints */
        XWMHints        *wmhints;

        /*
         * In X11 Release 4, the XWMHints structure
         * became dynamically allocated (so it can grow)
         * if R4 is in use, call XAllocWMHints(),
         * otherwise, use malloc().
         */
#ifdef X11R4
        wmhints    = XAllocWMHints();

#else   /* -- R3 or below */
        wmhints    = (XWMHints *)  malloc( sizeof( XWMHints ) );
#endif

        if ( wmhints != (XWMHints *) NULL )
                {
                /*
                 * Now, set up the hints
                 */
                wmhints->initial_state = NormalState;
```

```
            wmhints->input          = True;

            if ( icon != (Pixmap) None )
                    {
                    wmhints->icon_pixmap = icon;
                    wmhints->icon_mask   = icon;
                    wmhints->flags       =  StateHint      |
                                            InputHint      |
                                            IconPixmapHint |
                                            IconMaskHint;
                    }
            else
                    {
                    wmhints->flags       = StateHint | InputHint;
                    }

            /*
             * Send the hints to the window manager
             */
            XSetWMHints( display, window, wmhints );

            /*
             * Return the memory
             */
#ifdef X11R4
            XFree( wmhints );
#else
            free( wmhints );
#endif
            }

}       /* -- function SetWMHints */
```

`SetWMHints()` should isolate this incompatibility from your code (except for the X11R4 symbol), but the Release 4 issues get worse, unfortunately.

MAINTAINING NORMALCY OR SETTING THE NORMAL HINTS

After you set the `WM` (for `Window Manager`) hints, you need to set up the "normal" hints. These hints give information about the window when it is in the normal state.

You have two main choices to set these hints: `XSetNormalHints()` (obsolete in R4) or `XSetWMNormalHints()` (nonexistent in Release 3). Obsolete or nonexistent: what a choice.

Both of these routines use the `XSizeHints` structure:

```
typedef struct
        {
        long            flags;
        int             x, y;           /* obsolete in R4 */
        int             width, height;  /* obsolete in R4 */
        int             min_width, min_height;
        int             max_width, max_height;
        int             width_inc, height_inc;
        struct
                {
                int     x;      /* numerator */
                int     y;      /* denominator */
                } min_aspect, max_aspect;
        int             base_width, base_height;  /* new in R4 */
        int             win_gravity;              /* new in R4 */
        } XSizeHints;
```

As usual, the flags field gets a bit mask that defines which of the other fields are filled in, shown in the following table:

```
USPosition          (for user-specified x, y)
USSize              (for user-specified width,
                        height)
PPosition           (for program-specified x,y )
PSize               (for program-specified
                        width, height)
PMinSize            (min_width, min_height)
PMaxSize            (max_width, max_height)
PResizeInc          (width_inc, height_inc)
PAspect             (min_aspect, max_aspect)
PBaseSize           (base_width, base_height)
PWinGravity         (win_gravity)
```

In Release 4, the x, y, width, and height fields are declared obsolete. The new `base_width` and `base_height` fields act as the old width and height fields (we're sure there's a good reason for this base change, but we can't think of one). If you don't specify a `min` size, the base size may be used as a `min` size.

Note: Don't use the old `PAllHints` constant.

To set these hints, use `XSetWMNormalHints()` or `XSetNormalHints()`:

```
Display         *display;
Window          window;
XSizeHints      *sizehints;


XSetWMNormalHints( display, window, sizehints );
```

Or,

```
XSetNormalHints(   display, window, sizehints );
```

`XSetNormalHints()` is declared obsolete in Release 4. `XSetWMNormalHints()` is not in a pre-R4 Xlib.

To allocate an `XSizeHints` structure, use `XAllocSizeHints()`:

```
XSizeHints      *sizehints;

sizehints = XAllocSizeHints();
```

Use `XFree()` to free the memory when done. `XAllocSizeHints()` did not exist before Release 4.

`SetNormalHints()`, again, hides most of the incompatibilities in setting the `WM_NORMAL_HINTS` property. Be sure to define X11R4 if needed. The contents of `Set Normal Hints()` are as follows:

```
SetNormalHints( display, window, x, y, width, height )

Display         *display;
Window          window;
int             x, y, width, height;  /* size and location of the window */

{       /* -- function SetNormalHints  */
```

```
        XSizeHints                          *sizehints;

        /*
         * In X11 Release 4, the XSizeHints structure
         * became dynamically allocated (so it can grow)
         * if R4 is in use, call XAllocSizeHints(),
         * otherwise, use malloc().
         */
#ifdef X11R4
        sizehints  = XAllocSizeHints();

#else   /* -- R3 or below */
        sizehints  = (XSizeHints *)malloc( sizeof( XSizeHints ) );
#endif

        if ( sizehints != (XSizeHints *) NULL )
                {
                /*
                 * In R3 and below, most window managers
                 * expected the x, y, width, height fields
                 * to hold the desired x, y, width and height
                 * for the window.
                 *
                 * In Release 4, these are obsolete, but we'll
                 * fill them in anyway.
                 *
                 */
                sizehints->x             = x;         /* -- Obsolete in R4 */
                sizehints->y             = y;         /* -- Obsolete in R4 */
                sizehints->width         = width;     /* -- Obsolete in R4 */
                sizehints->height        = height;    /* -- Obsolete in R4 */

                /*
                 * You need to set a min width and height in R4,
                 * or the base size might become the min size.
                 */
                sizehints->min_width     = 100;
                sizehints->min_height    = 50;

                /*
                 * Now tell the window manager about the size and location.
                 * we want for our windows.  USPosition means we are
                 * stating the User chose the position, same with the
                 * size.  PPosition and PSize would mean that the program
                 * choose the size.  Note that we always tell the
                 * window manager that the user chose the size
```

```
                 * and location.
                 */

                sizehints->flags       = USPosition | USSize | PMinSize;

#ifdef X11R4
                /*
                 * In R4, we set the base width and height
                 * in place of the old width and height.
                 * We're sure there was a great reason for
                 * the change.
                 */
                sizehints->base_width  = width;     /* -- New in R4 */
                sizehints->base_height = height;    /* -- New in R4 */

                sizehints->flags       |= PBaseSize;

                XSetWMNormalHints( display, window, sizehints );

                XFree( sizehints );

#else
                /*
                 * Pre-R4
                 */
                XSetNormalHints  ( display, window, sizehints );

                free( sizehints );
#endif
                }

}       /* -- function SetNormalHints */
```

NAMING WINDOWS

The next step is to give the top level window a title. You also want to give your window an icon name and a class (a class name and a class type).

THE XClassHint STRUCTURE

Like other structures, the XClassHints structure should be dynamically allocated with XAllocClassHint():

```
XClassHint      *classhints;

classhints = XAllocClassHint();
```

Use XFree() to free the structure when done. XAllocClassHint() is new in Release 4.

The XClassHint structure contains fields for the class name and class type. This at least hasn't changed (but probably will).

The class name should be something like the application's name, like "xterm." The class type is usually the class name, but capitalized: "XTerm."

```
Display         *display;
Window          window;
XClassHint      *classhints;

classhints->res_name  = "xterm";
classhints->res_class = "XTerm";

XSetClassHint( display, window, classhints );
```

The class types registered with the X Consortium include:

Clock	XEyes
Listres	Xfd
Xbiff	XFontSel
XCalc	Xgc
Xcessory	XLogo
XClipboard	Xman
XCutsel	Xmh
Xditview	XTerm
Xedit	

TEXT PROPERTIES

One of the changes in Release 4 is the use of text properties. Text properties replace simple (ASCII) strings used in many functions, like setting a window's name. The main reason for this change seems to be helping make X work better with languages, especially Asian and Middle-Eastern languages.

Text properties are defined in the `XTextProperty` structure:

```
typedef struct
        {
        unsigned char   *value;
        Atom            encoding;
        int             format;   /* 8, 16 or 32-bit items */
        unsigned long   nitems;   /* number of items */
        } XTextProperty;
```

Text properties are new in Release 4.

`XStringListToTextProperty()` converts a list of character strings to a text property. `XTextPropertyToStringList()` converts a text property back to a list of character strings.

```
char            **string_list;
int             number_strings, status;
XTextProperty   *text_property;

status = XStringListToTextProperty( string_list,
                number_strings,
                text_property );

status = XTextPropertyToStringList( text_property,
                &string_list,
                &number_strings );
```

Both functions return a status of 0 if a failure occurs.

`XFreeStringList()` frees the string list memory when done.

```
char            **string_list;

XFreeStringList( string_list );
```

SETTING A WINDOW NAME

The new and improved method to give windows a name is the `XSetWMName()` function.

```
Display         *display;
Window          window;
XTextProperty   *text_property;

XSetWMName( display, window, text_property );
```

Previous to Release 4, the `XStoreName()` function was used:

```
Display *display;
Window  window;
char    *name;

XStoreName( display, window, name );
```

`XStoreName()` isn't on the obsolete list yet, is a lot simpler, and is backwardly compatible, so we used it to set a window's name. But if you want to set the window's title in Japanese, for example, use `XSetWMName()` instead.

ICON NAMES

Icon names are for the window manager to use, if the window manager wants to place a name by the icon (when the window is in iconic state).

```
Display         *display;
Window          window;
XTextProperty   *text_property;

XSetWMIconName( display, window, text_property );
```

Previous to Release 4, the `XSetIconName()` function was used.

```
Display *display;
Window  window;
char    *name;

XSetIconName( display, window, name );
```

THE NameWindow FUNCTION

To hide some of the incompatibilities, we've developed the `NameWindow()` function, which handles setting the window's name, icon name and class. It also depends on the symbol X11R4. We did not use any text-property routines in order to ensure a high level of compatibility. If you are developing applications for use outside of the United States (especially in Asian countries), you should take a long look at text properties.

```
NameWindow( display, window, name, class_name, class_type )

Display *display;
Window  window;
char    *name;
char    *class_name;
char    *class_type;

{       /* -- function NameWindow */
        XClassHint              *classhints;

#ifdef X11R4
        /*
         * XAllocClassHint() is new in R4
         */
        classhints = XAllocClassHint();

#else   /* -- R3 or below */
        classhints = (XClassHint *)malloc( sizeof( XClassHint ) );
#endif
        /*
         * Store Class hints
         */
        if ( classhints != (XClassHint *) NULL )
                {
                classhints->res_name  = class_name;
                classhints->res_class = class_type;

                XSetClassHint( display, window, classhints );

                /*
                 * Return the memory
                 */
#ifdef X11R4
                XFree( classhints );
#else
```

```
                free( classhints );
#endif
                }

        /*
         * Window and icon name--we're using
         * the pre-R4 routines here, for simplicity.
         */
        XStoreName( display, window, name );

        XSetIconName( display, window, name );

        /*
         * Save window name in global for later
         */
        (void) strcpy( AppName, name );

}       /* -- function NameWindow */
```

NameWindow() sets the window name and the icon name to be the same. It also stores the window name away in the global AppName for later use.

MAPPING WINDOWS

After the hinting and cajoling, it's now time to actually put the window on the screen, the end result of XCreateWindow() "creating" a window. Creating a window and mapping a window are two different things, however, so you need XMapWindow() or XMapRaised() to actually bring those pixels to life. If you just call XCreateWindow(), you'll never see your window.

XMapWindow() maps the window to the screen, which makes the window appear. XMapRaised() brings the window to the top of other windows. XMapWindow() usually does the same thing, but it's not explicit and can be overruled by the window manager. The contents of the XMapWindows() are as follows:

```
Display *display;
Window  window;

XMapWindow( display, window );
```

XMapRaised() maps a window and asks that it appear on top of all other windows:

```
XMapRaised( display, window );
```

You can later unmap a window with the XUnmapWindow() function, using the same parameters:

```
XUnmapWindow( display, window );
```

To map a number of subwindows at once, use XMapSubwindows(), which maps all subwindows with a given parent window. It, too, takes the same parameters.

```
XMapSubwindows( display, window );
```

You can also call XMapWindow() on any of your subwindows, but it would not be nice to call XMapSubwindows() on the root window.

Generally, when you create a top-level window you'd map the top-level window (and any subwindows). MapWindow() is a convenient routine for this task:

```
MapWindow( display, window )


Display *display;
Window  window;

{       /* -- function MapWindow */

        XMapRaised( display, window );

        XMapSubwindows( display, window );

        XFlush( display );

}       /* -- function MapWindow */
```

DESTROYING WINDOWS

Before exiting a program you should destroy all windows—this frees up the limited resources in the X server. `XCloseDisplay()` (covered in chapter 2) will normally destroy all windows, but it's better to be as explicit as possible (as always in X) and destroy all windows with the `XDestroyWindow()` function:

```
Display *display;
Window  window;

XDestroyWindow( display, window );
```

To destroy subwindows, use the following:

```
XDestroySubwindows( display, window );
```

SOURCE CODE FOR window.c

The `window.c` file contains a number of convenient routines for creating windows and sending hints to the window manager (refer to chapter 9 for the file `xbook.h`). If you are running under X11R4, define the symbol X11R4 (e.g., `#define X11R4` or `-DX11R4` on the cc command line). The contents of `window c.` are as follows:

window.c:

```
/*
 *      window.c
 *      X11 routines for the top-level window
 *      of an application.
 *      X11 routines to create windows and
 *      set basic window manager hints.
 *      You'll need more than these hints to be fully
 *      ICCCM-compliant (see icccm.c).
 *
 *      This module depends on the symbol X11R4.
 *      If X11R4 is defined, it will use the newer
 *      R4 functions for dynamically allocating
 *      Hint structures.
 *
 *      Written for Advanced X Window Applications Programming
 *
```

```
 */

#include  "xbook.h"

/*
 *      GLOBALS, used to later retrieve the application's
 *      name (stored from the title of the main application
 *      top-level window).
 */
char    AppName[ BUFSIZE + 1 ];

Window CreateWindow( display,parent,x,y,width,height,border,fore,back,
events )

Display         *display;
Window          parent;
int             x, y, width, height, border;
unsigned long   fore, back;
long            events;

/*
 *      CreateWindow() calls XCreateWindow() to
 *      create an X window.  It handles any window
 *      error as a fatal error (and closes the X connection).
 *      CreateWindow() also selects events on the window,
 *      based on the events mask.
 *
 *      A failure to create the window results in
 *      terminating the program, by calling QuitX().
 */

{       /* -- function CreateWindow */
        Window                  window;
        XSetWindowAttributes    attributes;
        unsigned long           attribute_mask;
        Visual                  *visual = CopyFromParent;

        /*
         *      Set up window attributes
         */
        attributes.background_pixel = back;
        attributes.border_pixel     = fore;
        attributes.event_mask       = events;
        attribute_mask              = CWBackPixel | CWBorderPixel |
                                            CWEventMask;

        /*
```

```
         *      Create the window
         */
        window = XCreateWindow( display,
                        parent,
                        x, y, width, height,    /* -- location, size */
                        border,
                        CopyFromParent,         /* -- Depth */
                        InputOutput,            /* -- window class */
                        visual,
                        attribute_mask,
                        &attributes );

        if ( window = = (Window) None )
                {
                QuitX( display, "",
                        "Error: Could not open window." );
                }

        return( window );

}       /* -- function CreateWindow */

CheckGeometry( argc, argv, screen_width, screen_height, x, y, width, height )

int     argc;
char    *argv[];
int     screen_width, screen_height;
int     *x, *y, *width, *height;

/*
 *      CheckGeometry() checks the command-line for
 *      a window geometry specification.
 *      This routine does nothing to x, y, width,
 *      height, unless set in the specification.
 *      So, it is best to pass default values
 *      to CheckGeometry().
 *
 */

{       /* -- function CheckGeometry */
        int     status;
        int     x1, y1, width1, height1;
        int     counter;

        counter  = 1;
        while( counter < argc )
```

```
                {
                if ( strncmp( argv[ counter ], "-geom", 5 ) = = 0 )
                        {
                        counter++;
                        if ( counter < argc )
                                {
                                status =
                                        XParseGeometry( argv[ counter ],
                                                &x1, &y1, &width1, &height1 );

                                if ( status & XValue )
                                        *x = x1;
                                if ( status & YValue )
                                        *y = y1;
                                if ( status & WidthValue )
                                        *width = width1;
                                if ( status & HeightValue )
                                        *height = height1;
                                if ( status & XNegative )
                                        *x = screen_width - *width + *x;
                                if ( status & YNegative )
                                        *y = screen_height - *height + *y;
                                }
                        }

                counter++;
                }

}       /* -- function CheckGeometry */

MapWindow( display, window )

Display *display;
Window  window;

/*
 *      MapWindow() combines three common
 *      Xlib calls for mapping a window
 *      together into one function, as
 *      a convenience.
 */

{       /* -- function MapWindow */

        XMapRaised( display, window );

        XMapSubwindows( display, window );
```

```
        XFlush( display );

}       /* -- function MapWindow */

NameWindow( display, window, name, class_name, class_type )

Display *display;
Window  window;
char    *name;
char    *class_name;
char    *class_type;

/*
 *      NameWindow() writes out properties that are used by the
 *      window manager for an application's top-level window,
 *      including the window name, the icon name and the
 *      application class (class name and class type).
 *      The window name is stored in a global AppName,
 *      so that the name can be asked for later.
 */

{       /* -- function NameWindow */
        XClassHint              *classhints;

#ifdef X11R4
        /*
         * XAllocClassHint() is new in R4
         */
        classhints = XAllocClassHint();

#else   /* -- R3 or below */
        classhints = (XClassHint *)malloc( sizeof( XClassHint ) );
#endif
        /*
         * Store Class hints
         */
        if ( classhints != (XClassHint *) NULL )
                {
                classhints->res_name  = class_name;
                classhints->res_class = class_type;

                XSetClassHint( display, window, classhints );

                /*
                 * Return the memory
```

```
                 */
#ifdef X11R4
                XFree( classhints );
#else
                free( classhints );
#endif
                }

        /*
         * Window and icon name--we're using
         * The pre-R4 routines here, for simplicity.
         */
        XStoreName( display, window, name );

        XSetIconName( display, window, name );

        /*
         * Save window name in global for later
         */
        (void) strcpy( AppName, name );

}       /* -- function NameWindow */

SetWMHints( display, window, icon )

Display *display;
Window  window;
Pixmap  icon;

/*
 *      SetWMHints() sets hints for the window
 *      manager, contained in an XWMHints structure.
 */

{       /* -- function SetWMHints */
        XWMHints        *wmhints;

        /*
         * In X11 Release 4, the XWMHints structure
         * became dynamically allocated (so it can grow)
         * if R4 is in use, call XAllocWMHints(),
         * otherwise, use malloc().
         */
#ifdef X11R4
        wmhints    = XAllocWMHints();

#else   /* -- R3 or below */
```

```
        wmhints    = (XWMHints *)  malloc( sizeof( XWMHints ) );
#endif

        if ( wmhints != (XWMHints *) NULL )
                {
                /*
                 * Now, set up the hints
                 */
                wmhints->initial_state = NormalState;
                wmhints->input         = True;

                if ( icon != (Pixmap) None )
                        {
                        wmhints->icon_pixmap = icon;
                        wmhints->icon_mask   = icon;
                        wmhints->flags       =  StateHint      |
                                                InputHint      |
                                                IconPixmapHint |
                                                IconMaskHint;
                        }
                else
                        {
                        wmhints->flags       = StateHint | InputHint;
                        }

                /*
                 * Send the hints to the window manager
                 */
                XSetWMHints( display, window, wmhints );

                /*
                 * Return the memory
                 */
#ifdef X11R4
                XFree( wmhints );
#else
                free( wmhints );
#endif
                }

}       /* -- function SetWMHints */

SetNormalHints( display, window, x, y, width, height )

Display         *display;
Window          window;
```

```
int             x, y, width, height;

/*
 *      SetNormalHints() sets the WM_NORMAL_HINTS
 *      property on an application's top-level window.
 *      WM_NORMAL_HITS is based on an XSizeHints structure.
 */

{       /* -- function SetNormalHints */
        XSizeHints              *sizehints;

        /*
         * In X11 Release 4, the XSizeHints structure
         * became dynamically allocated (so it can grow)
         * if R4 is in use, call XAllocSizeHints(),
         * otherwise, use malloc().
         */
#ifdef X11R4
        sizehints  = XAllocSizeHints();

#else   /* -- R3 or below */
        sizehints  = (XSizeHints *)malloc( sizeof( XSizeHints ) );
#endif

        if ( sizehints != (XSizeHints *) NULL )
                {
                /*
                 * In R3 and below, most window managers
                 * expected the x, y, width, height fields
                 * to hold the desired x, y, width and height
                 * for the window.
                 *
                 * In Release 4, these are obsolete, but we'll
                 * fill them in anyway.
                 *
                 */
                sizehints->x            = x;        /* -- Obsolete in R4 */
                sizehints->y            = y;        /* -- Obsolete in R4 */
                sizehints->width        = width;    /* -- Obsolete in R4 */
                sizehints->height       = height;   /* -- Obsolete in R4 */

                /*
                 * You need to set a min width and height in R4,
                 * or the base size might become the min size.
                 */
                sizehints->min_width    = 100;
```

```
                sizehints->min_height  = 50;

                /*
                 * Now tell the window manager about the size and location.
                 * we want for our windows.  USPosition means we are
                 * stating the User chose the position, same with the
                 * size.  PPosition and PSize would mean that the program
                 * choose the size.  Note that we always tell the
                 * window manager that the user chose the size
                 * and location.
                 */

                sizehints->flags       = USPosition | USSize | PMinSize;

#ifdef X11R4
                /*
                 * In R4, we set the base width and height
                 * in place of the old width and height.
                 * we're sure there was a great reason for
                 * the change.
                 */
                sizehints->base_width  = width;     /* -- New in R4 */
                sizehints->base_height = height;    /* -- New in R4 */

                sizehints->flags       |= PBaseSize;

                XSetWMNormalHints( display, window, sizehints );

                XFree( sizehints );

#else
                /*
                 * Pre-R4
                 */
                XSetNormalHints  ( display, window, sizehints );

                free( sizehints );
#endif
                }

}       /* -- function SetNormalHints */

GetAppName( name )

char    *name;
```

```
/*
 *      GetAppName() fills up the string name with
 *      the contents of the AppName GLOBAL.
 *      AppName contains the main window's title.
 */

{       /* -- function GetAppName */

        (void) strcpy( name, AppName );

}       /* -- function GetAppName */

/*
 *      end of file
 */
```

FUNCTIONS DEVELOPED IN THIS CHAPTER

CheckGeometry
CreateWindow
MapWindow
NameWindow
SetNormalHints
SetWMHints

XLIB FUNCTIONS AND MACROS INTRODUCED IN THIS CHAPTER

BlackPixel
DisplayHeight
DisplayWidth
WhitePixel
XAllocClassHint
XAllocSizeHints
XAllocWMHints
XCreateSimpleWindow
XCreateWindow
XDestroySubwindows
XDestroyWindow
XFree
XFreeStringList
XMapRaised
XMapSubwindows
XMapWindow
XParseGeometry
XSetClassHint

`XSetIconName`
`XSetNormalHints`
`XSetWMHints`
`XSetWMIconName`
`XSetWMName`
`XSetWMNormalHints`
`XStoreName`
`XStringListToTextProperty`
`XTextPropertyToStringList`
`XUnmapWindow`

SUMMARY

- Windows are rectangles on the screen that can be drawn, can overlap, and can be stacked on top of one another. Most X applications open one large window for the application and have a number of subwindows inside the main application window. By sending hints to the window manager, you can define the window's attributes—ranging from the thickness of the border to the window's location. Since you're sending hints to the window manager—instead of marching orders—most of your choices can be ignored by whatever window manager you're running.

- Two main Xlib calls create windows: `XCreateSimpleWindow()` and `XCreateWindow()`. `XCreateSimpleWindow()` inherits most values from the parent window. `XCreateWindow()` allows you to set these values. After creating a window, you must send hints to the window manager (a window manger may not be running, but send the hints anyway). The hints can be something as basic as the position and size of the new window. Of course, the window manager can ignore your hints and pick a different position and size.

- The `XSetWindowAttributes` structure allows you to specify more than you ever wanted about your window. Like many X structures, you can fill in what you want and leave the rest blank.

- The geometry specification, or geometry string, tells a program where to put its top-level window. With the X Window System, location 0, 0 is at the top left corner. You can also, through a bit of trickery, specify coordinates in relation to other sides of the screen. A x value of -0 means the right edge, a +0 means the left edge. A y value of -0 means the bottom of the screen, etc.

- Several Release 4-specific functions and operations are covered: setting the input flag, using the function `XAllocWMHints()` to dynamically allocate an

XWMHints structure, maintaining normalcy or setting the normal hints, allocating an XSizeHints structure with XAllocSizeHints(), the XAllocClassHint(), text properties, setting a window name with the XSetWMName() function, and establishing icon names with XSetWMIconName().

- Creating the window and mapping the window are two different things in X. XMapWindow() maps the window to the screen, and mapping makes the window appear. XMapRaised() brings the window to the top of other windows. To map a number of subwindows at once, use XMapSubwindows(), which maps all subwindows with a given parent window.
- Before exiting a program you should destroy all windows—this frees up the limited resources in the X server. XCloseDisplay() will destroy all windows, but it's better (as always in X) to be as explicit as possible and destroy all windows with the XDestroyWindow() function.

Chapter 4

The Graphics Context

Now that you've learned the basics of window creation you'll need to create a graphics context for a window. A graphics context contains the attributes of a "pen" with which you can draw. The graphics context, or `GC`, specifies how wide lines should be when drawn, what color lines should be drawn in, and so on. Each `GC` is associated with a `Drawable`—that is, a `Window` or a `Pixmap`. You can have a number of `GC`s per `Drawable`, but remember that a `GC` is a resource that takes up space in the X server and that some X servers, especially X terminals, have limited resources available (usually limited RAM).

CREATING A GRAPHICS CONTEXT

The pen parameters stored in a `GC` are available for setting in an `XGCValues` structure. The contents of the `XGCValues` structure are as follows:

```
typedef struct
        {
        int             function;       /* -- like GXcopy */
        unsigned long   plane_mask;
        unsigned long   foreground;
        unsigned long   background;
        int             line_width;
        int             line_style, cap_style, join_style;
        int             fill_style, fill_rule;
        int             arc_mode;
        Pixmap          tile;
        Pixmap          stipple;
        int             ts_x_origin, ts_y_origin;
        Font            font;
        int             subwindow_mode;
        Bool            graphics_exposures;
        int             clip_x_origin, clip_y_origin;
        Pixmap          clip_mask;
        int             dash_offset;
        char            dashes;
        } XGCValues;
```

As usual with one of these huge structures, you don't have to fill in the whole thing, but you need to tell the X library which fields you have filled in, using the bit masks as follows:

```
GCFunction                  (for the function field)
GCPlaneMask                 (plane_mask)
GCForeground                (foreground)
GCBackground                (background)
GCLineWidth                 (line_width)
GCLineStyle                 (line_style)
GCCapStyle                  (cap_style)
GCJoinStyle                 (join_style)
GCFillStyle                 (fill_style)
GCFillRule                  (fill_rule)
GCArcMode                   (arc_mode)
```

```
GCTile                  (tile)
GCStipple               (stipple)
GCTileStipXOrigin       (ts_x_origin)
GCTileStipYOrigin       (ts_y_origin)
GCFont                  (font)
GCSubwindowMode         (subwindow_mode )
GCGraphicsExposures     (graphics_exposures)
GCClipXOrigin           (clip_x_origin)
GCClipYOrigin           (clip_y_origin)
GCClipMask              (clip_mask)
GCDashOffset            (dash_offset)
GCDashList              (dashes)
```

To create a graphics context, pass an `XGCValues` structure to `XCreateGC()` and set up any values you want for when the `GC` is created. You can change those values later. Call `XCreateGC()` as follows:

```
Display          *display;
Drawable         drawable;
unsigned long    mask;
XGCValues        gcvalues;
GC               gc;

gc = XCreateGC( display,
                drawable,
                mask,
                &gcvalues );
```

The graphics context is associated with a particular `Drawable`, such as the top-level window. `GC`s may also be used on subwindows. `Windows` and `Drawables` are interchangeable for most X functions. The function `MakeGC()` handles the work of creating a graphics context. The `MakeCG()` contents are as follows:

```
GC MakeGC( display, drawable, fore, back )

Display          *display;
Drawable         drawable;
unsigned long    fore, back;

{       /* -- function MakeGC */
```

```
        GC              gc;
        XGCValues       gcvalues;

        gcvalues.foreground = fore;
        gcvalues.background = back;

        gc = XCreateGC( display, drawable,
                        ( GCForeground | GCBackground ),
                        &gcvalues );

        /*
         *      For this book, an error
         *      in creating a GC is considered
         *      a fatal error
         */
        if ( gc = = 0 )
                {
                QuitX( display,
                        "Error in creating a Graphics context", "" );
                }

        return( gc );

}       /* -- function MakeGC */
```

SETTING THE COLORS IN A GRAPHICS CONTEXT

Each graphics context has a foreground and a background color. The background color is used primarily for `XDrawImageString()` text output (see chapter 8). To set a `GC` to a certain color, you need a pixel value for that color (see chapter 14 for more on color, or use the `BlackPixel`, `WhitePixel` values described in chapter 3).

`XSetForeground()` sets the foreground color:

```
        Display         *display;
        GC              gc;
        unsigned long   fore, back;

        XSetForeground( display, gc, fore );
```

`XSetBackground()` sets the background color.:

```
XSetBackground( display, gc, fore );
```

The `SetGC()` function sets both the foreground and the background colors. This is a convenience routine, used mainly by code that wants to reverse video (set the background to fore and the foreground to back). The contents of the `SetGC()` function are as follows:

```
SetGC( display, gc, fore, back )

Display         *display;
GC              gc;
unsigned long   fore, back;

{       /* -- function SetGC */

        XSetForeground( display, gc, fore );

        XSetBackground( display, gc, back );

}       /* -- function SetGC */
```

FREEING A GRAPHICS CONTEXT

When you are done with a GC, call `XFreeGC()` to free the resources in the X server:

```
Display *display;
GC      gc;

XFreeGC( display, gc );
```

GC FUNCTIONS OR RASTER OPERATIONS

In this book, the term "function" usually means a C language function. However, each GC has a graphics mode that the designers of X called a "function." By far the most common "function" is the GXcopy mode. With GXcopy, any items you draw will appear in the window. GXcopy is the default.

Take a look at the Release 4 program called xgc, which shows how the various modes work.

The only other graphics mode in wide use is the GXxor mode. When drawing in exclusive-OR mode (XOR), each pixel drawn is XOR'ed with the pixel already in the window at that spot. The main use of the XOR mode is to make an item disappear by drawing it twice. XOR mode is used for what is called "rubber-band" lines.

RUBBER-BAND LINES

To set up a GC for drawing rubber-band lines, you need to do two things. First, set the GC's "function" to GXxor. Second, set the foreground color for XORing:

```
Display         *display;
GC              gc;
unsigned long   fore, back;

XSetFunction( display, gc, GXxor );

XSetForeground( display, gc, fore ^ back );
```

SOURCE CODE FOR gc.c

The file gc.c contains MakeGC() and SetGC(), two convenience functions for working with graphics contexts. The contents of gc.c are as follows:

```
gc.c:
/*
 *      gc.c
 *      X11 C routines to create a graphics context
 *      and fill in the fore and back ground
 *      color fields of the new GC.
 *
 *      Written for Advanced X Window Applications Programming
```

```
 *
 */

#include   "xbook.h"

GC MakeGC( display, drawable, fore, back )

Display         *display;
Drawable        drawable;
unsigned long   fore, back;

/*
 *      In all the programs in the book, each time a graphics
 *      context is created, the GC has its fore and back
 *      colors set.  This function does all that.
 *
 *      Any error is assumed to be a fatal error and
 *      the program is terminated by a call to QuitX().
 *
 */

{       /* -- function MakeGC */
        GC              gc;
        XGCValues       gcvalues;

        gcvalues.foreground = fore;
        gcvalues.background = back;

        gc = XCreateGC( display, drawable,
                        ( GCForeground | GCBackground ),
                        &gcvalues );

        /*
         *      For this book, an error
         *      in creating a GC is considered
         *      a fatal error
         */
        if ( gc = = 0 )
                {
                QuitX( display,
                        "Error in creating a Graphics context", "" );
                }

        return( gc );

}       /* -- function MakeGC */
```

```
SetGC( display, gc, fore, back )

Display          *display;
GC               gc;
unsigned long    fore, back;

/*
 *      SetGC() sets the foreground and background colors
 *      of a graphic context.
 */

{       /* -- function SetGC */

        XSetForeground( display, gc, fore );

        XSetBackground( display, gc, back );

}       /* -- function SetGC */

/*
 *      end of file
 */
```

FUNCTIONS DEVELOPED IN THIS CHAPTER

MakeGC
SetGC

XLIB FUNCTIONS AND MACROS INTRODUCED IN THIS CHAPTER

XCreateGC
XFreeGC
XSetBackground
XSetForeground
XSetFunction

SUMMARY

- A graphics context contains the attributes of a "pen" with which you can draw. The graphics context, or GC, specifies how wide lines should be when drawn, what color lines should be drawn in, and so on. Each GC is associated with a Drawable—that is, a Window or a Pixmap. The parameters stored in a GC are available for setting in an XGCValues structure.

- XCreateGC() creates a graphic context. When the GC is created you pass an XGCValues structure to XCreateGC() and set up for any values you want. You can change those values later.

- Each graphics context has a foreground and a background color. The background color is used primarily for XDrawImageString() text output. We have discussed a black-and-white GC so far, later we'll cover color pixel values.

- Each GC has a graphics mode called a "function." By far the most common "function" is the GXcopy mode. With GXcopy, any items you draw will appear in the window. GXcopy is the default.

Chapter 5

Events

In this chapter, we assume you have a basic familiarity with X events and event structures. We focus on filtering out unwanted events and general event-handling routines.

EVENTS

Events in X are asynchronous messages from the X server that are generated for key presses, mouse-button presses, and special client messages, among other things. Most X applications, in fact, event-driven; that is, the major processing is done in reaction to incoming events. Usually event-driven programs place a good deal of control in the hands of the user. Event-driven applications typically have an event loop in which the application gets the next event and processes the event.

This loop is repeated over and over again. In this chapter, we focus on filtering X events, so that your event loops don't have to do so much.

SELECTING EVENTS FOR WINDOWS

There are two basic mechanisms to tell an X server which events your application wants. First, you can pass a bit mask of desired events in the `XCreateWindow()` function. Second, you can call `XSelectInput()`, where the `event_mask` is built from the `OR` of the individual event masks your application wants.

```
Display *display;
Window  window;
long    event_mask;
XSelectInput( display, window, event_mask );
```

EVENT MASKS

Xlib's event masks include:

ColormapChangeMask	ExposureMask
ButtonMotionMask	FocusChangeMask
Button1MotionMask	KeymapStateMask
Button2MotionMask	KeyPressMask
Button3MotionMask	KeyReleaseMask
Button4MotionMask	LeaveWindowMask
Button5MotionMask	NoEventMask
ButtonPressMask	OwnerGrabButtonMask
ButtonReleaseMask	PointerMotionMask
EnterWindowMask	PointerMotionHintMask

PropertyChangeMask	SubstructureNotifyMask
ResizeRedirectMask	SubstructureRedirectMask
StructureNotifyMask	VisibilityChangeMask

Many of these events, in fact, can be filtered out. Most X applications really only need to ask for the following:

ButtonPressMask	a mouse button is pressed
ExposureMask	part of the window needs to be redrawn
KeyPressMask	a key has been pressed
StructureNotifyMask	the window has changed (looking for resizes)

FILTERING OUT EVENTS

When an application gets a MappingNotify event, you should always pass that event to XRefreshKeyboardMapping().

```
XEvent  *event;
XRefreshKeyboardMapping( event );
```

Not every event loop you write will need this line. The ParseEvent() function, explained later in this chapter, filters out MappingNotify events, among others.

Expose events usually come in a series. With each event on the same window, the count field decreases until a count of zero means that the last Expose event for that window has come in. If your application can refresh part of its windows but would rather refresh the whole window in one fell swoop, it is easier to ignore the Expose events until the last one in the series (where the count equals 0).

Depending on your application, you may not want Expose events until the count equals 0. Other applications might want all Expose events. The function

ParseEvent() takes a want_exposes flag. If the want_exposes flag is True, then ParseEvent will return all Expose events. If want_exposes is False, only the last Expose event is returned. The rest are eaten. ParseEvent() returns True for an "interesting" event and False for an event that should be ignored.

ConfigureNotify is another type of event where you may get many "uninteresting" events. Most applications want to know if their top-level window is resized. Most don't care if the top-level window is moved, though, so long as its size remains the same. ConfigureNotify events are generated for many things, most of them uninteresting. The way to check if the window has been resized is to compare the top-level window's previous width and height with the new width and height returned in the event.

In addition, on KeyPress events, ParseEvent() will translate the key code into a portable X KeySym, and return the KeySym value. Thus, ParseEvent() is a handy way to filter many X events so that your event loop need only deal with interesting events. The contents of the ParseEvent() are as follows:

```
/*
 *      GLOBAL
 */
Time    LastEventTime;  /* -- last known timestamp */

ParseEvent( event, want_exposes, width, height, keysym )

XEvent  *event;
int     want_exposes;
int     width, height;
KeySym  *keysym;

{       /* -- function ParseEvent */
        int     status;

        status = False;

        switch( event->type )
                {
                /*
                 * Events we want passed back
                 */
                case ButtonPress:
                        LastEventTime = event->xbutton.time;
```

```
        status = True;
        break;
case ClientMessage:
        status = True;
        break;
case PropertyNotify:
        LastEventTime = event->xproperty.time;

        status = True;
        break;
case SelectionClear:
        LastEventTime = event->xselectionclear.time;

        status = True;
        break;
case SelectionNotify:
        LastEventTime = event->xselection.time;

        status = True;
        break;
case SelectionRequest:
        LastEventTime = event->xselectionrequest.time;

        status = True;
        break;
case ConfigureNotify:
        /*
         * Was window resized?
         */
        if ( ( width != event->xconfigure.width ) ||
             ( height != event->xconfigure.height ) )
                {
                status = True;
                }
        break;
case Expose:
        status = True;

        if ( want_exposes = = False )
                {
                if ( event->xexpose.count != 0 )
                        {
                        status = False;
                        }
                }
        break;
```

```
            case KeyPress:
                    LastEventTime = event->xkey.time;

                    status  = True;
                    *keysym = Key2Keysym( event );
                    break;
            case MappingNotify:
                    XRefreshKeyboardMapping( event );
                    break;
            }

        return( status );

}       /* -- function ParseEvent */
```

WAITING FOR EVENTS

XNextEvent() waits until an event arrives from the X server.

```
        Display *display;
        XEvent  *event;
```

From XNextEvent(), you can build a routine that not only waits for an event from the X server, but also waits until an interesting event arrives. NextEvent() calls ParseEvent() to determine if the event is interesting or not. It takes the same parameters as ParseEvent() and loops until ParseEvent() returns True. The contents of NextEvent() are shown below:

```
NextEvent( display, want_exposes, width, height, event, keysym )

Display *display;
int     want_exposes;
int     width, height;  /* -- Size of application's top-level window */
XEvent  *event;
KeySym  *keysym;

{       /* -- function NextEvent */
        int     status;

        /*
         * Loop until we have an interesting event to return.
         */
```

```
        status = False;         /* -- No interesting event yet */

        while( status = = False )
                {
                XNextEvent( display, event );

                status = ParseEvent( event,
                                want_exposes,
                                width, height,
                                keysym );
                }

}       /* -- function NextEvent */
/
```

CHECKING FOR EVENTS, BUT NOT WAITING

Many times your application doesn't want to block until an event arrives. Instead, the application may want to do some form of processing while it awaits events from the X server.

However, if your application establishes connections to more than one X server, you cannot afford to wait until an event arrives on a particular X connection—you need to periodically check all connections. `XPending()` returns the number of events waiting in the event queue. The contents of `XPending()` are as follows:

```
Display *display;
int     number_events;

number_events = XPending( display );
```

`CheckEvent()` takes the same parameters as `NextEvent()`, but it does not block until an interesting event arrives. Instead, it returns `True` for an interesting event and `False` if no interesting event has arrived. The contents of `CheckEvent()` are as follows:

```
CheckEvent( display, want_exposes, width, height, event, keysym )

Display *display;
int     want_exposes;
int     width, height;  /* -- Size of application's top-level window */
XEvent  *event;
KeySym  *keysym;

{       /* -- function CheckEvent */
        int     status;

        status = False;

        /*
         * Are there any events in the event queue?
         */
        if ( XPending( display ) > 0 )
                {
                XNextEvent( display, event );

                status = ParseEvent( event,
                                want_exposes,
                                width, height,
                                keysym );

                }


        return( status );

}       /* -- function CheckEvent */
```

With the use of `NextEvent()` or `CheckEvent()`, your application can have a smaller event loop in most common applications.

KeySyms

The X Window System uses `KeySyms` to abstract the many different keyboards available. A `KeySym` is a name defined to a specific value for a key. This value remains the same no matter what keyboard system is in use. For example, `XK_Up` is the up arrow key, whether it is on an Apple Macintosh Extended keyboard on a Sun Type 4 keyboard. Each `KeyPress` event has the keyboard-specific (and system-specific) key code for that key.

A number of functions will convert Key events to KeySyms, but most require a special index value into a list of possible KeySyms. XLookupString(), however, does not, but it is not as efficient.

```
XComposeStatus  composestatus;
KeySym          keysym;
char            string[ 10 ];
int             max_characters = 9;
int             number_characters;

number_characters = XLookupString( event,
                        string,
                        max_characters,
                        &keysym,
                        &compose_status );
```

XLookupString() also converts the KeyPress event into an ASCII string. The ASCII string is useful, but KeySyms are often easier to deal with.

MAPPING KeyPress EVENTS TO KeySyms

Key2KeySym() converts an X event (KeyPress or KeyRelease event) into a KeySym:

```
KeySym  Key2Keysym( keyevent )

XKeyEvent         *keyevent;

{       /* -- function Key2Keysym */
        XComposeStatus  composestatus;
        KeySym          keysym;
        char            string[ 10 ];

        XLookupString( keyevent, string,
                       9, &keysym, &composestatus );

        return( keysym );

}       /* -- function Key2Keysym */
```

SOURCE CODE FOR event.c

The file event.c contains a number of utility routines for handling events. The contents of event c. are as follows:

```
event.c
/*
 *      event.c
 *      X11 event-handling utility functions.
 *
 *      Written for Advanced X Window Applications Programming
 *
 */

#include  "xbook.h"

/*
 *      Globals
 */
Time    LastEventTime = CurrentTime;

CheckEvent( display, want_exposes, width, height, event, keysym )

Display *display;
int     want_exposes;
int     width, height;  /* -- Size of application's top-level window */
XEvent  *event;
KeySym  *keysym;

{       /* -- function CheckEvent */
        int     status;

        status = False;

        /*
         * Are there any events in the event queue?
         */
        if ( XPending( display ) > 0 )
                {
                XNextEvent( display, event );

                status = ParseEvent( event,
                                want_exposes,
                                width, height,
                                keysym );
```

```
                }

        return( status );

}       /* -- function CheckEvent */

NextEvent( display, want_exposes, width, height, event, keysym )

Display *display;
int     want_exposes;
int     width, height;  /* -- Size of application's top-level window */
XEvent  *event;
KeySym  *keysym;

/*
 *      NextEvent() provides some event-handling functions.
 *      It first blocks until an X event arrives--calling
 *      XNextEvent().  Then, NextEvent() calls ParseEvent(),
 *      which either eats the event or passes it back.
 *
 */

{       /* -- function NextEvent */
        int     status;

        /*
         * Loop until we have an interesting event to return.
         */
        status = False;         /* -- No interesting event yet */

        while( status == False )
                {
                XNextEvent( display, event );

                status = ParseEvent( event,
                                want_exposes,
                                width, height,
                                keysym );
                }

}       /* -- function NextEvent */

ParseEvent( event, want_exposes, width, height, keysym )

XEvent  *event;
```

```
int     want_exposes;
int     width, height;
KeySym  *keysym;

/*
 *      ParseEvent() takes an X11 event and then determines
 *      if the event should be passed back.
 *
 *      ParseEvent() will either pass back
 *      the event, or eat the event.
 *
 *      Expose events are eaten unless the count field = = 0
 *      (which means all expose events are in for that window),
 *      if want_exposes = = False.  If want_exposes = = True,
 *      then all Expose events are returned.
 *
 *      KeyPress events are returned, and the keysym is determined.
 *
 *      ConfigureNotify events are eaten, unless the window
 *      size != the width and height passed.
 *
 *      ButtonPress events are returned. As are ClientMessage,
 *      SelectionClear, SelectionRequest.
 *
 *      MappingNotify events are eaten.
 *
 *      All other events are eaten.
 *
 *      ParseEvent() returns True for an event, and False if the
 *      event was eaten.
 *
 */

{       /* -- function ParseEvent */
        int     status;

        status = False;

        switch( event->type )
                {
                /*
                 * Events we want passed back
                 */
                case ButtonPress:
                        LastEventTime = event->xbutton.time;

                        status = True;
```

```
        break;
case ClientMessage:
        status = True;
        break;
case PropertyNotify:
        LastEventTime = event->xproperty.time;

        status = True;
        break;
case SelectionClear:
        LastEventTime = event->xselectionclear.time;

        status = True;
        break;
case SelectionNotify:
        LastEventTime = event->xselection.time;

        status = True;
        break;
case SelectionRequest:
        LastEventTime = event->xselectionrequest.time;

        status = True;
        break;
case ConfigureNotify:
        /*
         * Was window resized?
         */
        if ( ( width != event->xconfigure.width ) ||
             ( height != event->xconfigure.height ) )
                {
                status = True;
                }
        break;
case Expose:
        status = True;

        if ( want_exposes = = False )
                {
                if ( event->xexpose.count != 0 )
                        {
                        status = False;
                        }
                }
        break;

case KeyPress:
```

```
                        LastEventTime = event->xkey.time;

                        status  = True;
                        *keysym = Key2Keysym( event );
                        break;
                case MappingNotify:
                        XRefreshKeyboardMapping( event );
                        break;
                }

        return( status );

}       /* -- function ParseEvent */

KeySym  Key2Keysym( keyevent )

XKeyEvent       *keyevent;

/*
 *      Key2Keysym() converts a KeyPress event
 *      into a character keysym.
 */

{       /* -- function Key2Keysym */
        XComposeStatus  composestatus;
        KeySym          keysym;
        char            string[ 10 ];

        XLookupString( keyevent, string,
                        9, &keysym, &composestatus );

        return( keysym );

}       /* -- function Key2Keysym */

Time LastTimeStamp()

/*
 *      LastTimeStamp() returns the last-known timestamp
 *      for an event.  Some event types do not come with
 *      a timestamp.
 */

{       /* -- function LastTimeStamp */

        return( LastEventTime );
```

```
}       /* -- function LastTimeStamp */

/*
 *      end of file
 */
```

FUNCTIONS DEVELOPED IN THIS CHAPTER

CheckEvent
Key2Keysym
LastTimeStamp
NextEvent
ParseEvent

XLIB FUNCTIONS AND MACROS INTRODUCED IN THIS CHAPTER

XLookupString
XNextEvent
XPending
XSelectInput

SUMMARY

- Events in X are asynchronous messages from the X server that are generated for key presses, mouse-button presses, and special client messages, among other things. Most X applications are event-driven: the major processing is done in reaction to incoming events. Two basic mechanisms, `XCreateWindow()` and `XSelectInput()`, tell an X server which events your application is interested .

- Expose events usually come in a series. With each event on the same window, the count field decreases. A count of zero means that the last Expose event for that window has come in. If your application can refresh part of its windows and but would rather refresh the whole window in one fell swoop, it is easier to ignore the Expose events until the last one in the series (when the count equals 0).

- `XNextEvent()` waits until an event arrives from the X server. With it, you can build a routine that not only waits for an event from the X server, but also waits until an interesting event arrives.

- Many times your application doesn't want to block until an event arrives. Instead, the application may want to do some form of processing while it awaits events from the X server. `XPending()` returns the number of events waiting in the event queue.

- X uses `KeySyms` to abstract the many different keyboards available. A `KeySym` is a name for a key—a name that is defined to a specific value. This value remains the same no matter what keyboard system is in use. For example, `XK_Up` is the up arrow key on an Apple Macintosh Extended keyboard and a Sun Type 4 keyboard. Each `KeyPress` event has the keyboard-specific (and system-specific) key code for that key.

Chapter 6

Bitmaps, Pixmaps, and Icons

Once a window is created, you need to work with pixmaps, bitmaps and icons. A bitmap is a single-plane pixmap. Bitmaps are often used for icons or screen backgrounds. Pixmaps are like off-screen windows (not quite, but very close) and may have multiple color planes. Icons, often used by window managers, are really bitmaps. Sound confusing? It won't be after reading this chapter.

DRAWABLES

The main construct used in X is the window, an area for drawing on the screen. A window is considered a `Drawable` in X; that is, something that can be drawn in. A

Pixmap is also a Drawable. You can consider Pixmaps to be off-screen windows, or off-screen drawing areas.

Just about every drawing operation that works on windows also works on Pixmaps. You create a graphics context for the pixmap and you can draw lines, rectangles and other assorted fun shapes and text into pixmaps. You never see what you've drawn on a pixmap, though, until you copy the pixmap to the screen.

BITMAPS

As a single-plane pixmaps, a bitmap only has on and off information for its pixels. You may draw a bitmap onto a window (or multiplane pixmap) in a foreground color and a background color, but that's it. Bitmaps are often used for icons or screen backgrounds with the xsetroot program. A bitmap is shown in figure 6-1.

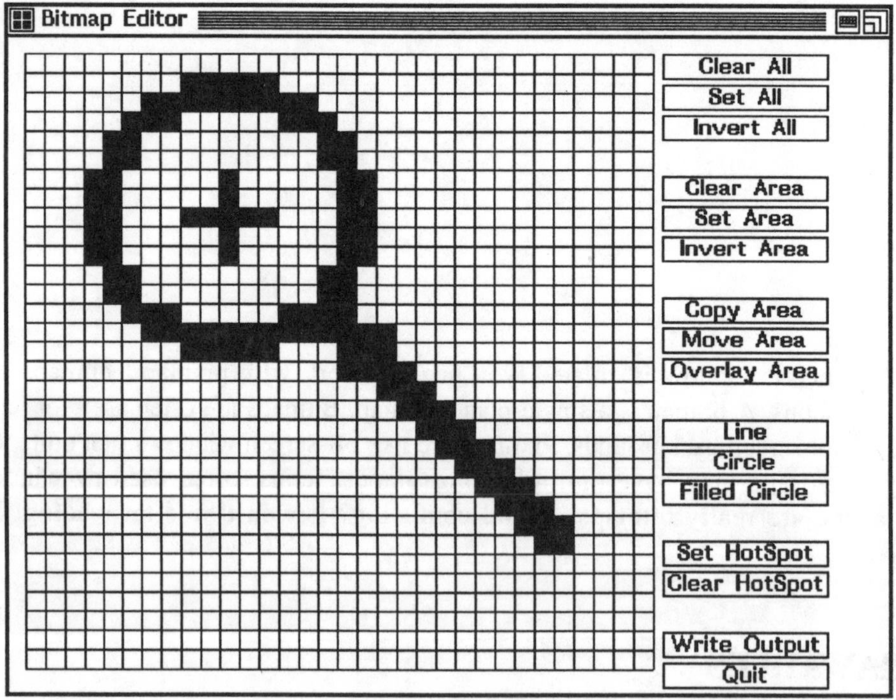

Figure 6-1. A Bitmap

ASCII Bitmap Files

Bitmaps can be stored in ASCII files. ASCII files are not storage-efficient, but they make life easy when you want to transport files between systems.

These ASCII files are used extensively by the X11 bitmap editor program, called `bitmap`. The ASCII file for the bitmap is pictured in figure 6-1.

```
#define bit_width 32
#define bit_height 32
static char bit_bits[] = {
   0x00, 0x00, 0x00, 0x00, 0x00, 0x1f, 0x00, 0x00, 0xc0, 0x7f, 0x00, 0x00,
   0xe0, 0xe0, 0x00, 0x00, 0x30, 0x80, 0x01, 0x00, 0x30, 0x80, 0x01, 0x00,
   0x18, 0x04, 0x03, 0x00, 0x18, 0x04, 0x03, 0x00, 0x18, 0x1f, 0x03, 0x00,
   0x18, 0x04, 0x03, 0x00, 0x18, 0x04, 0x03, 0x00, 0x30, 0x80, 0x01, 0x00,
   0x30, 0x80, 0x01, 0x00, 0xe0, 0xe0, 0x01, 0x00, 0xc0, 0xff, 0x07, 0x00,
   0x00, 0x1f, 0x07, 0x00, 0x00, 0x00, 0x0f, 0x00, 0x00, 0x00, 0x1c, 0x00,
   0x00, 0x00, 0x38, 0x00, 0x00, 0x00, 0x70, 0x00, 0x00, 0x00, 0xe0, 0x00,
   0x00, 0x00, 0xc0, 0x01, 0x00, 0x00, 0x80, 0x03, 0x00, 0x00, 0x00, 0x07,
   0x00, 0x00, 0x00, 0x0e, 0x00, 0x00, 0x00, 0x0c, 0x00, 0x00, 0x00, 0x00,
   0x00, 0x00, 0x00, 0x00, 0x00, 0x00, 0x00, 0x00, 0x00, 0x00, 0x00, 0x00,
   0x00, 0x00, 0x00, 0x00, 0x00, 0x00, 0x00, 0x00};
```

As you suspect, `Xlib` provides functions to read and write these ASCII bitmap files.

Reading A Bitmap File

`XReadBitmapFile()` will read in an ASCII bitmap file from disk and convert the data to a single-plane pixmap (a bitmap). Call `XReadBitmapFile()` as follows:

```
Display         *display;
Drawable        drawable;
char            filename[];
unsigned int    width, height;
Pixmap          pixmap;
int             xHotSpot, yHotSpot;
int             status;

status = XReadBitmapFile( display,
                drawable,
                filename,
```

```
                    &width, &height,
                    &pixmap,
                    &xHotSpot, &yHotSpot );

if ( status = = BitmapSuccess )
        {
        /* -- Yow! We did it. */

        ...

        }
else
        {
        /* -- Yech-o! An XReadBitmapFile() failed */

        ...

        }
```

Writing A Bitmap File

XWriteBitmapFile() is the opposite of XReadBitmapFile(). It writes a bitmap out to a disk file. Call XWriteBitmapFile () as follows:

```
Display         *display;
char            filename[];
unsigned int    width, height;
Pixmap          pixmap;
int             xHotSpot = (-1), yHotSpot = (-1);
int             status;

status = XWriteBitmapFile( display,
                filename,
                pixmap,         /* -- Note the different order! */
                width, height,
                xHotSpot, yHotSpot );

if ( status = = BitmapSuccess )
        {

        ...

        }
```

Note that if the hot spot is -1, -1, then no hot spot will be written out to disk. (Hot spots are for cursors.)

Source Code For bitmap.c

The file `bitmap.c` contains a function to load in ASCII bitmap files:

```
/*
 *      bitmap.c
 *      Utility routine for handling X11 bitmaps
 *      (single-plane pixmaps).
 *
 *      Written for Advanced X Window Applications Programming
 *
 */

#include  "xbook.h"

Pixmap LoadBitmap( display, window, filename, width, height )

Display *display;
Window  window;
char    filename[];            /* -- name of bitmap(1)-format file */
int     *width, *height;       /* -- returned size of the bitmap */

/*
 *      LoadBitmap() creates a 1-plane pixmap from an
 *      X bitmap file and then returns the pixmap, width
 *      and height.
 *
 *      The file should be in the text format used by the bitmap(1)
 *      application.
 *
 *      Errors: If the given bitmap file cannot be loaded,
 *      this function calls QuitX(), which will terminate
 *      the program.  You may want to recover from these
 *      errors instead.
 *
 */

{       /* -- function LoadBitmap */
        int     status;
        int     xHotSpot, yHotSpot;
        Pixmap  pixmap;
```

```
        status = XReadBitmapFile( display, window,
                        filename,
                        width, height,
                        &pixmap,
                        &xHotSpot, &yHotSpot );

        /*
         *      Exit on error
         */
        if ( status != BitmapSuccess )
                {
                QuitX( display, "Could not load bitmap ", filename );
                }

        return( pixmap );

}       /* -- function LoadBitmap */

/*
 *      end of file.
 */
```

PIXMAPS

Pixmaps are very similar to off-screen windows. They may have multiple color planes and can be used for things like backing storage for a window's image and as an animation buffer.

Creating Pixmaps

You can create pixmaps a number of ways, but the easiest is `XCreatePixmap()`.

When you create a pixmap, pay careful attention to the depth. Your options are limited for copying pixmaps onto windows (or other pixmaps) of different depths. It's best to use a depth that matches what you want to copy to. So, if you plan on copying the pixmap's contents onto a window, make both the pixmap and the window with the same depth. Call `XCreatePixmap()` as follows:

```
        Display         *display;
        Drawable        drawable;       /* -- usually your top-level window */
        unsigned int    width, height;
        unsigned int    depth;
```

```
Pixmap          pixmap;

pixmap = XCreatePixmap( display,
                drawable,
                width, height,
                depth );

if ( pixmap != (Pixmap) None )
        {
        /* -- Success */

        ...

        }
```

The drawable parameter is used to determine which screen the pixmap is created on. You cannot move pixmaps between screens. The depth parameter must be an acceptable depth for that screen.

Clearing Pixmaps

The first thing you should do with a pixmap is clear it out. Some earlier X servers, such as Release 2, cleared a pixmap on creation. That doesn't happen very much with later releases so you cannot depend on it. Instead you should create a graphics context for the pixmap and set the foreground color to the color you want to clear out the pixmap with. Then, call `XFillRectangle()`. You'll have to know how large the pixmap is, but if you clear the pixmap right after creation, your code already has the width and height values. Call `XFillRectangle()` as follows:

```
...
/* -- Create pixmap */

...

/* -- Create GC for pixmap */

...

/* -- Clear pixmap */
XFillRectangle( display, pixmap, gc,
        0, 0, width, height );
```

The function ClearPixmap() was developed to handle this task.

Copying Pixmaps to Windows

Two main functions exist for copying pixmap data, XCopyArea() and XCopyPlane():

```
Display          *display;
Drawable         src_drawable, dest_drawable;
GC               gc;
int              src_x, src_y;
unsigned int     width, height;
int              dest_x, dest_y;
unsigned long    plane;

XCopyArea( display,
        src_drawable, dest_drawable,
        gc,
        src_x, src_y,
        width, height,
        dest_x, dest_y );

XCopyPlane(  display,
        src_drawable, dest_drawable,
        gc,
        src_x, src_y,
        width, height,
        dest_x, dest_y,
        plane );
```

If you have an application that works fine on a monochrome system and has problems on a color system, you may be using these functions incorrectly. Since it can be a nasty issue, it's best to create pixmaps with the same depth as windows and then use XCopyArea(). XCopyArea() copies part (or all) of a drawable onto another drawable. Both drawables must have the same depth (and root, but the depth is usually the main issue). The bitview program, developed in chapter 9, uses this technique.

If you copy a bitmap onto a window or pixmap, use XCopyPlane(), which copies only one plane (bitmaps have just one plane). Usually the plane is set to 0x01.

Freeing Pixmaps When Done

Since pixmaps are resources in the X server, you should free them when you are through using the resource:

```
Display *display;
Pixmap  pixmap;

XFreePixmap( display, pixmap );
```

ICONS ARE BITMAPS

Icons, often used by window managers, are really bitmaps and bitmaps are really pixmaps. If you are confused, don't worry, it will soon become clear. You can load in an icon bitmap file from disk, with `XReadBitmapFile()`, or you can include the bitmap data right in your program. (You've already noticed that the ASCII bitmap files look a lot like a C program fragment, right? That's so you can include a bitmap file directly into your programs.)

For example, a small bitmap file could be called `"small.xb"`, shown in figure 6-2.

```
#define small_width 16
#define small_height 16
static char small_bits[] = {
   0x00, 0x80, 0xaa, 0xea, 0x54, 0xd5, 0xaa, 0xea, 0xd4, 0xd5, 0xea, 0xeb,
   0xf4, 0xd7, 0xfa, 0xef, 0xd4, 0xd5, 0xea, 0xeb, 0xd4, 0xd5, 0xea, 0xeb,
   0x54, 0xd5, 0xaa, 0xea, 0xfe, 0xff, 0xff, 0xff};
```

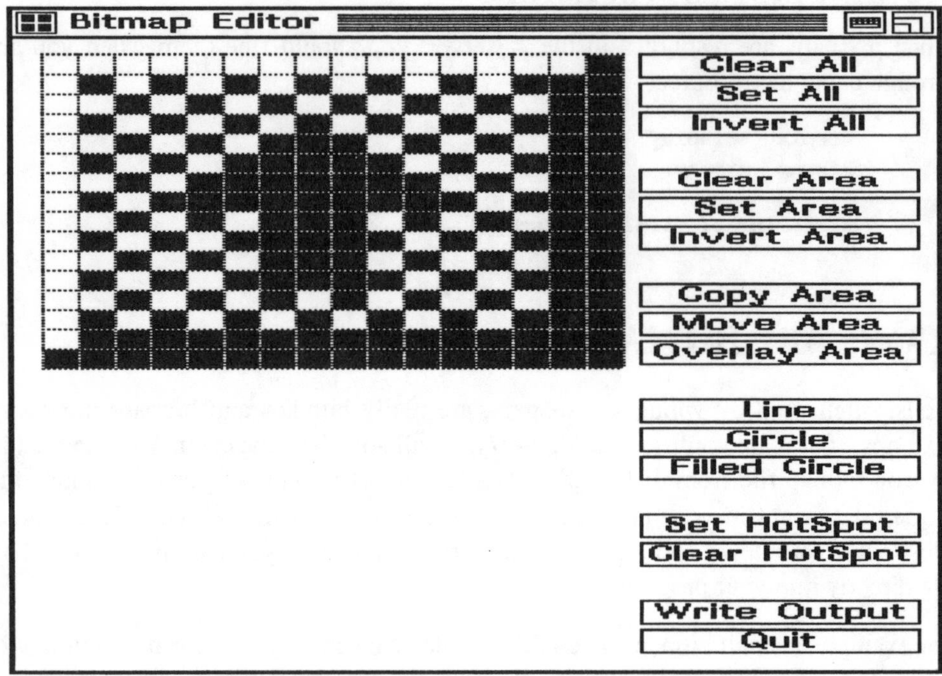

Figure 6-2. A Small Bitmap

You can include this ASCII bitmap into your program (directly or with the `#include` directive). The Xlib function `XCreateBitmapFromData()` will convert this data into a bitmap suitable for use as an icon:

```
#include "small.xb"

Display         *display;
Drawable        drawable;   /* -- usually your top-level window */
Pixmap          icon;

icon = XCreateBitmapFromData( display,
                drawable,
                small_bits,
                small_width, small_height );


if ( icon != (Pixmap) None )
```

```
{
/* -- Yeah, we did it */

...

}
```

ICON SIZES AND WINDOW MANAGERS

The main problem with icons is that a window manager may only support certain sizes for icons. Since you usually don't know what window manager all your users will be running, you'll have to guess on these sizes.

You can be fully responsible and include icons in your programs for every conceivable size (start with multiples of eight pixels in each direction), or you can punt.

We punted. Why? It isn't worth it. It just doesn't make sense to include four, eight or 100 different icons in an application, just to support someone's crazy window manager. No matter what, you have to guess what you think will be the common sizes. No matter what, you could guess wrong (of course, you may want to include a bitmap-scaling routine to handle any size). Some window managers don't even support icons. So, pick a size and just use that. If you guessed wrong for a significant number of users, they'll let you know. (You should make sure your icons were accepted by the Motif and `twm` window managers, and possibly the Open Look window manager, as these are becoming the most popular choices.)

SETTING THE ICON FOR A TOP-LEVEL WINDOW

As we described previously in `window.c` (chapter 3), you pass the icon pixmap to the window manager via the `XSetWMHints()` function. (Note that the code below requires Release 4. See `window.c` for more information and support for Release 3 and Release 2.) Call `XSetWMHints` as follows:

```
Display         *display;
Window          window;
XWMHints        *wmhints;

wmhints    = XAllocWMHints();
if ( wmhints != (XWMHints *) NULL )
```

```
{
wmhints->initial_state = NormalState;
wmhints->input         = True;

wmhints->icon_pixmap = icon;
wmhints->icon_mask   = icon;
wmhints->flags       =  StateHint      |
                        InputHint      |
                        IconPixmapHint |
                        IconMaskHint;
/*
 * Send the hints to the window manager
 */
XSetWMHints( display, window, wmhints );

XFree( wmhints );
}\
```

SOURCE CODE FOR pixmap.c

Pixmaps, which exist essentially as off-screen windows, can take up a lots of memory in the X server. You should be especially careful about creating large, multiplane pixmaps for use on X terminals (which typically have a small amount of RAM—the whole purpose of an X terminal is to cut the costs for using X).

The source code for `pixmap.c` is as follows:

```
pixmap.c:
/*
 *      pixmap.c
 *      Routines for creating and clearing X11 pixmaps.
 *
 *      Written for Advanced X Window Applications Programming.
 *
 */

#include  "xbook.h"

Pixmap CreatePixmap( display, window, width, height, depth, fore, back, gc )

Display         *display;
Window          window;
int             width, height, depth;
```

```
unsigned long   fore, back;
GC              *gc;

/*
 *      CreatePixmap() creates a pixmap and a graphics context
 *      for the pixmap. It will terminate the program if the
 *      pixmap cannot be created, with a call to QuitX().
 *
 */

{       /* -- function CreatePixmap */
        Pixmap  pixmap;

        pixmap = XCreatePixmap( display, window,
                        width, height, depth );

        /*
         *      If a failure,
         *      then exit
         */
        if ( pixmap = = (Pixmap) None )
                {
                QuitX( display,
                        "ERROR: Could not create pixmap",
                        " " );
                }

        /*
         *      If you get to here,
         *      you have succeeded.
         */
        *gc = MakeGC( display, pixmap, fore, back );

        /*
         *      Clear out pixmap
         */
        ClearPixmap( display, pixmap, *gc, fore, back, width, height );

        return( pixmap );

}       /* -- function CreatePixmap */

ClearPixmap( display, pixmap, gc, fore, back, width, height )

Display         *display;
Pixmap          pixmap;
```

```
GC              gc;
unsigned long   fore, back;
int             width, height;

/*
 *      ClearPixmap() clears a pixmap with its background
 *      color.  When done, ClearPixmap() resets the
 *      pixmap's GC to the proper foreground color.
 *
 */

{       /* -- function ClearPixmap */

        XSetForeground( display, gc, back );

        XFillRectangle( display, pixmap, gc,
                0, 0, width, height );

        XSetForeground( display, gc, fore );

}       /* -- function ClearPixmap */

/*
 *      end of file
 */
```

FUNCTIONS DEVELOPED IN THIS CHAPTER

ClearPixmap
CreatePixmap
LoadBitmap

XLIB FUNCTIONS AND MACROS INTRODUCED IN THIS CHAPTER

XCopyArea
XCopyPlane
XCreateBitmapFromData
XCreatePixmap
XFreePixmap
XReadBitmapFile
XWriteBitmapFile

SUMMARY

- Just about every drawing operation that works on windows also works on `pixmaps`. You create a graphics context for the pixmap—just like for windows. Then you can draw lines, rectangles and other shapes, and text into pixmaps.
- Bitmaps are single-plane pixmaps. That is, a bitmap only has on and off information for its pixels. You may draw a bitmap onto a window in a foreground color and a background color, but that's it. Bitmaps are often used for icons or screen backgrounds with the `xsetroot` program. Bitmaps can be stored in ASCII files. ASCII files are not storage-efficient, but they sure make life easy when you want to transport files between systems.
- Pixmaps are like off-screen windows (not quite, but very close). Pixmaps may have multiple color planes. You can create pixmaps a number of ways, but the easiest is `XCreatePixmap()`. You clear pixmaps using `ClearPixmap()`.
- Icons, often used by window managers, are really bitmaps. You can load in an icon bitmap file from disk, with `XReadBitmapFile()`, or you can include the bitmap data right in your program. The main problem with icons is that a window manager may only support certain sizes. Since you usually don't know what window manager all your users will be running, you'll have to guess on these sizes.

SUMMARY

Chapter 7

Cursors

We've shown you how to create a cursor in the very first program in this book, the now-famous gumby program. This chapter covers a bit more about cursors. In it, we show you how to build a function for cursor creation and a function for tying a cursor to a window.

The X Window System comes with a special font, called cursor, that contains a set of standard, if primitive, cursor shapes. The best thing about the cursor font is that it's available as a standard part of X. (An even better thing is that this font has been improved in Release 4.) Some X toolkits come with their own set of cursors, but in general, you should stick to the standard cursor font.

CREATING CURSORS

```
Display         *display;

unsigned int    which_cursor;
Cursor          cursor;

cursor = XCreateFontCursor( display, which_cursor );

if ( cursor != (Cursor) None )
        {
        /* -- the cursor was created */

        ...

        }
```

The which_cursor parameter comes from a list of symbols defined in <X11/cursorfont.h> and includes symbols like XC_gumby.

TYING A CURSOR TO A WINDOW

Once you create a cursor, you need to tie the cursor to a window. This means that whenever the mouse pointer enters the window, it will assume the shape of your cursor. Use XDefineCursor() to tie a cursor to a window:

```
DISPLAY *DISPLAY;
Window  window;
Cursor  cursor;

XDefineCursor( display, window, cursor );
```

You can call XDefineCursor() repeatedly. Each call overrides the previous call and allows you, for example, to have a busy cursor and a normal cursor. When your application is busy, it can define the busy cursor for your application's windows.

FREEING CURSORS

When finished with a cursor, free up the X server resource with `XFreeCursor()`:

```
Display *display;
Cursor  cursor;

XFreeCursor( display, cursor );
```

THE X11 CURSOR FONT

The cursor font shown in figures 7-1 and 7-2 is a standard part of X. You can use any of these cursors in your applications. Pass the symbol (for example, `XC_gumby`) as the `which_cursor` parameter to the `MakeCursor()` function. Be sure to include the X11 header file `<X11/cursorfont.h>` or you will have no fun.

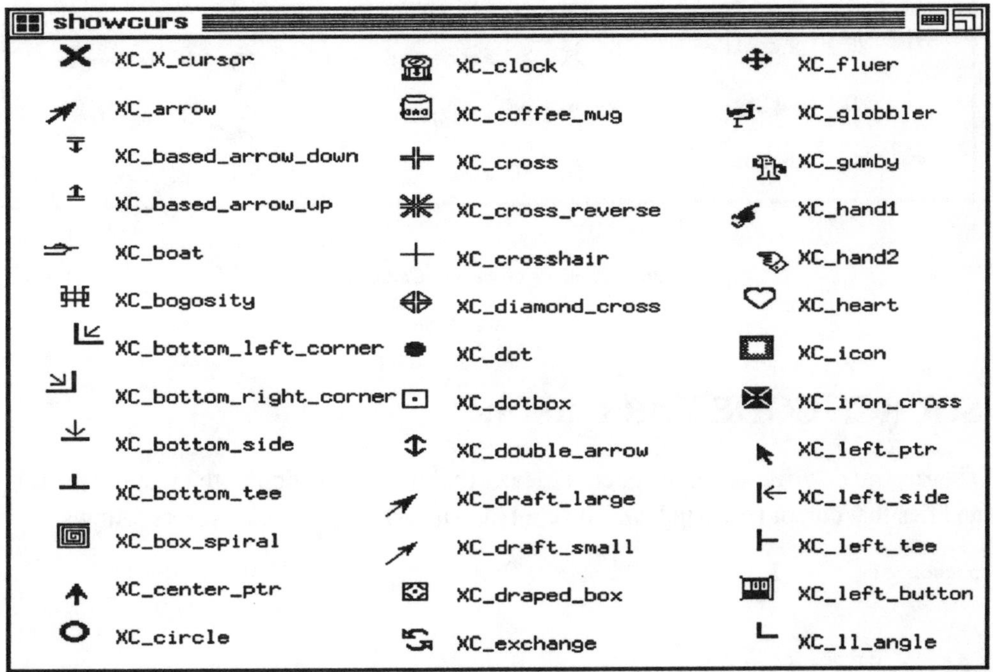

Figure 7-1. The X11 Cursor Font

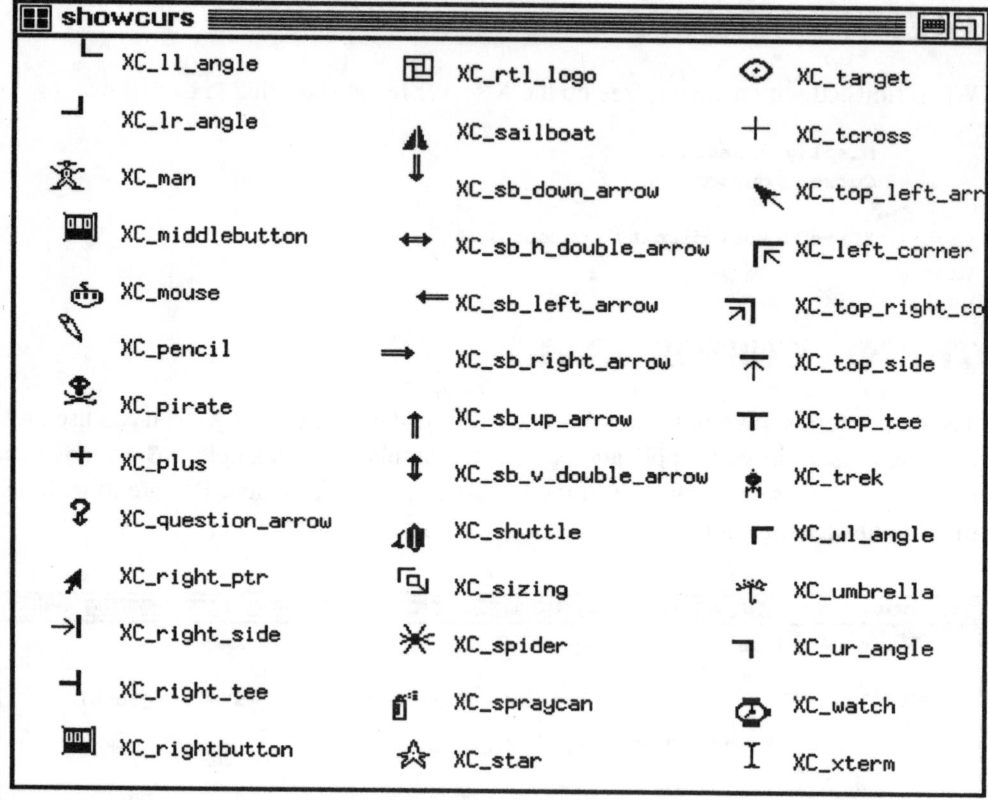

Figure 7-2. More of the X11 Cursor Font

SOURCE CODE FOR cursor.c

The `cursor.c` file has one function, `MakeCursor()`, which both creates a cursor and ties that cursor to a window. The contents of `MakeCursor()` are as follows:

cursor.c:

```
/*
 *      cursor.c
 *      X11 C routine for setting up a cursor for a window.
 *
```

```
 *      Written for Advanced X Window Applications Programming
 *
 */

#include  "xbook.h"

Cursor MakeCursor( display, window, which_cursor )

Display         *display;
Window          window;
unsigned int    which_cursor;

/*
 *      MakeCursor() creates a cursor resource in the X server
 *      and then sets a given window to use that cursor.
 *
 */

{       /* -- function MakeCursor */
        Cursor  cursor;

        /*
         *      Create the cursor from the standard
         *      cursor font
         */
        cursor = XCreateFontCursor( display, (unsigned) which_cursor );

        /*
         *      If we succeeded in creating
         *      the cursor, then set the
         *      window to use that
         *      cursor
         */
        if ( cursor != (Cursor) None )
                {
                XDefineCursor( display, window, cursor );
                }

        return( cursor );

}       /* -- function MakeCursor */

/*
 *      end of file.
 */
```

FUNCTIONS DEVELOPED IN THIS CHAPTER

```
MakeCursor
```

XLIB FUNCTIONS AND MACROS USED IN THIS CHAPTER

```
XCreateFontCursor
XDefineCursor
```

SUMMARY

- The X Window System comes with a special font, called cursor, that contains a set of standard cursor shapes. Once you create a cursor, you need to use `XDefineCursor()` and tie the cursor to a window. Whenever the mouse pointer enters the window, it will assume the shape of your cursor. When finished with a cursor, free up the X server resource with `XFreeCursor()`.

Chapter 8

Text and Fonts

Now that you've created windows, you need to fill the windows with text. This isn't necessarily a simple process, following the X Window dictum of mechanism, not policy. This chapter covers loading fonts, font structures, and the wise use of font resources.

FONT IDS AND FONT STRUCTURES

X fonts are stored as resources in the X server and take up precious server memory.

These fonts are identified two ways in Xlib routines: by font ID numbers and font structures. Font structures provide a better interface, since a font structure contains a font ID number as well as information regarding the size of the font. Font size will be discussed later in this chapter.

The contents of `XFontStruct` are as follows:

```
typedef struct
        {
        XExtData        *ext_data;        /* -- for X extensions */
        Font            fid;              /* -- Font ID */
        unsigned        direction;        /* -- just a HINT */
        unsigned        min_char_or_byte2;
        unsigned        max_char_or_byte2;
        unsigned        min_byte1;
        unsigned        max_byte1;
        Bool            all_chars_exist; /* -- flag for holes in font */
        unsigned        default_char;
        int             n_properties;     /* -- number of properties */
        XFontProp       *properties;      /* -- array of properties */
        XCharStruct     min_bounds;
        XCharStruct     max_bounds;
        XCharStruct     *per_char;        /* -- first to last char */
        int             ascent;           /* -- height above baseline */
        int             descent;          /* -- below baseline */
        } XFontStruct;
```

The `XFontProp` structure is defined as:

```
typedef struct
        {
        Atom            name;
        unsigned long   card32;
        } XFontProp;
```

The `XCharStruct` structure is defined as:

```
typedef struct
        {
        short           lbearing;
        short           rbearing;
        short           width;
        short           ascent;
        short           descent;
```

```
        unsigned short  attributes;
        } XCharStruct;
```

That's a lot of structures. You'll probably only ever use a few fields.

LOADING FONTS

There are two ways to load fonts. One way returns a font ID, the other way returns a pointer to an `XFontStruct` structure. `XLoadFont()` loads up a given font and returns its font ID. You pass the display pointer and the name of the font you want to use.

```
Display         *display;
char            *name;
Font            font_id;

font_id = XLoadFont( display, name );
```

Once you've loaded a font, you can get a structure that contains information about the font, including its height, by calling `XQueryFont()`:

```
XFontStruct     *font_struct;

font_struct     = XQueryFont( display, font_id );
```

Finally, if you know you'll need the font information returned by `XQueryFont()`, you can do both of the above operations at once with `XLoadQueryFont()`. `XLoadQueryFont()` loads up the named font, but returns a pointer to an `XFontStruct`, not just a font ID.

```
font_struct     = XLoadQueryFont( display, name );
```

Since we often want to find out how tall a font is, or how wide a given string is, we use `XLoadQueryFont()` exclusively in the source example in the section "Source Code for font.c"

COMMON FONT NAMES

Each X implementation comes with a host of fonts--more appear in every release. We've only seen two fonts consistently appear in X implementations: the cursor font, introduced in chapter 7, and the fixed font, a small fixed-width font. The cursor font contains the standard cursor shapes.

Another common font name is "variable" (usually looking like a version of Helvetica), but we have seen at least one system that didn't come with the variable font (the first release of Sun's OpenWindows X11/NeWS merged product). X11 Release 3 added a host of new fonts to the standard release and eliminated a few old fonts. More fonts were added in Release 4.

You must be prepared if the font you want is not available. If you choose a font that isn't on a user's X implementation, there's not much you can do. Your first step is avoiding the problem and letting the user choose a font name. This is done by specifying a font name on the Unix command line:

```
myprogram -font myfontname
```

The `-font` option is fairly standard in the X world. Also, `-fn` is often accepted.

If you can't load the desired font, use this three-step tier:

1) If the user specifies a font name on the command line, try that font first.

2) If 1) fails, try a default font name.

3) If 2) fails, try the font named "`fixed.`"

If all that fails, punt. There's not a lot you can do.

SETTING UP A GRAPHICS CONTEXT TO USE A FONT

Before you can draw text, you need to set up a graphics context with your desired font. `XSetFont()` sets a given `GC` to use the desired font for text output:

```
Display *display;
GC      gc;
```

```
Font    font_id;

XSetFont( display, gc, font_id );
```

If you called XLoadQueryFont(), then you have a font structure, not a font ID. You can access the fid field of the font structure in the call to XSetFont(), for example:

```
XFontStruct     *font_struct;

XSetFont( display, gc, font_struct->fid );
```

SOURCE CODE FOR font.c

The file font.c contains a function, LoadFont(), that handles the task of loading a font and setting up a graphics context to use that font. LoadFont() returns a pointer to an XFontStruct.

CheckFontName() checks the Unix command-line parameters (argc, argv) for a font name. Pass LoadFont(), a display pointer, a GC, the command-line parameters (argc, argv) and a default font name:

```
main( argc, argv )
int     argc;
char    *argv[];

{       /* -- main */

        Display         *display;
        GC              gc;
        XFontStruct     *font_struct;

        /*
         * Open display, create a top-level window and a GC
         */

        ...

        font_struct = LoadFont( display, gc,
                                argc, argv,     /* -- command-line */
                                "variable" );   /* -- default name */
```

```
        ...
```

font.c:

```
/*
 *      font.c
 *      X11 routines to load in a font
 *
 *      Written for Advanced X Window Applications Programming
 *
 */

#include   "xbook.h"

XFontStruct *LoadFont( display, gc, argc, argv, default_name )

Display *display;
GC      gc;
int     argc;
char    *argv[];
char    default_name[];

/*
 *      LoadFont()
 *              1) Checks the command-line for a font name
 *              (-font fontname or -fn fontname).
 *              The default_name is used if no font name
 *              is found.
 *              2) Tries to load a font.
 *              3) If all else fails, LoadFont()
 *              tries to load a font called "fixed".
 *              ("fixed" seems to be a common font name
 *              and is available on more systems than
 *              "variable", another common name. Sun's
 *              X11/NeWS OpenWindows 1.0 has "fixed" but not
 *              "variable".)
 *              4) If all this still fails to load a font,
 *              the program is terminated by a call to
 *              QuitX().
 *              5) If it succeeds, though, the font is
 *              set up in the given graphics context, gc,
 *              and is then suitable for drawing text.
 *
 */

{       /* -- function LoadFont */
```

```
XFontStruct       *font;
char              name[ BUFSIZE + 1 ];

/*
 * Get a user-specified font name
 */
(void) strcpy( name, default_name );

CheckFontName( argc, argv, name );

/*
 * Load in the user-specified font
 */
font = XLoadQueryFont( display, name );

/*
 *      If we couldn't find the font,
 *      try a default.
 */

if ( font = = (XFontStruct *) NULL )
        {
        font = XLoadQueryFont( display, default_name );

        /*
         *      If we still have a problem,
         *      try a common name
         */
        if ( font = = (XFontStruct *) NULL )
                {
                font = XLoadQueryFont( display, "fixed" );
                }
        }

if ( font != (XFontStruct *) NULL )
        {
        XSetFont( display, gc, font->fid );
        }
else
        {
        /*
         *      Not loading a font is
         *      considered a fatal error.
         */
        QuitX( display, "Error: could not load font ",
                name );
```

```
                }

        return( font );

}       /* -- function LoadFont */

CheckFontName( argc, argv, fontname )

int     argc;
char    *argv[];
char    fontname[];

/*
 *      CheckFontName() checks the command line for a
 *      font specification.
 *
 *      A default font should be passed to CheckFontName(),
 *      as it does nothing if no name is specified.
 *
 */

{       /* -- function CheckFontName */
        int     counter;

        counter  = 1;
        while( counter < argc )
                {
                if ( ( strncmp( argv[ counter ], "-font", 5 ) = = 0 ) ||
                   ( strncmp( argv[ counter ], "-fn", 3 ) = = 0 ) )
                        {
                        counter++;
                        if ( counter < argc )
                                {
                                (void) strcpy( fontname, argv[ counter ] );
                                }
                        else
                                {
                                (void) fprintf( stderr,
                                  "Error: usage is -font FontName\n" );
                                }
                        }

                counter++;
                }
```

```
}        /* -- function CheckFontName */

/*
 *      end of file
 */
```

THE SIZE OF THE LETTERS IN A FONT

Once you've loaded a font, you may want to do something with it—most probably output text. The first question, though, is how big the font is. You need to determine the size of the font to accurately space the text. This requires knowing both the height of the font and the width of a given string in the font.

The height bounds for a given font are in the font structure (`XFontStruct`). The height of a line of text should be:

```
int             height;
XFontStruct     *font_struct;

height = font_struct->ascent + font_struct->descent;
```

The width of a given character string in pixels in a given font is returned by `XTextWidth()`.

```
XFontStruct     *font_struct;
char            string[ 120 ];
int             number_letters;

strcpy( string, "I Like Ike" );

width = XTextWidth( font_struct, string, number_letters );
```

The value in width will be the number of pixels wide the string "I Like Ike" takes up using the given font. Note that in a proportional font, a string like "I Like Ike" will generally have less width that a string like "WOMBATS!!!," even though both strings have the same number of characters. "M" and "W" are typically the widest characters (at least in ASCII). "I" and "j" are typically among the thinnest characters.

Now that you can find out how big the text is, you may want to draw some text.

DRAWING TEXT

XDrawString() draws a text string onto a given drawable. It draws only the foreground of the text (that is, the text is drawn in the foreground color).

```
Display         *display;
Drawable        drawable;
GC              gc;
int             x, y;
char            *string;
int             string_length;


XDrawString( display,
                drawable,
                gc,
                x, y,
                string,
                string_length );
```

XDrawImageString() draws the foreground of the text and fills in the background of the letters with the GC's background color:

```
XDrawImageString( display,
                drawable,
                gc,
                x, y,
                string,
                string_length );
```

XDrawImageString() is especially important for terminal emulators and for drawing text over other text without the flickering caused by clearing the area.

FREEING FONTS WHEN DONE

A font, like any other X resource, should be freed when you are done with it. Since there are two ways to load fonts, there are, of course, two ways to free fonts.

If you used XLoadFont() to load up the font, use XUnloadFont() to free the font ID.

If you used `XLoadQueryFont()` and received a font structure, then call `XFreeFont()` to free the font:

```
Display         *display;
Font            font_id;

XUnloadFont( display, font_id );

Display         *display;
XFontStruct     *font_struct;

XFreeFont( display, font_struct );
```

FUNCTIONS DEVELOPED IN THIS CHAPTER

CheckFontName
LoadFont

XLIB FUNCTIONS AND MACROS INTRODUCED IN THIS CHAPTER

XDrawImageString
XDrawString
XFreeFont
XLoadFont
XLoadQueryFont
XQueryFont
XSetFont
XTextWidth
XUnloadFont

SUMMARY

- X fonts are stored as resources in the X server and are identified two ways in Xlib routines: by font ID numbers and font structures. There are two ways to load fonts: One way returns a font ID; the other way returns a pointer to a font structure.

- `XLoadFont()` loads up a given font and returns its font ID. `XQueryFont()` passes a structure that contains information about the font, including its height, once you've loaded a font. `XLoadQueryFont()` performs both operations at once.

- Each X implementation comes with a host of fonts and different vendors include different fonts. Two of the consistently appear in X implementations: the "cursor" font and the "fixed" font, a small fixed-width font. If your chosen font isn't available, you can either let the user choose a font name, try a default font name, or try the fixed font. After calling a font, you must set a graphics context with your desired font.

- You must determine the size of the font to accurately space the text. This requires knowing both the height of the font and the width of a given string in the font . The height bounds for a given font are in the font structure (`XFontStruct`); the width of a given character string in pixels in a given font is returned by `XTextWidth()`.

Chapter 9

A Sample Program to View Bitmaps

Chapter 9 pulls together all the code in section I into a library of routines that make writing Xlib-based applications easier. First, we flesh out the library and then we build a sample program called `Bitview` using the library. `Bitview` displays a number of X bitmaps in a window and mainly serves to illustrate the concepts of section I.

OPENING UP THE TOP-LEVEL WINDOW

Just about every X application creates one top-level window. A few create two or more top-level windows. No matter what your application, chances are that most of your top-level windows will be the same or at least have a number of features in common. For example, most top-level windows default to a white background and a black border.

The function `TopWindow()`, creates the top-level window, as well as a graphics context and an icon. `TopWindow()` gives the window:

- a black, 2-pixel wide border
- a white background
- a default cursor (an arrow cursor)
- a default event mask

Both the event mask and the cursor are defined in the file `xbook.h`, shown in a section to follow.

RESOURCES, DEFAULTS, AND COMPLEXITY

When we call `TopWindow()`, we're not trying to limit the flexibility of application programs. We've just noticed that for most applications, these defaults are sufficient. There's always a relationship between complexity and flexibility. Increase flexibility and you usually gain complexity. We'd rather have the complexity lie within the application rather than in the development of a window. The whole idea is to minimize the work at hand (the X overhead) so that your applications can go about their business.

The X Window System has a set of conventions called resources that allows users to customize X applications. The X resource data base can be built up from defaults and a set of resource files. These resource files are usually ASCII text files that follow a certain syntax. Unfortunately, sometimes the resource files exceed the size of the executable program. Moreover, few users know what resource files are or how to change them. Most users who do know about resource files don't want to be forced into this anyway. Should you use the resource-manager routines?

It's a trade off. If you use the resource-manager routines, you gain flexibility, but you add complexity. Some programs that should be relatively simple have resource files in excess of 15 kilobytes in size. If you are trying to port software to X or want to make life as easy as possible for your users (who most likely are unfamiliar with X), we advise skipping the use of X's resource-manager routines. As part of that philosophy, and due to lack of space, the X resource-manager is not covered in this book. (This was a long, hard decision. Whenever you make a choice like this you're stuck: the purists will hate you. However, the pragmatists will see where you are coming from. We're pragmatists. We've seen X users have too much trouble already because of the complexity of the system, while most despair at ever understanding how to customize it. The best advice we have is to make it simple.)

If you don't like this approach, just remember that the programs in this book were designed to highlight the concepts of X and not to replace commercial applications.

SOURCE CODE FOR topwind.c

The contents of `topwind.c` are as follows:

```
topwind.c:

#include  "xbook.h"

Window TopWindow( display, x, y, width, height,
        bitmap_data, bitmap_width, bitmap_height, icon, gc )

Display         *display;
int             x, y, width, height;
char            *bitmap_data;
int             bitmap_width, bitmap_height;
Pixmap          *icon;
GC              *gc;

/*
 *      TopWindow() creates an application's top-level window.
 *      It makes anumber of assumptions about how you want
 *      that window to look (change them if they bother you)
 *      and also takes care of a few details in setting up
 *      the top-level window.
 *
 *      TopWindow() creates the top-level window, a GC for the window
 *      and an Icon to pass to the window manager. A cursor is created
 *      and associated with the window.
 *
 *      TopWindow() assumes:
 *              default screen
 *              black border
 *              white background
 *              2-pixel border width
```

```
 *              fixed event mask (from xbook.h)
 *              fixed cursor (from xbook.h)
 *
 */

{       /* -- function TopWindow */
        int             screen;
        Window          rootwindow, window;
        unsigned long   black, white;
        Cursor          cursor;

        /*
         * Get defaults
         */
        screen     = DefaultScreen( display );

        rootwindow = RootWindow( display, screen );

        black      = BlackPixel( display, screen );
        white      = WhitePixel( display, screen );

        /*
         * Create window
         */
#define BORDER_WIDTH    2

        window  = CreateWindow( display,
                        rootwindow,
                        x, y, width, height,
                        BORDER_WIDTH,
                        black, white,
                        EVENT_MASK );

        /*
         * Create GC
         */
        *gc = MakeGC( display, window, black, white );

        /*
         * Create Icon Pixmap
         */
        *icon = XCreateBitmapFromData( display, window,
                        bitmap_data,
                        bitmap_width, bitmap_height );

        cursor  = MakeCursor( display, window, DEFAULT_CURSOR );
```

```
        XFreeCursor( display, cursor );

        XFlush( display );

        return( window );

}       /* -- function TopWindow */

/*
 *      end of file
 */
```

A COMMON HEADER FILE FOR THE EXAMPLE SOURCES

Since so many of the functions introduced in this book return odd types, like XFontStruct pointers or Window IDs, we decided to declare the return types in one place to maintain consistency. We put these definitions into a file called xbook.h. To make things easier, we also placed the include directives for the necessary Xlib header files in xbook.h and declared a few macros .

SOURCE CODE FOR xbook.h

The contents of xbook.h are as follows:

xbook.h:

```
/*
 *      Include the most common
 *      X11 header files. Note: Xos.h may
 *      give you some grief.  You may have to define
 *      a symbol like "sun" or "i386" to get this
 *      file to compile.  If you have problems (most likely
 *      the compiler bombing out on Xos.h), look into
 *      the file and see what definition you really need.
 *
 */
#include    <stdio.h>
#include    <memory.h>
```

```
#include   <X11/Xlib.h>
#include   <X11/Xutil.h>
#include   <X11/Xos.h>
#include   <X11/cursorfont.h>
#include   <X11/keysym.h>
#include   <X11/keysymdef.h>
#include   <X11/Xatom.h>

/*
 *      Default big string size
 */
#ifndef BUFSIZE
#define BUFSIZE 256
#endif

/*
 *      Define full size for properties. This is an X magic
 *      constant.
 */
#define  FULL_LENGTH    8192L

/*
 *      Property name for Property examples.  This is an arbitrary name.
 */
#define PROP_NAME   "__XBOOK"

/*
 *      Common event mask for top-level windows.
 *      Using this event mask just makes
 *      application development easier.
 */
#define EVENT_MASK      (long)( ButtonPressMask    | \
                                KeyPressMask       | \
                                ExposureMask       | \
                                StructureNotifyMask )


/*
 *      Default cursor
 */
#define DEFAULT_CURSOR  XC_left_ptr

/*
 *      Size of user interface buttons
 */
#define BUTTON_WIDTH    70
#define BUTTON_HEIGHT   24
```

```
/*
 *      Declare functions (old-style) that
 *      do not return an int type.
 *
 */

Atom ConvertTarget();

Cursor MakeCursor();

Display *SetUpDisplay();
Display *OpenDisplay();

GC MakeGC();

KeySym Key2Keysym();

Pixmap CreatePixmap();
Pixmap LoadBitmap();

Time LastTimeStamp();
Time PrimaryTimeStamp();

unsigned long Bytes2Long();
unsigned long GetColor();

Window BuildWList();
Window CheckWindow();
Window CreateWindow();

Window FindWindow();
Window FindSendWindow();
Window FindSubWindow();

Window GetParent();

Window PickWindow();
Window SearchWindowTree();
Window TopWindow();

XFontStruct *LoadFont();

/*
 *      end of file
 */
```

Bitview

Bitview is a program for displaying bitmaps. It ties together the example functions shown in the preceding eight chapters into a program that shows how to put all this stuff together. Much of the Bitview code is derived from the example code in the preceding chapters, so a minimum of explanation is provided. If you work through the code, you will see the routines for bitmaps, pixmaps, windows, and the rest in action.

The Bitview program displays a number of X ASCII bitmap files (figure 9-1) similar to those described in chapter 6.

Figure 9-1. The Bitview Program

STARTING Bitview

When Bitview starts up, it first checks to see if there are enough command-line parameters. Then it sets up a connection to an X server:

```
main( argc, argv )

int     argc;
char    *argv[];

{       /* -- main */
        Display         *display;
        int             screen;
        Window          rootwindow;
        unsigned long   black, white;

        display    = SetUpDisplay( argc, argv, &screen );
```

```
        rootwindow = RootWindow( display, screen );
        black      = BlackPixel( display, screen );
        white      = WhitePixel( display, screen );

        ...
```

LOADING BITMAPS

Next, Bitview checks the command-line parameters for names of ASCII bitmap files and loads these files into a global array of pixmaps. PixmapWidth and PixmapHeight are globals; their contents are as follows:

```
        GC      pixgc;
        int     num_bitmaps;
        int     width, height;
        Pixmap  pixmap;

        ...

        num_bitmaps = BuildPixmaps( display,
                                    rootwindow,
                                    argc, argv,
                                    &width, &height );
        /*
         *      Now, create a big Pixmap to
         *      hold all the bitmaps
         */
#define HEIGHT_OFFSET 20
        PixmapWidth    = width;
        PixmapHeight   = height + HEIGHT_OFFSET;

        /*
         * Notice how CreatePixmap() uses the DefaultDepth().
         * This is to make sure XCopyArea() can be called.
         */
        pixmap = CreatePixmap( display, rootwindow,
                        PixmapWidth, PixmapHeight,
                        DefaultDepth( display, screen ),
                        black, white, &pixgc );

        /*
         *      Copy all the bitmaps into
         *      the Pixmap for the whole window
```

```
         */
        FillNewPixmap( display, pixmap, pixgc, num_bitmaps );

        /*
         *      free resource
         */
        XFreeGC( display, pixgc );

        XFlush( display );
```

The function `BuildPixmaps()` goes through the Unix command line and loads in the desired ASCII bitmap files, placing the bitmaps in the global array `the_bitmaps[]`:

```
BuildPixmaps( display, rootwindow, argc, argv, sum_width, sum_height )

Display *display;
Window  rootwindow;
int     argc;
char    *argv[];
int     *sum_width, *sum_height;

{       /* -- function BuildPixmaps */
        int     i, max, num_bitmaps;
        int     width, height;
        Pixmap  pixmap;

        ...

        max          = argc -1;
        *sum_width   = 10;
        *sum_height  = 10;
        num_bitmaps  = 0;
        i            = 0;

        while( i < max )
                {
                the_bitmaps[ num_bitmaps ].x =  *sum_width;
                the_bitmaps[ num_bitmaps ].y = 10;

                /*
                 *      Jump over display, geometry
                 *      and font args
                 */
                if ( argv[ i + 1 ][ 0 ] = = '-' )
```

```
                {
                i += 2;
                continue;
                }

            pixmap = LoadBitmap( display, rootwindow,
                         argv[ i + 1 ],
                         &width, &height );

            if ( height >  *sum_height )
                {
                *sum_height = height + 5;
                }

            *sum_width   += ( width + 5 );

            the_bitmaps[ num_bitmaps ].width     = width;
            the_bitmaps[ num_bitmaps ].height    = height;
            the_bitmaps[ num_bitmaps ].bitmap    = pixmap;
            num_bitmaps++;

            i++;
            }

        return( num_bitmaps );

}       /* -- function BuildPixmaps */
```

`FillNewPixmap()` copies the one-plane pixmaps (also called bitmaps) stored in the `the_bitmaps[]` array into one large pixmap. The large pixmap is the size of the window `Bitview` creates. It serves as backing storage for the window. The bitmaps are copied onto the pixmap; there any part of the pixmap can be copied to the application's top-level window to refresh part of the window. The backing pixmap has the same depth as the top-level window, while the bitmaps all have one plane of depth. Since the bitmaps have one plane of depth, we use `XCopyPlane()` to copy the contents of the bitmaps onto the larger pixmap.This part of `bitview.c` is as follows:

```
FillNewPixmap( display, pixmap, pixgc, num_bitmaps )

Display *display;
Pixmap  pixmap;
GC      pixgc;
int     num_bitmaps;
```

```
/*
 *      Accesses the GLOBAL array of bitmaps,
 *      the_bitmaps, and copies each of these bitmaps
 *      into the given window-backing large pixmap.
 */

{       /* -- function FillNewPixmap */
        int     i;

        for( i = 0; i < num_bitmaps; i++ )
                {
                XCopyPlane( display,
                        the_bitmaps[ i ].bitmap,
                        pixmap, pixgc,
                        0, 0,                   /* -- Src X, y */
                        the_bitmaps[ i ].width,
                        the_bitmaps[ i ].height,
                        the_bitmaps[ i ].x,     /* -- Dest X, Y */
                        the_bitmaps[ i ].y,
                        0x01 );                 /* -- Only one plane */

                /*
                 *      Clean up
                 */
                XFreePixmap( display,
                        the_bitmaps[ i ].bitmap );
                }

}       /* -- function FillNewPixmap */
```

CREATING Bitview's TOP-LEVEL WINDOW

`CheckGeometry()` checks the command-line parameters for a window geometry string and sets x, y, width, and height accordingly. If no geometry string is given, then the x and y are defaulted to 10,10. The default width and height is roughly the size of the combined bitmap files (with a bit of padding).

```
Window  window;
GC      gc;
int     x, y;

...
```

```
/*
 *      Open a window to hold the pixmap
 */
x       = 10;
y       = 10;
height += HEIGHT_OFFSET;

CheckGeometry( argc, argv,
        DisplayWidth(  display, screen ),
        DisplayHeight( display, screen ),
        &x, &y, &width, &height );

window    = TopWindow( display, x, y, width, height,
                bit_bits, bit_width, bit_height,
                &icon, &gc );

/*
 * Pass hints to the window manager
 */
SetNormalHints( display, window,
        x, y, width, height );

SetWMHints( display, window, icon );

NameWindow( display, window,
        "bitview",
        "bitview",
        "Bitview" );
```

Bitview's Eventloop

`Bitview's EventLoop()` function is rather simple. It blocks awaiting an "interesting" event to arrive from the X server.

```
EventLoop( display, window, pixmap, gc, width, height )

Display *display;
Window  window;
Pixmap  pixmap;
GC      gc;
int     *width, *height;

{       /* -- function EventLoop */
        XEvent          event;
```

```
KeySym          keysym;

/*
 *      Block on input, awaiting
 *      an event from X.
 */
NextEvent( display, True,
        *width, *height,
        &event,
        &keysym );

...
```

EventLoop() calls Refresh() to redraw an exposed area, or checks if a KeyPress is a “q” (or “Q”) to quit the program. EventLoop() returns False to quit and True to continue. Eventloop() continues as follows:

```
...

/*
 *      Decode the event and call
 *      a specific routine to
 *      handle it.
 */
switch( event.type )
        {
        case  Expose:
                /*
                 *      Copy the necessary part of
                 *      the backing pixmap
                 *      to refresh the screen
                 */
                Refresh( display, window,
                        gc, pixmap,
                        event.xexpose.x,
                        event.xexpose.y,
                        event.xexpose.width,
                        event.xexpose.height );

                XFlush( display );
                break;
        case  KeyPress:
                /*
                 *      Quit on a
                 *      Q or q
```

```
                    */
                    if ( ( keysym = = XK_Q ) || ( keysym = = XK_q ) )
                            {
                            return( False );
                            }
                    break;

            ...

            }

        return( True );

}       /* -- function EventLoop */
```

REFRESHING AREAS OF THE WINDOW

When part of `Bitview`'s window needs to be redrawn—or refreshed—the `Refresh()` function copies the backing pixmap to the window. `Refresh()` is passed the rectangle that arrived with the `Expose` event—the area that needs to be redrawn. If this area is too large for the pixmap, then the refreshed area is made to fit the size of the pixmap. `XCopyArea()`, introduced in chapter 6, is used to copy part of the backing pixmap to the screen.

```
Refresh( display, window, gc, pixmap, x, y, width, height )

Display *display;
Window  window;
GC      gc;
Pixmap  pixmap;
int     x, y, width, height;    /* -- rectangle to refresh */

{       /* -- function Refresh */

        /*
         *      Window may be too big
         */
        if ( ( x > PixmapWidth ) || ( y > PixmapHeight ) )
                {
                return;
                }

        if ( ( x + width  ) > PixmapWidth  )
```

```
		{
		width = PixmapWidth - x;

		if ( width  < 0 )
			{
			return;
			}
		}

	if ( ( y + height ) > PixmapHeight )
		{
		height = PixmapHeight - y;

		if ( height < 0 )
			{
			return;
			}
		}

	/*
	 *	Copy the necessary part of
	 *	the backing pixmap
	 *	to refresh the screen
	 */
	 XCopyArea( display, pixmap,
		window, gc,
		x, y,
		width, height,
		x, y );

}	/* -- function Refresh */
```

CLEANING UP

When the program is ready to quit, it frees a few X resources, calls `CloseDisplay()` and then `exit()`:

```
	...

	/*
	 *	Close Connection to X Server
	 */
	XFreePixmap( display, pixmap );
	XFreePixmap( display, icon );
```

```
        CloseDisplay( display, window, gc );

        exit( 0 );
```

SOURCE CODE FOR bitview.c

The full source code for `bitview.c` is as follows:

bitview.c:

```
#include  "xbook.h"

/*
 *      Include Icon shape
 */
#include  "bit.xb"

/*
 *      Program-wide Globals.
 *
 */
#define         MAX_PIX         30      /* -- Max bitmaps */

typedef struct
        {
        Pixmap          bitmap;
        int             x, y;
        int             width, height;
        } BIT_STRUCT;

BIT_STRUCT      the_bitmaps[ MAX_PIX ];

/*
 *      Top-level window Globals
 */
int     PixmapWidth, PixmapHeight;

main( argc, argv )

int     argc;
char    *argv[];

{       /* -- function main */
        Display         *display;
```

```
        int             screen;
        Window          rootwindow, window;
        unsigned long   black, white;
        int             x, y, width, height;
        Pixmap          icon, pixmap;
        GC              pixgc, gc;
        int             num_bitmaps;

        /*
         *      Check on number of
         *      command-line arguments
         */
        if ( argc < 2 )
                {
                usage();
                exit( 1 );
                }

        /*
         *      Set up X connection
         */
        display    = SetUpDisplay( argc, argv, &screen );

        rootwindow = RootWindow( display, screen );
        black      = BlackPixel( display, screen );
        white      = WhitePixel( display, screen );

        /*
         *      Load up all Bitmap files
         *      specified on the command
         *      line. Width and height
         *      are overridden.
         */
        num_bitmaps = BuildPixmaps( display,
                                rootwindow,
                                argc, argv,
                                &width, &height );

        /*
         *      Now, create a big Pixmap to
         *      hold all the bitmaps
         */
#define HEIGHT_OFFSET 20
        PixmapWidth   = width;
        PixmapHeight  = height + HEIGHT_OFFSET;
```

```
pixmap = CreatePixmap( display, rootwindow,
                PixmapWidth, PixmapHeight,
                DefaultDepth( display, screen ),
                black, white, &pixgc );

/*
 *      Copy all the bitmaps into
 *      the Pixmap for the whole window
 */
FillNewPixmap( display, pixmap, pixgc, num_bitmaps );

/*
 *      free resource
 */
XFreeGC( display, pixgc );

XFlush( display );

/*
 *      Open a window to hold the pixmap
 */
x       = 10;
y       = 10;
height += HEIGHT_OFFSET;

CheckGeometry( argc, argv,
        DisplayWidth(  display, screen ),
        DisplayHeight( display, screen ),
        &x, &y, &width, &height );

window    = TopWindow( display, x, y, width, height,
                bit_bits, bit_width, bit_height,
                &icon, &gc );

/*
 * Pass hints to the window manager
 */
SetNormalHints( display, window,
        x, y, width, height );

SetWMHints( display, window, icon );

NameWindow( display, window,
        "bitview",
        "bitview",
        "Bitview" );
```

```
        MapWindow( display, window );

        /*
         *      Handle any events
         */
        while( EventLoop( display, window, pixmap, gc,
                &width, &height ) == True );

        /*
         *      Close Connection to X Server
         */
        XFreePixmap( display, pixmap );
        XFreePixmap( display, icon );

        CloseDisplay( display, window, gc );

        exit( 0 );

}       /* -- function main */

BuildPixmaps( display, rootwindow, argc, argv, sum_width, sum_height )

Display *display;
Window  rootwindow;
int     argc;
char    *argv[];
int     *sum_width, *sum_height;

/*
 *      BuildPixmaps() reads the command-line parameters for the
 *      names of bitmap files (every parameter is assumed to
 *      name a bitmap file, except for ones that start with
 *      "-" which precede a two-item command, such as
 *      -display attila:0.0).
 *
 *      These bitmaps are stored in a global array of structures
 *      which will later be combined into one large pixmap.
 *
 */

{       /* -- function BuildPixmaps */
        int     i, max, num_bitmaps;
        int     width, height;
        Pixmap  pixmap;

        /*
```

```
 *      Only allow a certain number
 *      of bitmaps to be displayed
 */
max = argc - 1;

if ( max > MAX_PIX )
        {
        max = MAX_PIX;
        }

*sum_width  = 10;
*sum_height = 10;
num_bitmaps = 0;
i           = 0;

while( i < max )
        {
        the_bitmaps[ num_bitmaps ].x =  *sum_width;
        the_bitmaps[ num_bitmaps ].y = 10;

        /*
         *      Jump over display, geometry
         *      and font args
         */
        if ( argv[ i + 1 ][ 0 ] = = '-' )
                {
                i += 2;
                continue;
                }

        pixmap = LoadBitmap( display, rootwindow,
                        argv[ i + 1 ],
                        &width, &height );

        if ( height >  *sum_height )
                {
                *sum_height = height + 5;
                }

        *sum_width   += ( width + 5 );

        the_bitmaps[ num_bitmaps ].width     = width;
        the_bitmaps[ num_bitmaps ].height    = height;
        the_bitmaps[ num_bitmaps ].bitmap    = pixmap;
        num_bitmaps++;
```

```
                i++;
                }

        return( num_bitmaps );

}       /* -- function BuildPixmaps */

EventLoop( display, window, pixmap, gc, width, height )

Display *display;
Window  window;
Pixmap  pixmap;
GC      gc;
int     *width, *height;

/*
 *      EventLoop() handles generic X events, but passes
 *      most events on to specific functions to handle
 *      the particular event.
 *
 */

{       /* -- function EventLoop */
        XEvent          event;
        KeySym          keysym;

        /*
         *      Block on input, awaiting
         *      an event from X.
         */
        NextEvent( display, True,
                *width, *height,
                &event,
                &keysym );

        /*
         *      Decode the event and call
         *      a specific routine to
         *      handle it.
         */
        switch( event.type )
                {
                case  Expose:
                        /*
                         *      Copy the necessary part of
                         *      the backing pixmap
```

```
                 *      to refresh the screen
                 */
                Refresh( display, window,
                        gc, pixmap,
                        event.xexpose.x,
                        event.xexpose.y,
                        event.xexpose.width,
                        event.xexpose.height );

                XFlush( display );
                break;
        case  KeyPress:
                /*
                 *      Quit on a
                 *      Q or Meta-Q
                 */
                if ( ( keysym = = XK_Q ) || ( keysym = = XK_q ) )
                        {
                        return( False );
                        }
                break;
        case ConfigureNotify:
                *width   = event.xconfigure.width;
                *height  = event.xconfigure.height;
                break;
        }

    return( True );

}       /* -- function EventLoop */

FillNewPixmap( display, pixmap, pixgc, num_bitmaps )

Display *display;
Pixmap  pixmap;
GC      pixgc;
int     num_bitmaps;

/*
 *      Accesses the GLOBAL array of bitmaps,
 *      the_bitmaps, and copies each of these bitmaps
 *      into the given window-backing large pixmap.
 *
 */

{       /* -- function FillNewPixmap */
```

```
        int     i;

        for( i = 0; i < num_bitmaps; i++ )
                {
                XCopyPlane( display,
                        the_bitmaps[ i ].bitmap,
                        pixmap, pixgc,
                        0, 0,                   /* -- Src X, y */
                        the_bitmaps[ i ].width,
                        the_bitmaps[ i ].height,
                        the_bitmaps[ i ].x,     /* -- Dest X, Y */
                        the_bitmaps[ i ].y,
                        0x01 );                 /* -- Only one plane */

                /*
                 *      Clean up
                 */
                XFreePixmap( display,
                        the_bitmaps[ i ].bitmap );
                }

}       /* -- function FillNewPixmap */

Refresh( display, window, gc, pixmap, x, y, width, height )

Display *display;
Window  window;
GC      gc;
Pixmap  pixmap;
int     x, y, width, height;    /* -- rectangle to refresh */

{       /* -- function Refresh */

        /*
         *      Window may be too big
         */
        if ( ( x > PixmapWidth ) || ( y > PixmapHeight ) )
                {
                return;
                }

        if ( ( x + width  ) > PixmapWidth  )
                {
                width = PixmapWidth - x;

                if ( width  < 0 )
```

```
                        {
                        return;
                        }
                }

        if ( ( y + height ) > PixmapHeight )
                {
                height = PixmapHeight - y;

                if ( height < 0 )
                        {
                        return;
                        }
                }

        /*
         *      Copy the necessary part of
         *      the backing pixmap
         *      to refresh the screen
         */
         XCopyArea( display, pixmap,
                window, gc,
                x, y,
                width, height,
                x, y );

}       /* -- function Refresh */

usage()

/*
 *      usage() prints out a message about what command-line
 *      parameters the program expects
 */

{       /* -- function usage */

        (void) fprintf( stderr,
                "ERROR: Usage is bitview bitfile1 ...\n" );
        (void) fprintf( stderr,
                "Where each bitfile is an X11 bitmap(1) file.\n" );

        (void) fprintf( stderr,
                "Or, usage is bitview -display displayname bitfile1 ...\n" );
```

```
}       /* -- function usage */

/*
 *      end of file
 */
```

Bitview's ICON

Every X application should have an icon, no matter how artistic you are. We certainly don't pretend to be artistic geniuses, but our icon appears in figure 9-2:

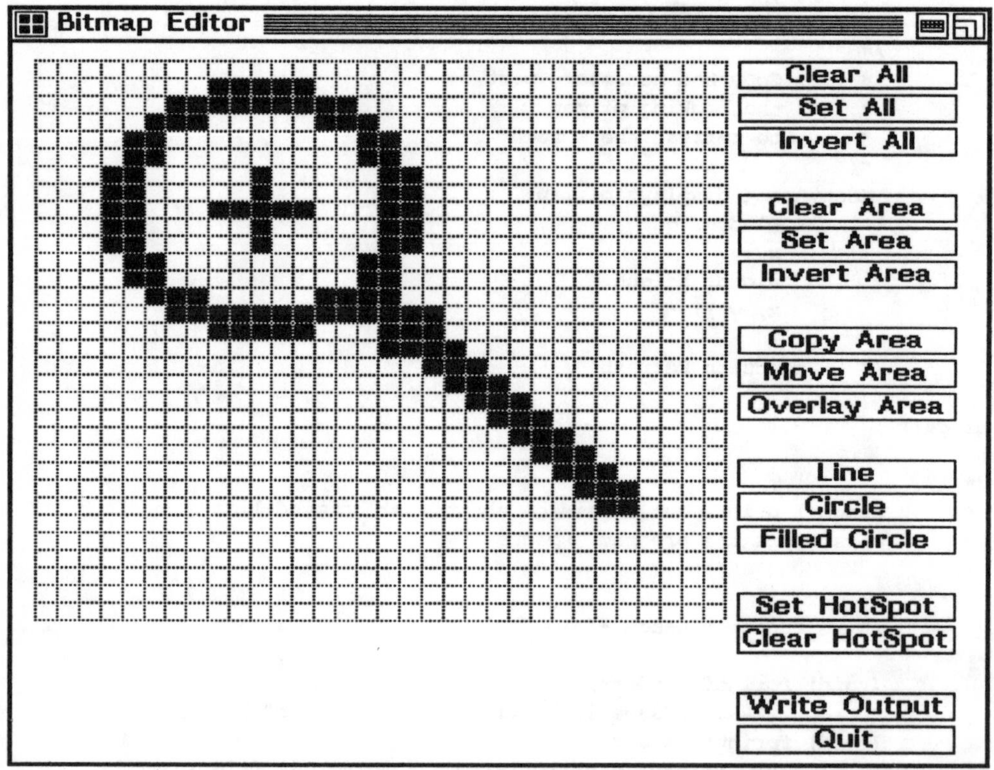

Figure 9-2. The Bitview Icon

You can create the bitmap file `bit.xb` with the standard X application called bitmap by typing in the text below, picking up the source code diskette that accompanies this book (see the order form in the back of the book), or by creating you own bitmap. You should name the file `bit.xb`, unless you want to dig out all references to "bit_width," "bit_height," "bit_bits," and "bit.xb." Anyway, have fun—it's just a bitmap.

SOURCE CODE FOR bit.xb

The source code for `bit.xb` is as follows:

bit.xb:

```
#define bit_width 32
#define bit_height 32
static char bit_bits[] = {
   0x00, 0x00, 0x00, 0x00, 0x00, 0x1f, 0x00, 0x00, 0xc0, 0x7f, 0x00, 0x00,
   0xe0, 0xe0, 0x00, 0x00, 0x30, 0x80, 0x01, 0x00, 0x30, 0x80, 0x01, 0x00,
   0x18, 0x04, 0x03, 0x00, 0x18, 0x04, 0x03, 0x00, 0x18, 0x1f, 0x03, 0x00,
   0x18, 0x04, 0x03, 0x00, 0x18, 0x04, 0x03, 0x00, 0x30, 0x80, 0x01, 0x00,
   0x30, 0x80, 0x01, 0x00, 0xe0, 0xe0, 0x01, 0x00, 0xc0, 0xff, 0x07, 0x00,
   0x00, 0x1f, 0x07, 0x00, 0x00, 0x00, 0x0f, 0x00, 0x00, 0x00, 0x1c, 0x00,
   0x00, 0x00, 0x38, 0x00, 0x00, 0x00, 0x70, 0x00, 0x00, 0x00, 0xe0, 0x00,
   0x00, 0x00, 0xc0, 0x01, 0x00, 0x00, 0x80, 0x03, 0x00, 0x00, 0x00, 0x07,
   0x00, 0x00, 0x00, 0x0e, 0x00, 0x00, 0x00, 0x0c, 0x00, 0x00, 0x00, 0x00,
   0x00, 0x00, 0x00, 0x00, 0x00, 0x00, 0x00, 0x00, 0x00, 0x00, 0x00, 0x00,
   0x00, 0x00, 0x00, 0x00, 0x00, 0x00, 0x00, 0x00};
```

COMPILING Bitview

Here comes the hard part: compiling the `Bitview` program. `Bitview` needs the following source modules:

`bitmap.c`	*(chapter 6)*
`bitview.c`	
`cursor.c`	*(chapter 7)*
`display.c`	*(chapter 2)*
`event.c`	*(chapter 5)*
`gc.c`	*(chapter 4)*
`pixmap.c`	*(chapter 6)*
`topwind.c`	
`window.c`	*(chapter 3)*

You can compile it with:

```
cc -O -o bitview bitmap.c bitview.c cursor.c display.c event.c \
      gc.c pixmap.c topwind.c window.c -lX11
```

Or, you can use the `Makefile` in Appendix C:

```
make bitview
```

CONFIGURING THE SOURCES FOR YOUR SYSTEM

To get the sources to compile on your system, you may need to define a special symbol or two (mainly to get the file `<X11/Xos.h>` to compile). You can use `#define SYMBOL` in a source file or `-DSYMBOL` on the `cc` (C compiler) command line.

For common operating systems, you can use symbols such as:

`i386`	for Interactive's 386/ix on 386 Unix clones
`macII`	for Apple's Macintosh II (running A/UX)
`sun`	for any of Sun Microsystem's CPUs, including SPARCs and 386is.
`hpux`	for Hewlett-Packard's 9000/300 series running HP-UX

These defines were found in `<X11/Xos.h>`. We've also added a special define to compile in support for the new routines in Release 4: `X11R4`.

Use:

`X11R4`	for systems running X11R4 (and above?)
`X11R3`	for systems running X11R3 (and below)

In general, if the compiler or linker doesn't complain, don't worry. See the `Makefile` in appendix C for more information.

RUNNING Bitview

To run `Bitview`, just give it the name of at least one ASCII bitmap file. If you have the source code diskette that accompanies this book, you can use the icon bitmap files for all the example programs:

```
bitview *.xb
```

or `bitview bit.xb`

where `bit.xb` is an ASCII bitmap file.

You can pass a display name and a geometry string, if you wish:

```
bitview -display flame:0.0 -geometry 500x400+10+1 bit.xb
```

FUNCTION DEVELOPED IN THIS CHAPTER

`TopWindow`

SUMMARY

- We pull together the programming examples in the first eight chapters into an application called `Bitview`. The `bitview.c` program displays a number of X ASCII bitmap files of the type described in chapter 6. One function is introduced, `TopWindow()`, which creates the top-level window, as well as a graphics context and an icon.
- This chapter completes the brief introduction to the X library. In section II we'll show you more of the X system and extract information from your X server. Displays, networking, windows, properties, and color will be covered. So, take a break, enjoy a gin and tonic and then turn to section II.

Section II

Exploring X

Section II jumps into the meat of Advanced X Window Applications Programming. It covers how to find out more information from the X server and how to interact with more advanced areas of X. The concepts developed here will be used in sections III and IV in developing X applications that communicate with other applications and more than one X server.

Topics covered in section II include:

- information on X servers
- window information

- The usage of X properties—typed collections of data bytes
- Host and network information
- Exploring color

Chapter 10

X Display Information

Since the X Window System is a networked beast, it's important for the X programmer to keep track of X displays across the network. The first step is identifying the X display, vendor, and release information—data that's passed along automatically when you connect to a server. After that, it's up to you to use programs provided with X or the tools outlined here to ferret out more information about your display—for example, whether it supports color (and how many planes), the number of screens it has and any possible extensions.

X DISPLAYS

X provides application portability—something few other graphics systems can boast. X servers run on anything from monochrome CISC Apple Macintosh SE/30s to color

RISC Data General Aviions to computers so expensive that their use by mere mortals is prohibitive.

This portability comes at a price. The X program must deal with screens having different pixel resolutions; monochrome, gray-scale, and color workstations; mice with one, two, three, and more buttons; and displays with one screen, two screens, and many screens.

Some of you may use only one model and brand of computer, with only one type of screen, keyboard, and mouse. For you, portability may not be a great concern. Others will have the same problem that faced the developers of X: many machines from many vendors, with an assortment of color and monochrome stations, running many different types of operating system software (and by now, probably many different versions of the X software).

The question is, how can software that works on the majority of X-based systems be written? The first step is to see what kinds of capabilities these displays (X servers) have.

FINDING OUT MORE ABOUT A DISPLAY

When you set up a connection to an X server, the server responds with a host of information about its capabilities. Many of these capabilities are stored in a `Display` structure and utilized by the display pointer in just about every Xlib function. Xlib provides a number of macros and functions to get at the information stored in the `Display` structure.

DISPLAY NAME

The first item about a display is its display name, which you probably already have. The `XOpenDisplay()` function takes a display name, or uses the `DISPLAY` environment variable. If you don't know the display name, use `XDisplayName()` to return the contents of the `DISPLAY` environment variable.

To print the display name to stdout:

```
char      *display_name;

if ( display_name = = (char *)NULL )
          {
          (void) printf( "Display Information for %s:\n",
                  XDisplayName( display_name ) );
          }
else
          {
          (void) printf( "Display Information for %s:\n",
                  display_name );
          }
```

VENDOR AND RELEASE INFORMATION

Setting up a connection to an X server also returns information on the company that wrote the particular X server. The ServerVendor() macro returns a string something like "MIT X Consortium" or "Hewlett-Packard Company." The macro VendorRelease() returns an integer with the vendor's release number. If your X server came from the MIT X Consortium, the VendorRelease() number may be the X release number (that is, 2 for X11 Release 2, 3 for X11 Release 3, 4 for X11 Release 4). However, other companies use this number for their own release-numbering scheme. If this is the case, there is no easy way to determine what release you are running under.

The ProtocolVersion() macro returns an integer with the major version number of the X connection protocol (this number should be 11). The ProtocolRevision() macro returns the minor number of the communications protocol (updated for changes in the communication protocol and not for updates in the X11 release).

```
Display          *display;

(void) printf( "The X server from %s at release %d, protocol %d.%d\n",
        ServerVendor( display ),
        VendorRelease( display ),
        ProtocolVersion( display ),
        ProtocolRevision( display ) );
```

CPU BYTE ORDERING

Some CPUs store integers with the most significant byte first; others store the least significant byte first. This may be an important issue when you try to write portable code. The macro ImageByteOrder() returns the required byte ordering for bitmaps and Z-format pixmaps. It returns LSBFirst or MSBFirst.

```
Display         *display;
int             byte_order;

byte_order = ImageByteOrder( display );

if ( byte_order = = MSBFirst )
        {
        (void) printf( "\tThe image byte order is MS Byte first.\n" );
        }
else
        {
        (void) printf( "\tThe image byte order is LS Byte first.\n" );
        }
```

In the source code example that follows in the next section, dinfo.c, the GetDisplayInfo() function prints information about a given display.

EXTENSIONS

The designers of X realized that X couldn't be the all-singing, all-dancing system for everyone, so they designed a standard way to link nonstandard extensions into the X server. This provides a means for vendors to add in features like Display Postscript, nonrectangular windows, VEX (the Video Extension to X), and PEX (the 3D Phigs Extension to X). The problem with X extensions is that you never know in advance if a system has a particular extension. If the extension you want is available on a given X server, you can find out at runtime, though.

The Xlib function XListExtensions() returns an array of character strings, each with the name of an extension:

```
Display *display;
int     number_extensions;
char    **extension_list;
```

```
extension_list = XListExtensions( display, &number_extensions );
```

If the extension_list is not NULL, and if the number of extensions is greater than zero, you can print out the names of the extensions:

```
for( i = 0; i < number_extensions; i++ )
        {
        (void) printf( "%s\n", extension_list[ i ] );
        }
```

For example, in the MIT X Consortium Release 4, the following extensions are available:

```
SHAPE

MIT-SHM

Multi-Buffering

MIT-SUNDRY-NONSTANDARD
```

(SHAPE is the fun one, as it provides for non-rectangular windows.)

When you are done with the list of extension names, free the list using XFreeExtensionList():

```
XFreeExtensionList( extension_list );
```

THE ListExtensions FUNCTION

The ListExtensions() function takes a display pointer and prints out the extension names available on that display:

```
ListExtensions( display )

Display *display;

{       /* -- function ListExtensions */
        int     i;
```

```
        int     number_extensions;
        char    **extension_list;

        extension_list = XListExtensions( display, &number_extensions );

        if ( ( extension_list != NULL ) && ( number_extensions > 0 ) )
                {
                (void) printf( "\tServer Extensions include:\n" );

                for( i = 0; i < number_extensions; i++ )
                        {
                        (void) printf( "\t\t%s\n", extension_list[ i ] );
                        }

                XFreeExtensionList( extension_list );
                }

}       /* -- function ListExtensions */
```

NUMBER OF SCREENS

Since any X server may have more than one screen, you might want to use the macro `ScreenCount()` to find out how many are available:

```
Display         *display;
int             screen;
int             num_screens;

num_screens = ScreenCount( display );
```

INFORMATION FOR EACH SCREEN

The X library has a number of macros and functions to extract information relating to each screen. Now that you know how to get the number of screens, you can loop for each screen and get information on that screen, starting with the pixel resolution. The function `GetScreenInfo()`, shown in the next section, takes a display pointer and a screen number and prints out information about a screen.

SCREEN RESOLUTION

The screen resolution is probably more important than the name of the display or most extensions. Each X server has a default screen, and some have multiple screens (either more than one physical monitor or one monitor that pretends to host more than one screen). Most X servers use only one screen, but you need to have a screen number to get the size of that screen.

Use the `DefaultScreen()` macro to get the number of the default screen:

```
Display *display;
int     screen;

screen     = DefaultScreen( display, screen );
```

The width and height (in pixels) for any screen can be determined using the `DisplayHeight()` and `DisplayWidth()` macros:

```
Display         *display;
int             screen;
unsigned int    width, height;

width      = DisplayWidth(  display, screen );
height     = DisplayHeight( display, screen );
```

To get the size in millimeters rather than pixels, you can use the following:

```
Display         *display;
int             screen;
unsigned int    widthmm, heightmm;

widthmm      = DisplayWidthMM(  display, screen );
heightmm     = DisplayHeightMM( display, screen );
```

Note that the accuracy of this value is in doubt. Most X servers have no way to ask a screen its physical size. Instead, these values are often programmed in.

COLOR INFORMATION

Color is one of the more obtuse areas of X, since X includes everything from monochrome to 24-bit (and more) color systems. In addition, a given screen can support a number of visuals, including monochrome and color visuals on the same monitor. The `DefaultDepth()` macro returns the number of color (or gray-scale) planes available on the default visual (the system may support another visual more to your liking if the default depth does not have enough color planes available). A depth of eight, for example, means that the default visual has 8-bit color (or 8-bit gray scale). The `DefaultDepth()` macro is:

```
Display         *display;
int             screen;
unsigned int    depth;

depth      = DefaultDepth(  display, screen );
```

You can determine the number of color cells actually available on the default visual of a screen with the macro `DisplayCells()`:

```
Display         *display;
int             screen;
int             num_cells;

num_cells  = DisplayCells( display, screen );
```

Note that some systems reserve color cells for things like overlay planes or hardware-supported cursors, so an 8-bit color system may not have 256 color cells available.

All X servers have predefined "black" and "white" colors. The "black" may not look black, but black and white are contrasting colors so you can, for example, draw black text on a white background and see the text. Many X applications just need two colors, so you don't have to worry about all the complexity of X's color model. Other applications, such as image-processing programs, may require color in oder to be useful. However, most X stations have only monochrome screens, so if you want your applications to be portable to the greatest number of machines, try to write monochrome applications using only the default `BlackPixel()` and `WhitePixel()` macros:

```
Display          *display;
int              screen;
unsigned long    black, white;

black       = BlackPixel( display, screen );
white       = WhitePixel( display, screen );
```

Since an X server could have a color screen and a monochrome screen, much of the color information is based on a screen. The `Display` structure has entries that point at the relevant `Screen` structures. You can get a pointer to the `Screen` structure with the macro `ScreenOfDisplay()`. With this `Screen` pointer, you can find out the maximum color maps available for that screen with the `MaxCmapsOfScreen()` macro:

```
Display          *display;
int              screen;
Screen           *screenptr;

screenptr   = ScreenOfDisplay( display, screen );

num_maps    = MaxCmapsOfScreen( screenptr );
```

Save Unders and Backing Store

The `Screen` pointer is also necessary to determine if the screen provides two nice features: `Save Unders` and `Backing Store`.

If you have a window that will be visible for only a short time (such as a pop-up menu), you normally want the menu to appear and disappear as fast as possible because once the menu is drawn on the screen, the menu will obscure the pixels underneath. When the menu goes away, the applications that own the windows underneath your menu need to redraw the formerly-obscured pixels. This can take time. One way to speed the redraw up is to ask the X server to save the area under the menu (hence `Save Unders`) and then restore that area when the menu goes away. (However, sometimes using `Save Unders` can be actually slower than skipping it entirely—depending on the server).

Note that the `Save Unders` request is just a request; the X server doesn't have to honor it. Just like with hinting, you never know if you'll get what you want.

```
Screen          *screenptr;

if ( DoesSaveUnders( screenptr ) = = True )
        {
        (void) printf( "The screen will provide save-unders.\n" );
        }
else
        {
        (void) printf( "The screen will not provide save-unders.\n" );
        }
```

Backing Store is similar to Save Unders. You use it to ask the X server to maintain a copy of any obscured areas of your window and restore those areas when the window becomes unobscured. Like Save Unders, Backing Store is a request that the X server does not have to honor. By using Backing Store instead of Save Unders, though, you can expect to receive fewer Expose events. If your application is on one machine and the X server on another, cutting the number of Expose events (and redraws) saves on a lot of network transmission time.

Backing Store may cut down on the number of Expose events, but your application will still get them. Any full-blown X application needs to handle Expose events and redraw all or part of its application windows.

The DoesBackingStore() macro returns WhenMapped, NotUseful, or Always to indicate what kind of Backing Store may be available:

```
Screen          *screenptr;
int             backing_type;

backing_type = DoesBackingStore( screenptr );

(void) printf( "\tBacking store " );
switch( backing_type )
        {
        case WhenMapped:
                (void) printf( "is provided for mapped windows.\n" );
                break;
        case Always:
                (void) printf( "is always provided.\n" );
                break;
        case NotUseful:
```

```
        default:
                (void) printf( "is not provided.\n" );
                break;
        }
```

INFORMATION ABOUT VISUALS

Each X screen on a display may support a number of visuals. These visuals can have a class of PseudoColor, DirectColor, TrueColor, StaticColor, GrayScale, or StaticGray. Each visual may support different depths of color planes.

XGetVisualInfo() returns a list of visuals that match a certain template. You can use it to find the visual you want or its closest match. Remember in chapter 3, we used CopyFromParent for the visual. You can, after calling XGetVisualInfo() to find the visual you want, specify a different visual when you create a window.

XGetVisualInfo() returns a list of XVisualInfo structures, which look like:

```
typedef struct
        {
        Visual          *visual;
        VisualID        visualid;
        int             screen;
        unsigned int    depth;
        int             class;          /* -- PseudoColor, etc. */
        unsigned long   red_mask;
        unsigned long   green_mask;
        unsigned long   blue_mask;
        int             colormap_size;
        int             bits_per_rgb;   /* -- bits per pixel */
        } XVisualInfo;
```

XGetVisualInfo() returns a list of all available visuals that match a given template. The template is an XVisualInfo structure. You fill in the fields you want to match, and of course, a bit mask of flags that tell Xlib which elements in the XVisualInfo structure you actually filled.

For example, if we wanted to find all visuals available for a given screen, we would fill in the screen field only:

```
Display          *display;
int              screen;
XVisualInfo      *visual_list;
XVisualInfo      visual_template;
int              number_visuals;
long             visual_mask;

visual_template.screen = screen;
visual_mask            = VisualScreenMask;

visual_list = XGetVisualInfo( display,
                              visual_mask,
                              &visual_template,
                              &number_visuals );

if ( ( visual_list != NULL ) && ( number_visuals > 0 ) )
        {
        /* -- success */

        ...

        }
```

The mask values include:

```
VisualNoMask
VisualIDMask
VisualScreenMask
VisualDepthMask
VisualClassMask
VisualRedMaskMask
VisualGreenMaskMask
VisualBlueMaskMask
VisualColormapSizeMask
VisualBitsPerRGBMask
VisualAllMask
```

As usual, OR the values together for all the fields you've filled in.

If you find the visual you want, the visual field can be used in the `XCreateWindow()` function.

When finished with the visual list, call `XFree()` to return the memory.

```
XFree( visual_list );
```

The class field will contain one of the following:

```
PseudoColor
DirectColor
TrueColor
StaticColor
GrayScale
StaticGray
```

A PROGRAM TO FIND OUT MORE ABOUT A DISPLAY

The code in the following section provides a program to discover and print information about an X server. Since there is such a variety of X-based systems, the first thing we usually do on an X system is run a program like `dinfo`, or the standard X program `xdpyinfo`. (Running `dinfo` has an advantage over running `xdpyinfo`, in that if it runs, it proves that you can compile an X program as well as run one.)

The `dinfo` program tells how many colors you can expect to use and the screen resolution, along with the other information in the preceding section.

`Dinfo` expects the command-line to contain a list of display names. For example:

```
dinfo flame:0.0 attila:0.0 THOR:0.0
```

In this example, `dinfo` will print out information about the three displays listed on the Unix command line.

`Dinfo` loops for each command-line argument and then tries to set up a display connection to each X server named on the command-line arguments. It prints out information on each display connection by calling the function `GetDisplayInfo()`.

SOURCE CODE FOR dinfo.c

The source code for `dinfo.c` is as follows:

dinfo.c:

```
/*
 *      dinfo.c
 *      dinfo is an X11 program which prints out information
 *      about displays (X servers). You can print out information
 *      about the default display (set in the DISPLAY environment
 *      variable), or about a list of displays (pass the list
 *      on the command line).  Dinfo is useful for finding
 *      out features of a given X11 server, such as screen resolution
 *      and number of visuals.
 *
 *      Usage:
 *      dinfo
 *      -or-
 *      dinfo displayname1 displayname2 ...
 *
 *      Written for Advanced X Window Applications Programming
 *
 */

#include  "xbook.h"

main( argc, argv )

int     argc;
char    *argv[];

{       /* -- function main   */
        int     i;

        /*
         *      Assume each command-line
         *      argument is a display
         *      name and try to get
         *      info on each display.
         */
        if ( argc > 1 )
                {
                for( i = 1; i < argc; i++ )
                        {
                        GetDisplayInfo( argv[ i ] );
```

```
                        }

                }
        else
                {
                /*
                 *      Use the dafult name
                 *      (set in the DISPLAY
                 *      environment variable).
                 *
                 */
                GetDisplayInfo( (char *)NULL );
                }

        exit( 0 );

}       /* -- function main   */

GetDisplayInfo( display_name )

char    *display_name;

/*
 *      GetDisplayInfo() sets up a display
 *      connection and then gets information about
 *      the given X display.  This information
 *      is printed to stdout.
 *
 */

{       /* -- function GetDisplayInfo */
        Display *display;
        int     screen, number_screens;
        int     i;

        /*
         *      1) Establish a connection to the
         *      X Server.
         */
        display = OpenDisplay( display_name, &screen );

        if ( display = = (Display *)NULL)
                {
                (void) printf( "Could not open connection to display [%s].\n",
                        display_name );
                return;
```

```
        }

/*
 *      2) Get info on X and print it.
 */

if ( display_name = = (char *)NULL )
        {
        (void) printf( "\n\nDisplay Information for %s:\n",
                XDisplayName( display_name ) );
        }
else
        {
        (void) printf( "\n\nDisplay Information for %s:\n",
                display_name );
        }

/*
 * Display information about the server.
 */
(void) printf( "\tThe X server from %s at release %d, protocol %d.%d\n",
        ServerVendor( display ),
        VendorRelease( display ),
        ProtocolVersion( display ),
        ProtocolRevision( display ) );

if ( ImageByteOrder( display ) = = MSBFirst )
        {
        (void) printf( "\tThe image byte order is MS Byte first.\n" );
        }
else
        {
        (void) printf( "\tThe image byte order is LS Byte first.\n" );
        }

/*
 * Find out about extensions
 */
ListExtensions( display );

/*
 * Display information for each screen
 */
number_screens = ScreenCount( display );

if ( number_screens < 1 )
```

```
                number_screens = 1;

        (void) printf( "\tNumber of screens is %d, default screen is %d.\n",
                number_screens, screen );

        for( i = 0; i < number_screens; i++ )
                {
                GetScreenInfo( display, i );
                }

        (void) printf( "\n\n" );

        /*
         *      4) Close connection
         */
        XCloseDisplay( display );

}       /* -- function GetDisplayInfo */

GetScreenInfo( display, screen )

Display *display;
int     screen;

/*
 *      GetScreenInfo() prints out information
 *      about a given screen on a given display.
 */

{       /* -- function GetScreenInfo */
        unsigned int    depth, width, height;
        unsigned long   black, white;
        Screen          *screenptr;

        black      = BlackPixel( display, screen );
        white      = WhitePixel( display, screen );

        width      = DisplayWidth(  display, screen );
        height     = DisplayHeight( display, screen );
        depth      = DefaultDepth(  display, screen );

        screenptr  = ScreenOfDisplay( display, screen );

        (void) printf( "\tScreen %d size is %d by %d pixels.\n",
                screen, width, height );
```

```
        (void) printf( "\t\t%d bit planes, ",
                depth );

        (void) printf( "%d color cells and %d colormaps.\n",
                DisplayCells( display, screen ),
                MaxCmapsOfScreen( screenptr ) );

        (void) printf( "\t\tBlack is defined as 0x%4.4lX; white as 0x%4.4lX.\n",
                black, white );

        if ( DoesSaveUnders( screenptr ) = = True )
                {
                (void) printf( "\t\tThe screen will provide save-unders.\n" );
                }
        else
                {
                (void) printf("\t\tThe screen doesn't provide save-unders.\n");
                }

        (void) printf( "\t\tBacking store " );
        switch( DoesBackingStore( screenptr ) )
                {
                case WhenMapped:
                        (void) printf( "is provided for mapped windows.\n" );
                        break;
                case Always:
                        (void) printf( "is always provided.\n" );
                        break;
                case NotUseful:
                default:
                        (void) printf( "is not provided.\n" );
                        break;
                }

        GetVisualInfo( display, screen );

}       /* -- function GetScreenInfo */

GetVisualInfo( display, screen )

Display *display;
int     screen;

/*
 *      GetVisualInfo() lists out the visuals
```

```
 *      available on a screen.
 */

{       /* -- function GetVisualInfo */
        XVisualInfo     *visual_list;
        XVisualInfo     visual_template;
        int             i, number_visuals;

        /*
         * Find all visuals for this screen
         */
        visual_template.screen = screen;

        visual_list = XGetVisualInfo( display,
                                VisualScreenMask,
                                &visual_template,
                                &number_visuals );

        if ( ( visual_list != NULL ) && ( number_visuals > 0 ) )
                {
                (void) printf( "\t\tScreen %d has %d Visuals:\n",
                        screen, number_visuals );

                for( i = 0; i < number_visuals; i++ )
                        {
                        (void) printf( "\t\t\t" );

                        switch( visual_list[ i ].class )
                                {
                                case PseudoColor:
                                        (void) printf( "PseudoColor " );
                                        break;
                                case DirectColor:
                                        (void) printf( "DirectColor " );
                                        break;
                                case TrueColor:
                                        (void) printf( "TrueColor " );
                                        break;
                                case StaticColor:
                                        (void) printf( "StaticColor " );
                                        break;
                                case GrayScale:
                                        (void) printf( "GrayScale " );
                                        break;
                                case StaticGray:
                                        (void) printf( "StaticGray " );
```

```
                                        break;
                                }

                        (void) printf( "visual with id 0x%lx.\n",
                                visual_list[ i ].visualid );

                        (void) printf( "\t\t\t\t%d planes depth\n",
                                visual_list[ i ].depth );

                        (void) printf( "\t\t\t\t%d colormap entries\n",
                                visual_list[ i ].colormap_size );

                        (void) printf( "\t\t\t\t%d Bits per pixel\n",
                                visual_list[ i ].bits_per_rgb );
                        }

                XFree( visual_list );
                }

}       /* -- function GetVisualInfo */

ListExtensions( display )

Display *display;

/*
 *      ListExtensions() lists out the names of the
 *      X server extensions available on a given display.
 *
 */

{       /* -- function ListExtensions */
        int     i;
        int     number_extensions;
        char    **extension_list;

        extension_list = XListExtensions( display, &number_extensions );

        if ( ( extension_list != NULL ) && ( number_extensions > 0 ) )
                {
                (void) printf( "\tServer Extensions include:\n" );

                for( i = 0; i < number_extensions; i++ )
                        {
                        (void) printf( "\t\t%s\n", extension_list[ i ] );
                        }
```

```
            XFreeExtensionList( extension_list );
            }

}       /* -- function ListExtensions */

/*
 *      end of file.
 */
```

COMPILING dinfo

The dinfo program uses the following C source modules:

display.c   *(chapter 2)*

dinfo.c

You can compile it with:

```
cc -O -o dinfo dinfo.c display.c -lX11
```

Or, you can use the Makefile from appendix C:

```
make dinfo
```

RUNNING dinfo

If you've set the DISPLAY environment variable, you can run dinfo with no command line arguments:

```
dinfo
```

Dinfo will then report information on your default X server (if it is running).

If you have a number of machines connected over a network, you can pass a number of display names on the command-line. For example:

```
dinfo display1 display2 display3
```

Typical display names look something like:

```
dinfo flame:0.0 attila:0.0 gondor:0.0
```

SAMPLE OUTPUT OF dinfo

This section shows the sample output of three X servers (one for Release 2, one for Release 3 and one for Release 4).

Apple Macintosh IIx, running A/UX 1.1 beta 3, with X11R2 from Apple on a monochrome system. The CPU is a Motorola 68030:

```
Display Information for Unix:0.0:
        The X server from Apple Computer, Inc. at release 0, protocol 11.0
        The image byte order is MS Byte first.
        Number of screens is 1, default screen is 0.
        Screen 0 size is 640 by 480 pixels.
                1 bit planes, 2 color cells and 1 colormaps.
                Black is defined as 0x0001; white as 0x0000.
                The screen will not provide save-unders.
                Backing store is not provided.
                Screen 0 has 1 Visuals:
                        StaticGray visual with id 0x80064.
                                1 planes depth
                                2 colormap entries
                                1 Bits per pixel
```

386 AT clone, running Interactive 386/ix 2.0, with X11R3 from Interactive on a 4-bit color system (enhanced VGA). The CPU is an Intel 80386. Note that black is 0 and white is 1.

```
Display Information for THOR:0.0:
        The X server from 386/ix X11 Release 0.0.2 at release 3, protocol 11.0
        The image byte order is LS Byte first.
        Number of screens is 1, default screen is 0.
        Screen 0 size is 800 by 600 pixels.
                4 bit planes, 16 color cells and 1 colormaps.
                Black is defined as 0x0000; white as 0x0001.
                The screen will not provide save-unders.
```

```
        Backing store is not provided.
        Screen 0 has 1 Visuals:
                PseudoColor visual with id 0x80064.
                        4 planes depth
                        16 colormap entries
                        4 Bits per pixel
```

Sun Microsystems SPARCStation-1, running SunOS 4.0.3c, with X11R4 from MIT on an 8-bit color system. The CPU is a SPARC RISC chip.

```
Display Information for flame:0.0:
        The X server from MIT X Consortium at release 4, protocol 11.0
        The image byte order is MS Byte first.
        Server Extensions include:
                SHAPE
                MIT-SHM
                Multi-Buffering
                MIT-SUNDRY-NONSTANDARD
        Number of screens is 1, default screen is 0.
        Screen 0 size is 1152 by 900 pixels.
                8 bit planes, 256 color cells and 1 colormaps.
                Black is defined as 0x0001; white as 0x0000.
                The screen will provide save-unders.
                Backing store is always provided.
                Screen 0 has 6 Visuals:
                        PseudoColor visual with id 0x80065.
                                8 planes depth
                                256 colormap entries
                                8 Bits per pixel
                        DirectColor visual with id 0x80066.
                                8 planes depth
                                8 colormap entries
                                8 Bits per pixel
                        GrayScale visual with id 0x80067.
                                8 planes depth
                                256 colormap entries
                                8 Bits per pixel
                        StaticGray visual with id 0x80068.
                                8 planes depth
                                256 colormap entries
                                8 Bits per pixel
                        StaticColor visual with id 0x80069.
                                8 planes depth
                                256 colormap entries
```

```
            8 Bits per pixel
TrueColor visual with id 0x8006a.
            8 planes depth
            8 colormap entries
            8 Bits per pixel
```

xdpyinfo

The MIT X Consortium Releases 3 and 4 include a program called `xdpyinfo`, which provides a more-detailed listing of information about an X server. `Xdpyinfo` is a lot like `dinfo` but the X release doesn't give you a step-by-step description of how `xdpyinfo` works.

In addition, some systems do not have this program with their X implementation.

FUNCTIONS DEVELOPED IN THIS CHAPTER

```
GetDisplayInfo
GetScreenInfo
GetVisualInfo
ListExtensions
```

XLIB FUNCTIONS AND MACROS INTRODUCED IN THIS CHAPTER

```
DisplayCells
DisplayHeightMM
DisplayWidthMM
DoesSaveUnders
DoesBackingStore
ImageByteOrder
MaxCmapsOfDisplay
ProtocolRevision
ProtocolVersion
ScreenCount
ScreenOfDisplay
ServerVendor
VendorRelease
XDisplayName
XFreeExtensionList
XGetVisualInfo
XListExtensions
```

SUMMARY

- Since portability is a prime reason for developing in X, you'll want to keep your code as portable as possible. This process starts with ferreting out information that's passed along automatically when you set up a connection to an X server. Many of these capabilities are stored in a `Display` structure and are utilized by the display pointer in just about every Xlib function.

- Xlib also provides a number of macros and functions to get at the information stored in the `Display` structure: display name (using `XDisplayName()` if the information wasn't passed along by `XOpenDisplay()`), vendor and release information (using `ServerVendor()`, `VendorRelease()` and `ProtocolVersion()`), CPU byte ordering (using `ImageByteOrder()`), extensions (such as Display Postscript, nonrectangular windows, VEX and PEX, using `XListExtensions()`), number of screens (using `ScreenCount()`), and screen resolution (using `DefaultScreen()`).

- Since color is one of the more obtuse areas of X, it requires special attention. There are grey-scale, TrueColor, and PseudoColor systems, among others. Also a given screen can support a number of visuals, including monochrome and color visuals on the same monitor. Use the macro `DefaultDepth()` to find the number of color (or grey-scale) planes available on the default visual. Remember, many X stations don't support color and most X applications don't really need more than black and white. In the interests of portability and programming simplicity, think hard before delving into X's color model.

- Using `Save Unders` saves the area under a menu that will be visible for only a short time, (such as a pop-up menu). Since `Save Unders` is merely a request, the X server doesn't need to respond to your wishes. `Backing Store` is similar; it maintains a copy of any obscured areas of your window and restores those areas when the window becomes unobscured. It, too, is a request. Since `Backing Store` cuts down on the number of `Expose` events, it saves network transmission time.

- Each X screen on a display may support a number of visuals: `PseudoColor`, `DirectColor`, `TrueColor`, `StaticColor`, `GrayScale` or `StaticGray`. Each visual may support different depths of color planes. Use `XGetVisualInfo()` to returns a list of visuals that match a certain template.

Chapter 11

Window Information

Windows form the major part of any X application—it isn't called the X Window System for nothing. Most applications pop up at least one main window and a number of subwindows.

Usually an application is aware of its own windows, but sometimes other X applications (namely the window manager) can alter the way windows appear on the screen. Normally, such interference is called something like "enforcing a user-interface policy," but for an X application program, it's really messing around with the application. In such cases, you may want to avoid this interference by making your applications retrieve information about your windows.

Other times, an application may want to know about the other windows on an X screen. This chapter covers finding information about a window and tracking the windows that appear on the screen. It ends with sample programs that allow the user to interactively pick a particular window on the screen.

GETTING WINDOW INFORMATION

The X Window System has a number of calls that retrieve information about any window on the screen. (Remember, an X display may drive multiple screens, often separate CRTs.)

GETTING A WINDOW'S NAME WITH XFetchName

Most window information is stored in properties associated with the window (see chapter 12). Therefore, you can get a lot of information with one call, `XGetWindowProperty()`, which unfortunately is rather complex. An easier way is to use many of the X convenience functions to get the value of a particular property such as the window name, which is stored in the `WM_NAME` property.

`XFetchName()` retrieves a window's name:

```
Display *display;
Window  window;
char    *name;

XFetchName( display, window, &name );

if ( name != (char *) NULL )
        {
        printf( "(%s) ", name );

        XFree( name );
        }
```

There's also the Release 4 routine that retrieves a window's name as a text property:

```
Display         *display;
Window          window;
XTextProperty   *text_property;
int             status;
```

```
status = XGetWMName( display, window, text_property );
```

`XGetWMName()` is the routine of the future. Unfortunately, it only exists starting with Release 4.

GETTING A WINDOW'S SIZE AND LOCATION WITH XGetGeometry

The Xlib function `XGetGeometry()` actually returns information on a `Drawable` (a `Window` or a `Pixmap`), but is usually used on a window, since `Pixmaps` have no location—they reside somewhere "off the screen."

```
Display         *display;
Drawable        window;
int             x, y;
unsigned int    width, height;
unsigned int    borderwidth, depth;

XGetGeometry( display,
        window,
        &rootwindow,
        &x, &y,         /* -- location, 0,0 for Pixmaps */
        &width, &height,
        &borderwidth,   /* -- 0 for Pixmaps, which have no border */
        &depth );
```

THE CLASS HINTS

Each window may have "hints" about the class of the window. (If X11 were truthful, Sun 386i windows would be listed as lower class and SPARCStation windows as upper-middle, but performance is another issue.) The class hints have two parts, and yes, there is a C structure for it:

```
typedef struct
        {
        char    *res_name;
        char    *res_class;
        } XClassHint;
```

The class hints are stored in the WM_CLASS property. The res_name field holds the application name (which is probably not the same as the window's name). The res_class field contains the application class type, such as XTerm for an xterm window. The name should be all lowercase and the first letter of the class should be capitalized. For example, the "emacs" application (res_name) has a class type of "Emacs."

These class hints can be used by the window manager when grabbing resources from the X resource manager (should you decide to use the X resource manager). See section 4.1.2.5 of the *Inter-Client Communication Conventions Manual* (ICCCM) for more information (also see chapter 15, "The ICCCM").

You can retrieve the class hints for a window with XGetClassHint(). Note the differences for Release 4. (Chapter 3 shows how to set the class hints.)

```
        Display         *display;
        Window          window;
        XClassHint      *classhint;
        int             status;

#ifdef X11R4
        classhint = XAllocClassHint();
#else
        classhint = (XClassHint *) malloc ( sizeof( XClassHint ) );
#endif

        if ( classhint != (XClassHint *) NULL )
                {

                status = XGetClassHint( display, window, classhint );

                if ( status != 0 )
                        {
                        /* -- Access the class name and type */

                        ...

                        XFree( classhint->res_name  );
                        XFree( classhint->res_class );
                        }

                /*
                 * Free memory for whole hint structure
                 */
#ifdef X11R4
```

```
                XFree( classhint );
#else
                free( classhint );
#endif
                }
```

Use XFree() to free the memory when finished with the res_name and res_class fields.

To put all this window information together, the wprint.c file contains a function to print out window information.

PRINTING WINDOW INFORMATION WITH wprint.c

The wprint.c file contains PrintWinInfo(), a function that prints information about a particular window. (The output is sent to stdout, so it will probably be best if the function is called from a program that has a valid stdout on which to write its output.)

PrintWinInfo() takes two parameters, a display connection, and a window ID. It calls functions to print out:

- the window name (if there is one)
- the window location (relative to its parent window)
- the window size (in pixels)
- the window's class hints (resource class and name, if there is one)

The contents of PrintWinInfo() are as follows:

wprint.c:

```
/*
 *      wprint.c
 *
 *      Prints out information on a given window to stdout.
 */

#include  "xbook.h"
```

```
PrintWinInfo( display, window )

Display *display;
Window  window;

/*
 *      PrintWinInfo() prints out information on a window to stdout.
 *
 */

{       /* -- function PrintWinInfo */
        char    string[ BUFSIZE + 1 ];

        GetWindowInfo( display, window, string );

        (void) printf( "%s\n", string );

}       /* -- function PrintWinInfo */

GetWindowInfo( display, window, string )

Display *display;
Window  window;
char    string[];

/*
 *      GetWindowInfo() builds up a character string
 *      with information about a given window:
 *              name
 *              class
 *              local geometry
 *
 */

{       /* -- function GetWindowInfo */
        int             x, y, width, height;
        char            name[ BUFSIZE + 1 ];
        int             status;
        char            st[ BUFSIZE + 1 ];

        /*
         *      Get Info on the Window
         */
        GetWindowName( display, window, name );

        if ( name[ 0 ] != '\0' )
```

```
                {
                (void) sprintf( string, "(%s)[0x%lx] ", name, window );
                }
        else
                {
                (void) sprintf( string, "[0x%lx] ", window );
                }

        GetClassHintAsText( display, window, st );
        strcat( string, st );

        status = GetGeometry( display, window,
                        &x, &y, &width, &height );

        if ( status != 0 )
                {
                (void) sprintf( st, "at local %d, %d; %d by %d",
                        x, y, width, height );

                (void) strcat( string, st );
                }

}       /* -- function GetWindowInfo */

GetGeometry( display, window, x, y, width, height )

Display *display;
Window  window;
int     *x, *y, *width, *height;

/*
 *      GetGeometry() calls XGetGeometry() and returns the
 *      x, y, width, height for the window.
 */

{       /* -- function GetGeometry */
        unsigned int    borderwidth, depth;
        Window          rootwindow;
        int             status;

        status = XGetGeometry( display, window, &rootwindow,
                        x, y, width, height,
                        &borderwidth, &depth );

        return( status );
```

```
}       /* -- function GetGeometry */

GetWindowName( display, window, name )

Display *display;
Window  window;
char    name[];

/*
 *      GetWindowName() returns the window's name.  It uses
 *      the old Release 3 routine, XFetchName() rather than
 *      XGetWMName() (new in Release 4) for compatibility reasons.
 */

{       /* -- function GetWindowName */
        char    *window_name;

        XFetchName( display, window, &window_name );    /* R3 routine */

        if ( window_name != (char *) NULL )
                {
                (void) strcpy( name, window_name );

                XFree( window_name );
                }
        else
                {
                name[ 0 ] = '\0';
                }

}       /* -- function GetWindowName */

GetClassHintAsText( display, window, string )

Display *display;
Window  window;
char    string[];

/*
 *      GetClassHintAsText() gets the window's
 *      class hint, if one is available, and
 *      places it into the given string,
 *      as:
 *      "CLASS: class name / class type"
 *
 *      This routine depends on the symbol X11R4.
```

```
 */

{       /* -- function GetClassHintAsText */
        XClassHint      *classhint;
        int             status;

        /*
         * Initialize string
         */
        string[ 0 ] = '\0';

#ifdef X11R4
        classhint = XAllocClassHint();
#else
        classhint = (XClassHint *) malloc ( sizeof( XClassHint ) );
#endif

        if ( classhint != (XClassHint *) NULL )
                {

                status = XGetClassHint( display, window, classhint );

                if ( status != 0 )
                        {
                        (void) sprintf( string, "CLASS %s/%s ",
                                classhint->res_name,
                                classhint->res_class );

                        XFree( classhint->res_name  );
                        XFree( classhint->res_class );
                        }

                /*
                 * Free memory for whole hint structure
                 */
#ifdef X11R4
                XFree( classhint );
#else
                free( classhint );
#endif
                }

}       /* -- function GetClassHintAsText */

/*
 *      end of file
 */
```

THE WINDOW HIERARCHY

As shown in chapter 3, windows on any screen are arranged in a hierarchy. The root window is the highest window in the hierarchy and covers the entire screen. Below the root window, many applications have their top-level windows.

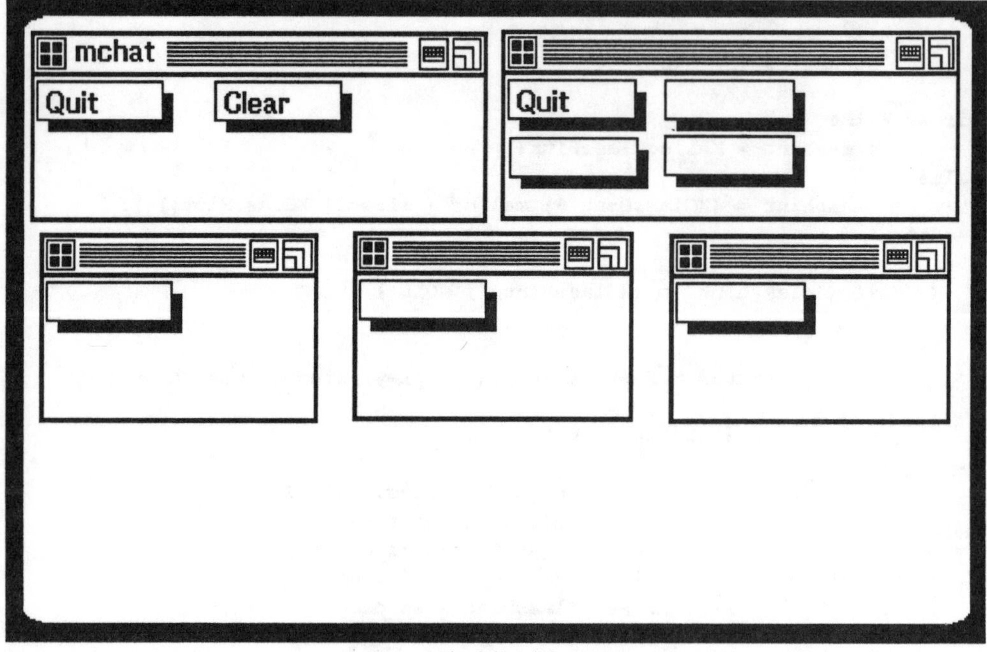

Figure 11-1. Top-Level Windows

A window manager (such as the Motif window manager `mwm`) usually interferes with these top-level windows. Sometimes, a window manager will reparent the top-level windows (that is, put in a window between the top-level window and the screen's root window). Window managers do this so they can place title bars and other resource-intensive gadgets to "decorate" the windows. The program `winfo`, shown in the following section, will demonstrate the windows a window manager places on the screen.

Every window (except for the root window) has a parent window one level above it. A window may have siblings: other windows at the same level which share the same parent. A window may also have children; that is, it may be a parent to the lower-level windows.

This ability to create many levels of windows helps in the creation of attractive user interfaces, but sometimes you want to see which windows are in use. The Xlib function `XQueryTree()` helps you do that.

TRACING DOWN THE WINDOW HIERARCHY WITH XQueryTree

`XQueryTree()` traces down the window hierarchy, or tree, and returns information about a given window: its parent, its root window, and the number of child windows.

```
Display *display;
Window  starting_window;          /* -- Window we are using */
Window  rootwindow;               /* -- starting_window's root */
Window  parent;                   /* -- starting_window's parent */
Window  *children;                /* -- start_window's children */
int     number_children;          /* -- how many children? */
int     status, i;

/*
 *      Search down the window tree
 *      in a depth-first fashion.
 */
children = (Window *)NULL;

status   = XQueryTree( display,
                       starting_window,
                       &rootwindow,
                       &parent,
                       &children,
                       &number_children );

if ( status = = 0 )
        {
        /*
         *      No children,
         *      or cannot get Window
         *      Tree.
         */

        ...

        }
else
```

```
{

/*
 *      Check the children,
 *      one at a time.
 */
for( i = 0; i < number_children; i++ )
        {
        /*
         *      children[ i ] contains
         *      the window ID of a child
         *      window.
         */

        ...

        }

/*
 *      Return memory resources
 *      to the Operating
 *      System
 */
if ( children )
        {
        XFree( children );
        }

}
```

`XQueryTree()` does not give you the whole hierarchy, but just information about the tree starting at one window and going down one level, as shown in figure 11-2.

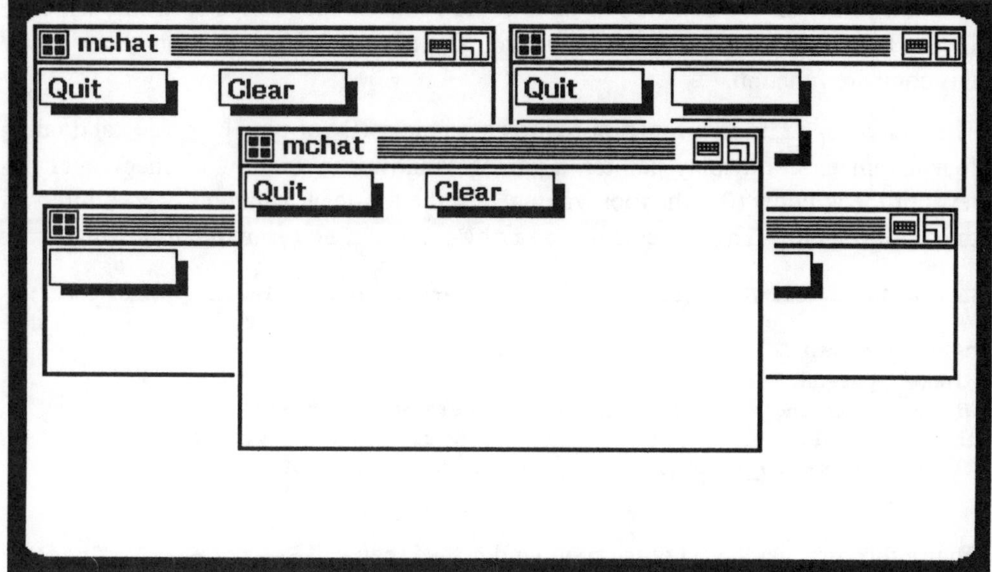

Figure 11-2. Down One Level of the Window Tree

Thus, to find out about the whole screen, you need to call `XQueryTree()` recursively, starting with the root window (typically ending up with a depth-first search).

SEARCHING FOR A WINDOW

Many X programs need to search through the window hierarchy. Window managers, for example, need to know about all application top-level windows. The X Window Dumper, `xwd`, has the user pick a window with the mouse. `Xlswins` lists out all the windows on the screen.

Sometimes you may want to traverse the entire window tree. Other times you may be interested in finding just one window. To make life easier, we created a function to help out, `SearchWindowTree()`.

The `SearchWindowTree()` function, returns a window ID (of type `Window`) or `None` if no matching window was found. It will call itself recursively to traverse depth-first down the window hierarchy. To avoid rewriting code, `SearchWindowTree()` takes a function pointer as a parameter, using it as the compare function to see if the window ID has been found and the task completed. You pass whatever function you want as this compare function.

The `compare_func()` function returns a window ID (of type `Window`) and takes four parameters: a display pointer, a parent window, the window to check, and the level of the window (0 = the root window, 1 = the top-level windows, 2 = children of the top-level, etc.). The contents of `SearchWindowTree()` are the following:

```
Window SearchWindowTree( display, parent, starting_window, level, compare_func )

Display *display;
Window  parent;
Window  starting_window;          /* -- Where we start */
int     level;                    /* -- How far down are we? */
Window  (*compare_func)();        /* -- is this the one? */
```

To use this, first get the ID of the root window and then call `SearchWindowTree()`. For each window in the tree, `SearchWindowTree()` will call your `compare_func()` to see if you have found your window yet. If so, the `SearchWindowTree()` is done. If your window wasn't found, `SearchWindowTree()` will call itself for each child window.

Your `compare_func()` should be defined something like:

```
Window  MyCompareFunction( display, parent, window, level )

Display *display;
Window  parent;
Window  window;          /* -- window to check */
int     level;           /* -- how far down in the tree is window? */
```

If you want to traverse the entire window tree, your compare function should always return `None` and should do whatever you want to do with each window ID as it comes by. The next section shows C source code to find a particular window (based on its name) and lists out all windows. Both programs call `SearchWindowTree()`.

SOURCE CODE FOR wsearch.c

The contents of `wsearch.c` are the following:

wsearch.c:

```
/*
 *      wsearch.c
 *
 *      Routines for a depth-first search
 *      of a display's window hierarchy.
 */

#include  "xbook.h"

Window SearchWindowTree( display, parent, starting_window, level,
compare_func )

Display *display;
Window  parent;
Window  starting_window;        /* -- Where we start */
int     level;                  /* -- How far down are we? */
Window  (*compare_func)();      /* -- is this the one? */

/*
 *      SearchWindowTree() performs a depth-first search of
 *      all the windows in the display's window hierarchy, until
 *      compare_func() returns a non-null (non-None)
 *      window.  Until that point, SearchWindowTree()
 *      will call itself recursively going down the
 *      window tree.  compare_func() is called with:
 *      display, parent window, window, level.
 */

{       /* -- function SearchWindowTree */
        Window  window, rootwindow, window_parent;
        int     num_children, status, i;
        Window  *children;

        /*
         *      First check the easy case,
         *      Is this window the one
         *      we are looking for?
         */
        window = (compare_func)(display,
                        parent,
```

```
                        starting_window, level );

        if ( window != (Window)None )
                {
                return( window );
                }

        /*
         *      Ok, we haven't found it yet.
         *      Now, search down the window tree
         *      in a depth-first fashion.
         */
        children = (Window *)NULL;

        status   = XQueryTree(  display,
                                starting_window,
                                &rootwindow,
                                &window_parent,
                                &children,
                                &num_children );

        if ( status == 0 )
                {
                /*
                 *      No more children,
                 *      or cannot get Window
                 *      Tree
                 */
                return( (Window) None );
                }

        /*
         *      Check the children
         */
        i = 0;

        while( ( i < num_children ) &&
            ( window == (Window) None ) )
                {
                window = SearchWindowTree( display,
                                starting_window,        /* -- parent */
                                children[ i ],
                                level + 1,
                                compare_func );

                i++;
```

```
                }

        /*
         *      Return memory resources
         *      to the Operating
         *      System
         */
        if ( children )
                {
                XFree( children );
                }

        return( window );

}       /* -- function SearchWindowTree */

/*
 *      end of file
 */
```

THE X11 PROGRAM xlswins

Later on, we will build a program to list all the windows on the screen. However, X11 (at least the MIT-originated version) contains a program that does much the same thing. This program, `xlswins`, can be used to make sure the program `winfo.c` shown in the section "Source Code for `winfo.c`" works correctly.

WRITING A PROGRAM TO LIST THE WINDOWS ON THE DISPLAY

Like `xlswins`, `winfo` lists out all the windows on the screen. `Winfo` shows how to put all the code shown in previous sections together into a working program.

`Winfo` is useful to see what windows are on the screen, and how many new windows a window manager uses. Some window managers, like `uwm`, do not reparent application windows. Others, like `twm` or `olwm` (the Open Look window manager), reparent application windows and create a bevy of new windows for all the fancy gadgets they place on a window's title bar. Figures 11-3 and 11-4 show the difference between the application window with decorations and without decorations.

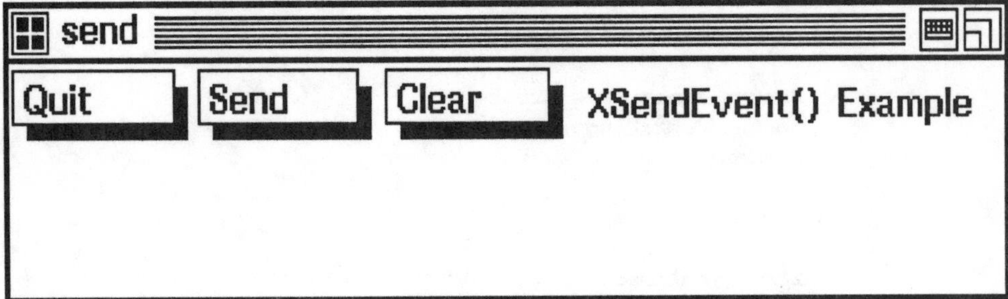

Figure 11-3. Application Window with Decorations

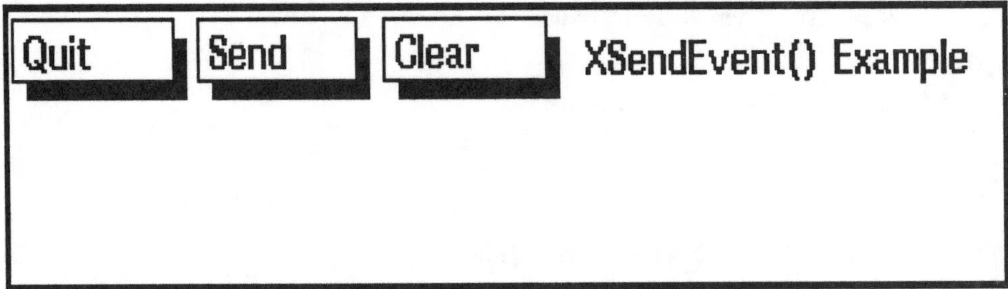

Figure 11-4. Application Window Without Decorations

The `winfo` program uses the `SearchWindowTree()` function to list all the windows on the display. Its compare function calls `PrintWinInfo()` (for `wprint.c`) to print information about each window in the hierarchy.

SOURCE CODE FOR winfo. c

The source code for `winfo.c` is the following:

winfo.c:

```
/*
 *      winfo.c
 *
 *      Program to list all the windows on a display/screen.
 */
```

```
#include  "xbook.h"

main( argc, argv )

int     argc;
char    *argv[];

{
        Display *display;
        int     screen;
        Window  rootwindow, window;

        /*
         *      Set up X connection
         */
        display    = SetUpDisplay( argc, argv, &screen );

        rootwindow = RootWindow( display, screen );

        /*
         *      Now, search the window tree.
         */
        window = SearchWindowTree( display, None, rootwindow, 0, CheckWindow );

        XCloseDisplay( display );

        exit( 0 );
}

Window CheckWindow( display, parent, window, level )

Display *display;
Window  parent;
Window  window;
int     level;

/*
 *      This function merely prints
 *      out information about the window.
 *      For searching programs you would
 *      use this function to test if the
 *      window was "interesting".
 *
 */

{       /* -- function CheckWindow */
```

```
        int     i;

        for( i = 0; i < level; i++ )
                printf( "  " );

        PrintWinInfo( display, window );

        return( (Window)None );

}       /* -- function CheckWindow */

/*
 *      end of file
 */
```

COMPILING winfo

The `winfo` program uses the following code modules:

```
display.c        (from chapter 2)
winfo.c
wprint.c
wsearch.c
```

On Unix-based systems, you can use the `Makefile` in appendix C, with:

```
make winfo
```

Or, you can compile with:

```
cc -o winfo winfo.c display.c wprint.c wsearch.c -lX11
```

RUNNING winfo

You can run `winfo` with no parameters:

```
winfo
```

You can also run `winfo` to accept a display parameter to connect to the first display on machine attila (and on the first screen of that display):

```
winfo -display attila:0.0
```

THE OUTPUT OF winfo

While running under a window manager that provides title bars (such as `twm`, the standard window manager in X11R4), you will notice many more windows on the display (created by the window manager) than while running under a visually simple window manager like `uwm` (the default window manager in X11R3).

We ran `winfo` with the same X applications, under both `twm` and `uwm` to provide an example of the output.

Running `winfo` under `uwm`:

```
( X Root Window ) [0x8006b] at local 0, 0; 640 by 480
  [0x40000f] at local 0, 0; 50 by 18
  (Window Manager) [0x400010] at local 0, 0; 114 by 192
  (X Time) [0x300006] at local 0, 337; 116 by 26
  (/users/erc/x2/src2) [0x200005] at local 1, 1; 499 by 316
    [0x200009] at local 0, 0; 499 by 316
      [0x200017] at local -1, -1; 14 by 316
  (/users/erc/x2/text) [0x500005] at local 135, 33; 499 by 420
    [0x500009] at local 0, 0; 499 by 420
      [0x500017] at local -1, -1; 14 by 420
```

Running `winfo` under `twm` showed in many more windows:

```
[0x8006b] at local 0, 0; 640 by 480
  [0x300016] at local 0, 0; 10 by 10
  [0x300017] at local 0, 0; 10 by 10
    [0x300020] at local -1, 0; 86 by 16
    [0x300021] at local 0, 18; 38 by 18
    [0x300022] at local 0, 36; 85 by 18
    [0x300023] at local 0, 54; 54 by 18
  [0x300018] at local 0, 0; 10 by 10
  [0x300019] at local 0, 0; 10 by 10
    [0x300024] at local -1, 0; 85 by 16
    [0x300025] at local 0, 18; 52 by 18
    [0x300026] at local 0, 36; 85 by 18
```

```
  [0x300027] at local 0, 54; 54 by 18
[0x30001a] at local 0, 0; 10 by 10
[0x30001b] at local 0, 0; 10 by 10
  [0x300028] at local -1, 0; 72 by 16
[0x30001c] at local 0, 0; 10 by 10
[0x30001d] at local 0, 0; 10 by 10
  [0x30001e] at local 0, 0; 7 by 18
  [0x30001f] at local 0, 18; 7 by 18
[0x300034] at local 0, 0; 62 by 65
  [0x300035] at local 7, 0; 48 by 48
[0x300039] at local 0, 0; 100 by 26
[0x300029] at local 1, 0; 499 by 335
  [0x30002a] at local -2, -2; 499 by 17
    [0x30002c] at local 1, 1; 15 by 15
    [0x30002e] at local 466, 1; 15 by 15
    [0x300030] at local 483, 1; 15 by 15
    [0x300032] at local 78, 1; 382 by 16
  (/users/erc/x2/src2) [0x200005] at local 0, 19; 499 by 316
    [0x200009] at local 0, 0; 499 by 316
      [0x200017] at local -1, -1; 14 by 316
[0x300045] at local 0, 0; 54 by 65
  [0x300046] at local 3, 0; 48 by 48
[0x30003a] at local 0, 337; 116 by 26
  [0x30003b] at local -2, -2; 116 by 17
    [0x30003d] at local 1, 1; 15 by 15
    [0x30003f] at local 83, 1; 15 by 15
    [0x300041] at local 100, 1; 15 by 15
    [0x300043] at local 74, 1; 3 by 16
  (X Time) [0x400006] at local 0, 0; 116 by 26
[0x300052] at local 0, 0; 78 by 65
  [0x300053] at local 15, 0; 48 by 48
[0x300047] at local 135, 14; 499 by 439
  [0x300048] at local -2, -2; 499 by 17
    [0x30004a] at local 1, 1; 15 by 15
    [0x30004c] at local 466, 1; 15 by 15
    [0x30004e] at local 483, 1; 15 by 15
    [0x300050] at local 94, 1; 366 by 16
  (/users/erc/x2/text) [0x500005] at local 0, 19; 499 by 420
    [0x500009] at local 0, 0; 499 by 420
      [0x500017] at local -1, -1; 14 by 420
[0x300036] at local 0, 0; 372 by 17
  [0x300038] at local 4, 1; 48 by 15
```

FINDING WINDOWS ON THE DISPLAY SCREEN

Listing all the windows on a screen may be informative, but it is really only useful for a small number of programs. A more useful task is finding a particular window, either based on some window information (such as a window's name) or chosen interactively with a mouse or other pointing device.

Finding a window is useful because many X programs act on other windows. For example, programs that "dump" the contents of a window to an image file (or to the printer) usually need the user to select which window to dump. Many window managers have menu choices that allow you to pick a window and then resize it (or move it, or iconify it, and so on).

The next sections show two programs, `wfind` and `wpick`, that find particular windows.

FINDING WINDOWS BY NAME

One way of choosing a window is to search for a particular name, class, or other information commonly held in a property associated with a window.

In the following example of source code, we'll search for a given window by name, but you, of course, can do anything you want.

SOURCE CODE FOR wfind c.

The contents of `wfind.c` are as follows:

```
wfind.c:
/*
 *      wfind.c
 *
 *      Takes a command-line parameter of the text information to
 *      find associated with a window. In other words, this program
 *      tries to find a window that has a given title.
 *
 */
```

```
#include  "xbook.h"

/*
 *      GLOBAL search string
 */
char    search_string[ BUFSIZE + 1 ];

main( argc, argv )

int     argc;
char    *argv[];

{
        Display *display;
        int     screen, counter;
        Window  rootwindow, window;

        /*
         *      Set up X connection
         */
        display    = SetUpDisplay( argc, argv, &screen );

        rootwindow = RootWindow( display, screen );

        /*
         *      Set up search string
         */
        (void) strcpy( search_string, "--" );

        counter = 1;
        while( counter < argc )
                {
                if ( argv[ counter ][ 0 ] = = '-' )
                        {
                        counter += 1;
                        }
                else
                        {
                        /* -- No match */
                        (void) strcpy( search_string, argv[ counter ] );
                        }
                counter += 1;
                }

        /*
         *      Now, find a window with matching information.
```

```
         */
        window = SearchWindowTree( display, None, rootwindow, 0, FindWindow );

        if ( window != (Window)None )
                {
                /*
                 *      We found it
                 */
                (void) printf( "A window matching %s is:\n    ",
                                search_string );

                PrintWinInfo( display, window );
                }
        else
                {
                (void) printf( "A window matching %s was not found\n",
                        search_string );
                }

        XCloseDisplay( display );

        exit( 0 );
}

Window FindWindow( display, parent, window, level )

Display *display;
Window  parent;
Window  window;
int     level;

/*
 *      This function is looking for a match
 *      between the window's name and the
 *      Global search_string.
 *
 */

{       /* -- function  FindWindow */
        char    *name;
        Window  found;

        found = (Window) None;

        /*
         *      Get the window's name, using the
         *      pre-R4 function.
```

```
         */
        XFetchName( display, window, &name );

        /*
         *      Check if there is a name
         */
        if ( name != (char *)NULL )
                {
                if ( strcmp( name, search_string ) = = 0 )
                        {
                        found = window;
                        }

                XFree( name );
                }

        return( found );

}       /* -- function  FindWindow */

/*
 *      end of file
 */
```

The `wfind.c` file looks much like `winfo.c`, but the `wfind` program is concerned with finding a particular window. A global character array, `search_string`, is set up with the value of the name string to search for (or "--" if no search string was specified).

If a window is found with a matching name, `PrintWinInfo()` is called to print out information about the chosen window.

COMPILING wfind

The `wfind` program uses the following code modules:

```
display.c          (from chapter 2)
wfind.c
wprint.c
wsearch.c
```

On Unix-based systems, you can use the `Makefile` in appendix C with:

```
make wfind
```

Or, you can compile with:

```
cc -o wfind wfind.c display.c wprint.c wsearch.c -lX11
```

RUNNING wfind

To be useful, `wfind` requires a name parameter that specifies what to search for. You can add in a display name, with the `-display` option.

```
wfind "X Time"
```

Searches for a window named `X Time`. Sample output could be:

```
A window matching X Time is:
    (X Time) [0x400006] at local 0, 0; 116 by 26
```

Or, if no window was found:

```
A window matching X Time was not found.
```

```
wfind xterm
```

searches for a window named xterm.

```
wfind xterm -display attila:0.0
```

searches for a window named `xterm` on display `attila:0.0`.

CHOOSING WINDOWS INTERACTIVELY WITH THE MOUSE POINTER

The most common approach to choosing windows is by use of the mouse. This approach presents some tricky code, because you need to take control of the mouse pointer while the user is selecting a window. You want the user to be able to move the mouse all over the screen to locate a window. You also want the mouse-pointer cursor to have a particular shape, and when the user clicks a mouse button, you want your program to catch the click (the `ButtonPress` event).

The code shown in the following section shows how a user can choose a window interactively using the mouse pointer .

GRABBING THE X MOUSE POINTER FOR EXCLUSIVE ACCESS

To prevent other code from messing with the mouse while the user selects a window using the mouse, we grab control of the mouse pointer. This means all mouse-based events can be picked up by our application—and no one else's if we want. To other X client applications, the mouse pointer appears to "freeze" and these other programs never "see" the mouse movements while the pointer is grabbed.

Use `XGrabPointer()` to take control of the pointer:

```
int            status;
Display        *display;
window         rootwindow;      /* -- rootwindow of a display screen */
Cursor         cursor;          /* -- What cursor you want */
unsigned int   mask;
Bool           pointer_mode;
Bool           keyboard_mode;
Window         confine_to;
Time           server_time;

mask          = ButtonPressMask; /* -- only event we want */
pointer_mode  = GrabModeSync;    /* -- freeze pointer for clients */
keyboard_mode = GrabModeAsync;   /* -- Leave keyboard alone */
confine_to    = None;            /* -- want to move all over screen */
server_time   = CurrentTime;     /* -- do it now */
```

```
status = XGrabPointer( display,
                    rootwindow,
                    False,          /* -- Don't Report events as usual */
                    mask,
                    pointer_mode,
                    keyboard_mode;
                    confine_to,     /* -- no need to confine mouse */
                    cursor,
                    server_time );

if ( status = = GrabSuccess )
        {
        /*
         *      Do you stuff with the
         *      mouse here
         */

        ...

        /*
         *      Always, Always, Always
         *      restore the system after
         *      you have grabbed anything.
         */
        XUngrabPointer( display,
                CurrentTime );
        }
```

In the preceding example, we specified that we wanted to grab the mouse pointer on the root window, which means our program owns the pointer for the whole screen (since the root window covers the screen). Therefore, we had no need to confine the mouse to any window (other programs may want to do this though; for example during menu handling). The pointer events are reported with respect to the root window. The only event we care about is the button-press mask, and we want to take total control of the pointer for the duration of choosing a window (we don't care about the keyboard).

`XGrabPointer()` will return `GrabSuccess` if everything worked out OK and the pointer is grabbed successfully.

Normally, when you need to specify a time to the X server, use `CurrentTime`. This avoids time-dependent problems when multiple programs try to grab the pointer.

When done, always ungrab the pointer, so the rest of the X applications can continue normally. If your program crashes during a grab on the mouse, you may be in for some tough luck.

DETECTING THE MOUSE CLICK

Once you grab the mouse pointer, the next step is to wait until the user clicks a mouse button. Once the mouse is clicked, find out which window the mouse was in when the button was clicked .

The first step is to allow events with `XAllowEvents()`, a rather strange Xlib function that, in this particular mode, frees queued-up events and allows event-processing to proceed as usual until the next `ButtonPress` or `ButtonRelease` events—just the ticket for the `wpick` program. Using the `SyncPointer` mode will make after the next `ButtonPress` or `ButtonRelease` event. Pointer events appear to "freeze" again.

Then we wait for an event from the X server. Since we're only interested in one event (a `ButtonPress` event) we use `XWindowEvent()` with an event mask of `ButtonPressMask` to wait for a `ButtonPress` event on the rootwindow.

```
Display         *display;
XButtonEvent    event;
Window          rootwindow, window;
int             status;

...
if ( status = = GrabSuccess )
        {
        XAllowEvents( display,
                SyncPointer,
                CurrentTime );

        XWindowEvent( display,
                rootwindow,
                ButtonPressMask,
                &event );

        if ( event.type = = ButtonPress )
                {
                /*
                 *      Find lowest
```

```
             *       child.
             */
            window = FindSubWindow( display,
                          rootwindow,
                          event.xbutton.subwindow,
                          event.xbutton.x,
                          event.xbutton.y );

            /*
             *       If no window is found,
             *       then the user clicked
             *       in the screen background,
             *       so use the root window,
             *       since it covers the screen
             *       and is always valid.
             */
            if ( window = = (Window) None )
                     {
                     window = rootwindow;
                     }
            }

        XUngrabPointer( display, CurrentTime );
        }

...
```

Once a `ButtonPress` event is detected, we want to find the window the pointer is over. `FindSubWindow()` finds the lowest-level window that contains the coordinates x and y (as passed in the event structure: `event.xbutton.x` and `event.xbutton.y`). `FindSubWindow()` is explained in following sections.

Putting it all together, we get the function `PickWindow()` in the `pickwind.c` file:

```
Window PickWindow( display, rootwindow, cursor )

Display *display;
Window  rootwindow;
Cursor  cursor;
```

`PickWindow()` grabs control of the mouse pointer and waits until the user presses a mouse button. It then searches through the window hierarchy to find the lowest window in the hierarchy that the mouse pointer is over. If no such window is found, `PickWindow()` returns the rootwindow.

SOURCE CODE FOR pickwind.c

The source code for `pickwind.c` is as follows:

pickwind.c:

```
/*
 *      pickwind.c
 *      Routine to pick a window on the
 *      display interactively with
 *      a mouse.  The mouse pointer is
 *      grabbed until a button is pressed,
 *      and the window selected is the
 *      window the mouse is in.
 */

#include   "xbook.h"

Window PickWindow( display, rootwindow, cursor )

Display *display;
Window  rootwindow;
Cursor  cursor;

{       /* -- function PickWindow */
        Window  window;
        int     status;
        XEvent  event;

        window = (Window) None;

        status = XGrabPointer( display, rootwindow,
                        False,
                        ButtonPressMask,
                        GrabModeSync,
                        GrabModeAsync,  /* -- Leave keyboard alone */
                        None,           /* -- no need to confine mouse */
                        cursor,
                        CurrentTime );

        if ( status = = GrabSuccess )
                {
                XAllowEvents( display, SyncPointer, CurrentTime );

                XWindowEvent( display, rootwindow,
                        ButtonPressMask, &event );
```

```
                if ( event.type = = ButtonPress )
                        {
                        /*
                         *      Find lowest
                         *      child.
                         */
                        window = FindSubWindow( display,
                                        rootwindow,
                                        event.xbutton.subwindow,
                                        event.xbutton.x,
                                        event.xbutton.y );

                        if ( window = = (Window) None )
                                {
                                window = rootwindow;
                                }
                        }

                XUngrabPointer( display, CurrentTime );
                }

        return( window );

}       /* -- function PickWindow */

PrintPickMsg()

/*
 *      Prints out a message to ask the
 *      user to pick a window.
 */

{       /* -- function PrintPickMsg */

        (void) printf( "\nMove the mouse pointer over the window" );
        (void) printf( "\nyou want, then press a mouse button\n" );

}       /* -- function PrintPickMsg */

/*
 *      end of file.
 */
```

TRACING DOWN THE WINDOW HIERARCHY WITH XTranslateCoordinates

Once we have the location of the mouse pointer, we find out which window the pointer is in. XTranslateCoordinates() asks the X server to map an x, y location from one window's coordinates to another—in this case, from that of topwindow to the coordinate system of window_to_check. If the window_to_check has a child window, then the variable window will be filled with the child window's ID. Otherwise the window will be set to None.

We start with the Root window of a screen and a top-level application window (returned by the ButtonPress event). We then ask XTranslateCoordinates() to translate the root x, y location (again, passed by the ButtonPress event) to the child window's coordinate space (making newx and newy the position of the local coordinates of the child window). If there is another lower-level child window (returned in the variable window), we call XTranslateCoordinates() again.

```
Display *display;
Window  topwindow;                /* -- we start with the root window */
Window  window_to_check;          /* -- a child of topwindow */
int     x, y;                     /* -- original coords */
int     newx, newy;
Window  window;                   /* -- a child of window_to_check */

window = window_to_check;

while ( ( XTranslateCoordinates( display, topwindow,
        window_to_check, x, y, &newx, &newy, &window ) != 0 ) &&
      ( window != (Window) None ) )
        {
        if ( window != (Window) None )
                {
                topwindow       = window_to_check;
                window_to_check = window;
                x               = newx;
                y               = newy;
                }
        }
```

The subwind.c file introduces a function developed to find the lowest-level window on the window hierarchy that contains a given point.

```
Window FindSubWindow( display, topwindow, window_to_check, x, y )

Display *display;
Window  topwindow, window_to_check;
int     x, y;
```

It will return the window ID of the lowest-level window, or `None`.

SOURCE CODE FOR subwind.c

The source code for `subwind.c` is as follows:

```
subwind.c:

/*
 *      subwind.c
 *
 *      Routine to find the lowest child window (called
 *      a subwindow), for a given set of coordinates in
 *      a parent window.
 *
 *      If no child window can be found in the given
 *      coordinates, then the lowest window is the
 *      parent.
 */

#include  "xbook.h"

Window FindSubWindow( display, topwindow, window_to_check, x, y )

Display *display;
Window  topwindow, window_to_check;
int     x, y;

/*
 *      FindSubWindow() finds the child
 *      window lowest on the window
 *      hierarchy, that the given x, y
 *      coordinates are in.
 *
 */

{       /* -- function FindSubWindow */
```

```
        int     newx, newy;
        Window  window;

        /*
         *      Check for bad input
         */
        if ( topwindow = = (Window) None )
                return( (Window) None );

        if ( window_to_check = = (Window) None )
                return( topwindow );

        /*
         *      Check for children
         */
        window = window_to_check;

        while ( ( XTranslateCoordinates( display, topwindow,
                window_to_check, x, y, &newx, &newy, &window ) != 0 ) &&
              ( window != (Window) None ) )
                {
                if ( window != (Window) None )
                        {
                        topwindow       = window_to_check;
                        window_to_check = window;
                        x               = newx;
                        y               = newy;
                        }
                }

        if ( window = = (Window) None )
                {
                window = window_to_check;
                }

        return( window );

}       /* -- function FindSubWindow */

/*
 *      end of file.
 */
```

SOURCE CODE FOR wpick. c

The `wpick.c` file contains the main function for the program to interactively select any window on the screen with a mouse. Its contents are as follows:

wpick.c:

```
/*
 *      wpick.c
 *
 *      Allows the user to pick a window interactively with
 *      the mouse.
 */

#include  "xbook.h"

main( argc, argv )

int     argc;
char    *argv[];

{
        Display *display;
        int     screen;
        Window  rootwindow, window;
        Cursor  cursor;

        /*
         *      Set up X connection
         */
        display    = SetUpDisplay( argc, argv, &screen );

        rootwindow = RootWindow( display, screen );

        cursor     = XCreateFontCursor( display, XC_gumby );

        /*
         *      Now, find a window with the pointer
         */
        PrintPickMsg();

        window = PickWindow( display, rootwindow, cursor );

        if ( window != (Window) None )
                {
```

```
                PrintWinInfo( display, window );
                }
        else
                {
                (void) printf( "A window was not found.\n" );
                }

        XFreeCursor( display, cursor );

        XCloseDisplay( display );

        exit( 0 );
}

/*
 *      end of file
 */
```

COMPILING wpick

The `wpick` program uses the following code modules:

`display.c`	*(from chapter 2)*
`pickwind.c`	
`subwind.c`	
`wpick.c`	
`wprint.c`	

On Unix-based systems, you can use the `Makefile` in appendix C with:

```
make wpick
```

Or, you can compile with:

```
cc -o wpick wpick.c display.c wprint.c pickwind.c subwind.c -lX11
```

RUNNING wpick

`Wpick` will optionally take a display name.

You can run `wpick` with:

```
wpick
or
wpick -display attila:0.0
```

FUNCTIONS DEVELOPED IN THIS CHAPTER

```
PickWindow
FindSubWindow
PrintWinInfo
SearchWindowTree
```

XLIB FUNCTIONS AND MACROS INTRODUCED IN THIS CHAPTER

```
XAllowEvents
XFetchName
XGetClassHint
XGetGeometry
XGrabPointer
XQueryTree
XTranslateCoordinates
XUngrabPointer
XWindowEvent
```

SUMMARY

- The X Window system contains a number of calls that retrieve information about any window on the screen. Most window information is stored in properties associated with the window. You can get a lot of information with one call, `XGetWindowProperty()`, which is unfortunately rather complex. We recommend using the X convenience functions to get the value of a particular property. `XFetchName()`, for instance, retrieves a window's name.

- Each window may have hints about the class of the window. These hints are stored in the `WM_CLASS` property. The `res_name` field holds the application name. These class hints can be used by the window manager and wnen grabbing resources from the X resource manager, should you decide to use the X resource manager). `PrintWinInfo()` prints out information about a particular window.
- Windows on any screen are arranged in a hierarchy. The root window is the highest window in the hierarchy and covers the entire screen. Below the root window, many applications have their top-level windows. A window may have siblings: other windows at the same level which share the same parent. A window may also have children; that is, it may be a parent to the lower-level windows. While the ability to create many levels of windows helps in the creation of elaborate user interfaces, you sometimes want to see which windows are in use. `XQueryTree()` traces down the window hierarchy, or tree, and returns information about a given window: its parent, its root window and the number of child windows.
- Many X programs need to search through the window hierarchy. Sometimes you may want to traverse the entire window tree. Other times you may be interested in finding just one window. The function, `SearchWindowTree()`, returns a window ID (of type `Window`) or `None` if no matching window was found. `SearchWindowTree()` will call itself recursively to traverse depth-first down the window hierarchy. Another program, `winfo`, lists the windows that are on the screen and how many new windows a window manager uses.
- It's also useful for the programmer to be able to find a particular window, either based on some window information or interactively with a mouse. Many X programs act on other windows. For example, programs that "dump" the contents of a window to an image file (or to the printer) usually need the user to select which window to dump. Many window managers have menu choices that allow you to pick a window and then do a number of things with it including resize it, move it, and iconify it. The most common approach will have the user choose a window using the mouse. This approach presents some tricky code, because you need to take control of the mouse pointer while the user is selecting a window, and

you want the user to be able to move the mouse all over the screen to locate a window. After that, you must wait until the user clicks a mouse button. Then you want to find out where the mouse was when the button was clicked and which window the mouse was in.

Chapter 12

Property Information

Property in X has nothing to do with real estate. Instead, an X property is a collection of data bytes with a type and a name. Properties are of arbitrary length and are used through the Xlib for things like window names (the `WM_NAME` property) and application classes (the `WM_CLASS` property).

These properties are also used in most X mechanisms for program-to-program communication (as you'll see in section III).

Properties have a text name, a type, and raw bytes of data (which can be interpreted various ways depending on the type). Since dealing with text names is often expensive in terms of CPU time, the X server keeps a table of string names for things, and a magic number for each thing. These magic numbers are called `atoms`.

ATOMS

In X, an atom is a 32-bit integer stored in the X server. Each atom represents a name, properties, and types of properties. It is a general mechanism for identifying some named thing using a 32-bit integer. In other words, you can convert a string to an atom and then use that atom as shorthand for the name.

Each property has a name, although usually that name is converted to an atom to speed processing. The important part, though, is that each property has an atom to identify it.

To convert a name to an atom, use XInternAtom():

```
Display *display;
Atom    atom;
char    *propname;
Bool    only_if_exists;

/*
 *      We want to create an Atom if it doesn't
 *      exist yet. A True would mean to return None
 *      if the Atom does not exist yet.
 */
only_if_exists = False;

atom = XInternAtom( display, propname, only_if_exists );

if ( atom != (Atom) None )
        {
        /*
         *      We have success!
         */


        ...

        }
```

To convert back from an atom to a name, use XGetAtomName(). XGetAtomName() returns a character pointer, pointing to the name (a NULL-terminated string).

```
char    *name;
Display *display;
Atom    atom;

name = XGetAtomName( display, atom );

if ( name != (char *) NULL )
        {
        /*
         *      Success! You can now
         *      use the atom's name
         *      as a character string
         */

        ...

        /*
         *      When done,
         *      use XFree() to free
         *      the storage for the name
         */
        XFree( name );
        }
```

Predefined Atoms

A number of atoms are predefined in the include file <X11/XAtom.h>. These atoms include XA_STRING (used as a string type) and XA_INTEGER, a signed 32-bit integer. You may use these predefined names directly, without making a round trip to the X server with XInternAtom().

Atom Conventions

The main convention for predefined atoms is that they begin with XA_ and are followed by the name. Also, each word in an atom name is separated by an underscore (_). For example, XA_CUT_BUFFER0 is the predefined atom for the name "CUT_BUFFER0".

Some of the predefined names include:

ARC
ATOM
BITMAP
CAP_HEIGHT
CARDINAL
COLORMAP
COPYRIGHT
CURSOR
CUT_BUFFER0
CUT_BUFFER1
CUT_BUFFER2
CUT_BUFFER3
CUT_BUFFER4
CUT_BUFFER5
CUT_BUFFER6
CUT_BUFFER7
DRAWABLE
END_SPACE
FAMILY_NAME
FONT
FONT_NAME
FULL_NAME
INTEGER
ITALIC_ANGLE
MAX_SPACE
MIN_SPACE
NORM_SPACE
NOTICE
PIXMAP
POINT
POINT_SIZE
PRIMARY *(see chapter 19)*
QUAD_WIDTH
RECTANGLE
RESOLUTION
RESOURCE_MANAGER
RGB_BEST_MAP
RGB_BLUE_MAP
RGB_COLOR_MAP
RGB_DEFAULT_MAP
RGB_GRAY_MAP
RGB_GREEN_MAP
RGB_RED_MAP
SECONDARY *(see chapter 19)*
STRIKEOUT_ASCENT
STRIKEOUT_DESCENT
STRING
SUBSCRIPT_X
SUBSCRIPT_Y
SUPERSCRIPT_X
SUPERSCRIPT_Y
UNDERLINE_POSITION
UNDERLINE_THICKNESS
VISUALID
WEIGHT
WM_CLASS
WM_CLIENT_MACHINE
WM_COMMAND
WM_HINTS
WM_ICON_NAME
WM_ICON_SIZE
WM_NAME
WM_NORMAL_HINTS
WM_TRANSIENT_FOR
WM_ZOOM_HINTS
X_HEIGHT

Joining the Atomic Club

If your organization comes up with its own set of atoms for use in applications, you should begin each atom name with an underscore to prevent naming conflicts. (For example, we call the atom used in chapter 19 "__XBOOK".) You can register these names with the X Consortium if you are serious about the naming schemes you use.

Identifying with Atoms

Atoms aren't much good on their own. They usually serve to identify a type of item, like XA_STRING for a character string type; properties, like XA_WM_NAME for a window's name property (used by the window manager); and selections, like XA_PRIMARY for the "PRIMARY" selection (used for program-to-program communication in chapter 19).

PROPERTY

A property is a collection of bytes associated with a window. The property has a name which is tied to an atom. This atom is used to identify the property in most cases. Each property also has a type, also identified by an atom.

Each window can have many properties associated with it. Additionally, each of those properties is unique to the window so that two windows may have unique names stored in the WM_NAME property. Window managers, in fact, use a large number of properties (most of them begin with "WM_").

When you create an application's top-level window, you typically create a number of properties for use by the window manager. When you create these properties you tell the window manager several things including the name you want for the window, how small it can go, a name for its icon, and a pixmap for its icon.

You can list out the properties to see what kinds of properties are associated with a window.

LISTING THE NAMES OF PROPERTIES ASSOCIATED WITH A WINDOW

The XListProperties() Xlib function will return a list (an array) of the atoms identifying the properties associated with a window. Since the atoms are used to get and put property data, you could then use these atoms to access the data stored within the properties.

```
Display *display;

Window  window;
Atom    *properties;
int     num_properties;

properties = XListProperties( display,
                window,
                &num_properties );
```

You can then access each atom by indexing from the start. For example, to print out the names of all the properties associated with a window, you could:

```
...

int     i;
...

if ( ( num_properties > 0 ) && ( properties != NULL ) )
        {
        (void) printf( "Number of Properties: %d.\n",
                num_properties );

        for( i = 0; i < num_properties; i++ )
                {
                (void) printf( "\t[%4ld]   ",
                        properties[ i ] );

                name = XGetAtomName( display, properties[ i ] );

                if ( name != (char *) NULL )
                        {
                        (void) printf( "%s", name );

                        XFree( name );
```

```
                    }
                (void) printf( "\n" );
                }
        }
```

The lsprop.c source file contains code that does exactly that, in the function ListWProperties().

SOURCE CODE FOR lsprop. c

The contents of lsprop.c are as follows:

lsprop.c:

```
/*
 *      lsprop.c
 *      Routines to list out all the property names associated with
 *      a given window on a given display.
 *
 *      Written for Advanced X Window Application Programming
 */

#include    "xbook.h"

/*
 *      20 Blank spaces
 */
#define    SPACES        "                    "

ListWProperties( display, window, string )

Display         *display;
Window          window;
char            string[];

/*
 *      ListWProperties() lists out the names of all properties
 *      associated with the given window on the given display.
 *      This information is printed to stdout.
 *
 */

{       /* -- function ListWProperties */
        Atom    *properties;
        int     num_properties, i, length;
```

```
        char    *name;

        /*
         * Initialize string
         */
        string[ 0 ] = '\0';

        /*
         * Get list of properties
         */
        properties = XListProperties( display,
                        window, &num_properties );

        if ( ( num_properties > 0 ) && ( properties != NULL ) )
                {
                for( i = 0; i < num_properties; i++ )
                        {
                        name = XGetAtomName( display, properties[ i ] );

                        if ( name != (char *) NULL )
                                {
                                (void) strcat( string, name );

                                if ( ( i > 0 ) && ( ( i % 3 ) = = 0 ) )
                                        {
                                        (void) strcat( string, "\n" );
                                        }
                                else
                                        {
                                        length = 20 - strlen( name );

                                        if ( length > 0 )
                                                {
                                                (void) strncat( string,
                                                                SPACES,
                                                                length );
                                                }
                                        }

                                XFree( name );
                                }

                        }
                }

}       /* -- function ListWProperties */
```

```
/*
 *      end of file.
 */
```

THE X11 PROGRAM xprop

The X11 release from the MIT X Consortium includes a program called `xprop` that lists the properties associated with a window and the contents of those properties. Some properties include binary information, which, of course, leads to a very complex program. If `xprop` is available on your system, try it out.

In the program below, we will be a little less ambitious than the writers of `xprop`.

LISTING PROPERTY NAMES FOR A WINDOW

`Propinfo` is a program that has the user interactively pick a window using the mouse (using routines developed in chapter 11). `Propinfo` then lists out the atom names for the properties on that window. `Propinfo` uses the `PickWindow()` function (created in chapter 11) to have the user interactively pick a window.

Source Code for propinfo. c

The contents for `propinfo.c` are as follows:

propinfo.c:

```
/*
 *      propinfo.c
 *
 *      Program to display the names of all properties associated
 *      with a given window.
 *
 *      The user picks the window interactively with the mouse.
 *
 *      Written for Advanced X Window Applications Programming.
 *
 */

#include  "xbook.h"

main( argc, argv )
```

```
int     argc;
char    *argv[];
{
        Display         *display;
        int             screen;
        Window          window, rootwindow;
        Cursor          cursor;
        char            string[ BUFSIZE + 1 ];

        /*
         *      Set up X connection
         */
        display    = SetUpDisplay( argc, argv, &screen );

        rootwindow = RootWindow( display, screen );

        cursor     = XCreateFontCursor( display, XC_gumby );

        /*
         *      Now, pick a window
         */
        PrintPickMsg();

        window = PickWindow( display, rootwindow, cursor );

        if ( window != (Window) None )
                {
                PrintWinInfo( display, window );

                ListWProperties( display, window, string );

                (void) printf( "%s\n", string );
                }
        else
                {
                (void) printf( "No window was found.\n" );
                }

        XFreeCursor( display, cursor );

        XCloseDisplay( display );

        exit( 0 );
}
```

```
/*
 *      end of file
 */
```

Compiling propinfo

The `propinfo` program uses the following code modules:

```
display.c       (from chapter 2)
wprint.c        (from chapter 11)
subwind.c       (from chapter 11)
pickwind.c      (from chapter 11)
lsprop.c
propinfo.c
```

On Unix-based systems, you can use the `Makefile` in appendix C, with:

```
make propinfo
```

Or, you can compile with:

```
cc -o propinfo propinfo.c display.c pickwind.c lsprop.c \
        wprint.c subwind.c -lX11
```

Running propinfo

You can pass a display name to `propinfo`, or run the program without any command-line arguments:

```
propinfo
```

Or:

```
propinfo -display attila:0.0
```

First, `propinfo` will prompt you to position the mouse over a window and then to press a mouse button:

```
Move the mouse pointer over the window
you want, then press a mouse button
```

The cursor will change in shape to the XC_gumby shape.

The output of propinfo looks something like the following:

```
(X Time)[0x400006] at local 0, 0; 116 by 26
WM_CLASS  WM_ICON_NAME  WM_NAME  WM_NORMAL_HINTS
WM_HINTS
```

Note that these properties are all for use of the window manager. However, the root window usually has the most interesting properties. We'll go into much more depth in chapter 18 on using properties to communicate with other X applications.

FUNCTIONS DEVELOPED IN THIS CHAPTER

ListWProperties

XLIB FUNCTIONS AND MACROS INTRODUCED IN THIS CHAPTER

XGetAtomName
XInternAtom
XListProperties

SUMMARY

- An X property is a collection of data bytes of arbitrary length with a type and a name. Properties are used through Xlib for things like window names and application classes. These properties are used in most X mechanisms for program-to-program communication. Properties have a text name, a type, and raw bytes of data (which can be interpreted various ways depending on the type).
- The X server maintains a table of string names and a magic number for each thing. These magic numbers are called atoms. They are 32-bit integers used to represent

properties and types of properties. They act as a general mechanism for identifying some named thing using a 32-bit integer.

- To convert a name to an `atom`, use `XInternAtom()`. To convert back from an `atom` to a name, use `XGetAtomName()`.
- To list the `atoms` that identify the properties associated with a window, use `XListProperties()`. You can use these `atoms` to access the data stored within the properties, since the atoms are used to get and put property data.
- The X11 release from the MIT X Consortium includes a program called `xprop` that lists the properties associated with a window and the contents of those properties. Some properties include binary information, which, of course, leads to a very complex program. Included in this chapter is a less-ambitious program that lists the atom names for the properties a user-defined window.

Chapter 13

Host/Network Information

X is a network-oriented graphical windowing system. Programs running on one machine may display their output on another machine. This really helps if you have a Unix workstation at your desk and a Cray Y-MP supercomputer in the basement. You can let the Cray do the major calculations and let the workstation display the results.

Other times, you can test whether X software runs on various machines by sending the output to your display—without getting up from your desk. (This doesn't test if the software will run on the other machines' displays, but rather whether the software will run at all on the other machine.)

All in all, the networking features of X come in very handy, especially when you have multiple `xterm` sessions remotely logged in to a number of machines on the network.

This chapter shows how X controls this access and how to get information about which machines are allowed to access your X server on your workstation. Some of the material is Unix-specific, much of it is Ethernet TCP/IP-specific. While that probably fits the majority of readers, those running VMS or AmigaDOS will have to bear with us. (Most of this system-specific material is just in converting the X format for machine addresses into an ASCII format; it shouldn't be too hard to swap in the necessary code for your system.)

ALLOWING HOST ACCESS

Basic X provides virtually no access-protection mechanisms. Any X client can munge (and even destroy) X resources stored in the server (including windows and pixmaps).

Instead of providing access-protection, the designers of X choose to allow you to layer your own security and authentication system. The issues involved in allowing programs from other machines access to a host over a network are not merely graphics or X issues, so the approach of offloading most authentication and security issues is valid. No one wants zillions of authentication methods (one for X, one for databases, and so on) to access programs over a network.

Even so, the MIT server provides two types of access control. The first is when each client must send a special value (often called a "magic cookie") to the server to be allowed a connection. The second involves a list of other hosts that each server maintains, called the access list. The server allows connections from any client on one of the hosts on the access list.

Unfortunately, for those who desire more security, most X servers provide only control over the access list. (The authentication schemes are new to Release 4.)

CONTROLLING THE X ACCESS LIST

Xlib provides three basic functions to control access to your server, all of which result in the same X protocol message, `SetAccessControl`. These functions are:

```
Display *display;
int     access_mode;      /* -- EnableAccess or DisableAccess */
```

```
XSetAccessControl( display, access_mode );

XEnableAccessControl( display );

XDisableAccessControl( display );
```

Set `access_mode` to `EnableAccess` or `DisableAccess`. Of course, you must have access to the server to set the access control.

WHICH MACHINES HAVE ACCESS?

The X access control is based on machine access. This means that you can allow a particular machine to have access, or you can make a machine have no access to a particular server. The access is for the whole machine, i.e., any program on a given "trusted" machine can access your X server.

When an X server starts up, access is allowed for the machine on which the server is running.

On Unix-based systems, a file in the `/etc` directory may contain extra host names, which are allowed access.

This file has one host name per line (DECnet machine names need to end with two colons: "::"). There is one file per display and the names are numbered by the displays:

```
/etc/X0.hosts
/etc/X1.hosts
/etc/X2.hosts
```

and so on, where `/etc/X0.hosts` is the file for server zero. For example, `:0`, `unix:0` or `hostname:0`, and `/etc/X1.hosts` is the file for server one.

These files just set up the initial access list. Other machines can be listed as "trusted" or removed from the trusted list with the `xhost` program.

THE X11 xhost PROGRAM

The MIT X Consortium release contains a program called `xhost` that allows you to list, add, or remove hosts from the default list of hosts with access to your X server.

Calling `xhost` with no command-line parameters lists out the names of the hosts with access (much like the hosts program developed below). Calling `xhost` with a machine (host) name adds that machine to the access list. You can also call `xhost` with a plus sign ("+") and the machine name.

```
xhost attila
```

adds `host attila` to the list of hosts that can access your X server.

```
xhost +attila
```

does the same thing.

```
xhost -attila
```

removes `machine attila` from the list of hosts with access to your X server.

```
xhost
```

lists out the hosts with access to your X server.

THE XHostAddress STRUCTURE

X uses the `XHostAddress` structure to represent the hosts in the access-control list:

```
typedef struct
        {
        int     family;
        int     length;         /* -- number of bytes in address */
        char    *address;
        } XHostAddress;
```

The family field can be one of:

```
FamilyInternet
FamilyDECnet
FamilyChaos
```

FINDING WHICH HOSTS HAVE ACCESS

From an X client program, you can find out which machines can access a display.

To find out which hosts have access to a display, use the Xlib function `XListHosts()`. `XListHosts()` returns a pointer to a list of `XHostAddress` structures, one for each host machine with access.

```
Display         *display;
Bool            access_enabled; /* -- is access enabled? */
int             num_hosts;      /* -- number of hosts */
XHostAddress    *hosts;

hosts = XListHosts( display, &num_hosts, &access_enabled );
```

If `access_enabled` is `True`, then access is enabled for the list of machines returned in the variable hosts.

The `hosts` program prints out the list of hosts that have access to your X server.

SOURCE CODE FOR lshosts.c

The source code for `lshosts.c` is the following:

lshosts.c:

```
/*
 *      lshosts.c
 *      Lists all the hosts with X access permission.
 *
 *      This is Unix and TCP/IP specific.
 *
 *      Note: define the symbol hpux in the Makefile, if your
 *      system runs Hewlett-Packard's implementation of Unix
 *      (HP-UX).
```

```
 *
 */

/*
 *      Include the necessary X11 files
 */
#include    "xbook.h"

/*
 *      Include the necessary networking files
 */
#include    <sys/socket.h>
#include    <netdb.h>

#ifndef hpux
#include    <arpa/inet.h>
#endif

#include    <netinet/in.h>

ListHosts( display )

Display *display;

/*
 *      ListHosts() calls the Xlib routine XListHosts() to
 *      get an array of structures, one for each host
 *      with access permission for the given X display.
 *
 */

{       /* -- function ListHosts */
        XHostAddress     *hosts;
        Bool             access_enabled;
        int              num_hosts, i;
        struct hostent   *thehostent;
        char             string_address[ BUFSIZE + 1 ];

        hosts = XListHosts( display, &num_hosts, &access_enabled );

        if ( ( access_enabled = = True ) && ( num_hosts > 0 ) )
                {
                (void) printf( "Access is enabled to:\n" );
                }

        for( i = 0; i < num_hosts; i++ )
```

```
            {
            if ( hosts[ i ].family == FamilyInternet )
                    {
                    thehostent = gethostbyaddr( hosts[ i ].address,
                                    hosts[ i ].length, AF_INET );

                    GetIPAddress( hosts[ i ].address,
                            string_address );

                    (void) printf( "%40s %s\n",
                            thehostent->h_name,
                            string_address );

                    }
            else
                    {
                    switch( hosts[ i ].family )
                            {
                            case FamilyDECnet:
                                    (void) printf( "Family is DECnet\n" );
                                    break;
                            case FamilyChaos:
                                    (void) printf( "Family is Chaos\n" );
                                    break;
                            default:
                                    (void) printf( "Family is Unknown\n");
                                    break;
                            }
                    }
            }

        if ( hosts != (XHostAddress *) NULL )
                {
                XFree( hosts );
                }

}       /* -- function ListHosts */

GetIPAddress( address, string_address )

char    *address;
char    *string_address;

/*
 *      GetIPAddress() converts an Internet Protocol-style
 *      address number into its string "dot" representation,
```

```
 *      e.g., 192.1.1.1
 *
 *      If you use something other than TCP/IP, this
 *      probably won't work for you.
 *
 */

{       /* -- function GetIPAddress */
        char            *inet_ntoa();

        (void) strcpy( string_address,
                inet_ntoa( (*(struct in_addr *)address) ) );

}       /* -- function GetIPAddress */

/*
 *      end of file
 */
```

SOURCE CODE FOR hosts.c

The file `hosts.c` contains a `main()` function that sets up the connection to the X server and then calls the `ListHosts()` function (in `lshosts.c`). We split up the example so that it would be easier for you to include `ListHosts()` in your own programs.

hosts.c:

```
/*
 *      hosts.c
 *      Program to list all the hosts with X access permission.
 *
 *      This is Unix and TCP/IP specific.
 *
 */

#include    "xbook.h"

main( argc, argv )

int     argc;
char    *argv[];
```

```
{
        Display *display;
        int     screen;

        /*
         *      Open display connection.
         */
        display = SetUpDisplay( argc, argv, &screen );

        /*
         *      List out Unix hosts
         */
        ListHosts( display );

        /*
         *      Clean up
         */
        XCloseDisplay( display );

        exit( 0 );

}

/*
 *      end of file
 */
```

COMPILING hosts

The `hosts` program uses the following code modules:

```
display.c        (from chapter 2)
hosts.c
lshosts.c
```

On Unix-based systems, you can use the `Makefile` in appendix C, with:

```
make hosts
```

You can also compile with:

```
cc -o hosts hosts.c display.c lshosts.c -lX11
```

Some Unix-based systems, notably HP-UX (Hewlett-Packard's implementation of Unix), do not have a certain include file, or change the names of the include files needed. Under HP-UX, add a `-Dhpux` to the compilation command in the `Makefile` (see appendix C for more information).

If you have problems compiling `lshosts.c`, consult your system manuals. You will also have problems if your system does not have a Berkeley-style socket library.

RUNNING hosts

Hosts can take an optional display parameter, with the `-display displayname` option:

```
hosts
```

You can also use:

```
hosts -display attila:0.0
```

The output of `hosts` looks something like the following:

```
Access is enabled to:
                                              THOR 192.6.1.110
                                             flame 192.6.1.111
                                           attila 192.6.1.112
                                           gondor 192.6.1.113
```

THE UNIX SELECT FUNCTION

In addition to the networking provided by X, your applications may set up their own network connections. To do this, if your applications run on a Unix-based system, you may want to call the Unix function `select()`.

The `ConnectionNumber()` X macro will return the file descriptor of the X socket connection (on a Unix-based system).

```
int     fd;

fd = ConnectionNumber( display );
```

The connection file descriptor helps mainly if you are using Berkeley-style sockets within your application, in addition to the connection to the X server.

FUNCTIONS DEVELOPED IN THIS CHAPTER

ListHosts

XLIB FUNCTIONS AND MACROS INTRODUCED IN THIS CHAPTER

ConnectionNumber
XDisableAccessControl
XEnableAccessControl
XListHosts
XSetAccessControl

SUMMARY

- X provides virtually no access-protection mechanisms. Almost any X client can munge (and even destroy) X resources stored in the server (including windows and pixmaps). Most protection issues are up to the application programmer.
- The MIT server provides two types of access control. The first is when each client must send a special value to the server to be allowed a connection. The second involves a list of other hosts that each server maintains, called the access list. The server allows connections from any client on one of the hosts on the access list. Unfortunately for those who wish for more security, most X servers provide only control over the access list. Xlib provides three basic functions to control access to

your server, all of which result in the same X protocol message (SetAccessControl).

- The X access control is based on machine access; that is, you can allow a particular machine to have access. When an X server starts up, access is allowed for the machine on which the server is running. On Unix-based systems, there may be a file in the /etc directory that contains extra host names, which are allowed access.

- The MIT X Consortium release contains a program called xhost that allows you to list, add, or remove hosts from the default list of hosts with access to your X server.

- From an X client program, you can find out which machines can access a display with the Xlib function XListHosts(). XListHosts() returns a pointer to a list of XHostAddress structures, one for each host machine with access.

- In addition to the networking provided by X, your applications may set up their own network connections. In such cases, you may want to call the Unix function select() if your applications run on a Unix-based system. The X macro ConnectionNumber() will return the file descriptor of the X socket connection (on a Unix-based system).

Chapter 14

Living Color

When creating a portable application, using color can be a pitfall in many operating environments. This is not the case with X, however. The X designers wisely created a colormap common to every X-equipped computer (if, of course, the computer supports color). While a colormap ensures the consistency of colors between different implementations of X applications, the colormap can also be a dangerous temptation to those wanting to create custom colors. This chapter shows how to view the default X colormap and why using the default colormap is wise.

THE COLORMAP

A colormap is a table that contains color cells. Each color cell represents a color that is in use on the screen. Most colormaps have default entries for black and white. For a monochrome system, that's all you'll have. For a full-blown color system, you might have anywhere from 16 entries (VGA) to 256 entries to 16 million entries (rare and very expensive).

COLORS ARE PIXEL VALUES

Individual colors in X are called pixel values. These pixel values are unsigned longs and index to a colormap cell. When you want to draw in a given color, you need the pixel (unsigned long index into the colormap in use) value. You can then pass this value to `XSetForeground()`, which sets a graphics context to draw in the given color. So, to get a color—for example, red—you need to first find an entry in a colormap that corresponds to the RGB (Red, Green, Blue) values for red, or allocate a cell in a colormap and set the values in the cell to the RGB values for red.

From then on, whenever you want to draw in red you can set the GC to the cell number (the pixel value) that holds red in the colormap. You can get much more complex (and a lot closer to the hardware) with color, but using the simple model of color presented here is not only easier, but more portable. X also adds another simplification for color through the use of color names.

DEFAULT COLOR NAMES

The X Window System comes with a database of English color names, such as blue and lime green, usually stored in `/usr/lib/X11/rgb.txt`. Each color name in this database has associated red, green, and blue values (usually 8 bits for each) that specify the color in numeric terms (in an RGB color model). You can use any of these color names, and X will use a color as close as possible to the requested RGB values associated with that color name. Using these color names makes for more portable code and allows X users to tweak the color database locally. For example, if the color associated with "pink" doesn't really look pink on a particular monitor, you can change the entry for "pink" in the color database. Then, anytime someone asks for pink they will get your new pink. This use of color names makes your applications both look better and makes them more portable at the same time.

The Release 4 set of color names doesn't match the Release 3 set. This is both good and bad. It's good in that the Release 3 (and 2) default colors didn't look good on most monitors. The pink, for example, looked wretched on most Sun monitors. The Release 4 default colors look much better and contain a much larger set of color names. That's also the bad news. The Release 3 color names don't include colors like "gainsboro" or "mistyrose." For the greatest portability, stick to the Release 3 names for now.

No matter what color name you choose, though, you still have to convert the color name to an X pixel value in a colormap.

CONVERTING COLOR NAMES TO PIXEL VALUES

Converting a color name to a pixel value is a two-step process. First, call `XLookupColor()` to find the closest match to your color available on your hardware:

```
Display         *display;
Colormap        colormap;
char            *name="LimeGreen";
XColor          rgbcolor, hardwarecolor;
int             status;

status = XLookupColor( display, colormap, name,
                &rgbcolor, &hardwarecolor );

if ( status != 0 )
        {
        /* -- We found a match */

        ...

        }
```

`XLookupColor()` returns the RGB definition `(rgbcolor)` of the given color name from the color database. `XLookupColor()` also returns the closest match to that RGB definition that is supported by the color hardware in use `(hardwarecolor)`.

Then, call XAllocColor() to allocate a cell in the colormap:

```
unsigned long color;

status = XAllocColor( display, colormap,
                      &hardwarecolor );

if ( status != 0 )
        {
        /*
         * Success, now hardware.pixel is a
         * pixel value we can use to set a GC
         * foreground, etc.
         */
        color = hardwarecolor.pixel;
        }
```

XAllocColor() allocates a "read-only" cell in the colormap. This means another X application can share the colormap cell. If you use the default colormap and another application already allocated the same color, XAllocColor() will return that color cell. This way, you can share common colors—if you use the same (usually the default) colormap.

XAllocColor() checks the given colormap. If a read-only cell in the colormap matches the color you want, it returns that cell's pixel value. If no read-only cell matches the color you want and there is an available read-write cell, then XAllocColor() will allocate that cell for you (as a read-only cell, so it can be shared later) and return that cell's pixel. If hardware doesn't support read-write colormap cells, then XAllocColor() can just check the read-only cells for the closest match.

If it all fails, XAllocColor() returns a zero.

SOURCE CODE FOR color c.

The file color.c contains a function, GetColor(), that converts a color name to a pixel value. It is passed as a default color if no color cells are available in the colormap, or if the color database does not have the color you want. The contents of color.c are as follows:

color.c:

```
/*
 *      color.c
 *      X11 routine to convert color name to color.
 */

#include   "xbook.h"

unsigned long GetColor( display, name, colormap, default_color )

Display         *display;
char            name[];         /* -- name of color we want, like LimeGreen */
Colormap        colormap;         /* -- Colormap to use */
unsigned long   default_color;  /* -- What to return on failure */

/*
 *      GetColor() converts a color name into a pixel
 *      value in the given colormap.  Ideally, the color
 *      is already in the colormap.
 *
 *      If no there is no close match in the colormap,
 *      or the colormap is full, GetColor() will return
 *      the default_color
 *
 */

{       /* -- function GetColor */
        unsigned long   color;
        XColor          rgbcolor, hardwarecolor;
        int             status;

        color = default_color;

        status = XLookupColor( display, colormap, name,
                        &rgbcolor, &hardwarecolor );

        if ( status != 0 )
                {
                status = XAllocColor( display, colormap,
                                &hardwarecolor );

                if ( status != 0 )
                        {
                        color = hardwarecolor.pixel;
                        }
                }
```

```
        return( color );

}       /* -- function GetColor */

/*
 *      end of file.
 */
```

USING THE DEFAULT COLORMAP

Many X stations just have one hardware colormap, so it is a good idea to share colormaps and colormap entries. For most workstations or X terminals, color is very expensive and very few colors will be available. Most X color stations have only 256 color cells (that is, eight color planes or an 8-bit depth). Many 386 PCs running X have only sixteen colors available on VGA or EGA screens. So, the first rule is to only use the colors your application absolutely needs. The second rule is to use the default colormap if possible.

If you are writing a program to analyze medical imagery, then you probably want to create your own colormap. Most programs don't need really fancy colors, although colors can certainly enhance a user interface. For most applications, such as business spreadsheet charts, statistical analysis or industrial-process control, you can probably get away with using the default colormap.

X has a macro, called `DefaultColormap()`, that will return the default colormap for a given screen:

```
Display         *display;
int             screen;
Colormap        colormap;

colormap = DefaultColormap( display, screen );
```

Combined with the `GetColor()` function, the default colormap will improve the appearance of your X applications.

VIEWING THE DEFAULT COLORMAP

We've created an example program, called `colort` (for Color Table), that displays a set of color names from the color database in a window. It uses, of course, the default colormap on the default screen with the default visual.

COLOR NAMES FOR RELEASE 4

In Release 4, the following include file contains the English names of a number of the Release 4 colors. We included only 256, since most X color systems have only 256 colors (8-bit planes). The full Release 4 default color list has over 600 entries and is located in appendix E. The Release 3 list of color names contained only 66 basic entries (some servers added a number of gray scales to the 66 basic entries). You'll notice the Release 4 list contains many more pastel colors and fixed the wretched pink.

For the `colort` program, we've built two include files, `colort.h` and `colortr4.h` (the last one contains Release 4 color names). Both include files that use the same array, `colornames`, to contain the names used by the `colort` program. The contents of `colortr4.h` are as follows:

colortr4.h:

```
/*
 *      colortr4.h
 *      Global color name definitions for the Color Table
 *      program.
 *
 *      colort.h contains the default (pre-X11R4) definitions
 *      of 66 colors.
 *
 *      colortr4.h contains the X11R4 version, highly edited.
 *
 */


/*
 *      Global color name definitions, edited from X11R4 rgb database.
 *
 */
#define MAX_COLORS      255
```

```
char     *colornames[ MAX_COLORS ] =
                        {
                        "black",
                        "navyblue",
                        "mediumblue",
                        "blue",
                        "darkgreen",
                        "deepskyblue",
                        "darkturquoise",
                        "green2",
                        "springgreen2",
                        "cyan2",
                        "turquoise1",
                        "mediumspringgreen",
                        "green",
                        "springgreen",
                        "cyan",
                        "midnightblue",
                        "dodgerblue",
                        "lightseagreen",
                        "forestgreen",
                        "seagreen",
                        "darkslategrey",
                        "limegreen",
                        "mediumseagreen",
                        "turquoise",
                        "royalblue",
                        "royalblue2",
                        "steelblue",
                        "darkslateblue",
                        "royalblue1",
                        "mediumturquoise",
                        "seagreen2",
                        "seagreen1",
                        "darkolivegreen",
                        "steelblue2",
                        "cadetblue",
                        "steelblue1",
                        "cornflowerblue",
                        "mediumaquamarine",
                        "dimgrey",
                        "slateblue",
                        "olivedrab",
                        "slategrey",
                        "chartreuse2",
                        "aquamarine2",
```

```
"lightslategrey",
"slateblue2",
"mediumslateblue",
"lawngreen",
"skyblue2",
"chartreuse",
"aquamarine",
"slateblue1",
"lightslateblue",
"skyblue",
"lightskyblue",
"skyblue1",
"blueviolet",
"saddlebrown",
"darkslategray2",
"cadetblue2",
"darkseagreen",
"palegreen2",
"purple2",
"mediumpurple",
"darkviolet",
"darkslategray1",
"cadetblue1",
"palegreen",
"darkorchid",
"yellowgreen",
"palegreen1",
"purple1",
"mediumpurple2",
"purple",
"sienna",
"lightskyblue2",
"brown",
"mediumpurple1",
"lightblue",
"greenyellow",
"paleturquoise2",
"paleturquoise",
"maroon",
"lightsteelblue",
"powderblue",
"lightskyblue1",
"firebrick",
"darkorchid2",
"lightblue2",
"olivedrab2",
```

```
"darkseagreen2",
"darkgoldenrod",
"slategray2",
"mediumorchid",
"paleturquoise1",
"rosybrown",
"lightsteelblue2",
"darkolivegreen2",
"darkkhaki",
"darkorchid1",
"lightblue1",
"grey",
"olivedrab1",
"darkseagreen1",
"slategray1",
"mediumvioletred",
"lightsteelblue1",
"darkolivegreen1",
"red3",
"indianred",
"chocolate3",
"peru",
"rosybrown3",
"burlywood3",
"lemonchiffon3",
"violetred",
"mediumorchid2",
"lightcyan2",
"chocolate",
"tan",
"lightgrey",
"thistle",
"orchid",
"goldenrod",
"palevioletred",
"gainsboro",
"plum",
"burlywood",
"mediumorchid1",
"honeydew2",
"azure2",
"lightcyan",
"lavender",
"darksalmon",
"red2",
"magenta2",
```

```
"deeppink2",
"firebrick2",
"maroon2",
"violetred2",
"brown2",
"orangered2",
"tomato2",
"indianred2",
"coral2",
"hotpink2",
"darkorange2",
"chocolate2",
"sienna2",
"palevioletred2",
"orchid2",
"salmon2",
"violet",
"lightsalmon2",
"orange2",
"tan2",
"lightpink2",
"pink2",
"darkgoldenrod2",
"plum2",
"goldenrod2",
"rosybrown2",
"burlywood2",
"gold2",
"peachpuff2",
"navajowhite2",
"thistle2",
"bisque2",
"mistyrose2",
"wheat2",
"lightgoldenrod2",
"lightgoldenrod",
"antiquewhite2",
"lavenderblush2",
"seashell2",
"khaki2",
"palegoldenrod",
"cornsilk2",
"lemonchiffon2",
"snow2",
"yellow2",
"lightyellow2",
```

```
"ivory2",
"lightcoral",
"khaki",
"aliceblue",
"honeydew",
"azure",
"sandybrown",
"wheat",
"beige",
"whitesmoke",
"mintcream",
"ghostwhite",
"salmon",
"antiquewhite",
"linen",
"lightgoldenrodyellow",
"oldlace",
"red",
"magenta",
"deeppink",
"firebrick1",
"maroon1",
"violetred1",
"brown1",
"orangered",
"tomato",
"hotpink",
"indianred1",
"hotpink1",
"coral1",
"darkorange1",
"chocolate1",
"coral",
"sienna1",
"palevioletred1",
"orchid1",
"darkorange",
"salmon1",
"lightsalmon",
"orange",
"tan1",
"lightpink1",
"pink1",
"lightpink",
"darkgoldenrod1",
"plum1",
```

```
                        "pink",
                        "goldenrod1",
                        "rosybrown1",
                        "burlywood1",
                        "gold",
                        "peachpuff",
                        "navajowhite",
                        "thistle1",
                        "moccasin",
                        "bisque",
                        "mistyrose",
                        "wheat1",
                        "blanchedalmond",
                        "lightgoldenrod1",
                        "papayawhip",
                        "antiquewhite1",
                        "lavenderblush",
                        "seashell",
                        "khaki1",
                        "cornsilk",
                        "lemonchiffon",
                        "floralwhite",
                        "snow",
                        "yellow",
                        "lightyellow",
                        "ivory",
                        "white"
        };

/*
 *      end of file
 */
```

COLOR NAMES FOR RELEASE 3

Release 3 had only sixty-six standard colors, plus a number of shades of gray on some systems. The contents of the file that shows these colors, `colort.h`, are as follows:

colort.h:

```
/*
 *      colort.h
```

```
 *      Global color name definitions for the Color Table
 *      program.
 *
 *      colort.h contains the default (pre-X11R4) definitions
 *      of 66 colors.
 *
 *      colortr4.h contains the X11R4 version, highly edited.
 *
 */

/*
 *      Global color name definitions, based somewhat by color.
 *
 */

#define MAX_COLORS        66

char                      *colornames[ MAX_COLORS ] =
                          {       "White",                 /* -- 0  */
                                  "LightGrey",             /* -- 1  */
                                  "Grey",                  /* -- 2  */
                                  "DimGrey",               /* -- 3  */
                                  "DarkSlateGrey",         /* -- 4  */
                                  "Black",                 /* -- 5  */
                                  "Turquoise",             /* -- 6  */
                                  "MediumTurquoise",       /* -- 7  */
                                  "DarkTurquoise",         /* -- 8  */
                                  "LightBlue",             /* -- 9  */
                                  "Blue",                  /* -- 10 */
                                  "MediumBlue",            /* -- 11 */
                                  "LightSteelBlue",        /* -- 12 */
                                  "SteelBlue",             /* -- 13 */
                                  "CadetBlue",             /* -- 14 */
                                  "SkyBlue",               /* -- 15 */
                                  "Cyan",                  /* -- 16 */
                                  "Navy",                  /* -- 17 */
                                  "CornflowerBlue",        /* -- 18 */
                                  "MidnightBlue",          /* -- 19 */
                                  "SlateBlue",             /* -- 20 */
                                  "MediumSlateBlue",       /* -- 21 */
                                  "DarkSlateBlue",         /* -- 22 */
                                  "Aquamarine",            /* -- 23 */
                                  "MediumAquamarine",      /* -- 24 */
                                  "GreenYellow",           /* -- 25 */
                                  "SpringGreen",           /* -- 26 */
                                  "MediumSpringGreen",     /* -- 27 */
```

```
                        "Green",                  /* -- 28  */
                        "LimeGreen",              /* -- 29  */
                        "PaleGreen",              /* -- 30  */
                        "SeaGreen",               /* -- 31  */
                        "MediumSeaGreen",         /* -- 32  */
                        "ForestGreen",            /* -- 33  */
                        "MediumForestGreen",      /* -- 34  */
                        "DarkGreen",              /* -- 35  */
                        "DarkOliveGreen",         /* -- 36  */
                        "Yellow",                 /* -- 37  */
                        "YellowGreen",            /* -- 38  */
                        "Salmon",                 /* -- 39  */
                        "Thistle",                /* -- 40  */
                        "Coral",                  /* -- 41  */
                        "Orange",                 /* -- 42  */
                        "OrangeRed",              /* -- 43  */
                        "Red",                    /* -- 44  */
                        "Pink",                   /* -- 45  */
                        "Violetred",              /* -- 46  */
                        "MediumVioletRed",        /* -- 47  */
                        "Firebrick",              /* -- 48  */
                        "IndianRed",              /* -- 49  */
                        "Violet",                 /* -- 50  */
                        "Magenta",                /* -- 51  */
                        "Maroon",                 /* -- 52  */
                        "BlueViolet",             /* -- 53  */
                        "Plum",                   /* -- 54  */
                        "Orchid",                 /* -- 55  */
                        "MediumOrchid",           /* -- 56  */
                        "DarkOrchid",             /* -- 57  */
                        "Gold",                   /* -- 58  */
                        "Goldenrod",              /* -- 59  */
                        "MediumGoldenrod",        /* -- 60  */
                        "Wheat",                  /* -- 61  */
                        "Tan",                    /* -- 62  */
                        "Khaki",                  /* -- 63  */
                        "Sienna",                 /* -- 64  */
                        "Brown"                   /* -- 65  */
            };

/*
 *      end of file
 */
```

THE colort PROGRAM

The colort program puts up a basic top-level window that contains 256 squares. Each square can potentially contain a different color, based on the color names in either colortr4.h or colort.h. When the user presses a mouse button in one of the squares, the colort program prints the name of that color in the top of the window.

This program uses only one window. We could have used 256 subwindows, one for each color, but decided against that because 256 is an extremely large number of subwindows. After watching performance on the Sun 386i (always slow with X) and a 386 PC running Interactive's 386/ix, we figured one main window was fine.

The main reason to use subwindows is for detecting ButtonPress events, since each ButtonPress event comes with a window ID for the window in which the event took place—which solves the hit-detection problem in one fell swoop. However, since we're not using subwindows in the colort program, we added a few routines to determine which square (and therefore which color) a ButtonPress event occurred. That's the purpose of the LocateColor(), ColorX(), and ColorY() functions, which are rather simplistic.

The whole colort program is rather simple, as its main purpose is to show how some of the available colors look and how the color database names correspond to actual colors on the screen.

Colort first initializes 256 or sixty-six colors (256 if you compile under a Release 4 system). Then it creates a top-level window and calculates the size of each color square based on the size of the window.

Next, colort loops on events. When the user presses a "q" (or "Q")—generating a KeyPress event—the program quits. Any other KeyPress events are ignored. On ButtonPress events, LocateColor() is called to determine the square in which the mouse button was pressed. If a square is determined, the color name is extracted and displayed at the top of the window, along with a solid rectangular bar of the given color.

If a ConfigureNotify event comes in (remember, we are filtering out ConfigureNotify's except for window resizes), we recalculate the size of the individual color squares and redraw the window. We also redraw the window on

Expose events. Note that the NextEvent() function filters out all Expose events except for the last in a series, that is when the count field equals zero (see chapter 5 for more information).

Finally, colort releases the X resources it acquired and shuts down the connection to the X server.

This explanation is rather brief as the code is not very complex (especially for readers of a book that has a first name of Advanced).

The function InitColours() bears a closer look, though. InitColours() initializes the 256 or sixty-six colors based on the names in the global colornames array (filled in either colort.h or colortr4.h) and fills in the pixel field in the global array of structures called colours.

Note that we use a simplistic test for a monochrome system. A depth of one indicates a monochrome visual (again we are using the default visual). However, there may be many other visuals available on your X server. If the default visual is not to your liking you can check for a better visual. We didn't here for two reasons: one, simplicity, and, secondly because we wanted to stress that unimportant applications, like colort—which may already grab 256 color cells—shouldn't try to mess much with the color options available for more important applications like finite element analysis programs or, of course, games.

If you do use another visual, be sure to use that visual when you open your top-level window. (See the use of XGetVisualInfo() in chapter 10 on display information).

You could use XGetVisualInfo() to find the list of visuals (it could be a null list) that hold the required attributes:

```
Display         *display;
int             screen;
XVisualInfo     *visual_list;
XVisualInfo     visual_template;
int             number_visuals;
long            visual_mask;

visual_template.screen = screen;
visual_template.class  = PseudoColor;
visual_template.depth  = 8;

visual_mask  = VisualScreenMask | VisualClassMask |
```

```
                                VisualDepthMask;
        visual_list = XGetVisualInfo( display,
                                visual_mask,
                                &visual_template,
                                &number_visuals );

        if ( ( visual_list != NULL ) && ( number_visuals > 0 ) )
                {
                /* -- success */

                ...

                }
```

Here, we ask for a visual with a class of PseudoColor and 8-bit planes of depth. You may get lucky and have the choice of a whole list of visuals, but chances are you can expect one at most. If you do find a visual, you can use the visual field that points to the proper Visual structure. (That's the ticket: the visual field is a pointer to a Visual—confused yet?)

You could also use XMatchVisualInfo():

```
        Display         *display;
        int             screen;
        int             depth = 8;
        int             class = PseudoColor;
        int             status;
        XVisualInfo     visinfo;

        status = XMatchVisualInfo( display, screen,
                        depth, class, &visinfo );

        if ( status != 0 )
                {
                /*
                 * We found one.
                 * visinfo.visual
                 * now points to the
                 * Visual we want
                 */

                ...

                }
```

XMatchVisualInfo() will find one of the possibly many visuals that could match the required depth and class.

This is what InitColours() looks like. If any color allocation fails, we use white as a default (white is set to the screen's WhitePixel):

```
InitColours( display, screen, depth, black, white )

Display         *display;
int             depth, screen;
unsigned long   black, white;

{       /* -- function InitColours */
        int             i;
        Colormap        colormap;

        colormap = DefaultColormap( display, screen );

        for( i = 0; i < MAX_COLORS; i++ )
                {
                /*
                 *      The depth is not a good
                 *      determinant for whether a
                 *      display has color or not.
                 *      You should travel down the
                 *      list of available Visuals.
                 */
                if ( depth > 1 )
                        {
                        colours[ i ].pixel =
                                GetColor( display,
                                        colornames[ i ],
                                        colormap,
                                        white );

                        }
                else
                        {
                        /*
                         *      Monochrome system, maybe
                         */
                        if ( strcmp( "black", colornames[ i ] ) = = 0 )
                                {
                                colours[ i ].pixel =  black;
                                }
```

```
                        else
                                {
                                colours[ i ].pixel =  white;
                                }
                        }

                }

}       /* -- function InitColours */
```

Source Code for colort.c

The `colort.c` file contains the program to display a color table window:

colort.c:

```
/*
 *      colort.c
 *      X11 Color Table Program.
 *      You may use this program with the X11R4 or
 *      X11R3 (X11R2) color database.
 */

#include  "xbook.h"

/*
 *      Color Table icon
 */
#include  "table.xb"

/*
 *      Include color name definitions, different if X11R4
 */
#ifdef X11R4

#include  "colortr4.h"

#else

#include  "colort.h"

#endif
```

```
#define  NUMBER_BOXES   16      /* -- We use a square of boxes */

/*
 *      Globals for the color table
 */
typedef struct
        {
        unsigned long   pixel;
        } ColourStruct;

ColourStruct    colours[ MAX_COLORS + 1 ];

int             box_width;              /* -- width of each box */
int             box_height;             /* -- height of each box */
int             current_color = 0;      /* -- which color was last chosen */
unsigned long   black;

main( argc, argv )

int     argc;
char    *argv[];

{       /* -- main */
        Display         *display;
        int             screen, depth;
        Window          window;
        XFontStruct     *font;
        GC              gc;
        int             x, y, width, height;
        Pixmap          icon;


        /*
         *      Set up connection with X server
         */
        display    = SetUpDisplay( argc, argv, &screen );

        black      = BlackPixel( display, screen );

        /*
         * This program uses the default visual.
         * You could search down the visual tree
         * and pick the one you want.
         */
```

```
depth      = DefaultDepth( display, screen );

/*
 * Set up colors
 */
InitColours( display, screen, depth,
        black, WhitePixel( display, screen ) );

/*
 * Create main window
 */
x      = 10;
y      = 10;
width  = NUMBER_BOXES * 33;
height = NUMBER_BOXES * 37;

CheckGeometry( argc, argv,
                DisplayWidth ( display, screen ),
                DisplayHeight( display, screen ),
                &x, &y, &width, &height );


window    = TopWindow( display,
                x, y, width, height,
                table_bits, table_width, table_height,
                &icon, &gc );

/*
 * Load font
 */
font = LoadFont( display, gc, argc, argv, "variable" );

XFlush( display );

/*
 * Map main window
 */
XSetWindowBackground( display, window, black );

SetNormalHints( display, window,
        x, y, width, height );

SetWMHints( display, window, icon );
```

```
        NameWindow( display, window,
                "colort", "colort", "Colort" );

        MapWindow( display, window );

        /*
         * Use main window's size to
         * box sizes
         */
        CalculateBoxSizes( width, height );

        /*
         * Handle events
         */
        while( EventLoop( display, window, gc,
                &width, &height ) = = True );

        /*
         * Shut down X connection
         */
        XFreePixmap( display, icon );
        XFreeFont(   display, font );

        CloseDisplay( display, window, gc );

        exit( 0 );

}       /* -- main */

EventLoop( display, window, gc, width, height )

Display *display;
Window  window;         /* -- application's window */
GC      gc;
int     *width, *height;

{       /* -- function EventLoop */
        XEvent          event;
        int             status, which_color;
        KeySym          keysym;

        /*
         *      Block on input, awaiting an event from X
         */
        NextEvent( display,
```

```
                False,          /* -- miminize expose events */
                *width,
                *height,
                &event,
                &keysym );

        /*
         *      Decode the event and call a
         *      specific routine to  handle it.
         */
        status = True;
        switch( event.type )
                {
                case Expose:
                        Refresh( display,
                                window,
                                gc,
                                *width,
                                *height );

                        break;
                case KeyPress:
                        /*
                         * Quit program when user
                         * types a "q".
                         */
                        if ( ( keysym = = XK_Q ) || ( keysym = = XK_q ) )
                                {
                                status = False;
                                }
                        break;
                case ButtonPress:
                        /*
                         * Locate color where hit occurred.
                         */
                        which_color = LocateColor( &event );

                        /*
                         * Select color
                         */
                        if ( which_color >= 0 )
                                {
                                current_color = which_color;

                                ShowColor( display,
                                        window, gc,
```

```
                                        *width,
                                        which_color );
                        }

                break;
        case ConfigureNotify:
                /*
                 * Recalculate sizes of the boxes
                 */
                *width  = event.xconfigure.width;
                *height = event.xconfigure.height;

                CalculateBoxSizes( *width, *height );
                XClearWindow( display, window );

                Refresh( display,
                        window,
                        gc,
                        *width,
                        *height );
                break;
        }

        return( status );

}       /* -- function EventLoop */

Refresh( display, window, gc, width, height )

Display *display;
Window  window;
GC      gc;
int     width, height;

{       /* -- function Refresh */
        int             i, j;
        int             x, y;
        int             count;
        unsigned long   pixel;

        /*
         * Draw black lines around areas
         */
        ShowColor( display, window, gc, width, current_color );

        XSetForeground( display, gc, black );
```

```
x = 0;
y = 0;

for( i = 0; i < NUMBER_BOXES; i++ )
        {
        x += box_width;
        y += box_height;

        XDrawLine( display, window, gc,
                x, box_height, x, height );

        XDrawLine( display, window, gc,
                0, y, width, y );
        }


/*
 * Draw colored squares
 */
x       = 0;
y       = box_height + 1;
count   = 0;

for( i = 0; i < NUMBER_BOXES; i++ )
        {
        x = 0;
        for( j = 0; j < NUMBER_BOXES; j++ )
                {
                if ( count < MAX_COLORS )
                        {
                        pixel = colours[ count ].pixel;

                        XSetForeground( display, gc, pixel );

                        XFillRectangle( display, window, gc,
                                x, y,
                                box_width - 1, box_height - 1 );

                        x += box_width + 1;
                        }

                count++;
                }

        y += box_height + 1;
        }
```

```
        XFlush( display );

}       /* -- function Refresh */

InitColours( display, screen, depth, black, white )

Display         *display;
int             depth, screen;
unsigned long   black, white;

/*
 *      InitColours() sets up the array colours.
 *
 */

{       /* -- function InitColours */
        int             i;
        Colormap        colormap;

        /*
         *      We use the default colormap, to be
         *      as nice as possible to the other
         *      applications on the display.
         *      Color-hoarding is not nice unless
         *      you really need the colors (e.g.,
         *      in an image-processing program, etc.)
         *
         */
        colormap = DefaultColormap( display, screen );

        /*
         *      Get Pixel/RGB for colour
         */
        for( i = 0; i < MAX_COLORS; i++ )
                {
                /*
                 *      The depth is not a good
                 *      determinant for whether a
                 *      display has color or not.
                 *      You should travel down the
                 *      list of available Visuals.
                 */
                if ( depth > 1 )
                        {
                        colours[ i ].pixel =
                                GetColor( display,
```

```
                                        colornames[ i ],
                                        colormap,
                                        white );

                        }
                else
                        {
                        /*
                         *      Monochrome system, maybe
                         */
                        if ( strcmp( "black", colornames[ i ] ) = = 0 )
                                {
                                colours[ i ].pixel =  black;
                                }
                        else
                                {
                                colours[ i ].pixel =  white;
                                }
                        }

                }
}       /* -- function InitColours */

NameColor( display, window, gc, string )

Display *display;
Window  window;
GC      gc;
char    string[];

/*
 *      NameColor() is called to display the name
 *      of a color in the main window of the
 *      application.
 *
 */

{       /* -- function NameColor */

        XDrawImageString( display, window, gc,
                10, 15,
                string, strlen( string ) );

}       /* -- function NameColor */
```

```
ShowColor( display, window, gc, width, which_color )

Display *display;
Window  window;
GC      gc;
int     width, which_color;

/*
 *      ShowColor() shows the currently-selected
 *      color by making the main window have that
 *      color as a background.
 *
 *      ShowColor() then calls NameColour() to display
 *      the name of the color, too.
 */

{       /* -- function ShowColor */

        /*
         *      Show color
         */
        XSetForeground( display, gc,
                colours[ which_color ].pixel );

        XFillRectangle( display, window, gc,
                0, 0, width, box_height );

        /*
         *      Show Name
         */
        XSetForeground( display, gc, black );

        NameColor( display, window, gc, colornames[ which_color ] );
        /*
         *      Save the choice for later in GLOBAL
         */
        current_color = which_color;

        XFlush( display );

}       /* -- function ShowColor */

CalculateBoxSizes( width, height )

/*
 *      CalculateBoxSizes() calculates
 *      the size of each box, (also Globals)
```

```
 *      box_width and box_height.  It is called
 *      whenever the main application window
 *      changes size.
 */

{       /* -- function CalculateBoxSizes */

        box_width  = width  / ( NUMBER_BOXES + 2 );
        box_height = height / ( NUMBER_BOXES + 2 );

}       /* -- function CalculateBoxSizes */

LocateColor( event )

XButtonEvent    *event;

/*
 *      Locates which color the ButtonPress occurred in.
 *      Returns color number or -1 for none.
 */

{       /* -- function LocateColor */
        register int    i;
        int             x, y;

        for( i = 0; i < MAX_COLORS; i++ )
                {
                x = ColorX( i );
                y = ColorY( i );
                if ( ( event->x >= x ) &&
                        ( event->x <= ( x + box_width ) ) )
                        {
                        if ( ( event->y >= y ) &&
                                ( event->y <= ( y + box_height ) ) )
                                {
                                return( i );
                                }
                        }
                }

        return( -1 );

}       /* -- function LocateColor */

ColorX( which_color )

int     which_color;
```

```
{       /* -- function ColorX */
        int     x;
        int     level;

        level = which_color / NUMBER_BOXES;

        /*
         * Remainder
         */
        which_color = which_color - ( level * NUMBER_BOXES );

        x =  which_color * ( box_width  + 1 );

        return( x );

}       /* -- function ColorX */

ColorY( which_color )

int     which_color;

{       /* -- function ColorY */
        int     y;

        y = ( box_height + 1 ) +
                ( which_color / NUMBER_BOXES ) * ( box_height + 1 );

        return( y );

}       /* -- function ColorY */

/*
 *      end of file
 */
```

An Icon for colort

The color table icon looks vaguely like a table, as shown in figure 14-1.

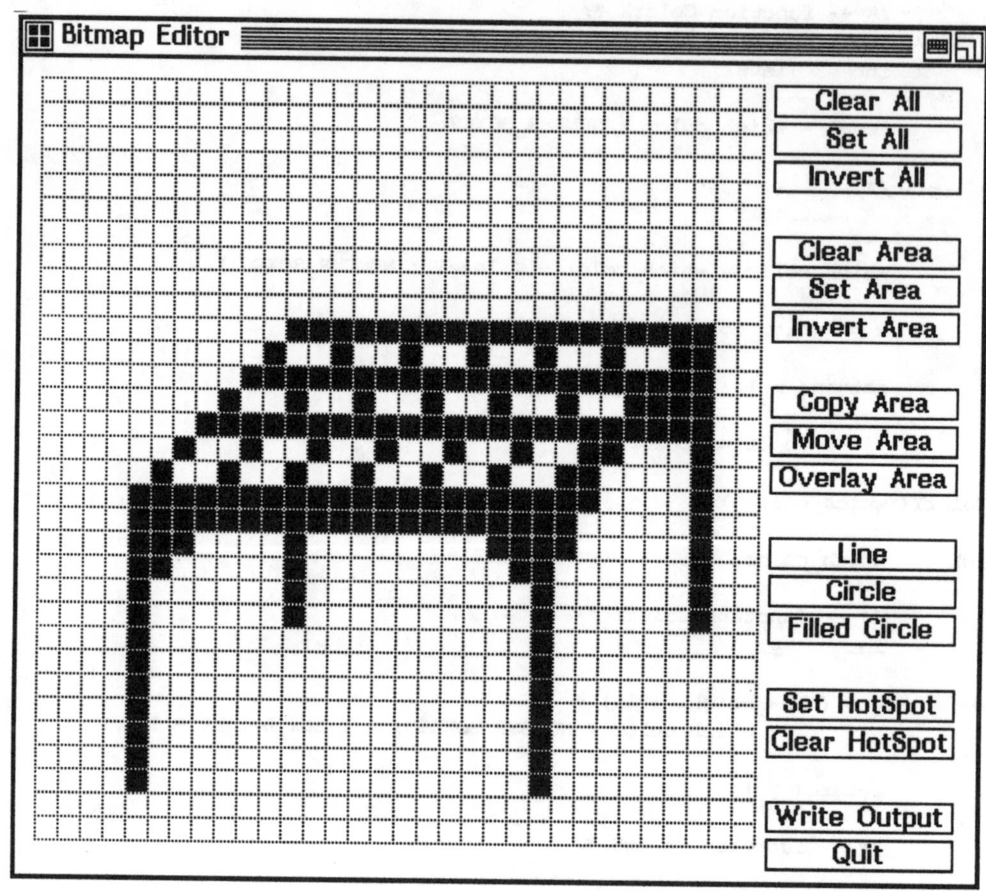

Figure 14-1. The Color Table Icon

The bitmap file `table.xb` is as follows:

```
#define table_width 32
#define table_height 32
static char table_bits[] = {
   0x00, 0x00, 0x00, 0x00, 0x00, 0x00, 0x00, 0x00, 0x00, 0x00, 0x00, 0x00,
   0x00, 0x00, 0x00, 0x00, 0x00, 0x00, 0x00, 0x00, 0x00, 0x00, 0x00, 0x00,
   0x00, 0x00, 0x00, 0x00, 0x00, 0x00, 0x00, 0x00, 0x00, 0x00, 0x00, 0x00,
   0x00, 0x00, 0x00, 0x00, 0x00, 0xf8, 0xff, 0x3f, 0x00, 0x24, 0x49, 0x32,
   0x00, 0xfe, 0xff, 0x3f, 0x00, 0x49, 0x92, 0x3c, 0x80, 0xff, 0xff, 0x3f,
   0x40, 0x92, 0x24, 0x23, 0x20, 0x49, 0x92, 0x21, 0xf0, 0xff, 0xff, 0x21,
   0xf0, 0xff, 0xff, 0x20, 0x70, 0x08, 0xf0, 0x20, 0x30, 0x08, 0x60, 0x20,
```

```
0x10, 0x08, 0x40, 0x20, 0x10, 0x08, 0x40, 0x20, 0x10, 0x00, 0x40, 0x00,
0x10, 0x00, 0x40, 0x00, 0x10, 0x00, 0x40, 0x00, 0x10, 0x00, 0x40, 0x00,
0x10, 0x00, 0x40, 0x00, 0x10, 0x00, 0x40, 0x00, 0x10, 0x00, 0x40, 0x00,
0x00, 0x00, 0x00, 0x00, 0x00, 0x00, 0x00, 0x00};
```

Compiling colort

The `colort` color table program uses the following code modules:

`color.c`	
`colort.c`	
`cursor.c`	*(from chapter 7)*
`display.c`	*(from chapter 2)*
`event.c`	*(from chapter 5)*
`font.c`	*(from chapter 8)*
`gc.c`	*(from chapter 4)*
`topwind.c`	*(from chapter 9)*
`window.c`	*(from chapter 3)*
`table.xb`	*(bitmap file above)*

On Unix-based systems, you can use the `Makefile` in appendix C, with:

```
make colort
```

Or, you can compile with:

```
cc -o colort color.c colort.c cursor.c display.c event.c font.c gc.c \
       topwind.c window.c -lX11
```

Running colort

`Colort` needs no command-line parameters. You may specify a window geometry, a display name, and a font name, all in the usual manner:

```
-display display_name
-geometry geometry_spec
        (e.g., 120x300+40+13)
-font font_name
```

FUNCTIONS DEVELOPED IN THIS CHAPTER

```
GetColor
```

XLIB FUNCTIONS AND MACROS USED IN THIS CHAPTER

```
XAllocColor
XLookupColor
XMatchVisualInfo
```

SUMMARY

- A colormap is a table that contains color cells. Each color cell represents a color that is in use on the screen. You might have anywhere from sixteen entries (VGA) to 16 million entries (rare and very expensive).

- Individual colors in X are called pixel values. These pixel values are unsigned longs and index to a colormap cell. When you want to draw in a given color, you need the pixel (unsigned long index into the colormap in use) value. You can then pass this value to `XSetForeground()`, which sets a graphics context to draw in the given color.

- The X Window System comes with a database of English color names, such as blue and lime green. Each color name has associated red, green, and blue values (usually eight bits for each) that specify the color in numeric terms in an RGB color model. You can use any of these color names. X will then use a color as close as possible to the requested RGB values associated with that color name. Using these color names makes for more portable code and allows X users to tweak the color database locally.

- You must convert the color name to an X pixel value in a colormap. First, call `XLookupColor()` to find the closest match to your color available on your hardware. `XLookupColor()` returns the RGB definition `(rgbcolor)` of the given color name from the color database. Then, call `XAllocColor()` to allocate a cell in the colormap.

- Many X stations just have one hardware colormap, so it is a good idea to share colormaps and colormap entries. For most workstations or X terminals, color is very expensive and very few colors will be available. Use the colors your application absolutely needs, and use the default colormap if possible. `DefaultColormap()` returns the default colormap for a given screen.

Section III

Communicating Between X Applications

Section III travels into one of the most difficult areas of X: making X applications communicate with each other. Application interoperability is a big, hot issue, and X provides many features to help make your programs talk to one another.

In addition, a multitasking windowed environment raises user expectations for what applications should be able to do. For example, users have come to expect to be able to copy and paste data between windowed applications and have the debugger talk to the compiler and editor. This means applications are expected more and more to operate intelligently together in the X environment.

Of course, the task of making applications communicate is never as easy as it sounds. The X Window System is not a general purpose inter-process communication system, but X does have a number of features that help with copy and paste operations (and general data exchange between X applications).

Section III covers X standards that applications should meet (described in a document titled Inter-Client Communications Conventions Manual) and three methods for communication: appending to properties, sending events, and using selections. Selections are by far the most important, most difficult, and the most feared.

Chapter 15

The ICCCM

As we're reminded every few minutes, X provides mechanism but not policy. X's designers work very hard to avoid interface issues, merely providing the underlying facilities to create a user interface. The problem is, though, that users now expect programs to work together, to provide "interoperability" (a term that is almost as ridiculous as GUI).

From this desire for programs to work together, a set of conventions was created to specify how X applications should act together.

It doesn't matter if you run your applications under Motif or Open Look or just plain X; all applications should follow the conventions described in the ICCCM—the Inter-Client Communications Conventions Manual. Your applications can leverage a lot of power from following these conventions, but be warned—there's much work to do.

The ICCCM covers a lot of ground and creates more confusion than any other topic in the X Window System. Included in the ICCCM are mechanisms for applications to communicate with other applications and cooperate in dealing with shared resources, window managers, and session managers. The application-to-application communication will be covered in the following chapters. For now, we'll concentrate on what you need to do for your applications to be considered "good citizens" in the X world, and we'll reference sections of the ICCCM where you can look for more information.

X SESSION MANAGERS

Window managers aren't hard to understand (not impossible, at least), but session managers are an evolving concept. Basically, a session manager manages a *session*—a group of X applications doing some particular form of work.

Session managers are responsible for starting up the group of applications, saving the state of the applications (so that they can be restarted from where they left off), and closing down the programs.

As it sounds, exactly what session managers do is fairly ambiguous and many of the tough decisions (like how to save the state of an application) are left for applications to deal with (which means that most applications won't deal with it at all). The whole concept of session managers is still evolving, so it will take some time before everyone reaches a consensus on what session managers should look like.

For now, you have to do two things to make the session manager happy: first set a `WM_COMMAND` and then a `WM_CLIENT_MACHINE` property on your application's top-level window. Even if you are not running a session manager, you should still set these properties. (As you'll see, most of the work done for window and session managers is to place certain properties on your application's top-level windows.)

WM_COMMAND

The `WM_COMMAND` property should contain the command necessary to start the application, at least on Unix-based systems. That is, the command-line parameters, usually called `argv` and `argc` (`argv` contains the parameters—a list of strings—and argc the number of parameters). Each application should place a WM_COMMAND property on one (and only one) top-level window. You may place a zero-length WM_COMMAND property on other top-level windows, but only one with a length greater than zero.

You can use XSetCommand() to create the WM_COMMAND property:

```
Display *display;
Window window;
char *argv[];
int argc;

XSetCommand( display, window, argv, argc );
```

This is done in the function SetICCCM(), in icccm.c, shown later in this chapter.

At various times, your application may be asked to update the WM_COMMAND property (see the section on Window Manager Protocols). When asked, your application should update WM_COMMAND so it reflects a command that could restart the application in its current state. When you do this, you always want to update WM_COMMAND—that is, you always want to write something out to the WM_COMMAND property. This may mean appending zero bytes to the WM_COMMAND property if the current state hasn't changed. Unfortunately, the definition of "current state" is still rather vague. (See section 5.1.1.1 in the ICCCM for more information.)

WM_CLIENT_MACHINE

The WM_CLIENT_MACHINE property should be the name of the machine (CPU) on which your application is running—as seen from the machine on which the X server is running. For example, if the application is running on "attila," but sets up a connection to the X server at flame:0.0 (on machine flame), then WM_CLIENT_MACHINE should be set to the string "attila", the name of the machine on which your application is running. The problem here is how to get your hostname in terms of the other machine (the machine the X server is running on).

GETTING THE HOSTNAME

If you have X11 Release 4, you don't have to worry about getting the hostname—the routine `XSetWMProperties()` will do it for you. Everyone else will need a way to get the hostname.

On a Unix machine, you can call `gethostname()`, as we did here:

```
GetHostName( name )

    char     *name;

{   /* -- function GetHostName */

    if ( gethostname( name, 64 ) = = (-1) )
        {
        (void) strcpy( name, "Unknown" '
        }

}   /* -- function GetHostName */
```

You also need the hostname to respond to selection requests (see chapter 19).

SETTING WM_Client_Machine

The function `SetWMClientMachine()` sets the `WM_CLIENT_MACHINE` property on a given window:

```
SetWMClientMachine( display, window )

Display *display;
Window window;

{   /* -- function SetWMClientMachine */
    char     hostname[ BUFSIZE + 1 ];
    Atom     client_machine;

    GetHostName( hostname );

    client_machine = XInternAtom( display,
"WM_CLIENT_MACHINE", False );
```

```
    if ( client_machine != (Atom) None )
        {
        AppendProperty( display, window,
            client_machine,
            XA_STRING,
            8,
            hostname,
            strlen( hostname ) );

        }

}   /* -- function SetWMClientMachine */
```

Note that we append a string (XA_STRING) to the property and ask the X server to Intern the string "WM_CLIENT_MACHINE" and return an atom. The function above should work for all X11 releases. The function AppendProperty() hides some of the gory details of appending data bytes to a property. (This will be explained in chapter 17. For now, don't worry about it.)

Those with Release 4 who want to use a more international machine name can call XSetWMClientMachine():

```
Display        *display;
Window          window;
XTextProperty  *text_property;

XSetWMClientMachine( display, window, text_property );
```

(See section 5.1.1.2 of the ICCCM for more information.)

X WINDOW MANAGERS

By now, you should be very familiar with X's window managers. Chapter 3 covered what you need to do to keep window managers happy (and meet the requirements of the ICCCM). However, there are a few more things you can do so the window manager will make your application happy. Most of these are special protocols for communicating certain requests to the window manager.

WINDOW MANAGER PROTOCOLS

Each window manager is different and many support special private protocols. For example, the Motif and Open Look window managers (mwm and olwm, respectively) each support certain conventions that follow their respective interface style guides.

Your applications, though, shouldn't need to know which window manager, if any, is running. Also, your applications should be able to interact with any window manager to at least some degree. The user is allowed to choose any window manager, which is one of the nice features of X.

The ICCCM protocols all work in basically the same way. First, you tell the window manager the protocols you support. Then, when the window manager wants to notify you about the use of the protocols (i.e., when you should be doing something special) the window manager will send your application a ClientMessage event. When you get such an event, do your stuff.

The ICCCM defines three special protocols for window managers to send events to clients: WM_TAKE_FOCUS, WM_SAVE_YOURSELF, and WM_DELETE_WINDOW.

The WM_TAKE_FOCUS Protocol

WM_TAKE_FOCUS is confusing. You now need to set WM_TAKE_FOCUS if your application wants to control the keyboard focus. In X, the keyboard focus is normally set to whatever window the mouse pointer is in (the lowest-level window that meets the criteria).

Some window managers use a click-to-type style interface where you click the mouse in a top-level window and then the input focus is set to that window. You shouldn't really mess with the input focus unless you are writing a window manager, since you will be messing up the user interface. However, you may have to. For example, if your application calls XSetInputFocus(), you should support the WM_TAKE_FOCUS protocol. When you call XSetInputFocus(), use the timestamp received with the WM_TAKE_FOCUS ClientMessage (more on that later). Also use Revert to Parent for the revert_to window. For example:

```
Display   *display;
Window     new_focus_window;
```

```
    int          revert_to_window;
    Time         timestamp;

revert_to_window = RevertToParent;

XSetInputFocus( display,
                new_focus_window,
                revert_to_window,
                timestamp );
```

Note that timestamp came from the ClientMessage event.

Now, if you follow the basic input model, you will set the input field of an XWMHints structure to True (see chapter 3). That means your application wants keyboard input. Again, only use WM_TAKE_FOCUS if you want to mess with the normal keyboard focus method.

If the input field of the XWMHints structure is True and you set the WM_TAKE_FOCUS protocol, then the input model is locally active. This means you should call XSetInputFocus() only if the pointer is already in one of your application's windows.

If you set the XWMHints input field to False and set WM_TAKE_FOCUS, then the input model is globally active. This means you can call XSetInputFocus() at any time, even if the mouse pointer is in another window. Pretty confusing, right? We advise you to leave well enough alone.

WM_TAKE_FOCUS is described in section 4.1.7 of the ICCCM.

The WM_SAVE_YOURSELF Protocol

WM_SAVE_YOURSELF is closely related to X session managers. If your application supports WM_SAVE_YOURSELF, you will get a ClientMessage when the window manager (or session manager) wants your application to save its "state"—whatever "state" is.

When this message arrives, your application should save its internal state so that it can be restarted. (This should imply that you may very well get this event just before the session manager shuts your application down.) The proper response is to save the application's state and then update the WM_COMMAND property on the application's top-level window. The WM_COMMAND should reflect the command needed to restart the application in its current state.

If the state hasn't changed, then append zero bytes to the WM_COMMAND property. Note that your application is supposed to write to this property (even with zero bytes of additional data) which signals your application has saved its state.

WM_SAVE_YOURSELF is described in section 5.2.1 of the ICCCM.

The WM_DELETE_WINDOW Protocol

Some window managers may have a menu choice to delete a window. This can be nasty, since some window managers may just up and delete your application's top-level window out from under your program, generating lots of X protocol errors and terminating your program. This is no fun.

To make this approach a bit nicer, the ICCCM has the WM_DELETE_WINDOW protocol. If your application supports this protocol, the window manager shouldn't delete your window. Instead, the window manager should ask nicely for your application to delete its own window.

When this message arrives (see the next section for more information on this), your application should save any work and perhaps prompt the user to save a file and close down the window. If your application has only one top-level window, this probably means shutting down the whole program. You may also ask the user to confirm the delete window choice. If the user cancels the delete window operation don't delete the window.

WM_DELETE_WINDOW gives your application a little foreknowledge of impending doom. We use that knowledge to clean up and shut down the programs in the example applications throughout the rest of this book.

WM_DELETE_WINDOW is described in section 5.2.2 of the ICCCM.

SETTING WM_PROTOCOLS

All of the protocols shown thus far in this chapter are set the same way: if your application supports a protocol, you need to create a special property, WM_ PROTOCOLS, on your top-level window. WM_PROTOCOLS is a property with a type of XA_ATOM—that is, a list of atoms. Each atom in the list is a protocol your application supports. For example, if your application supports WM_DELETE_WINDOW, you would place the atom for WM_DELETE_WINDOW in the WM_PROTOCOLS property. If your application supports all three of the protocols, you should place all thre e atoms in the WM_PROTOCOLS property.

In Release 4, you can call XSetWMProtocols() to create the WM_PROTOCOLS property and take care of all the details.

```
Display         *display;
Window           window;
Atom             protocols[ 4 ];         /* -- only need three */
int              number_protocols;
int              status;

status = XSetWMProtocols( display,
                 window,
                 protocols,
                 number_protocols );

if ( status != 0 )
{
/* -- OK */

...

}
```

You pass XSetWMProtocols() an array of atoms. These are the protocols your application supports, which can include any—or all—of the WM_TAKE_FOCUS, WM_SAVE_YOURSELF and WM_DELETE_WINDOW properties.

The SetProtocols() function sets up the WM_PROTOCOLS for the given window on the given display. It is used in all the example applications to follow. Note that we only support the WM_DELETE_WINDOW protocol.

Define X11R4 if your system supports Release 4. `SetProtocols()` has special code if your X system is not updated to Release 4 yet.

First, we intern atoms for "`WM_PROTOCOLS`" and "`WM_DELETE_WINDOW.`" Then, if the interning works, we call `XSetWMProtocols()` to set just one protocol, `WM_DELETE_WINDOW`. If `SetProtocols()` is compiled on a pre-Release 4 system, we handle the append to the `WM_PROTOCOLS` property manually (see chapter 17 for more information on appending data to a property).

The contents of `SetProtocols()` are as follows:

```
SetProtocols( display, window )

Display *display;
Window  window;

/*
*       SetProtocols() tells a window manager
*       that our application supports the
*       ICCCM WM_DELETE_WINDOW protocol.
*/

{       /* -- function SetProtocols */
        Atom    protocol_atom;
        Atom    delete_atom;
        char    data[ 25 ];

    delete_atom = XInternAtom( display, "WM_DELETE_WINDOW", False );
protocol_atom = XInternAtom( display, "WM_PROTOCOLS", False );

    if ( ( delete_atom = = (Atom) None ) ||
        ( protocol_atom = = (Atom) None ) )
        {
        return;
        }

#ifdef X11R4
    XSetWMProtocols( display, window, &delete_atom, 1 );

#else
    /*
     * Pre-R4 xlib
     */
    Long2Bytes( (long) delete_atom, data );
```

```
    AppendProperty( display, window,
        protocol_atom,
        XA_ATOM,
        32,
        data, 1 );

#endif

}   /* -- function SetProtocols */
```

RECEIVING MESSAGES FOR WINDOW MANAGER PROTOCOLS

A window-manager protocol only kicks in when you receive a special ClientMessage event. Your code may call XSetWMProtocols() but never receive any ClientMessage events. Don't worry. If your program needs the message, the message will arrive.

ClientMessage events carry up to twenty bytes of data. If the message_type is the WM_PROTOCOLS atom, then you have received one of these protocol messages. In this case, the first data element (four bytes) will contain an atom. If that atom is WM_DELETE_WINDOW, then your application has just been asked to delete its window. The same principle applies for WM_TAKE_FOCUS and WM_SAVE_YOURSELF.

A ClientMessage event structure looks like the following:

```
    typedef struct
        {
        int             type;  /* -- ClientMessage, obviously */
        unsigned long   serial;
        Bool            send_event; /* -- most likely True */
        Display         *display;
        Window          window; /* -- window event occurred on */
        Atom            message_type;
        int             format; /* -- 32 in our case */
        union       {
                    char b[ 20 ];
                    short s[ 10 ];
                    long l[ 5  ];
                    } data;
        } XClientMessageEvent;
```

The function `IsDeleteWindow()` checks if an incoming `ClientMessage` event is really a `WM_PROTOCOLS` request for deleting the window (`WM_DELETE_WINDOW`). The contents of `IsDeleteWindow()` are as follows:

```
IsDeleteWindow( display, event )

Display                *display;
XClientMessageEvent    *event;

{   /* -- function IsDeleteWindow */
    Atom    protocols_atom;
    Atom    delete_atom;

    protocols_atom = XInternAtom( display, "WM_PROTOCOLS", False );
delete_atom = XInternAtom( display,
"WM_DELETE_WINDOW", False );

    if ( ( event->message_type = = protocols_atom ) &&
           ( event->data.l[ 0 ] = = delete_atom ) &&
           ( event->format = = 32 ) )
           {
           return( True );
           }
    else
           {
           return( False );
           }

}   /* -- function IsDeleteWindow */
```

PROPERTIES EVERY APPLICATION SHOULD SET FOR THEIR TOP-LEVEL WINDOWS

The following chart summarizes the various properties your application should set on its top-level windows to remain in ICCCM-compliance.

PROPERTY NAME	PURPOSE	XlibFUNCTIONS	EXAMPLE FUNCTIONS	ICCCM SECTION
WM_ICON_NAME	window's name	XSetWMName XStoreName	NameWindow (chapter 3)	4.1.2.1
WM_NAME	icon name	XSetWMIconName XSetIconName	NameWindow (chapter 3)	4.1.2.2

WM_NORMAL_HINTS	size hints in normal state	XSetWMNormalHints XSetNormalHints	SetNormalHints	4.1.2.3
WM_HINTS	input and icon hints, etc.	XSetWMHints	SetWMHints (chapter 3)	4.1.2.4
WM_CLASS	type of application	XSetClassHint	NameWindow (chapter 3)	4.1.2.5
WM_PROTOCOLS	any special window manage protocols supported	XSetWMProtocols	SetProtocols (chapter 15)	4.1.2.7
WM_COLORMAP_WINDOWS	Windows that need special colormaps	XSetWMColormapWindows		4.1.2.8
WM_COMMAND	command-line used to launch program to current state	XSetCommand	SetICCCM (chapter 15)	5.1.1.1
WM_CLIENT_MACHINE	machine program is running on	XSetWMClientMachine	SetWMClientMachine (chapter 15)	5.1.1.2

PROPERTIES SET BY WINDOW MANAGER

Like your applications, the window manager is required to place a number of properties on your top-level windows. Your applications shouldn't change these properties, but you may want to look at them.

WM_STATE

The window should place a `WM_STATE` property on every top-level window. The `WM_STATE` property should contain at least the state of the window (a 32-bit value) and the icon's window ID. The state should be one of:

```
WithdrawnState    0
NormalState       1
IconicState       2
```

The best thing about `WM_STATE`, though, is that you can use its presence to search for the top-level windows of your application.

For more information see ICCCM sections 4.1.3.1, 5.1.1.3.

WM_ICON_SIZE

If a window manager only supports certain sizes for icons, it should place a `WM_ICON_SIZE` property on the Root window.

For more information, see ICCCM section 4.1.3.2.

OTHER ICCCM-RELATED CONVENTIONS

Most of the ICCCM is devoted to the concept of selections, which are used for application-to-application communication (described in chapter 19) . But the ICCCM also changed the way in which your applications can go about changing the state they are in.

Normally, it is up to the user working through the window manager to change the state of windows (from normal to iconic, for example). But, your applications can also try to change the state. Remember, though, all such changes are really requests and the window manager can deny your requests.

ICONIFYING A WINDOW

If your application wants to turn its window into an icon, it should send a special `ClientMessage` event to the Root window:

```
Display                     *display;
Window                      window;       /* -- your top-level window */
XClientMessageEvent         event;
Atom                        change_state;

change_state        = XInternAtom( display,
                            "WM_CHANGE_STATE",
                            False );

if ( change_state != (Atom) None )
    {
    event.type              = ClientMessage;
    event.window            = window;
```

```
event.message_type    = change_state;
event.format          = 32;
event.data.l          = IconicState;

...

/*
 * Use XSendEvent() to
 * send the event to
 * the root window
 */

...

}
```

RELEASE 4 GRAPHIC

In Release 4, you can also call `XIconifyWindow()`. `XIconifyWindow()` does the same thing as the code above.

```
Display     *display;
int         screen;
Window      window;
int         status;

status = XIconifyWindow( display, window, screen );

if ( status != 0 )
          {
          /*
           * At least the message was sent.
           * We don't know if a window manager
           * will accept it, though.
           */

           ...

           }
```

For more information see ICCCM section 4.1.4.

OBTAINING THE INFAMOUS ICCCM

We've used the ICCCM version 1.0 by David S. H. Rosenthal (which came with X11 Release 4 from the MIT X Consortium). The best way to get the ICCCM is to get the whole Release 4 release. If you are writing X applications, you really should read the ICCCM, no matter how confusing it is (see appendix B on obtaining X).

GETTING THE USER NAME

We've added an extra routine here, `GetUserName()`, which is needed to respond to certain selection requests. We thought it fit in `icccm.c` since it is a response for ICCCM-compliant applications. We cover selections in chapter 19, so don't worry about it now.

SOURCE CODE FOR icccm.c

The source code for `iccm.c` is as follows:

icccm.c:

```
/*
 *      icccm.c
 *      X11 routines to set the required
 *      properties on an application's
 *      top-level window, as per the infamous
 *      ICCCM.
 *
 *      This file is different for X11R4
 *      or X11R3 (and below). If you are running
 *      an R4 (or higher) system, your
 *      Makefile should define the symbol
 *      X11R4.
 *
 *      Written for Advanced X Window Applications Programming
 *
 */

/*
 *      Unix include file for getting the user name
```

```
 */
#include    <pwd.h>

#include    "xbook.h"

/*
 *     GLOBALS for ICCCM-related data
 */

Window  AppWindow;       /* -- top-level window */

SetICCCM( display, window, argc, argv )

Display     *display;
Window      window;
int         argc;
char        *argv[];

/*
 *          SetICCCM() sets properties associated with
 *          an application's top-level window for both
 *          a session manager and a window manager.
 *          It complements the hinting done in window.c
 *
 */

{           /* -- function SetICCCM */

            /*
             * WM_COMMAND
             */
            XSetCommand( display, window, argv, argc );

            /*
             * Store protocols. The only protocol
             * we support is WM_DELETE_WINDOW.
             */
            SetProtocols( display, window );


            /*
             * Store WM_CLIENT_MACHINE
             */
            SetWMClientMachine( display, window );

            /*
```

```
             * Store window IF in a global
             * for later reference.
             */
            AppWindow = window;

}           /* -- function SetICCCM */

GetHostName( name )

char        *name;

/*
 *          GetHostName() gets the current machine's
 *          hostname, by calling the Unix C lib function
 *          gethostname().
 */

{           /* -- function GetHostName */

            if ( gethostname( name, 64 ) = = (-1) )
                   {
                   (void) strcpy( name, "Unknown" );
                   }

}           /* -- function GetHostName */

GetUserName( name )

char        *name;

/*
 *          GetUserName() gets the current user name,
 *          if possible.
 *
 */

{           /* -- function GetUserName */
            struct  passwd  *pw;
            char        *login_name, *getlogin();
            int         uid;

            login_name = getlogin();

            if ( login_name = = NULL )
                   {
                   uid = getuid();
```

```
                pw = getpwuid( uid );

                (void) strcpy( name, pw->pw_name );
                }
        else
                {
                (void) strcpy( name, login_name );
                }

}           /* -- function GetUserName */

IsDeleteWindow( display, event )

Display                         *display;
XClientMessageEvent             *event;

/*
 * IsDeleteWindow() checks a ClientMessage
 * event to see if the event contains a
 * request from the window manager to delete
 * the window (part of the WM_PROTOCOLS in the
 * ICCCM).
 *
 * IsDeleteWindow() returns True if the message
 * is asking the application to delete its window,
 * and False if the message was something else.
 *
 */

{   /* -- function IsDeleteWindow */
    Atom    protocols_atom;
    Atom    delete_atom;

    protocols_atom = XInternAtom( display, "WM_PROTOCOLS", False );
delete_atom = XInternAtom( display, "WM_DELETE_WINDOW", False );

    if ( ( event->message_type = = protocols_atom ) &&
        ( event->data.l[ 0 ] = = delete_atom ) &&
        ( event->format = = 32 ) )
        {
        return( True );
        }
    else
        {
        return( False );
        }
```

```
}   /* -- function IsDeleteWindow */

SetWMClientMachine( display, window )

Display     *display;
Window      window;

/*
 * SetWMClientMachine() sets the
 * WM_CLIENT_MACHINE property on a
 * top-level window for a
 * session manager.
 */

{   /* -- function SetWMClientMachine */
    char     hostname[ BUFSIZE + 1 ];
    Atom     client_machine;

    GetHostName( hostname );

    client_machine = XInternAtom( display,"WM_CLIENT_MACHINE", False );

    if ( client_machine != (Atom) None )
        {
        AppendProperty( display, window,
            client_machine,
            XA_STRING,
            8,
            hostname,
            strlen( hostname ) );

        }

}   /* -- function SetWMClientMachine */

SetProtocols( display, window )

Display     *display;
Window      window;

/*
 * SetProtocols() tells a window manager
 * that our application supports the
 * ICCCM WM_DELETE_WINDOW protocol.
 */
```

```
{   /* -- function SetProtocols */
    Atom    protocol_atom;
    Atom    delete_atom;
    char    data[ 25 ];

    delete_atom = XInternAtom( display, "WM_DELETE_WINDOW", False );
protocol_atom = XInternAtom( display, "WM_PROTOCOLS", False );

    if ( ( delete_atom = = (Atom) None ) ||
        ( protocol_atom = = (Atom) None ) )
        {
        return;
        }

#ifdef X11R4
    XSetWMProtocols( display, window, &delete_atom, 1 );

#else
    /*
     * Pre-R4 xlib
     */
    Long2Bytes( (long) delete_atom, data );

    AppendProperty( display, window,
        protocol_atom,
        XA_ATOM,
        32,
        data, 1 );

#endif

}   /* -- function SetProtocols */

/*
 * end of file
 */
```

SOURCE CODE FOR bytes c.

The `bytes.c` file contains a few simple routines to convert 4-byte (32-bit) numbers—particularly atoms—to four character bytes. Its contents are as follows:

```
bytes.c:

/*
 * bytes.c
 * Routines to convert byte streams to and from 4-byte integers.
 *
 */

#include  "xbook.h"

unsigned long Bytes2Long( data )

char   *data;

/*
 * Bytes2Long converts four bytes on data
 * into a long number.  We're sure you can
 * create a more efficient function.
 */

{   /* -- function Bytes2Long */
    int     i;
    union {
        long   l;
        char   bytes[ 4 ];
        } converter;

    for( i = 0; i < 4; i++ )
        {
        converter.bytes[ i ] = data[ i ];
        }

    return( converter.l );

}   /* -- function Bytes2Long */

Long2Bytes( l, data )

long   l;
char   data[];

/*
 * Long2Bytes converts the four bytes of
 * a long integer into four straight bytes
 * of data.
 */

{   /* -- function Long2Bytes */
```

```
    int     i;
    union {
        long    l;
        char    bytes[ 4 ];
        } converter;

    converter.l = l;

    for( i = 0; i < 4; i++ )
        {
        data[ i ] = converter.bytes[ i ];
        }

}   /* -- function Long2Bytes */

ConvertIntegers( data, number_items, string, format )

char    data[];
long    number_items;
char    string[];
Atom    format;

/*
 * ConvertIntegers() takes a stream of data bytes
 * (data) and converts the data into 4-byte (32-bit)
 * integers, and then converts the integers to text
 * strings.  If the format is XA_WINDOW, then the
 * text strings will be in hex.
 */

{   /* -- function ConvertIntegers */
    char    st[ BUFSIZE + 1 ];
    long    number, position;
    int     i, length = 0;

    string[ 0 ] = '\0';

    position    = 0L;

    for( i = 0; i < number_items; i++ )
        {
        number = Bytes2Long( &data[ position ] );

        if ( format = = XA_WINDOW )
            {
            (void) sprintf( st, "0x%lx\n", number );
```

```
            }
        else    /* -- XA_INTEGER, etc. */
            {
            (void) sprintf( st, "%ld\n", number );
            }

        position += 4L;

        if ( ( length + strlen( st ) ) < BUFSIZE )
            {
            (void) strcat( string, st );

            length = strlen( string );
            }

        }

    return( length );

}   /* -- function ConvertIntegers */

/*
 * end of file
 */
```

FUNCTIONS DEVELOPED IN THIS CHAPTER

```
Bytes2Long
ConvertIntegers
GetHostName
GetUserName
IsDeleteWindow
Long2Bytes
SetICCCM
SetProtocols
SetWMClientMachine
```

XLIB FUNCTIONS AND MACROS INTRODUCED IN THIS CHAPTER

XSetCommand
XSetWMClientMachine
XSetWMProtocols

SUMMARY

- X provides mechanism but not policy. To make applications work together, however, X's designers came up with a policy: the ICCCM–the Inter-Client Communications Conventions Manual. By following ICCCM conventions, your applications can leverage a lot of power. However, the ICCCM covers a lot of ground and creates more confusion than any other topic in the X Window System.
- The ICCCM covers session manager, which manages a group of X applications doing some particular form of work. Session managers are responsible for starting up the group of applications, saving the state of the applications (so that they can be restarted from where they left off), and closing down the programs. However, the whole concept of session managers is still evolving, so it will take some time before everyone reaches a consensus on what session managers should resemble.
- Use WM_COMMAND and a WM_CLIENT_MACHINE to keep the session manager happy. Even if you are not running a session manager, you should still set these properties. The WM_COMMAND property should contain the command necessary to start the application. The WM_CLIENT_MACHINE property should be the name of the machine (CPU) your application is running on–as seen from the X server.
- X contains special ICCCM protocols for communicating certain requests to the window manager. These protocols all work in basically the same way. First, you tell the window manager the protocols you support. Then, when the window manager wants to notify you about t he use of the protocols (i.e., when you should be doing something special), the window manager will send your application a ClientMessage event. When you get one of these ClientMessage events, do your stuff.
- The ICCCM defines three special protocols for window managers to send events to clients: WM_TAKE_FOCUS, WM_SAVE_YOURSELF, and WM_DELETE_WINDOW. You now need to set WM_TAKE_FOCUS if your application wants to control the

keyboard focus. If your application supports WM_SAVE_YOURSELF, you will get a ClientMessage when the window manager (or session manager) wants your application to save its state.WM_DELETE_WINDOW prevents the window manager from deleting an application's window; instead, the window manager asks that the application delete its own window. If your application supports one of these protocols, you need to create a special property, WM_PROTOCOLS, on your top-level window.

- A window-manager protocol only kicks in when you receive a special ClientMessage event. ClientMessage events carry up to twenty bytes of data. If the message_type is the atom WM_PROTOCOLS, then you have received one of these protocol messages. In this case, the first data element (four bytes) will contain an atom. If that atom is WM_DELETE_WINDOW, then your application has just been asked to delete its window. The same principle applies for WM_TAKE_FOCUS and WM_SAVE_YOURSELF.
- The ICCCM defines how your applications can change their state. Normally, it is up to the user working with the window manager to change the state of windows Your applications can also try to change the state of your windows.

Chapter 16

Strategies for X Program-to-Program Communication

In the chapter 15 we covered the infamous ICCCM, which dictates how X programs operate together. Those were the ground rules; the next few chapters cover methods for directly exchanging data between X applications, including writing to properties on windows, sending events to application windows, and using selections. This chapter looks at the basic strategies and includes a common format for example programs. To make the example programs in section III simpler, we chose to make the programs as much the same as possible.

PROGRAM-TO-PROGRAM COMMUNICATION WITH X

X was designed as a graphical windowing system, not as a general purpose Inter-Process Communication (IPC) mechanism. Therefore, X is not designed to complete massive data transfers. Instead, program-to-program communication with X usually involves things like cut and paste, or communication related to the interface. All of these communication mechanisms involve round trips to the X server, using the server to provide something akin to a star network. If two programs want to communicate using X, each program must go through the X server to get to the other program. This is slower than a direct link, but much easier because the Xlib maintains the link for you; you only have one link to the server.

There are four main methods for program-to-program communication in X: appending to properties on some window, sending X events to a window, using the scary concept of selections, and using the old-style cut buffers.

APPENDING TO PROPERTIES

A good portion of the process to create windows involves sending hints to the window manager. These hints are "sent" to the window manager by writing to specific properties on the application's top-level window. The window manager, a separate process, then picks up the contents of these properties, and follows the hints (you hope). A good degree of X program-to-program communication involves writing to properties.

When writing to properties, both sides must agree on what properties to write to, what windows these properties will be on (since properties are tied to windows), who will read the properties, and who will write the properties. It's definitely a good idea to have only one reader and one writer for a given property.

SENDING X EVENTS

Just about every X application has a central event loop. In this loop, incoming events are received, parsed, and acted upon. Thus, just about every application is already set up for communication if you just send X events to that application. You can either send "normal" events, like `KeyPress` events and simulate a user typing at the keyboard, or you can send special events, like `ClientMessage` events. If you send `ClientMessage` events to another application, though, you must be sure that both applications have agreed on the format and content of these events. Chapter 15 covered one use of `ClientMessage` events. It showed how the window manager may send your application special events, like `WM_DELETE_WINDOW`.

The main problem with sending events to an application is finding out the correct window IDs. Since window IDs are created when windows are created, they will probably be different each time a program is executed. One solution for this is to combine appending to properties and sending events.

One way this can be accomplished is for each application to write out their window IDs to a special property on the root window. Other applications can then read this property and know to which window IDs events should be sent.

USING SELECTIONS FOR CUT AND PASTE

Selections are X's answer to cut-and-paste clipboard operations offered on the Macintosh, the Amiga, and Microsoft Windows. Whereas most cut-and-paste systems are passive (you cut data to the clipboard and paste it later from the clipboard), selections are active. With X's selections, an application owns the "clipboard" and not the X server. Many applications can own many different "clipboards" (selections). When you want to paste data, ask the owner of a given selection for the data you want (also ask the owner of the selection to format the data).

Active cut and paste makes selections in X much more powerful than most passive cut-and-paste systems. However, it also makes it a lot more complex (although Dynamic Data Exchange has a similar complexity).

You can also view selections as an X-based IPC mechanism with timeouts, requests for transmission, and everything else that a "real" IPC mechanism would have.

The really neat thing about selections is that you can play twenty questions with them. For example, if you have an X-aware debugger and select (the magic word) a breakpoint, a text editor (also X-aware) can ask the debugger (owner of the selection) for the file name in use and the line number selected.

Thus, you can ask for the selected "data" to be given to your application in a number of formats, including the file name the data came from, the current line number, and the actual line that is selected. It's complex, but very powerful.

CUT BUFFERS

A simpler method of cut and paste involves using X's cut buffers. Eight cut buffers can exist in the X server (actually implemented as eight properties on the root window). These cut buffers can be used to exchange limited amounts of text data only.

The best thing about cut buffers is the fact that a number of Xlib routines directly support cut buffers, making the programmer's task simple. The worst thing about cut buffers is that no one should use them anymore. The cut buffers were added for historical reasons and are now superseded by selections. (If only selections were as simple as the cut buffers). Oh well. Remember that the rule for cut buffers now is don't use them.

The next three chapters will explain appending properties, sending events, and using selections in excruciating detail, providing example programs using each method for data exchange. We've tried to make the basic format for each example program the same, so that you can concentrate on the data exchange method and don't have to worry over too many silly program details.

A COMMON APPLICATION FORMAT

The four applications that appear in the next few chapters follow a common format. First, each application sets up a connection to the X server and creates a top-level window. Then, a number of push-buttons are created: usually one to quit the application, one to send (or receive) the data, and one to clear out the data.

Each application's event loop looks mainly for push-button events and reacts accordingly (for example, quitting when the quit button is chosen). The data to be exchanged is stored in a global character string, so that it is really simple to respond to `Expose` events. We don't advise everyone to populate their programs with globals; however, we wanted a simple way to show the current data and not get in the way of describing data exchange.

To create the data to send, most of the programs ask the user to type in some data. This requires, of course, a few routines to handle the delete key and so on. Simple.

EDITING TEXT STRINGS

`TextEdit()` is a simple function that edits text strings. You pass `TextEdit()` a `KeySym` that was generated by a `KeyPress` event. `TextEdit()` then handles delete (and backspace, too—both are treated the same here) or plain ASCII characters. Readers in countries that use other character sets (basically the whole world) will need to modify two lines of code below.

When the user presses a delete key, the last character entered should be wiped out (this is a one-line text editing function). In addition, you also want to clear the display of that character in the window. `TextEdit()` handles this by outputting four blank spaces to cover the deleted character.

Because it needs to know the width of a text string, you need to pass an `XFontStruct` for the font currently in use. `TextEdit()` determines where the current text string ends. This simple function is located in `textedit.c`.

SOURCE CODE FOR textedit.c

The source code for `textedit.c` is as follows:

textedit.c:

```
/*
 * textedit.c
 * A simple routine for handling a user-entered
 * text string and allowing the use of backspace
 * and delete keys
 *
 */

#include  "xbook.h"

TextEdit( display, window, gc, font, x, y, keysym, data, max_size )

Display    *display;
```

```
Window          window;         /* -- Where to do the editing */
GC              gc;             /* -- How to draw the text */
XFontStruct     *font;          /* -- for checking widths of strings */
int             x, y;           /* -- Where the data string starts */
KeySym          keysym;         /* -- Key entered */
char            data[];         /* -- the current data string */
int             max_size;       /* -- The largest #bytes for data
*/

/*
 * TextEdit() handles common text-editing chores.
 * The routine:
 *     1) checks a KeyPress event packet for
 *     usable characters
 *     2) Handles backspaces
 *     3) Redraws the text, if need be.
 * This routine is obviously not very efficient
 * and is used for simplicity, not speed.
 *
 */

{   /* -- function TextEdit */
    int     length;
    char    string[ 10 ];

    length  = strlen( data );

    switch( keysym )
            {
            case XK_BackSpace:
            case XK_Delete:
                if( length > 0 )
                    {
                    length--;

                    data[ length ] = '\0';

                    x += XTextWidth( font, data, length );

                    XDrawImageString( display,
                        window, gc,
                        x, y,
                        "  ", 4 );

                    }
                break;
```

```
        default: /* -- normal keystroke */
            if ( ( keysym >= ' ' )    &&
               ( keysym <= '~' ) )
               {
               if ( ( length + 1 ) < max_size )
                   {
                   data[ length ] = keysym;

                   x += XTextWidth( font, data, length );

                   length++;
                   data[ length ] = '\0';

                   (void) sprintf( string, "%c", keysym );
                   XDrawImageString( display,
                       window, gc,
                       x, y,
                       string, 1 );
                   }
               }
        }

}   /* -- function TextEdit */

/*
 * end of file
 */
```

DISPLAYING MULTIPLE LINES OF TEXT

Often a text string read in from a property contains a number of lines of text, each separated by a newline character `(\n)`. In addition, many text strings have embedded tabs. Neither is handled well by X fonts and `XDrawImageString()`. The `DrawStrings()` function draws out a text string in multiple lines.

`DrawStrings()` is stored in `xstring.c` and exists because we don't know in advance the format in which the text will appear. `DrawStrings()` cleans up common cases, albeit in a manner that is not very efficient.

`DrawStrings()` calls `DrawString()`, which detabs the source string.

SOURCE CODE FOR xstring.c

The source code for `xstring.c` is as follows:

xstring.c:

```
/*
 * xstring.c
 * X11 string and multiple string drawing routines.
 */

#include  "xbook.h"

DrawStrings( display, window, gc, font_height, x, y, string, length )

Display   *display;
Window    window;
GC        gc;
int       font_height;
int       x, y;
char      string[];
int       length;

/*
 * DrawStrings() takes one character string that most likely
 * contains a number of newlines (\n) and draws the string as
 * a number of lines of text in a window.  It uses font_height
 * to determine the spacing between lines of text.
 */

{   /* -- function DrawStrings */
    int     c, i, j;
    char    st[ BUFSIZE + 1 ];

#define COLUMN_WIDTH  80         /* -- 80-char wide columns */

    i = 0;
    while( i < length )
        {
        c = string[ i ];
        j = 0;
        while( ( i < length ) && ( j < COLUMN_WIDTH ) &&
            ( c != '\r' ) && ( c != '\n' ) )
            {
            st[ j ] = string[ i ];
            j++;
```

```
            i++;

            if ( i < length )
                {
                c = string[ i ];
                }
            }

        if ( j > 0 )
            {
            st[ j ] = '\0';

            DrawString( display, window, gc, x, y, st );
            }

        y += font_height;
        i++; /* -- beyond newline */
        }

    XFlush( display );

}   /* -- function DrawStrings */

DrawString( display, window, gc, x, y, string )

Display     *display;
Window      window;
GC          gc;
int         x, y;
char        string[];

/*
 * DrawString() draws a given text string
 * into the given window.  First, DrawString()
 * untabs the text (since X fonts aren't too
 * good about tab characters).
 *
 */

{   /* -- function DrawString */

    detab( string, BUFSIZE );

    XDrawImageString( display, window, gc,
        x, y, string, strlen( string ) );
```

```
}   /* -- function DrawString */

detab( st, max_size )

char    st[];
int     max_size;

/*
 *  detab() expands the TABs in a given string.
 *
 */

{   /* -- function detab */
    register int    i, j;
    int             l, place;
    char            st1[ BUFSIZE + 5 ];

#define TAB      '\t'

    l = strlen( st );
    j = 0;
    i = 0;
    while( ( i < l ) && ( j < max_size ) )
        {
        if ( st[ i ] = = TAB ) /* -- Tab */
            {
                place = tabstop( j, max_size );

                while( j < place )
                    {
                    st1[ j ] = ' ';
                    j++;
                    }
                }
            else
                {
                st1[ j ] = st[ i ];
                j++;
                }
            i++;
            }

    st1[ j ] = '\0';

    /*
     * Copy string back onto original
```

```
     */
    (void) strcpy( st, st1 );

}   /* -- function detab */

tabstop( column, max_size )

int      column, max_size;

/*
 *  tabstop() determines how many spaces
 *  are needed from a given column to get to the
 *  next tab stop
 */

{   /* -- function tabstop */
    register int    i;

#define  TABSIZE        8              /* -- Space between tab stops */

    for( i = 0; i < max_size; i += TABSIZE )
        {
        if ( column < i )
            break;
        }

    return( i );     /* -- next stop */

}   /* -- function tabstop */

/*
 *  end of file
 */
```

A PUSH-BUTTON INTERFACE

In addition to editing and drawing text strings, we need to create a simple push-button interface. A push button, at least as the term is used here, is a small area in a window that contains a text message (like "Push Me"). The user moves the mouse pointer on top of the push button and then presses any mouse button, generating a `ButtonPress` event over the "push button." (It's a lot easier to use a push button than to describe one.) Figure 16-1 shows typical push buttons.

Figure 16-1. Push Buttons

CREATING PUSH BUTTONS

The first step in using a push button is creating one. We choose to implement push buttons as subwindows of an application's top-level window. The reason for this is simple: since each push button is a window, the X server will handle hit detection for us, and we will get `Expose` events for each button. This will tell us when to redraw each button.

We created a structure, called `ButtonStruct`, that contains information for each push button. We need the display the button is on (especially for the multiple-display program in part 4), its window, its parent window (usually the application's top-level window), and a graphics context to draw in the push button. To provide some feedback to the user when the button is pressed, we need a foreground and background color, so we can highlight the button when pressed. We also need a text string to display in the button, such as "Quit" or "Push Me." Finally, we need a function to call when the push button is pushed. Since we want to assign many uses to these buttons, we have a function for each button that is called when the button is pushed. This function is passed as a function pointer to the `CreateButton()` function. The contents of `ButtonStruct()` are as follows:

```
typedef struct
        {
        Display          *display;
        Window           w;
        Window           parent;
        GC               gc;
        unsigned long    fore, back;
        char             text[ BUFSIZE + 1 ];
        int              length; /* strlen of text */
        int              (*function)(); /* To call when pressed*/
        } ButtonStruct;
```

We build an array of these push button structures, one for each possible push button. We could have used `malloc()` to dynamically create the storage for each button, but using an array is simpler.

These buttons are stored in a global array called `AppButtons`. The global `buttons_used` is an index to the next available (free) button slot. The contents of `AppButtons` are as follows:

```
#define MAX_BUTTONS     20

ButtonStruct        AppButtons[ MAX_BUTTONS + 1 ];
int                 buttons_used = 0;
```

The function `CreateButton()` creates a push button and stores all the necessary information in the `AppButtons` array. Each button requires a GC and that a window be created. The contents of `CreateButton()` are as follows:

```
CreateButton( display, window, x, y, fore, back, font_id, text, function )

Display             *display;
Window              window;         /* -- bounding window, e.g., parent */
int                 x, y;
unsigned long       fore, back;
Font                font_id;
char                text[];
int                 (*function)();

{   /* -- function CreateButton */
    Window      w;
    GC          gc;

    /*
     * Find an available slot
     */
    if ( buttons_used < ( MAX_BUTTONS - 1 ) )
        {
        /*
         * Create window
         */
        w = CreateWindow( display, window, x, y,
            BUTTON_WIDTH, BUTTON_HEIGHT, 0,
            fore, back,
            ExposureMask | ButtonPressMask );
```

```
        /*
         * Create GC
         */
        gc = MakeGC( display, w, fore, back );

        XSetFont( display, gc, font_id );

        /*
         * Store values
         */
        AppButtons[ buttons_used     ].display     = display;
        AppButtons[ buttons_used     ].w           = w;
        AppButtons[ buttons_used     ].parent      = window;
        AppButtons[ buttons_used     ].gc          = gc;
        AppButtons[ buttons_used     ].fore        = fore;
        AppButtons[ buttons_used     ].back        = back;
        AppButtons[ buttons_used     ].function = function;

        if ( strlen( text ) <  BUFSIZE )
            {
            (void) strcpy( AppButtons[ buttons_used ].text, text );
            }
        else
            {
            (void) strncpy( AppButtons[ buttons_used ].text, text,
                BUFSIZE );
            AppButtons[ buttons_used ].text[ BUFSIZE ] = '\0';
            }

            AppButtons[ buttons_used ].length =
                strlen( AppButtons[ buttons_used ].text );

            XFlush( display );

            /*
             * Increment slot pointer
             */
            buttons_used++;

            return( True );
            }

        return( False );

}       /* -- function CreateButton */
```

PUSH BUTTONS' LOOK AND FEEL

Each push button is built within a rectangular window. We add a shadow for a three-dimensional effect and place the text in a smaller box. The shadow is really just two filled rectangles drawn in `Button3d()`.

The `ButtonRedraw()` function calls `Button3d()` as well as drawing the text name of the button (see the code for `button.c`, shown in the section "Source Code for `button.c`").

PUSH BUTTON EVENTS AND CALL-BACK FUNCTIONS

The push buttons here respond to only two events: `Expose` and `ButtonPress`. On `Expose` events, the button's window is merely redrawn. On `ButtonPress` events, the `ButtonExec()` function is called to execute the function that will implement the button's task. This was passed as a function pointer to `CreateButton()`. This type of function-calling is usually referred to as call-back functions, since the button system calls back your function whenever a button is pressed.

Each call-back function will be called with the display pointer and a window ID. This window ID will be the ID of the parent window (the parent window for the push-button's window). The contents of `ButtonExec()` are as follows:

```
ButtonExec( display, which_button )

Display     *display;
int         which_button;

{           /* -- function ButtonExec */

            ButtonHighlight( display, which_button );

            (AppButtons[ which_button ].function)( display,
                   AppButtons[ which_button ].parent );

            XClearWindow( display,
                AppButtons[ which_button ].w );
```

```
        ButtonRedraw( display, which_button );

}       /* -- function ButtonExec */
```

ButtonExec() first highlights the button, calling ButtonHighlight(), so that the user gets some feedback. Then, ButtonExec() executes the function stored for that button. Finally, when the function is complete, ButtonExec() clears the button and redraws it, thus telling the user that the function is complete.

PUSH-BUTTON EVENT HANDLING

ButtonEvent() is a function that traps events for push buttons. It examines an incoming event and determines if the event pertains to any push-buttons in use. If there is a pertinent event, ButtonEvent() acts on the event and returns True. A return of True tells the main application event loop that ButtonEvent() handled the event. A return of False means that the event did not pertain to any push button. The contents of ButtonEvent() are as follows:

```
ButtonEvent( display, event )

Display     *display;
XEvent      *event;

{           /* -- function ButtonEvent */
            int         which_button;

            switch( event->type )
                {
                case Expose:
                    which_button = ButtonFind( display,
                                        event->xexpose.window );

                    if ( which_button >= 0 )
                        {
                        ButtonRedraw( display, which_button );
                        return( True );
                        }
                    break;
                case ButtonPress:
                    which_button = ButtonFind( display,
                                        event->xbutton.window );
```

```
                if ( which_button >= 0 )
                    {
                    ButtonExec( display, which_button );

                    return( True );
                    }
                break;
            }

        XFlush( display );

        return( False );

}       /* -- function ButtonEvent */
```

USER FEEDBACK FOR PUSHING A PUSH BUTTON

User feedback is provided by drawing over most of the button with a black rectangle. This highlights the push button until the button's function is complete. Thus a long disk operation will be highlighted for a long time and a short calculation will be highlighted for only a short time. This gives the user some idea of what is going on.

SOURCE CODE FOR button.c

All the push button functions are stored in the file `button.c`:

```
/*
 *      button.c
 *      X11 button routines for handling simple
 *      "push-button" user input
.*
 */

#include  "xbook.h"

/*
 * Structure for information stored
 * on each button.
 *
 * A Global array of these structures is maintain, one
 * element for each push button in use.
```

```
 */

typedef struct
        {
        Display           *display;
        Window            w;
        Window            parent;
        GC                gc;
        unsigned long     fore, back;
        char              text[ BUFSIZE + 1 ];
        int               length;           /* strlen of text */
        int               (*function)();    /* To call when pressed */
        } ButtonStruct;

/*
 *      Global array to store button information.  A MAX_BUTTONS
 *      of 20 is a purely arbitrary number.
 */
#define MAX_BUTTONS 20

ButtonStruct  AppButtons[ MAX_BUTTONS + 1 ];
int           buttons_used = 0;

CreateButton( display, window, x, y, fore, back, font_id, text, function )

Display           *display;
Window            window;        /* -- bounding window, e.g., parent */
int               x, y;
unsigned long     fore, back;
Font              font_id;
char              text[];
int               (*function)();

{       /* -- function CreateButton */
        Window     w;
        GC         gc;

        /*
         * Find an available slot
         */
        if ( buttons_used < ( MAX_BUTTONS - 1 ) )
                {
                /*
                 * Create window
                 */
                w = CreateWindow( display, window, x, y,
```

```
        BUTTON_WIDTH, BUTTON_HEIGHT, 0,
        fore, back,
        ExposureMask | ButtonPressMask );

    /*
     * Create GC
     */
    gc = MakeGC( display, w, fore, back );

    XSetFont( display, gc, font_id );

    /*
     * Store values
     */
    AppButtons[ buttons_used ].display      = display;
    AppButtons[ buttons_used ].w            = w;
    AppButtons[ buttons_used ].parent       = window;
    AppButtons[ buttons_used ].gc           = gc;
    AppButtons[ buttons_used ].fore         = fore;
    AppButtons[ buttons_used ].back         = back;
    AppButtons[ buttons_used ].function     = function;

    if ( strlen( text ) <  BUFSIZE )
        {
        (void) strcpy( AppButtons[ buttons_used ].text, text );
        }
    else
        {
        (void) strncpy( AppButtons[ buttons_used ].text, text,
            BUFSIZE );
        AppButtons[ buttons_used ].text[ BUFSIZE ] = '\0';
        }

    AppButtons[ buttons_used ].length =
        strlen( AppButtons[ buttons_used ].text );

    XFlush( display );

    /*
     * Increment slot pointer
     */
    buttons_used++;

    return( True );
    }
```

```
          return( False );

}         /* -- function CreateButton */

ButtonEvent( display, event )

Display   *display;
XEvent    *event;

{         /* -- function ButtonEvent */
          int     which_button;

          switch( event->type )
              {
              case Expose:
                  which_button = ButtonFind( display,
                                    event->xexpose.window );

                  if ( which_button >= 0 )
                      {
                      ButtonRedraw( display, which_button );
                      return( True );
                      }
                  break;
              case ButtonPress:
                  which_button = ButtonFind( display,
                                    event->xbutton.window );

                  if ( which_button >= 0 )
                      {
                      ButtonExec( display, which_button );

                      return( True );
                      }
                  break;
              }

          XFlush( display );

          return( False );

          /* -- function ButtonEvent */
```

```
ButtonExec( display, which_button )

Display     *display;
int         which_button;

{           /* -- function ButtonExec */

            ButtonHighlight( display, which_button );

            (AppButtons[ which_button ].function)( display,
                     AppButtons[ which_button ].parent );

            XClearWindow( display,
                  AppButtons[ which_button ].w );

            ButtonRedraw( display, which_button );

}           /* -- function ButtonExec */

ButtonHighlight( display, which_button )

Display*display;
int         which_button;

{           /* -- function ButtonHighlight */

            XFillRectangle( display,
               AppButtons[ which_button ].w,
               AppButtons[ which_button ].gc,
               0, 0,
               BUTTON_WIDTH - 5, BUTTON_HEIGHT - 5 );

            SetGC( display,
               AppButtons[ which_button     ].gc,
               AppButtons[ which_button     ].back,
               AppButtons[ which_button     ].fore );

            Button3d( display,
               AppButtons[ which_button ].w,
               AppButtons[ which_button ].gc );

            ButtonText( display,
               AppButtons[ which_button     ].w,
               AppButtons[ which_button     ].gc,
               AppButtons[ which_button     ].text,
               AppButtons[ which_button     ].length );
```

```
            SetGC( display,
                AppButtons[ which_button    ].gc,
                AppButtons[ which_button    ].fore,
                AppButtons[ which_button    ].back );

            XFlush( display );

}           /* -- function ButtonHighlight */

ButtonRedraw( display, which_button )

Display *display;
int         which_button;

{           /* -- function ButtonHighlight */

            XDrawRectangle( display,
                AppButtons[ which_button ].w,
                AppButtons[ which_button ].gc,
                0, 0,
                BUTTON_WIDTH - 6, BUTTON_HEIGHT - 6 );

            Button3d( display,
                AppButtons[ which_button ].w,
                AppButtons[ which_button ].gc );

            ButtonText( display,
                AppButtons[ which_button    ].w,
                AppButtons[ which_button    ].gc,
                AppButtons[ which_button    ].text,
                AppButtons[ which_button    ].length );

}           /* -- function ButtonHighlight */

ButtonText( display, window, gc, text, length )

Display     *display;
Window      window;
GC          gc;
char        text[];
int         length;

{           /* -- function ButtonText */

            XDrawImageString( display, window, gc,
                5, 15,
```

```
                text, length );

}           /* -- function ButtonText */

ButtonFind( display, window )

Display *display;
Window      window;

{           /* -- function ButtonFind */
            int     which_button;

            for( which_button = 0; which_button < buttons_used; which_button++ )
                    {
                    if ( ( window = = AppButtons[ which_button ].w ) &&
                        ( display = = AppButtons[ which_button ].display ) )
                            {
                            return( which_button );
                            }
                    }

            return( -1 );

}           /* -- function ButtonFind */

Button3d( display, window, gc )

Display     *display;
Window      window;
GC          gc;

{           /* -- function Button3D */

            XFillRectangle( display,
                    window, gc,
                    6, BUTTON_HEIGHT - 5,
                    BUTTON_WIDTH - 10, BUTTON_HEIGHT - 5 );

            XFillRectangle( display,
                    window, gc,
                    BUTTON_WIDTH - 5, 6,
                    6, BUTTON_HEIGHT - 5 );

}           /* -- function Button3D */
```

```
/*
 *        end of file
 */
```

FUNCTIONS DEVELOPED IN THIS CHAPTER

```
ButtonEvent
CreateButton
TextEdit
```

SUMMARY

- X was designed as a graphical windowing system—not as a general purpose Inter-Process Communication (IPC) mechanism. Program-to-program communication with X involves things like cut and paste and communication related to the interface. All of these communication mechanisms involve round trips to the X server, using the server to provide something akin to a star network. There are four main methods for program-to-program communication in X: appending to properties on some window, sending X events to a window, using the scary concept of selections, and using the old-style cut buffers.

- You've already been writing to properties in earlier chapters by creating windows, which involves sending hints to the window manager. These hints are "sent" to the window manager by writing to specific properties on the application's top-level window. The window manager, a separate process, then picks up the contents of these properties and follows the hints (you hope). A lot of X program-to-program communication involves writing to properties. When writing to properties, both sides must agree on what properties to write to, what windows these properties will be on (since properties are tied to windows), who will read the properties and who will write the properties. It's definitely a good idea to only have one reader and one writer for a given property.

- In a central event loop, incoming events are received, parsed and acted upon. Thus, just about every application is already set up for communication, if you just send X events to that application. The main problem with sending events to an application is finding out the correct window IDs. One solution is combining appending to properties and sending events. One way to do this is for each application to write out their window IDs to a special property on the root window. Other applications can then read this property and know which window IDs to send events to.

- Selections are X's answer to cut-and-paste clipboard operations offered on other windowing systems. Whereas most cut-and-paste systems are passive (you cut data to the clipboard and paste it later from the clipboard), selections are active. With X's selections, an application owns the "clipboard" and not the X server. Many applications can own many different "clipboards"—called selections. This use of active cut and paste makes selections in X much more powerful that most passive systems.

- Don't use cut buffers. Never. Nada.

Chapter 17

Cut and Paste Using Properties

This chapter covers the exchange of data between programs, using X's concept of properties. Programs can write data to arbitrary properties on arbitrary windows. Other programs can then read this data. There's a lot of code in this chapter because dealing with properties is rather complex. Properties are extremely important as they touch so many aspects of X.

In addition, this long chapter deals with error handling.

EXCHANGING DATA VIA PROPERTIES

The first major means of X program-to-program communication involves properties. Properties are named, typed data that are stored with a window in the X server. Any program with a window ID and a property name can store data in a property. If two programs agree on the window and property, they can exchange data.

To use properties to exchange data, you need two things: a window ID and a property ID.

The property ID comes from a property name (a text string) and programs must agree on the name beforehand. The window ID is harder, since X does not force windows to have unique names. So, the best idea is to have all the programs that want to exchange data agree on a window, and then choose a common window such that all programs can get the necessary window ID.

APPENDING DATA TO A PROPERTY ON THE ROOT WINDOW

The root window stands out in this regard, because every application knows how to get the Window ID of the root window of a screen, using the macro `RootWindow()`:

```
Display     *display;
int         screen;
Window      rootwindow;

rootwindow = RootWindow( display, screen );
```

Every screen has a root window. In fact, the root window is the only window you can be sure will always exist. This makes the root window a good candidate for use so properties can exchange data.

GETTING A PROPERTY (atom) ID

For a property ID, applications need to agree beforehand which name will be used for the property. Use `XInternAtom()` to get the proper `atom` ID for the property:

```
Display     *display;
char        *property_name = "__XBOOK"; /* -- our name */
Atom        property;

property = XInternAtom( display, property_name, False );
```

```
if ( property != (Atom) None )
    {
    /* -- success */

    ...

    }
```

FUNCTIONS FOR WORKING WITH atoms

To work with properties, you must first learn to work with atoms. Atoms are 32-bit indentifiers used to represent a text string in some sort of hashed format (the actual format used by the server to look up the names is unimportant here). The first thing to note about atoms is that many X functions will return atom values. These values will most likely be different from one run of a program to the next.

How do we compare a variable atom with a known value? We decided to use the atom's name. Since each atom really represents a text string, and the text string (like "WM_DELETE_WINDOW") remains constant, we can intern the given name, getting an atom back. Then, we can compare this new atom with the atom returned in an X event or from XGetWindowProperty().

COMPARING AN atom AND AN atom NAME

CompareAtomWithName() compares an atom ID with an atom name and returns True if both resolve to the same atom ID. False is returned otherwise. Each call to XInternAtom() results in a round trip to the X server, so this function is not at all efficient (we could have interned each name once and then cached the atoms in some global data, but we would have had to cache each atom for each display we connect to, as explained in section IV).

The contents of CompareAtomWithName() are as follows:

```
CompareAtomWithName( display, atom, name )

Display     *display;
Atom        atom;
char        *name;
```

```
{   /* -- function CompareAtomWithName */
    Atom      compare_atom;
    int       status = False;

    compare_atom = XInternAtom( display, name, False );

    if ( compare_atom != (Atom) None )
            {
            if ( compare_atom = = atom )
                    {
                    status = True;
                    }
            }

    return( status );

}   /* -- function CompareAtomWithName */
```

CONVERTING A LIST OF atoms TO A LIST OF atom NAMES

The next function we need for dealing with atoms is to convert an array of data bytes representing atoms into the corresponding atoms, then convert the atoms into a text string containing the names of these atoms.

GetAtomsFromData() goes through an array of bytes which probably came from raw data stored in a property, converting each set of four bytes into a 32-bit atom ID, and then converting that atom ID to an atom name with GetAtomName().

The function Bytes2Long() (from chapter 15) converts the data bytes into an atom ID (really just into a 32-bit integer). GetAtomName() converts the atom ID to an atom name (a process also described in chapter 15). Finally, these names are appended to the end of the text string, with a newline (\n) character separating each name.

The contents of GetAtomName() are as follows:

```
GetAtomsFromData( display, data, number_items, string )

Display     *display;
char char  *data;              /* -- input bytes */
long number_items; /* -- number of 32-bit items, i.e., num bytes / 4 */
*string;           /* -- output text */

{   /* -- function GetAtomsFromData */
    int      i, length;
    long     position;
    char     name[ BUFSIZE + 1 ];
    long     atom;

    string[ 0 ] = '\0';
    length        = 0;
    position      = 0L;
    for( i = 0; i < number_items; i++ )
        {
        atom = Bytes2Long( &data[ position ] );

        position += 4L;

        GetAtomName( display, (Atom) atom, name );

        if ( length > 0 )
            {
            (void) strcat( string, "\n" );
            }

        if ( ( length + strlen( name ) ) < ( BUFSIZE - 10 ) )
            {
            (void) strcat( string, name );
            }

        length = strlen( string );
        }

    return( strlen( string ) );

}   /* -- function GetAtomsFromData */
```

CONVERTING A LIST OF atoms TO RAW DATA BYTES

Atoms2Data() is sort of the opposite of GetAtomsFromData(). It converts an array of atom IDs into a byte stream so the atom ID data can be written out to a property. The contents of Atoms2Data() are as follows:

```
Atoms2Data( atoms, number_atoms, data )

Atom    atoms[];
int     number_atoms;
char    *data;

{       /* -- function Atoms2Data */
        int     i, length, position;

        position = 0;
        length   = 0;

        for( i = 0; i < number_atoms; i++ )
                {
                Long2Bytes( (long) atoms[ i ], &data[ position ] );

                position += 4;
                }

        length = number_atoms * 4;

        return( length );

}       /* -- function Atoms2Data */
```

SOURCE CODE FOR atom.c

All the functions showing this code are covered in previous sections except GetAtomName(), which is just a convenient shell over XGetAtomName().

The contents of `atom.c` are as follows:

```
atom.c:

/*
 *      atom.c
 *      X11 routines for working with atoms
 *
 */

#include  "xbook.h"

CompareAtomWithName( display, atom, name )

Display     *display;
Atom        atom;
char        *name;

/*
 *      CompareAtomWithName() takes an
 *      Atom and a text string.  The routine
 *      interns the text string and compares the
 *      two atoms. If they match, True is returned,
 *      otherwise False.
 */

{       /* -- function CompareAtomWithName */
        Atom    compare_atom;
        int     status = False;

        compare_atom = XInternAtom( display, name, False );

        if ( compare_atom != (Atom) None )
                {
                if ( compare_atom = = atom )
                        {
                        status = True;
                        }
                }

        return( status );

}       /* -- function CompareAtomWithName */

GetAtomName( display, atom, string )
```

```
Display     *display;
Atom        atom;
char        string[];

/*
 *      GetAtomName() handles the messy part
 *      of getting a name for an atom.
 */

{       /* -- function GetAtomName */
        char    *name;

        string[ 0 ] = '\0';

        if ( atom != (Atom) None )
                {
                name = XGetAtomName( display, atom );

                if ( name )
                        {
                        (void) strcpy( string, name );

                        XFree( name );
                        }
                }

}       /* -- function GetAtomName */

GetAtomsFromData( display, data, number_items, string )

Display     *display;
char        *data;              /* -- input bytes */
long        number_items;
char        *string;            /* -- output text */

{       /* -- function GetAtomsFromData */
        int     i, length;
        long    position;
        char    name[ BUFSIZE + 1 ];
        long    atom;

        string[ 0 ] = '\0';
        length      = 0;
        position    = 0L;
        for( i = 0; i < number_items; i++ )
                {
```

```
            atom = Bytes2Long( &data[ position ] );

            position += 4L;

            GetAtomName( display, (Atom) atom, name );

            if ( length > 0 )
                  {
                  (void) strcat( string, "\n" );
                  }

            if ( ( length + strlen( name ) ) < ( BUFSIZE - 10 ) )
                  {
                  (void) strcat( string, name );
                  }

            length = strlen( string );
            }

      return( strlen( string ) );

}     /* -- function GetAtomsFromData */

Atoms2Data( atoms, number_atoms, data )

Atom  atoms[];
int   number_atoms;
char  *data;

{     /* -- function Atoms2Data */
      int     i, length, position;

      position = 0; length = 0;

      for( i = 0; i < number_atoms; i++ )
            {
            Long2Bytes( (long) atoms[ i ], &data[ position ] );

            position += 4; }

      length = number_atoms * 4;

      return( length );

}     /* -- function Atoms2Data */

/*
 *    end of file
 */
```

APPENDING DATA TO A PROPERTY

Once you've got how to convert atoms down pat, the next step is to use atoms to define a property ID. Then you'll start the real fun—munging with properties.

The two major operations with properties are appending data to a property and reading data back in from a property. The act of appending to a property—even appending with zero bytes of data—creates a property. In fact, zero-length appends are a primary means for creating properties.

Conversely, the act of reading a property may destroy the property data. This is one reason why you usually want only one process to write to a property and one process to read from a property.

To append data to a property, call XChangeProperty():

```
Display         *display;
Window          window;
Atom            property;
Atom            target;    /* -- type of data, e.g., XA_STRING */
int             format;    /* -- e.g., 8, 16, 32 */
int             append_mode;
unsigned char   *data;
int             number_items;

append_mode = PropModeAppend;

XChangeProperty( display,
                window,
                property,
                target,
                format,
                append_mode,
                data,
                number_items );
```

The append_mode can be PropModeAppend (appends the new data to the end of whatever data is already stored in the property), PropModePrepend (places new data in the beginning of any preexisting data), or PropModeReplace (replaces all the data—if any—stored in the property with the new data).

The number of items (number_items) is not the number of bytes, but the number of items. That is, if the format is 32 (32 bits per item of data), the number of bytes will equal number_items * 4.

HANDLING PROPERTY APPEND ERRORS

The nastiest thing about using XChangeProperty() is that when you try to append to a property, an error may be generated by the X server, particularly a BadAlloc—out of memory—error. Any code that appends data to properties needs an X error handler, to trap and stop these errors from trapping your program. The default X error handler causes your program to exit, which is normally no fun.

X errors fall into two classes: not so bad and really bad. The really bad errors are called IO errors. They are generated when your program unexpectedly loses its connection to the X server or when another operating system call fails. IO errors are no fun to deal with. In fact, in this book, we'll let IO errors stop our programs, because there is really nothing for X example programs to do if the X server connection is broken. You, though, may want to trap these errors in your applications.

To trap the really nasty errors, first create a really nasty X error handler function. This function will be called with one parameter, a display pointer:

```
int ReallNastyXErrorHandler( display )

Display *display;

{       /* -- function ReallyNastyXErrorHandler */

...

/*
 *      This routine should not return.  Use
 *      setjmp/longjmp or just call exit()
 *      after you've cleaned up.
 */

...

exit( 1 );

}       /* -- function ReallyNastyXErrorHandler */
```

The ReallyNastyXErrorHandler() should not return. (If it does, X takes care of this for you and calls exit—again, no fun.) There's not much you can do, but if your program has more than one display connection, then you probably should handle X's IO errors.

Once you've created a function to handle these really nasty errors, you need to set your error handler to be called on IO or system call errors:

```
int      ReallyNastyXErrorHandler();

(void)   XSetIOErrorHandler( ReallyNastyXErrorHandler );
```

In Release 4, `XSetIOErrorHandler()` returns a pointer to the function that was the old error handler. In Release 3 and before, `XSetIOErrorHandler()` does not do this. If you are running all systems at Release 4 or higher, then you can save and reset the old error handler after going through a critical or special region. If some systems are at Release 3 or before, you're stuck.

The same situation exists for `XSetErrorHandler()`, shown in the next section. We've decided to ignore the return of `XSetErrorHandler()` and not count on the ability to save (and restore) the old error handlers. Again, one of those fun differences between releases. Returning the old error handler is a really useful thing to do, but it's too bad Xlib didn't do this from day one. (It's hard to complain about added functionality, but you must consider that many X users are still on Release 3 or Release 2 systems.)

TRAPPING NOT-SO-BadAlloc ERRORS

The second type of X error, the not-so-bad error (including the `BadAlloc` errors that were mentioned previously), can be trapped with a different error-handler function:

```
ErrorHandler( display, error_event )

Display        *display;
XErrorEvent    *error_event;

{   /* -- function ErrorHandler */

... Take care of errors here...

}   /* -- function ErrorHandler */
```

This error-handler function should return. It gets passed a display pointer and an XErrorEvent, which contains information about what caused the error:

```
typedef struct
    {
    int               type;
    Display           *display;
    unsigned long     serial;
    unsigned char     error_code;    /* -- BadAlloc, etc.*/
    unsigned char     request_code;  /* -- Protocol request */
    unsigned char     minor_code;    /* -- Minor request number */
    XID               resourceid;    /* -- Window, Atom, etc. */
    } XErrorEvent;
```

The resourceid, an XID, is the ID of the offending resource, such as a Window or Pixmap. It is usually defined as an unsigned long (check the include file <X11/X.h> to see how your system defines it). The serial field is the serial number of the request, which usually isn't very helpful unless you are debugging an X server.

The request_code is the major op-code of the failed request, and the minor_code is the minor op-code of the failed X request.

The error_code field will be one of the following bad things:

BadAccess

BadAlloc

BadAtom

BadColor

BadCursor

BadDrawable

BadFont

BadGC

BadIDChoice

BadImplmentation

BadLength

BadMatch

BadName

BadPixmap

BadRequest

BadValue

BadWindow

You set up your error handler with `XSetErrorHandler()`:

```
int      ErrorHandler();

(void) XSetErrorHandler( ErrorHandler );
```

Again, in Release 4, `XSetErrorHandler()` returns the previous error handler function.

GETTING MORE INFORMATION ABOUT ERRORS

Once you've received an error, you can call `XGetErrorText()` to get a terse text string about the error.

`XGetErrorText()` pulls out a line of text that helps describe the error. It puts the text in a character-string buffer, for which you must allocate space. You also need to pass the maximum length for a buffer that your code can accept. The contents of `XGetErrorText()` are as follows:

```
Display    *display;
int        error_code;
char       string[ BUFSIZE + 1 ];
int        max_string_length = BUFSIZE;

XGetErrorText( display,
           error_code,
           string,
           max_string_length );
```

`ErrorHandler()` calls `XGetErrorText()` to get an error message and then prints this message to `stderr`. We augment the message by converting the `error_code` field into a string—for example, `"BadAlloc"` for a `BadAlloc` error. Finally, we set two global values (`ErrorFlag` to `True` because an error occurred and `LastError` to the contents of the `error_code` field). These globals can be checked later, to see if we had an error.

Note, since X errors are typically generated by bad parameters passed to an Xlib function and X resources are usually used over and over again, one error will probably generate many more errors. This is because the `ErrorHandler()` error handler function does not really deal with the error except to report it. In your code, you may want to put in something to deal more with the error. This code just shows how to set the function up. The contents of `ErrorHandler()` are as follows:

```
ErrorHandler( display, error_event )

Display         *display;
XErrorEvent     *error_event;

{   /* -- function ErrorHandler */
    char    string[ BUFSIZE + 1 ];

    /*
     * Just store that we had an error in
     * a global that can be accessed later.
     */
    ErrorFlag = True;
    LastError = (int) error_event->error_code;

    /*
     * Find out the error message and print it.
     */
    XGetErrorText( display,
        error_event->error_code,
        string,
        BUFSIZE );

    fprintf( stderr, "X Error on display %s.\nResource %ld:  ",
        DisplayString( display ),
        error_event->resourceid );

    if ( ( error_event->error_code > 0 ) &&
        ( error_event->error_code < NUMBER_ERRORS ) )
        {
        fprintf( stderr, "%s (%s).\n", string,
            ErrorCodes[ error_event->error_code ] );
        }
    else
        {
        fprintf( stderr, "%s.\n", string );
        }

    fprintf( stderr, "Op code %d.%d, Error code %d\n",
        error_event->request_code,
```

```
        error_event->minor_code,
        error_event->error_code );

    /*
     * Place any special error-processing here
     */

    /* ...your code here... */

}   /* -- function ErrorHandler */
```

SOURCE CODE FOR error.c

The `error.c` file contains the `ErrorHandler()` function, as well as a number of functions to manipulate the global `ErrorFlag`. `ResetErrorFlag()` sets the variable `ErrorFlag` to `False` (no error). `NoError()` returns `True` if there is no error (i.e., `ErrorFlag = False`) and `False` if there is an error.

`SetErrorHandler()` is the initialization routine. It sets up `ErrorHandler()` as the Xlib error handler function. The contents of `error.c` are as follows:

error.c:

```
/*
 *      error.c
 *      X11 basic error handler.
 *      This code just handles normal errors
 *      like BadAlloc, and not fatal (IO)
 *      errors.
 *
 *      Routines:
 *      ErrorHandler( display, error_event )
 *      NoError()
 *      ResetErrorFlag()
 *      SetErrorHandler()
 */

#include  "xbook.h"

/*
 *      GLOBALS to keep the last error status
 */
```

```
int     ErrorFlag = False;
int     LastError = None;

/*
 * Global strings for error codes, numbers are defined in <X11/X.h>
 */
#define NUMBER_ERRORS   18

char    *ErrorCodes[ NUMBER_ERRORS ] =
            {
            "Success",                  /* -- 0 */
            "BadRequest",               /* -- 1 */
            "BadValue",                 /* -- 2 */
            "BadWindow",                /* -- 3 */
            "BadPixmap",                /* -- 4 */
            "BadAtom",                  /* -- 5 */
            "BadCursor",                /* -- 6 */
            "BadFont",                  /* -- 7 */
            "BadMatch",                 /* -- 8 */
            "BadDrawable",              /* -- 9 */
            "BadAccess",                /* -- 10 */
            "BadAlloc",                 /* -- 11 */
            "BadGC",                    /* -- 13 */
            "BadIDChoice",              /* -- 14 */
            "BadName",                  /* -- 15 */
            "BadLength",                /* -- 16 */
            "BadImplementation"         /* -- 17 */
        };

ErrorHandler( display, error_event )

Display         *display;
XErrorEvent     *error_event;

/*
 *      ErrorHandler() handles normal X errors.  It does
 *      not handler fatal IO errors (such as termination
 *      of the display connection).
 */

{       /* -- function ErrorHandler */
        char    string[ BUFSIZE + 1 ];

        /*
         * Just store that we had an error in
         * a global that can be accessed later.
```

```
     */
    ErrorFlag = True;
    LastError = (int) error_event->error_code;

    /*
     * Find out the error message and print it.
     */
    XGetErrorText( display,
        error_event->error_code,
        string,
        BUFSIZE );

    fprintf( stderr, "X Error on display %s.\nResource %ld:  ",
        DisplayString( display ),
        error_event->resourceid );

    if ( ( error_event->error_code > 0 ) &&
        ( error_event->error_code < NUMBER_ERRORS ) )
        {
        fprintf( stderr, "%s (%s).\n", string,
            ErrorCodes[ error_event->error_code ] );
        }
    else
        {
        fprintf( stderr, "%s.\n", string );
        }

    fprintf( stderr, "Op code %d.%d, Error code %d\n",
        error_event->request_code,
        error_event->minor_code,
        error_event->error_code );

    /*
     * Place any special error-processing here
     */

    /* ...your code here... */

}   /* -- function ErrorHandler */

NoError()

/*
 *      NoError() returns True if the GLOBAL ErrorFlag
 *      does not store an X error.  NoError() is usually
 *      combined with ResetError() so that you can reset
```

```
 *      the ErrorFlag with ResetError(), perform an X
 *      call that could generate an error, especially
 *      property-writing routines, and then call NoError()
 *      to check and see if an error occurred.
 */

{       /* -- function NoError */

        if ( ErrorFlag = = True )
           {
           return( False );
           }
        else
           {
           return( True );
           }

}       /* -- function NoError */

ResetErrorFlag()

{       /* -- function ResetErrorFlag */

        ErrorFlag = False;
        LastError = None;

}       /* -- function ResetErrorFlag */

SetErrorHandler()

/*
 *      SetErrorHandler() overrides the default
 *      Xlib error handler with the function ErrorHandler(),
 *      above.
 *      Note that in X11R4, XSetErrorHandler() returns
 *      the previous error-handler function.  In Release
 *      3 and below, though, XSetErrorHandler() does not
 *      return the previous handler.  So, to write portable
 *      code, we ignore the previous error handler.
 */

{       /* -- function SetErrorHandler */
        int     ErrorHandler();

        (void) XSetErrorHandler( ErrorHandler );

}       /* -- function SetErrorHandler */

/*
```

```
 *     end of file
 */
```

A FUNCTION FOR APPENDING DATA ONTO A PROPERTY

You need all those error-handling functions if you intend to append data to properties. Since appending data is the whole point of using properties for communication, we must set up an error handler.

AppendProperty() makes sure that ErrorHandler() will trap normal X errors, and then resets the global ErrorFlag. This way, if ErrorFlag later indicates an error (and we've only executed one Xlib function) we have a pretty good idea what caused the error. Next, AppendProperty() calls XChangeProperty() to write out the data bytes to the property, and then returns with True if ErrorHandler() has not been called with an error. We still may get an error later, but for now we'll assume everything went OK if the ErrorFlag is not yet set to True (in error.c).

AppendProperty() writes out the given data to the given property on the given window. The format parameter indicates whether the data consists of 8, 16, or 32-bit items (the server will swap bytes for different "endian" architectures). Remember that number_items is the number of items in data, not necessarily the number of bytes in data (they only match if the format is eight).

The contents of AppendProperty() are as follows:

```
AppendProperty( display, window, property, target, format, data, number_items )

Display     *display;
Window      window;
Atom        property;
Atom        target; int format;
char        *data;
int         number_items;

{           /* -- function AppendProperty */
            int     status = False;

            /*
             * Any routine that appends properties
             * can generate a BadAlloc error.
             */
```

```
        SetErrorHandler();

        if ( number_items > 0 )
        {
        ResetErrorFlag();

        XChangeProperty( display,
                window,
                property,
                target,
                format,
                PropModeAppend,
                data,
                number_items );

        /*
         * XChangeProperty() could generate
         * an error, especially a BadAlloc
         * error (if the server ran out of
         * memory). Only if no error was
         * generated are we OK.
         */
        status = NoError();
        }

    return( status );

}   /* -- function AppendProperty */
```

READING DATA FROM A PROPERTY

After all the work it takes to write out data to a property, you'll be happy to know that reading from a property takes a lot less effort.

`XGetWindowProperty()` reads data from a property. Its contents are as follows:

```
Display         *display;
Window          window;
Atom            property;
Atom            target;
int             format;
Atom            actual_target;
Atom            new_target;     /* -- XA_STRING, etc. */
```

```
    int                 actual_format, status;
    unsigned long       bytes_remaining;
    unsigned long       number_items;
    unsigned char       *data;
    long                position_offset;
    long                length_to_read;
    Bool                delete_flag;

#define FULL_LENGTH     8192L

    position_offset = 0L;           /* -- Read from beginning */
    length_to_read  = FULL_LENGTH;  /* -- read whole thing    */
    delete_flag     = True;         /* -- Delete when read    */

    status = XGetWindowProperty( display,
                window,
                property,
                position_offset,
                length_to_read,
                delete_flag, /* -- delete when read */
                new_target,
                &actual_target,
                &actual_format,
                &number_items,
                &bytes_remaining,
                &data );

    if ( ( status = = Success ) && ( number_items > 0 ) )
            {
            /* -- We have made it */

            ...

            /*
             */
             * Call XFree() on data when done with it
            if ( data )
            {
            XFree( data );
            }
    }
```

FULL_LENGTH is a magic value that states we want all the data in the property.

CONVERTING TARGETS

You have to be careful about what type of "target" you ask for. The target parameter to `XGetWindowProperty()` specifies what kind of data you want. `Target` is an atom and could be `XA_STRING` for a string type, `XA_INTEGER` for an integer type (32 bits per integer), and so on.

Many possible targets exist, but most are built on top of other `atoms`. For example, the `"LENGTH"` target (use `"LENGTH"` for the name passed to `XInternAtom)` is really stored in the `"INTEGER"` format `("INTEGER"` corresponds to the built-in atom, `XA_INTEGER)`. So, you need to convert the desired target into a form more palatable to the X server.

We've chosen to convert all the types used in later source code examples, and they include:

Desired target	Convert to	Built-in Atom
TIMESTAMP	INTEGER	XA_INTEGER
LENGTH	INTEGER	XA_INTEGER
CHARACTER_POSITION	SPAN	(really sets of two integers)
TARGETS	ATOM	XA_ATOM
CLIENT_WINDOW	WINDOW	XA_WINDOW

`ConvertTarget()` converts a given desired target atom to a better atom for use with reading property data. Its contents are as follows:

```
Atom ConvertTarget( display, target )

Display    *display;
Atom       target;

{       /* -- function ConvertTarget */
        Atom    new_target = XA_STRING; /* -- default */

        /*
         *      Compare for simple cases
         */
        if ( ( target = = XA_INTEGER ) || ( target = = XA_WINDOW ) ||
                  ( target = = XA_ATOM ) )
                  {
                  return( target );
                  }
```

```
        if ( ( CompareAtomWithName( display, target, "TIMESTAMP" ) = = True ) ||
        ( CompareAtomWithName( display, target, "LENGTH" ) = = True ) )
            {
            new_target = XA_INTEGER;
            }

        if ( CompareAtomWithName( display, target,
            "CHARACTER_POSITION" ) = = True )
            {
            new_target = XInternAtom( display, "SPAN", False );
            }

        if ( CompareAtomWithName( display, target, "TARGETS" ) = = True )
            {
            new_target = XA_ATOM;
            }

        if ( CompareAtomWithName( display, target, "CLIENT_WINDOW" ) = = True )
            {
            new_target = XA_WINDOW;
            }

        return( new_target );

}       /* -- function ConvertTarget */
```

A FUNCTION TO READ DATA FROM A PROPERTY

GetWindowProperty() reads data from a given property on a given window. It returns True if successful and False if not. It will also change the target atom to a value more appropriate (the actual value read in from the property).

The contents of GetWindowProperty() are as follows:

```
GetWindowProperty( display, window, property, target, number_items, data )

Display         *display;
Window          window;
Atom            property;
Atom            *target;
```

```
unsigned long  *number_items;
unsigned char  **data;

{   /* -- function GetWindowProperty */
    Atom                actual_target;
    Atom                new_target;
    int                 actual_format, status;
    unsigned long       bytes_remaining;

    new_target = ConvertTarget( display, *target );

    status = XGetWindowProperty( display,
                        window,
                        property,
                        0L,             /* -- offset */
                        FULL_LENGTH,
                        True,           /* -- delete when read */
                        new_target,
                        &actual_target,
                        &actual_format,
                        number_items,
                        &bytes_remaining, data );

if ( ( status != Success ) || ( *number_items < 1 ) )
            {
            if ( data )
                        {
                        XFree( data );
                        }

            return( False );
            }

    *target = actual_target;

    return( True );

}   /* -- function GetWindowProperty */
```

CONVERTING PROPERTY DATA TO A STRING

`Property2String()` converts data read in from a property into a text string. You can pass this text string to the `DrawStrings()` function described in chapter 16. `Property2String()` is a good help for debugging programs and is useful anytime you want to view the data in a property. It doesn't convert every property type, just a few common types which are used later on in the text.

`Property2String()` takes a display pointer, a target type (the type of property data you have), the property data, and a number of items you have in the data and returns a text string. Where the data contains lists of items, like many atom IDs, each item in the list is separated by a new line in the output string.

The contents of `Property2String()` are as follows:

```
Property2String( display, target, data, number_items, string )

Display     *display;
Atom        target;
char        *data;
int         number_items;
char        string[];

{           /* -- function Property2String */
            int      length = 0;

            if ( target = = XA_ATOM )  /* -- list of atoms */
                {
                length = GetAtomsFromData( display,
                                    data,
                                    number_items,
                                    string );
                }

            if ( target == XA_STRING )
                {
                (void) memcpy( string, data, number_items );

                length = number_items;
                }

            if ( ( target = = XA_INTEGER )   ||
                   ( target  == XA_WINDOW )  ||
                   ( CompareAtomWithName( display, target, "SPAN" ) = = True ) )
```

```
                {
                length = ConvertIntegers( data,
                                          number_items,
                                          string,
                                          target );
                }

        if ( CompareAtomWithName( display, target, "TIMESTAMP" ) == True )
                {
                length = ConvertIntegers( data,
                                          number_items,
                                          string,
                                          target );
                }

        return( length );

}       /* -- function Property2String */
```

SOURCE CODE FOR prop.c

The file `prop.c` contains a number of useful utility functions for working with properties on windows. Its contents are as follows:

prop.c:

```
/*
 *      property.c
 *      X11 Property functions
 */

#include  "xbook.h"

AppendProperty( display, window, property, target, format, data, number_items )

Display    *display;
Window     window;
Atom       property;
Atom       target;
int        format;
char       *data;
int        number_items;

/*
 *      AppendProperty() appends the given property onto
```

```
 *          the given window.  It returns True if no errors were
 *          generated, False if an error was generated.
 */

{           /* -- function AppendProperty */
            int      status = False;

            /*
             *      Any routine that appends properties
             *      can generate a BadAlloc error.
             */
            SetErrorHandler();

            if ( number_items > 0 )
                    {
                    ResetErrorFlag();

                    XChangeProperty( display,
                        window,
                        property,
                        target,
                        format,
                        PropModeAppend,
                        data,
                        number_items );

                    /*
                     * XChangeProperty() could generate
                     * an error, especially a BadAlloc
                     * error (if the server ran out of
                     * memory). Only if no error was
                     * generated are we OK.
                     */
                    status = NoError();
                    }

            return( status );

}           /* -- function AppendProperty */

GetWindowProperty( display, window, property, target, number_items, data )

Display             *display;
Window              window;
Atom                property;
Atom                *target;
```

```
unsigned long      *number_items;
unsigned char      **data;

/*
 *     GetWindowProperty() calls XGetWindowProperty()
 *     to get the given property.
 *
 *     If the return is True, call XFree( data ) when done
 *     with the data *
 */

{      /* -- function GetWindowProperty */
       Atom                    actual_target;
       Atom                    new_target;
       int                     actual_format, status;
       unsigned long           bytes_remaining;

       new_target = ConvertTarget( display, *target );

       status = XGetWindowProperty( display,
                    window,
                    property,
                    0L, /* -- offset */
                    FULL_LENGTH,
                    True, /* -- delete when read */
                    new_target,
                    &actual_target,
                    &actual_format,
                    number_items,
                    &bytes_remaining,
                    data );

       if ( ( status != Success ) || ( *number_items < 1 ) )
           {
           if ( data )
               {
               XFree( data );
               }

           return( False );
           }

       *target = actual_target;

       return( True );
```

```
}       /* -- function GetWindowProperty */

Atom ConvertTarget( display, target )

Display    *display;
Atom       target;

/*
 *      ConvertTarget() converts a target
 *      from a specific request to a general
 *      data type, needed for a call
 *      to XGetWindowProperty().  The
 *      Default type is XA_STRING.*
 */

{   /* -- function ConvertTarget */
    Atom    new_target = XA_STRING;

    /*
    *       Compare for simple cases
     */
    if ( ( target = = XA_INTEGER ) || ( target = = XA_WINDOW ) ||
            ( target = = XA_ATOM ) )
            {
            return( target );
            }

    if ( ( CompareAtomWithName( display, target, "TIMESTAMP" ) = = True ) ||
            ( CompareAtomWithName( display, target, "LENGTH" ) = = True ) )
            {
            new_target = XA_INTEGER;
            }

    if ( CompareAtomWithName( display, target,
            "CHARACTER_POSITION" ) = = True )
            {
            new_target = XInternAtom( display, "SPAN", False );
            }

    if ( CompareAtomWithName( display, target, "TARGETS" ) = = True )
            {
            new_target = XA_ATOM;
            }

    if ( CompareAtomWithName( display, target, "CLIENT_WINDOW" ) = = True )
            {
```

```
            new_target = XA_WINDOW;
            }

    return( new_target );

}   /* -- function ConvertTarget */

GetFormat( target )

Atom    target;

/*
 *      GetFormat() returns the format for
 *      a given data type: 8, 16, or 32.
 *      Since we support only a few types,
 *      the default format is assumed to be 32.
 */

{       /* -- function GetFormat */
        int     format = 32;

        if ( target == XA_STRING )
                {
                format = 8;
                }

        return( format );

}   /* -- function GetFormat */

Property2String( display, target, data, number_items, string )

Display     *display;
Atom        target;
char        *data;
int         number_items;
char        string[];

/*
 *          Property2String() converts raw data from a property
 *          into an ASCII string.  This string may have a number
 *          of newlines ('\n') in it, separating numbers and
 *          Atom names.  returns number of bytes placed in string,
 *          or 0 for failure.
 */
```

```
{           /* -- function Property2String */
            int     length = 0;

            if ( target = = XA_ATOM )  /* -- list of atoms */
                    {
                    length = GetAtomsFromData( display,
                                               data,
                                               number_items,
                                               string );
                    }

            if ( target = = XA_STRING )
            {
            (void) memcpy( string, data, number_items );

            length = number_items;
            }

        if ( ( target = = XA_INTEGER )||
            ( target = = XA_WINDOW )   ||
            ( CompareAtomWithName( display, target, "SPAN" ) =  = True ) )
        {
            length = ConvertIntegers( data,
                                      number_items,
                                      string,
                                      target );
            }

        if ( CompareAtomWithName( display, target, "TIMESTAMP" ) = = True )
            {
            length = ConvertIntegers( data,
                                      number_items,
                                      string,
                                      target );
            }

        return( length );

}       /* -- function Property2String */

/*
 * end of file
 */
```

STRATEGY FOR EXCHANGING DATA WITH PROPERTIES

Any program with a property ID (`Atom`) and a Window ID can write data to that property on that window. Any program can call `XSelectInput()`, specify an interest in `PropertyNotify` events (pass a `PropertyChangeMask`), and therefore be notified when any data is written to that property. This is the key to exchanging data with properties.

Generally, one application will be chosen as a data producer. The producer writes to a given property on the root window.

The consumer of the data selects an interest in `PropertyNotify` events. When a `PropertyNotify` event arrives, the consumer reads the data from the property using the delete mode (of `True`). (The delete mode specifies that the data is to be deleted after reading, so the data will not be read twice.)

This, of course, is only one scheme for exchanging data via properties. For two-way communication, you could have a second property and reverse roles for the second property—the producer would become the consumer, and so on. You could also have multiple producers, with many programs writing to a particular property.

The programs that follow use the first, simplest method: one program, `propsend`, acts as a producer and writes to a given property on the root window. The second program, `reminder`, acts as a consumer and reads the data from the property. Like the rest of the programs in section III, both `propsend` and `reminder` place a window on the screen where you can manipulate the data.

SENDING DATA TO ANOTHER PROGRAM WITH Propsend

`Propsend` appends data to a given property on the root window of a screen. The data is text typed in by the user. When a line of text is typed in, the user can press a mouse button over the "Send" push-button window and `propsend` will do the rest. Figure 17-1 shows the `propsend` push-button windows.

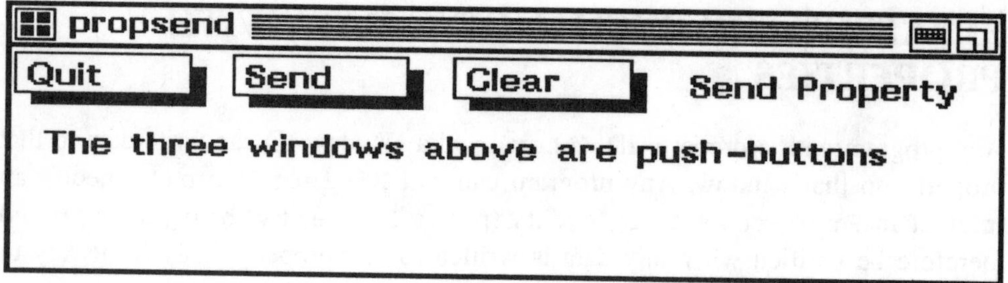

Figure 17-1. The Propsend Program

THE propsend EVENT LOOP

`Propsend` is similar to most of the programs in section III and follows the basic outline described in chapter 16. (The whole purpose of this similarity is to allow us space to describe the methods for data interchange, rather than the details of the part of the program that X requires to allow for an interactive user interface.) The most interesting part of `propsend` is its event-handling function, `EventLoop()`.

On a `ButtonPress` event in the `Send` push-button window, `propsend` will append the current data (stored in the global `PropertyData`) onto the property on the root window, using `AppendProperty()`, as developed previously in this chapter. In this (and all cases here) the data sent is text data.

`KeyPress` events are fed to the `TextEdit()` function (which edits the global string `PropertyData`). `ClientMessage` events are sent to `IsDeleteWindow()` to determine if the program should exit or not. Setting the global `QuitFlag` to `True` (also done in the `QuitApplication` function) will cause the program to break out of the event loop, clean up, and quit.

```
...

case ClientMessage:
        if( IsDeleteWindow( display, &event ) = = True )
                {
                QuitFlag = True;
                }
        break;

...
```

The SendData() function handles the job of appending the text entered by the user onto a property on the root window. Since communication involves both a sender and a receiver, we expect another program (reminder, later on) to read the data in this property. We use a name of "__XBOOK" for our property, under the assumption that no one else will be using this name.

The contents of SendData() are as follows:

```
SendData( display, window )

Display     *display;
Window      window;

{           /* -- function SendData */
            Window  rootwindow;
            Atom    xbook_atom;
            int     status;

            rootwindow = RootWindow( display,
                   DefaultScreen( display ) );

            xbook_atom = XInternAtom( display, PROP_NAME, False );

            if ( xbook_atom != (Atom) None )
                {
                status = AppendProperty( display,
                        rootwindow,
                        xbook_atom, /* -- property */
                        XA_STRING, /* -- target */ 8, /* -- 8 bits per item */
                        PropertyData,
                        PropertyLength );
                }
            else
                {
                status = False;
                }

            if ( status = = False )
                {
                XBell( display, 0 );
                }

}           /* -- function SendData */
```

SOURCE CODE FOR propsend.c

The file `propsend.c` contains the `main()` function for the `propsend` program, as well as functions to implement `propsend`'s interface. The code is fairly straightforward, so we won't go into detail here. `QuitApplication()`, `SendData()`, and `ClearData()` are call-back functions for the push-button interface. Again, it's easier to use a push-button interface than to describe one.

The contents of `propsend.c` are as follows:

```
propsend.c:
/*
 * propsend.c
 *
 * Program to send text-string information
 * via a property on the root window of a given display.
 */

#include  "xbook.h"

/*
 * Propsend's Icon
 */
#include "propsend.xb"

 /*
 * This message will be displayed in the window
 */
#define  MESSAGE     "Send Property"

/*
 * Top-level window Globals
 */
int         RefreshFlag = False;      /* -- do we need to redraw? */
int         QuitFlag    = False;      /* -- should we quit now?   */

/*
 * Global data to send to __XBOOK property
 * on root window.
 */
char        PropertyData[ (4 * FULL_LENGTH) + 1 ];
int         PropertyLength = 0;

main( argc, argv )
```

```
int     argc;
char    *argv[];

{       /* -- main */
        Display         *display;
        int             screen;
        Window          window;
        GC              gc;
        int             x, y, width, height;
        XFontStruct     *font;
        Pixmap          icon;
        int             font_height;
        unsigned long   black, white;

        /*
         *      Set up X connection
         */
        display= SetUpDisplay( argc, argv,
                                &screen );

        black       = BlackPixel( display, screen );
        white       = WhitePixel( display, screen );

        /*
         * Check size and location of window
         */
        x           = 10;
        y           = 10;
        width       = 360;
        height      = 100;
        CheckGeometry( argc, argv,
            DisplayWidth( display, screen ),
            DisplayHeight( display, screen ),
            &x, &y, &width, &height );

        /*
         * Create Window
         */
        window      = TopWindow( display, x, y, width, height,
                        propsend_bits, propsend_width, propsend_height,
                    &icon, &gc );

/*
 * Load font
 */
font = LoadFont( display, gc, argc, argv, "variable" );
```

```
font_height = font->ascent + font->descent;

/*
 * Store values for window manager
 */
SetNormalHints( display, window,
        x, y, width, height );

SetWMHints( display, window, icon );

NameWindow( display, window,
        "propsend", "propsend", "Propsend" );

SetICCCM( display, window,
        argc, argv );

/*
 * Clear out property text global
 */
PropertyData[ 0 ] = ' ';
PropertyLength = 1;

XFlush( display );

/*
 * Create buttons of ruser interface items */
MakeButtons( display, window,
        black, white, font->fid );

/*
 * Map windows
 */
MapWindow( display, window );

/*
 *      Handle any events
 */
while( QuitFlag = = False )
        {
        EventLoop( display,
                window, gc, font,
                &width, &height );

        if ( RefreshFlag = = True )
                {
```

```
                Refresh( display, window, gc, font_height );

                RefreshFlag = False;
                }

            }

        /*
         * Shut down
         */
        XFreeFont( display, font );
        XFreePixmap( display, icon );

        CloseDisplay( display, window, gc );

        exit( 0 );

}       /* -- main */

SendData( display, window )

Display     *display;
Window      window;

{       /* -- function SendData */
        Window  rootwindow;
        Atom    xbook_atom;
        int     status;

        rootwindow = RootWindow( display,
                            DefaultScreen( display ) );

        xbook_atom = XInternAtom( display, PROP_NAME, False );

        if ( xbook_atom != (Atom) None )
                {
                status = AppendProperty( display,
                                rootwindow,
                                xbook_atom, /* -- property */
                                XA_STRING, /* -- target */
                                8, /* -- 8 bits per item */
                                PropertyData,
                                PropertyLength );

                }
        else
                {
```

```
                status = False;
                }

        if ( status = = False )
                {
                XBell( display, 0 );
                }

}       /* -- function SendData */

ClearData( display, window )
Display *display;
Window  window;

{       /* -- function ClearData */

        /*
         * Clear out property text global
         */
        (void) strcpy( PropertyData, " " );
        PropertyLength = 1;

        XClearWindow( display, window );

        RefreshFlag = True;

}       /* -- function ClearData */

EventLoop( display, window, gc, font, width, height )

Display         *display;
Window          window;
GC              gc;
XFontStruct     *font;
int             *width, *height;

/*
 *      EventLoop() handles generic X events, but passes
 *      most events on to specific functions to handle
 *      the particular event.
 *
 *
 */

{       /* -- function EventLoop */
        XEvent  event;
```

```
KeySym  keysym;

/*
 *      Block on input, awaiting
 *      an event from X.
 */
NextEvent( display, False,
        *width, *height,
        &event,
        &keysym );

/*
 * Check if the event was taken care of by
 * the push-button interface.
 */
if ( ButtonEvent( display, &event ) == True )
        {
        return( True );
        }

/*
 *      Decode the event and call
 *      a specific routine to
 *      handle it.
 */
switch( event.type )
        {
        case ClientMessage:
                if( IsDeleteWindow( display, &event ) == True )
                        {
                        QuitFlag = True;
                        }
                break;
        case Expose:
                RefreshFlag = True;
                break;

        case ConfigureNotify:
                *width = event.xconfigure.width;
                *height = event.xconfigure.height;
                break;
        case KeyPress:
                TextEdit( display, window,
                        gc, font,
                        5, 2 * BUTTON_HEIGHT,
```

```
                                        keysym,
                                        PropertyData, BUFSIZE );

                                PropertyLength = strlen( PropertyData );
                                break;
                        }

        return( True );

}       /* -- function EventLoop */

QuitApplication( display, window )

Display *display;
Window  window;

{       /* -- function QuitApplication */

        QuitFlag = True;

}       /* -- function QuitApplication */

MakeButtons( display, window, fore, back, font_id )

Display                 *display;
Window                  window;
unsigned long           fore, back;
Font                    font_id;

{       /* -- function MakeButtons */
        int             QuitApplication();
        int             SendData();
        int             ClearData();

        CreateButton( display, window,
                        1, 2,
                        fore, back, font_id,
                        "Quit",
                        QuitApplication );

        CreateButton( display, window, BUTTON_WIDTH + 11, 2,
                        fore, back, font_id,
                        "Send",
                        SendData );

        CreateButton( display, window,
```

```
                ( 2 *BUTTON_WIDTH ) + 22, 2,
                fore, back, font_id,
                "Clear",
                ClearData );

}       /* -- function MakeButtons */

Refresh( display, window, gc, font_height )

Display         *display;
Window          window;
GC              gc;
int             font_height;

{       /* -- function Refresh */

        XDrawImageString( display, window, gc,
                ( 3 * ( BUTTON_WIDTH + 11 ) ) + 5,
                BUTTON_HEIGHT - 5,
                MESSAGE, strlen( MESSAGE ) );

        DrawStrings( display, window, gc,
                font_height,
                5, 2 * BUTTON_HEIGHT,
                PropertyData, PropertyLength );

        /*
         * Display any selection data
         */
        XFlush( display );

}       /* -- function Refresh */

/*
 *      end of file
 */
```

AN ICON FOR propsend

`Propsend`'s icon shown in figure 17-2 is stored in `propsend.xb`.

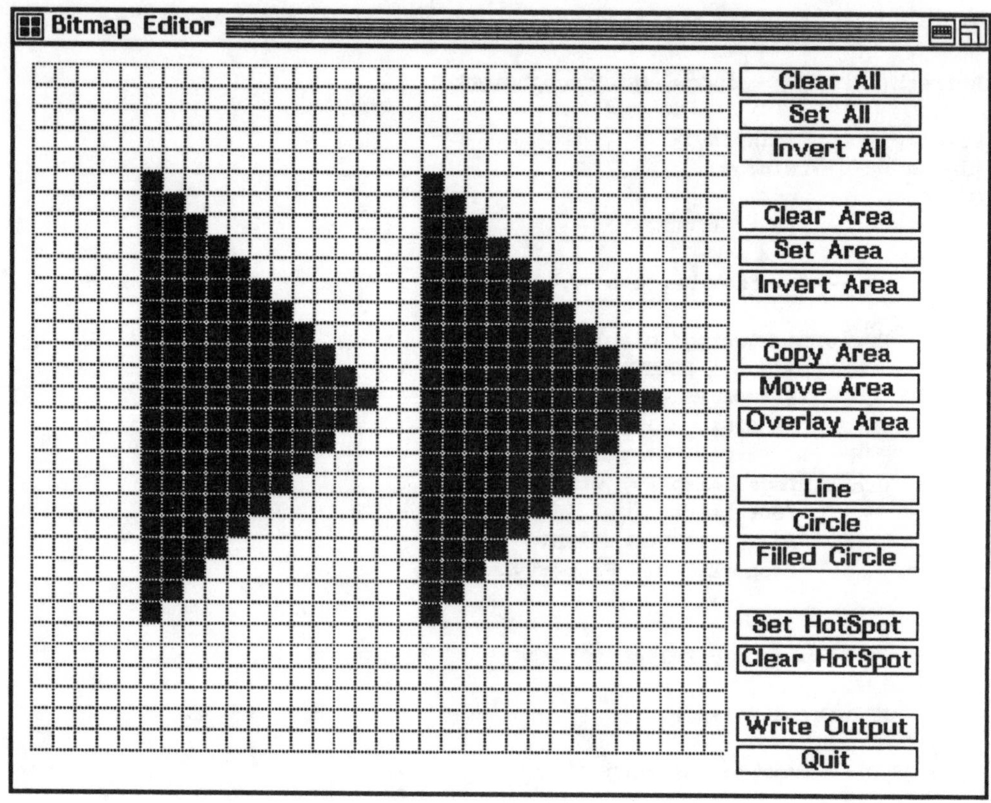

Figure 17-2. Bitmap Icon for Propsend

The contents for `propsend.xb` are as follows:

```
propsend.xb:
#define propsend_width 32
#define propsend_height 32
static char propsend_bits[] = {
0x00, 0x00, 0x00, 0x00, 0x00, 0x00, 0x00, 0x00, 0x00, 0x00, 0x00, 0x00,
0x00, 0x00, 0x00, 0x00, 0x00, 0x00, 0x00, 0x00, 0x20, 0x00, 0x04, 0x00,
0x60, 0x00, 0x0c, 0x00, 0xe0, 0x00, 0x1c, 0x00, 0xe0, 0x01, 0x3c, 0x00,
0xe0, 0x03, 0x7c, 0x00, 0xe0, 0x07, 0xfc, 0x00, 0xe0, 0x0f, 0xfc, 0x01,
```

```
0xe0, 0x1f, 0xfc, 0x03, 0xe0, 0x3f, 0xfc, 0x07, 0xe0, 0x7f, 0xfc, 0x0f,
0xe0, 0xff, 0xfc, 0x1f, 0xe0, 0x7f, 0xfc, 0x0f, 0xe0, 0x3f, 0xfc, 0x07,
0xe0, 0x1f, 0xfc, 0x03, 0xe0, 0x0f, 0xfc, 0x01, 0xe0, 0x07, 0xfc, 0x00,
0xe0, 0x03, 0x7c, 0x00, 0xe0, 0x01, 0x3c, 0x00, 0xe0, 0x00, 0x1c, 0x00,
0x60, 0x00, 0x0c, 0x00, 0x20, 0x00, 0x04, 0x00, 0x00, 0x00, 0x00, 0x00,
0x00, 0x00, 0x00, 0x00, 0x00, 0x00, 0x00, 0x00, 0x00, 0x00, 0x00, 0x00,
0x00, 0x00, 0x00, 0x00, 0x00, 0x00, 0x00, 0x00};
```

COMPILING propsend

`Propsend` uses the following source files:

`atom.c`	
`button.c`	*(from chapter 16)*
`bytes.c`	*(from chapter 15)*
`cursor.c`	*(from chapter 7)*
`display.c`	*(from chapter 2)*
`error.c`	
`event.c`	*(from chapter 5)*
`font.c`	*(from chapter 8)*
`gc.c`	*(from chapter 4)*
`icccm.c`	*(from chapter 15)*
`pixmap.c`	*(from chapter 6)*
`prop.c`	
`propsend.c`	
`textedit.c`	*(from chapter 16)*
`topwind.c`	*(from chapter 9)*
`xstring.c`	*(from chapter 16)*
`window.c`	*(from chapter 3)*
`propsend.xb`	

On Unix-based systems, you can use the `Makefile` in appendix C, with:

```
make propsend
```

Or, you can compile with:

```
cc -o propsend atom.c button.c bytes.c cursor.c display.c error.c \
      event.c font.c gc.c icccm.c pixmap.c prop.c propsend.c \
      textedit.c topwind.c xstring.c window.c -lX11
```

As you can tell, its a lot easier to use the Makefile.

RUNNING propsend

Propsend needs no command-line parameters. You may specify a window geometry, a display name and a font name, all in the usual manner:

```
-display display_name
-geometry geometry_spec
        (e.g., 120x300+40+13)
-font font_name
```

DETECTING WHEN A PROPERTY HAS BEEN WRITTEN TO

To detect when property data changes on a given window, pass a PropertyChangemask to XSelectInput(). When a property on that window changes, your application will receive a PropertyNotify event:

```
Display    *display;
Window     rootwindow;

XSelectInput( display, rootwindow, PropertyChangeMask );
```

Note that more than one program can select PropertyNotify events on the same window (in this case, the root window).

PropertyNotify EVENTS

A PropertyNotify event appears as follows:

```
typedef struct
        {
        int                 type;   /* --PropertyNotify */
        unsigned long       serial;
        Bool                send_event;
        Display             *display;
        Window              window;
        Atom                atom;
        Time                time;
        int                 state;
        } XPropertyEvent;
```

In our case, we're only interested in a certain property ("__XBOOK") changing. The root window typically has many properties on it, so we have to filter out PropertyNotify events. We look at the atom field to see if the property changed matches the property we are interested in ("__XBOOK" again).

The state field can be PropertyNewValue or PropertyDelete. We're only interested in PropertyNewValue states.

In the EventLoop() function the code looking at PropertyNotify events appears as follows:

```
Display     *display;
XEvent      event;
Window      rootwindow, window;
Atom        xbook_atom;

...

case PropertyNotify:
            /*
             * Intern "__XBOOK" atom
             */
            xbook_atom = XInternAtom( display,
                                      PROP_NAME, False );

            if ( xbook_atom = = (Atom) None )
                {
                break;
                }
```

```
                if ( ( xbook_atom == event.xproperty.atom) &&
                    ( event.xproperty.state == PropertyNewValue ) )
                        {
                        RefreshFlag = GetReminderData( display, rootwindow,
                                                       xbook_atom );

                        if ( RefreshFlag = = True )
                                {
                                /*
                                 * Clear window if data has changed
                                 */
                                XClearWindow( display, window );
                                }
                    }
            break;

        ...
```

Note that `RefreshFlag` is a global int.

READING IN THE __XBOOK PROPERTY DATA

`GetReminderData()` calls `GetWindowProperty()` to grab the new data in the `"__XBOOK"` property on the root window. This data will have been written there by the `propsend` program. We assume that the property data was stored as a text string (using the built-in atom ID of `XA_STRING` or the atom for `"STRING"`). We store the new data in the global character string `PropertyData`. The global int `PropertyLength` is the number of bytes used in `PropertyData`.

The contents of `GetReminderData()` are as follows:

```
GetReminderData( display, window, property )

Display *display;
Window      window;
Atom        property;

{           /* -- function GetReminderData */
            Atom        target;
            char        *data;
```

```
        int         number_items;
        int         status;

        target = XA_STRING;

        status = GetWindowProperty( display, window,
                        property,
                        &target,
                        &number_items,
                        &data );

        if ( ( status = = True ) && ( number_items > 0 ) &&
                ( data != (char *) NULL ) )
                {
                if ( number_items > FULL_LENGTH )
                    {
                    number_items = FULL_LENGTH;
                    }

                (void) memcpy( PropertyData, data, number_items );

                PropertyLength = number_items;

                XFree( data );
                }

        return( status );

}       /* -- function GetReminderData */
```

Reminder, A PROGRAM TO READ DATA FROM A PROPERTY

Reminder, like propsend, uses the same base interface code. It first appends one byte (a blank space) to the "__XBOOK" property. This creates the property if it doesn't yet exist. Then, reminder waits until the "__XBOOK" property on the root window has been changed. When that happens, reminder reads in and displays the contents of the property with the GetReminderData() function.

On Release 4 systems, pressing the "Hide" push button will cause the window to be withdrawn. This creates a program that can pop up when a message is received (perhaps from another display, as seen in section IV).

HIDING A WINDOW

The `HideWindow()` function (a push-button call-back function) "hides" the given window by changing the window to what is called withdrawn state. A window is in withdrawn state when the window is unmapped (usually via `XWithdrawWindow` or `XUnmapWindow`). Unmapped windows are not visible on the display.

`HideWindow()` depends on the Xlib function `XWithdrawWindow()`, a function that is only available on Release 4 (and later) systems.

```
Display    *display;
Window     window;
int        screen;

XWithdrawWindow( display, window, screen );
```

The contents of `HideWindow()` are as follows:

```
HideWindow( display, window )

Display    *display;
Window     window;

{          /* -- function HideWindow */

#ifdef     X11R4
           HideFlag = True;

           XWithdrawWindow( display, window,
              DefaultScreen( display ) );

#endif

}          /* -- function HideWindow */
```

To restore the withdrawn window, call `MapWindow()`:

```
Display    *display;
Window     window;

MapWindow( display, window );
```

We call `MapWindow()` whenever we want to refresh the window (and it has been hidden).

SOURCE CODE FOR reminder.c

The contents of `reminder.c` are as follows:

reminder.c:

```
/*
 *      reminder.c
 *      X11 program that pops up a window and draws text
 *      whenever a given property on the root window
 */

#include    "xbook.h"

/*
 *      Include Icon shape
 */
#include    "reminder.xb"

/*
 *      Message to be displayed in top-level window
 */
#define   MESSAGE   "A Reminder message:"

/*
 *      Top-level window Globals
 */
int     RefreshFlag = False;        /* -- do we need to redraw window?  */
int     QuitFlag    = False;        /* -- should we quit now?           */
int     HideFlag    = False;        /* -- should the window go away now? */

/*
 *      Global data received from __XBOOK property
 *      on root window. FULL_LENGTH = 8192
 */
char    PropertyData[ (4 * FULL_LENGTH) + 1 ];
int     PropertyLength = 0;

main( argc, argv )
```

```
int     argc;
char    *argv[];

{       /* -- function main */
        Display         *display;
        int             screen;
        Window          rootwindow, window;
        GC              gc;
        int             x, y, width, height;
        XFontStruct     *font;
        Pixmap          icon;
        int             font_height;
        unsigned long   black, white;
        Atom            xbook_atom;

        /*
         *      Set up X connection
         */
        display= SetUpDisplay( argc, argv,
                                &screen );

        rootwindow = RootWindow( display, screen );
        black      = BlackPixel( display, screen );
        white      = WhitePixel( display, screen );

        /*
         * Check size and location of window
         */
        x       = 10;
        y       = 10;
        width   = 350;
        height  = 100;
        CheckGeometry( argc, argv,
            DisplayWidth( display, screen ),
            DisplayHeight( display, screen ),
            &x, &y, &width, &height );

        /*
         * Create Window
         */
        window     = TopWindow( display, x, y, width, height,
                        reminder_bits, reminder_width, reminder_height,
                        &icon, &gc );

        /*
         * Load font
         */
```

```
font = LoadFont( display, gc, argc, argv, "variable" );

font_height = font->ascent + font->descent;

/*
 * Store values for window manager
 */
SetNormalHints( display, window,
       x, y, width, height );

SetWMHints( display, window, icon );

NameWindow( display, window,
       "reminder", "reminder", "Reminder" );

SetICCCM( display, window,
       argc, argv );

XFlush( display );

/*
 * Create buttons of ruser interface items
 */
MakeButtons( display, window,
       black, white, font->fid );

/*
 * Watch for Property changes on root
 */
XSelectInput( display, rootwindow, PropertyChangeMask );

/*
 * Check for initial data
 */
PropertyData[ 0 ] = ' ';
PropertyData[ 1 ] = '\0';
PropertyLength = 1;

xbook_atom = XInternAtom( display, PROP_NAME, False );

if ( xbook_atom != (Atom) None )
    {
    /*
     * Make sure property exists
     */
    AppendProperty( display, rootwindow, xbook_atom,
          XA_STRING, 8, PropertyData,PropertyLength );
```

```
            }

        /*
         * Map windows
         */
        MapWindow( display, window );

        /*
         *      Handle any events
         */
        while( QuitFlag = = False )
                {
                EventLoop( display,
                        rootwindow, window,
                        &width, &height );

                if ( RefreshFlag = = True )
                        {
                        if ( HideFlag = = True )
                                {
                                MapWindow( display, window );

                                HideFlag = False;
                                }

                        Refresh( display, window, gc, font_height );

                        RefreshFlag = False;
                        }

                }

        /*
         * Shut down
         */
        XFreeFont( display, font );
        XFreePixmap( display, icon );
        CloseDisplay( display, window, gc );

        exit( 0 );

}       /* -- function main */

EventLoop( display, rootwindow, window, width, height )

Display         *display;
```

```
Window          rootwindow, window;
int             *width, *height;

/*
 *      EventLoop() handles generic X events, but passes
 *      most events on to specific functions to handle
 *      the particular event.
 *
 *
 */

{       /* -- function EventLoop */
        XEvent          event;
        KeySym          keysym;
        Atom            xbook_atom;

        /*
         *      Block on input, awaiting
         *      an event from X.
         */
        NextEvent( display, False,
                *width, *height,
                &event,
                &keysym );

        /*
         * Check if button interface handles the
         * event.
         */
        if ( ButtonEvent( display, &event ) = = True )
                {
                return( True );
                }

        /*
         *      Decode the event and call
         *      a specific routine to
         *      handle it.
         */
        switch( event.type )
                {
                case ClientMessage:
                        if( IsDeleteWindow( display, &event ) = = True )
                                {
                                QuitFlag = True;
                                }
```

```
                    break;
                case PropertyNotify:
                    xbook_atom = XInternAtom( display,
                                    PROP_NAME,
                                    False );

                    if ( xbook_atom = = (Atom) None )
                        {
                        break;
                        }

                    if ( ( xbook_atom = = event.xproperty.atom) &&
                         ( event.xproperty.state = = PropertyNewValue ) )
                        {
                        RefreshFlag = GetReminderData( display,
                                        rootwindow,
                                        xbook_atom );

                        if ( RefreshFlag = = True )
                            {
                            XClearWindow( display, window );
                            }
                        }
                    break;
                case Expose:
                    RefreshFlag = True;
                    break;

                case ConfigureNotify:
                    *width = event.xconfigure.width;
                    *height = event.xconfigure.height;
                    break;
                }

        return( True );

}       /* -- function EventLoop */

QuitApplication( display, window )

Display     *display;
Window      window;

{       /* -- function QuitApplication */
```

```
        QuitFlag = True;

}       /* -- function QuitApplication */

HideWindow( display, window )

Display *display;
Window     window;

{       /* -- function HideWindow */

#ifdef X11R4
        HideFlag = True;

        XWithdrawWindow( display, window,
            DefaultScreen( display ) );

#endif

}       /* -- function HideWindow */

MakeButtons( display, window, fore, back, font_id )

Display            *display;
Window             window;
unsigned long      fore, back;
Font               font_id;

{       /* -- function MakeButtons */
            int    QuitApplication();
            int    HideWindow();

        CreateButton( display, window,
                   1, 2, fore, back,
                   font_id, "Quit",
                   QuitApplication );

#ifdef X11R4
        CreateButton( display, window, BUTTON_WIDTH + 11, 2,
                   fore, back, font_id,
                   "Hide", HideWindow );
#endif

}       /* -- function MakeButtons */
```

```
Refresh( display, window, gc, font_height )

Display             *display;
Window              window;
GC                  gc;
int                 font_height;

{       /* -- function Refresh */

        XDrawImageString( display, window, gc,
                    ( 2 * ( BUTTON_WIDTH + 5 ) ) + 5,
                    BUTTON_HEIGHT - 5, MESSAGE,
                    strlen( MESSAGE ) );

        DrawStrings( display, window, gc,
                    font_height, 5, 2 *
                    BUTTON_HEIGHT, PropertyData,
                    PropertyLength );

        XFlush( display );

}       /* -- function Refresh */

GetReminderData( display, window, property )

Display     *display;
Window      window;
Atom        property;

/*
 *          GetReminderData() gets the data from
 *          the given property on the given window
 *          and then sets the global PropertyData
 *          to contain that data.
 */

{       /* -- function GetReminderData */
            Atom    target;
            char    *data;
            int     number_items;
            int     status;

        target = XA_STRING;
```

```
        status = GetWindowProperty( display, window,
                        property,
                        &target, &number_items,
                        &data );

        if ( ( status = = True ) && ( number_items > 0 ) &&
            ( data != (char *) NULL ) )
            {
          if (number_items > FULL_LENGTH )
              {
              number_items = FULL_LENGTH;
              }

        (void) memcpy( PropertyData, data, number_items );

        PropertyLength = number_items;

        XFree( data ); }

    return( status );

}       /* -- function GetReminderData */

/*
 * end of file
 */
```

AN ICON FOR reminder

`Reminder`'s icon is shown in figure 17-3.

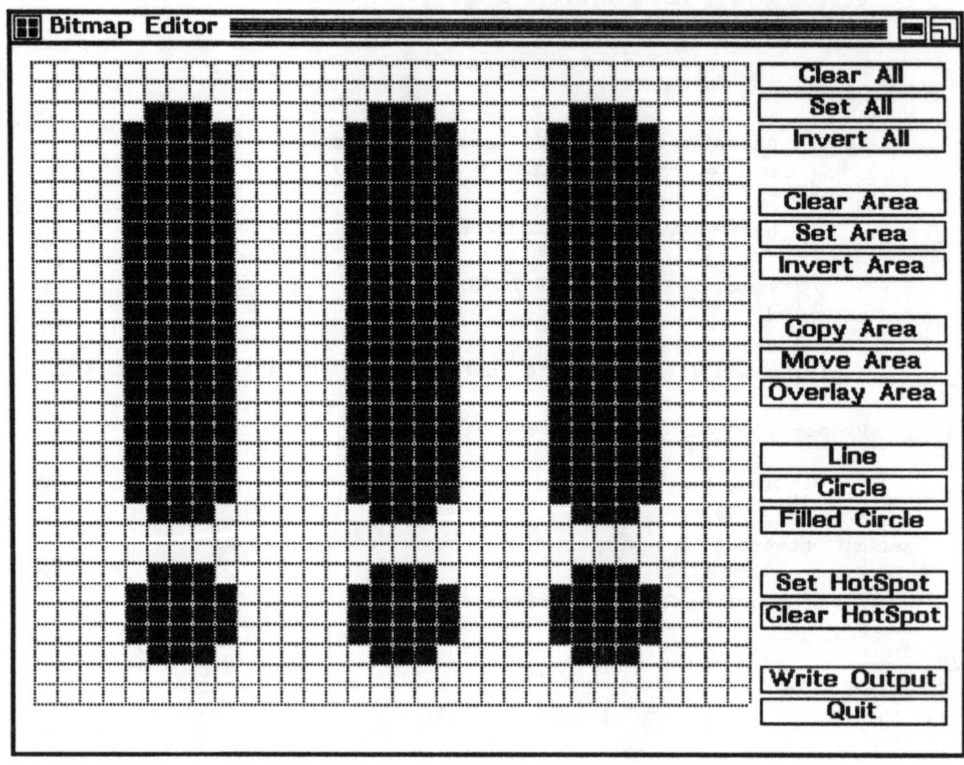

Figure 17-3. Icon Bitmap for Reminder

The `icon` bitmap's contents are as follows:

```
reminder.xb:
#define reminder_width 32
#define reminder_height 32
static char reminder_bits[] = {
0x00, 0x00, 0x00, 0x00, 0x00, 0x00, 0x00, 0x00, 0xe0, 0x80, 0x03, 0x07,
0xf0, 0xc1, 0x87, 0x0f, 0xf0, 0xc1, 0x87, 0x0f, 0xf0, 0xc1, 0x87, 0x0f,
0xf0, 0xc1, 0x87, 0x0f, 0xf0, 0xc1, 0x87, 0x0f, 0xf0, 0xc1, 0x87, 0x0f,
0xf0, 0xc1, 0x87, 0x0f, 0xf0, 0xc1, 0x87, 0x0f, 0xf0, 0xc1, 0x87, 0x0f,
0xf0, 0xc1, 0x87, 0x0f, 0xf0, 0xc1, 0x87, 0x0f, 0xf0, 0xc1, 0x87, 0x0f,
0xf0, 0xc1, 0x87, 0x0f, 0xf0, 0xc1, 0x87, 0x0f, 0xf0, 0xc1, 0x87, 0x0f,
0xf0, 0xc1, 0x87, 0x0f, 0xf0, 0xc1, 0x87, 0x0f, 0xf0, 0xc1, 0x87, 0x0f,
0xf0, 0xc1, 0x87, 0x0f, 0xe0, 0x80, 0x03, 0x07, 0x00, 0x00, 0x00, 0x00,
0x00, 0x00, 0x00, 0x00, 0xe0, 0x80, 0x03, 0x07, 0xf0, 0xc1, 0x87, 0x0f,
0xf0, 0xc1, 0x87, 0x0f, 0xf0, 0xc1, 0x87, 0x0f, 0xe0, 0x80, 0x03, 0x07,
0x00, 0x00, 0x00, 0x00, 0x00, 0x00, 0x00, 0x00};
```

COMPILING reminder

Like `propsend`, `reminder` uses a large number of source files:

```
atom.c
button.c        (from chapter 16)
bytes.c         (from chapter 15)
cursor.c        (from chapter 7)
display.c       (from chapter 2)
error.c
event.c         (from chapter 5)
font.c          (from chapter 8)
gc.c            (from chapter 4)
icccm.c         (from chapter 15)
pixmap.c        (from chapter 6)
prop.c
reminder.c
textedit.c      (from chapter 16)
topwind.c       (from chapter 9)
xstring.c       (from chapter 16)
window.c        (from chapter 3)
reminder.xb
```

On Unix-based systems, you can use the `Makefile` in appendix C, with:

```
make reminder
```

Or, you can compile with:

```
cc -o reminder atom.c button.c bytes.c cursor.c display.c error.c \
      event.c font.c gc.c icccm.c pixmap.c prop.c reminder.c \
   textedit.c topwind.c xstring.c window.c -lX11
```

As you can tell, it's a lot easier to use the `Makefile`.

RUNNING reminder

`Reminder` needs no command-line parameters. You may specify a window geometry, a display name and a font name, all in the usual manner:

```
-display display_name
-geometry geometry_spec
        (e.g., 120x300+40+13)
-font font_name
```

`Reminder` appears in figure 17-4.

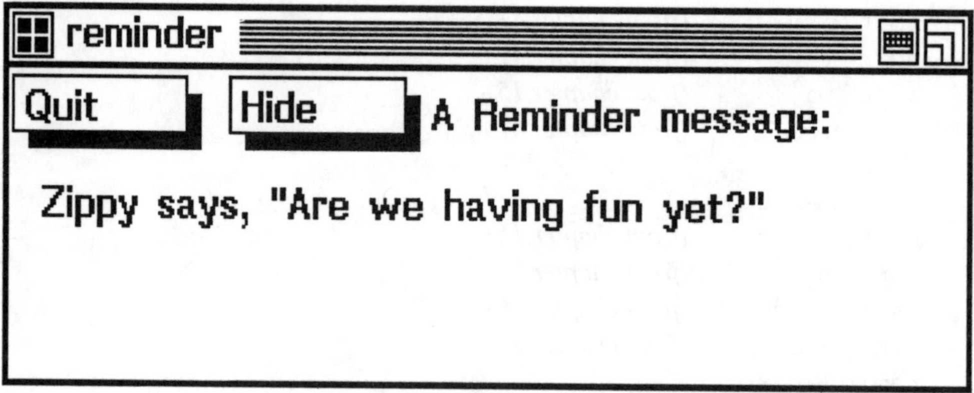

Figure 17-4. Reminder Program

FUNCTIONS DEVELOPED IN THIS CHAPTER

```
AppendProperty
ErrorHandler
NoError
ResetErrorHandler
SetErrorHandler
```

XLIB FUNCTIONS AND MACROS INTRODUCED IN THIS CHAPTER

XChangeProperty
XGetErrorText
XGetWindowProperty
XSetErrorHandler
XSetIOErrorHandler
XWithdrawWindow

SUMMARY

- The first step when communicating between programs is using properties properly. Programs can write data to arbitrary properties on arbitrary windows. Other programs can then read this data. Properties are named, typed data, stored with a window in the X server. Any program with a Window ID and a property name can store data in a property. If two programs agree on the window and property, they can exchange data.

- When discussing properties, it's also necessary to use atoms properly. Atoms are 32-bit indentifiers used to represent a text string in some sort of hashed format. Many X functions will return atom values, although these values will most likely be different from one run of a program to the next. Since each atom really represents a text string which, like "WM_DELETE_WINDOW", remains constant, we can intern the given name, getting an atom back. CompareAtomWithName() compares an atom ID with an atom name, and returns True if both resolve to the same atom ID. Next, we convert an array of data bytes representing atoms into the corresponding atoms, then into a text string containing the names of these atoms with GetAtomsFromData(), GetAtomName(), Bytes2Long(), and Atoms2Data().

- The major two operations with properties are appending data to a property and reading data back in from a property. The act of appending to a property—even appending with zero bytes of data—creates the property. To append data to a property, call XChangeProperty(). The append_mode can be PropModeAppend (append the new data to the end of whatever data is already stored in the property), PropModePrepend (place in the beginning of any preexisting data) or PropModeReplace (replace all the data—if any—stored in the property with the new data).

- The nastiest thing about XChangeProperty() is that it can generate an error, particularly a BadAlloc error. X errors fall into two classes: not so bad and really bad. The really bad errors are IO errors, which can be trapped with a really nasty X error handler function. The second type of X error, the not-so-bad error (including the BadAlloc errors) can be trapped with a different error-handler function. Once you've received an error, you can call XGetErrorText() to get a text string about the error.

- AppendProperty() makes sure that ErrorHandler() traps normal errors, and then resets the global ErrorFlag. AppendProperty() writes out the given data to the given property on the given window. The format parameter indicates whether the data consists of 8, 16 or 32-bit items (the server will swap bytes for different "endian" architectures). XGetWindowProperty() reads data from a property.

- In this process you must ask for a "target," which can be tricky. The target parameter to XGetWindowProperty() specifies what kind of data you want. Many possible targets exist, but most are built on top of other atoms. You need to convert the desired target into a form more palatable to the X server. ConvertTarget() converts a given desired target atom to a better atom for use with reading property data.

- Property2String() converts data read in from a property into a text string. Property2String() is a good help for debugging programs, and it is useful anytime you want to view the data in a property. It takes a display pointer, a target type (the type of property data you have) the property data, and a number of items you have in the data and returns a text string.

- Any program with a property ID (Atom) and a Window ID can write data to that property on that window. Any program can call XSelectInput(), specify an interest in PropertyNotify events (pass a PropertyChangeMask) and therefore be notified when any data is written to that property. Generally, one application will be chosen as a data producer. The consumer of the data selects an interest in PropertyNotify events. When a PropertyNotify event arrives, the consumer reads the data from the property using the delete mode (of True).

- To detect when property data changes on a given window, pass a `PropertyChangeMask` to `XSelectInput()`. When a property on that window changes, your application will receive a `PropertyNotify` event.

Chapter 18

Sending X Events Between Applications

The second major method for sending data between applications is to send events through application windows. Unfortunately, not every X application is set up to talk to other X clients. However, since most X applications must be built around an event loop, you can communicate with an X application by faking some events. In other words, by making the program send some events that look like the events generated by the X server, you can have a rudimentary form of interprocess communications. Luckily, Xlib contains the tools for such low-level trickery.

SENDING EVENTS

Most X applications are event-driven; they react to events sent to them from the X server. This includes events that signal a need to refresh a window (Expose events) and events that indicate the keyboard has been pressed (KeyPress events). Every X program must communicate with the X server, but that may be the extent of that program's interoperability with other applications. To transcend that low-level communication, you need to trick X with the XSendEvent() function.

USING XSendEvent

XSendEvent() sends an event packet to the given send_to_window. It is up to you to choose the event type and fill in the XEvent structure.

```
Status      status;

Display     *display;
Window      send_to_window;
Bool        propagate;
long        event_mask;
XEvent      event;

/*
 *          Set up event structure
 */

...

status = XSendEvent( display,
                     send_to_window,
                     propagate,
                     event_mask,
                     &event );

if ( status != 0 )
        {
        /*
         *      A non-zero status means the event
         *      was SENT ok, not necessarily
         *      received by anything.
         */
```

```
        ...

        }
else
        {
        /*
         * Error-handling goes here
         */

        ...

        }
```

When you use `XSendEvent()`, you can use an `event_mask` that does not contain the event type you are actually sending. You can also send an `event_mask` of zero, which means that the event will go to the application that created the `send_to_window`.

WHICH WINDOW TO SEND TO

`XSendEvent()` sends an X11 event packet to the given `send_to_window`, instead of to a given application program. This may be a problem if you know you want to send an event to an application, such as a word processor, but don't know any of that application's window IDs.

The key to using `XSendEvent()` is figuring out which window to send the event to. This is not always easy. If you are sending a `SelectionNotify` event, then you already had a `SelectionRequest` event that holds the receiving window to send to (see chapter 19).

However, in most cases, you will have to do some work to get the proper receiving window ID.

Xlib offers two easy ways out. You can avoid the selection of a specific window ID if you are aiming for the "current" application instead of a particular application. To do this, you can send the constant `PointerWindow` (which delivers the event to the window the mouse pointer is currently in) or you can send `InputFocus` (which delivers the event to whatever window currently has the keyboard focus).

In the program shown later in this chapter, we make the user interactively pick the receiving window. In most of your applications, choosing the right window will involve more work.

PROPAGATION

As described in chapter 5, events may propagate up the hierarchy of windows, until an application has indicated interest in that type of events. If you send an event to a window, and that window is not interested in the type of event you sent, then the event will propagate up the window hierarchy to the window's parent. If you pass propagate as `True`, the event will propagate up the window hierarchy. If the parent isn't interested, the event will propagate up to the parent's parent, and so on up to the root window.

If you pass propagate as `False`, then the event will not propagate up the window hierarchy. Instead, it will be sent to every window that has called `XSelectInput()` on `send_to_window` with a mask that matches any of the bits set in the `event_mask` parameter.

Adding even more complexity, the `event_mask` may be empty (set to zero). In that case, the event goes to the creator of `send_to_window`. If the creator application no longer exists, then no event is sent.

The events sent by `XSendEvent()` look just like normal events sent from the X server, except that the `send_event` field is set to `True` (this field is set to `False` on "real" events).

Some applications, like xterm in some modes, may not accept `KeyPress` events that have the `send_event` field set to `True`. This is to prevent applications from faking keyboard input (which could be a security problem if someone is logged in as `root` on a Unix box, using an xterm window). For testing an application, though, you may find faking events helps to simulate user input. Either way, xterm is configurable to accept or reject these events.

When you send an event using `XSendEvent()`, be sure to flesh out the entire event structure with good values for the particular type of event you want to send, or you may have problems.

ClientMessage EVENTS

ClientMessage is a special event type that exists so applications may exchange private data. Since most X applications don't deal with ClientMessage events, you must plan ahead to be sure the target application will act on incoming ClientMessages. ClientMessages have no mask to pass to XSelectInput(), so your application will always receive ClientMessage events. However, your application may not have any code to handle a ClientMessage event, so the message may be ignored.

Each ClientMessage event can carry up to twenty bytes of application-specific data, as you saw in chapter 15 on the infamous ICCCM. The contents of the ClientMessage event are as follows:

```
typedef struct
        {
        int                 type;   /* -- ClientMessage */
        unsigned long       serial;
        Bool                send_event;
        Display             *display;
        Window              window;
        Atom                message_type;
        int                 format;
        union   {
                char    b[ 20 ];
                short   s[ 10 ];
                long    l[ 5  ];
                } data;
        } XClientMessageEvent;
```

ClientMessage events can be handy for exchanging data between applications, but you have to get both applications to agree beforehand on how the data will be formatted.

SENDING A PRETEND KeyPress EVENT

Even though few applications are willing to deal with ClientMessage events, most will accept KeyPress events since the keyboard is an integral part of most workstations. While the data bandwidth of KeyPress events is pretty small (essentially one key per event), a KeyPress event raises interesting possibilities for use in a program that exercises other programs as part of testing.

You could, for example, create a program that sends many random KeyPress events to whatever application has the current input focus. If your applications can survive this kind of abuse, you can be more confident that they will survive the abuse heaped on them by end users.

To aid such a task, the SendKeyCode() function, developed in this chapter, sends a KeyPress event to a given window on a given display. To keep up with the symmetry in X, SendKeyCode() also sends a KeyRelease event to better mimic the action of a real keyboard (with a very fast typist).

SendKeyCode() sends a KeyPress/KeyRelease event pair to the given window on the given display. You also need to pass the keycode and the state of the modifier keys (for example, Shift, or more precisely, Shift1Mask).

The first thing you'll notice is the amount of data fields that must be filled in to create a KeyPress event that will be accepted by the X server (which forwards the event) and the applications (which receives the event). We only send a KeyRelease event if the first call to XSendEvent() was successful (returned a nonzero value). This return code does not indicate the event was received, but rather merely that it was properly sent.

The contents of SendKeyCode() are as follows:

```
SendKeyCode( display, window, keycode, state )

Display     *display;
Window      window;
KeyCode     keycode;
int         state;

{           /* -- function SendKeyCode */
            XKeyEvent           event;
            int                 status;

            event.type          = KeyPress;
            event.display       = display;
            event.window        = window;
            event.root          = RootWindow( display, DefaultScreen( display));
            event.keycode       = keycode;
```

```
        event.state       = state;
        event.time        = CurrentTime;
        event.same_screen = True;
        event.x           = 0;
        event.y           = 0;
        event.x_root      = 0;
        event.y_root      = 0;
        event.subwindow   = (Window)None;

        status = XSendEvent( display, window, True, KeyPressMask, &event );

        if ( status != 0 )
                {
                event.type =        KeyRelease;
                event.time =        CurrentTime;

                status = XSendEvent( display, window, True,
                                     KeyReleaseMask, &event );
                }

        return( status );

}       /* -- function SendKeyCode */
```

This function takes a `KeyCode` as a parameter. A `KeyCode` is a number that usually refers to a position on the keyboard (some magic vendor-specific number). Since each vendor's keyboards are different, `KeyCodes` are inherently unportable. Unfortunately, though, this is what a `KeyPress` event wants.

SENDING A KeySym

To make `SendKeyCode()` more portable, we layer another function, `SendKeysym()`, on top. Since `KeySyms` are X's portable key identifiers, `SendKeysym()` provides a much nicer interface to `SendKeyCode()`. `SendKeysym()` first checks if the given character is uppercase (using a U.S. ASCII-based test, so users in other countries will need to watch out for this) and sets the proper modifier state for the call to `SendKeyCode()`. Next, `SendKeysym()` calls `XKeysymToKeycode()` to translate the portable `KeySym` to a system-specific `KeyCode`. This is basically the opposite of the `XLookupString()` function used in chapter 5 on events.

```
Display     *display;
KeySym      keysym;
KeyCode     keycode;

keycode =XKeysymToKeycode( display, keysym );
```

If `XKeysymToKeyCode()` fails, it returns a zero.

The code for `SendKeySym()` is as follows:

```
SendKeysym( display, window, keysym )

Display     *display;
Window      window;
KeySym      keysym;

{           /* -- functions SendKeysym */
            KeyCode     keycode;
            int                 status;
            int                 state;

            status  = 0;        /* -- default */

            if ( keysym != NoSymbol )
                    {
                    if ( ( keysym >= XK_A ) && ( keysym <= XK_Z ) )
                            {
                            state = ShiftMask;
                            }
                    else
                            {
                            state = 0x00;
                            }

                    keycode = XKeysymToKeycode( display, keysym );

                    if ( keycode != 0 )
                            {
                            status = SendKeyCode( display, window, keycode, state );
                            }
                    }

            XFlush( display );
```

```
        return( status );

}       /* -- functions SendKeysym */
```

As you'll notice, sending a KeySym is still a low-level function. What we really need is the ability to send a whole character string and not worry about KeySyms or KeyCodes.

SENDING A CHARACTER STRING

We'll add a utility function to send several characters as a string to a particular window, layering on top of SendKeysym() and SendKeyCode(). This simple function calls SendKeysym() for each character in the input string and adds a carriage return at the end. (We're assuming that you want to send a full command to a Unix shell inside an xterm window.) The XK_Return KeySym translates to a carriage return. The contents of SendString() are as follows:

```
SendString( display, window, string )

Display     *display;
Window      window;
char        string[];

{           /* -- function SendString */
            int     i, length, status;

            length = strlen( string );
            status = 1;
            i      = 0;
            while ( ( i < length ) && ( status != 0 ) )
                    {
                    status = SendKeysym( display, window, string[ i ] );

                    i++;
                    }

            status = SendKeysym( display, window, XK_Return );

            return( status );

}           /* -- function SendString */
```

These `SendKeyCode()`, `SendKeysym()`, and `SendString()` functions are collected together in the file `sendev.c`.

SOURCE CODE FOR sendev.c

The source code contents for `sendev.c` are as follows:

```
sendev.c:
/*
 *      sendev.c
 *
 *      X11 code to send an event to
 *      a window on the display.
 */

#include  "xbook.h"

SendString( display, window, string )

Display    *display;
Window     window;
char       string[];

/*
 *         SendString() sends a text string as KeyPress/KeyRelease
 *         events to a given window.
 *
 */

{          /* -- function SendString */
           int    i, length, status;

           length = strlen( string );
           status = 1;
           i      = 0;
           while ( ( i < length ) && ( status != 0 ) )
               {
               status = SendKeysym( display, window, string[ i ] );

               i++;
               }

           status = SendKeysym( display, window, XK_Return );
```

```
            return( status );

}           /* -- function SendString */

/*
 *          SendKeySym() sends a given keysym to
 *          the given window.
 *
 */

SendKeysym( display, window, keysym )

Display     *display;
Window      window;
KeySym      keysym;

{           /* -- functions SendKeysym */
            KeyCode     keycode;
            int                 status;
            int                 state;

            status  = 0;        /* -- default */

            if ( keysym != NoSymbol )
                    {
                    if ( ( keysym >= XK_A ) && ( keysym <= XK_Z ) )
                    {
                    state = ShiftMask;
                    }
            else
                    {
                    state = 0x00;
                    }

            keycode = XKeysymToKeycode( display, keysym );

            if ( keycode != 0 )
                    {
                    status = SendKeyCode( display, window, keycode, state );
                    }
            }

        XFlush( display );

        return( status );

}       /* -- functions SendKeysym */
```

```
/*
 *      SendKeyCode() sends a keycode to
 *      a window.
 *
 */

SendKeyCode( display, window, keycode, state )

Display     *display;
Window      window;
KeyCode     keycode;
int         state;

{           /* -- function SendKeyCode */
            XKeyEvent           event;
            int                 status;

            event.type          = KeyPress;
            event.display       = display;
            event.window        = window;
            event.root          = RootWindow( display, DefaultScreen( display ) );
            event.keycode       = keycode;
            event.state         = state;
            event.time          = CurrentTime;
            event.same_screen = True;
            event.x             = 0;
            event.y             = 0;
            event.x_root        = 0;
            event.y_root        = 0;
            event.subwindow     = (Window)None;

            status = XSendEvent( display, window, True, KeyPressMask, &event );

            if ( status != 0 )
                   {
                   event.type          = KeyRelease;
                   event.time          = CurrentTime;

                   status = XSendEvent( display, window, True,
                                        KeyReleaseMask, &event );
                   }

            return( status );

}           /* -- function SendKeyCode */
```

```
/*
 *        end of file.
 */
```

A PROGRAM TO SEND CHARACTER STRINGS TO WINDOWS

We'll use the utility functions developed in `sendev.c` to create a program called `send`. The `send` program puts up a window where you can type in a character string. You can press the `"Send"` push-button to send the character string to another window, the `"Clear"` button to start over on a new character string, or the `"Quit"` button to quit the program. It's all pretty easy.

The whole `send` program looks suspiciously like the `propsend` program introduced in the last chapter—so suspiciously that we'll only go into the differences here.

To select a window to send the character string, we use the `PickWindow()` routine developed in `pickwind.c` (in chapter 11).

FINDING A WINDOW TO SEND THE CHARACTER STRING TO

The `FindSendWindow()` function calls the `PickWindow()` routine to find a window to send the character string to. `FindSendWindow()`'s basic purpose is to set up the necessary parameters to `PickWindow()` and clean up afterward. `FindSendWindow()` also displays a prompt to give the user at least a vague idea of what is expected. The contents of `FindSendWindows` are as follows:

```
Window FindSendWindow( display, window )

Display    *display;
Window     window;

{          /* -- function FindSendWindow */
           int      screen;
           Window   rootwindow, send_window;
           Cursor   cursor;
```

```
        /*
         * Display message to user
         */
        XDrawImageString( display, window, AppGC,
                ( 3 * ( BUTTON_WIDTH + 5 ) ) + 5,
                BUTTON_HEIGHT - 5,
                PRESS_MESSAGE, strlen( PRESS_MESSAGE ) );

        XFlush( display );

        /*
         * Pick a window to send characters to
         */
        screen = DefaultScreen( display );
        rootwindow = RootWindow( display, screen );

        cursor = XCreateFontCursor( display, XC_gumby );

        send_window = PickWindow( display,
                                  rootwindow,
                                  cursor );

        XFreeCursor( display, cursor );

        return( send_window );

}       /* -- function FindSendWindow */
```

SENDING THE TEXT STRING TO A WINDOW

The `SendData()` function is a call-back function from the `"Send"` push-button. Its job is to find a window to send the text data to, and then use `XSendEvent()` to send the data. The routine calls `FindSendWindow()`, shown in the preceding code, to figure out which window to send to, and then `SendString()` (from `sendev.c`, also in the preceding code) to get the data out. The character string to send is stored in a global variable, `SendText`:

```
char    SendText[ BUFSIZE + 1 ];

SendData( display, window )

Display *display;
Window    window;
```

```
{           /* -- function SendData */
            Window  send_window;

            send_window = FindSendWindow( display, window );

            if ( send_window != (Window) None )
                    {
                    SendString( display, send_window, SendText );
                    }

            RefreshFlag = True;

            XFlush( display );

            XClearWindow( display, window );

}           /* -- function SendData */
```

SOURCE CODE FOR send.c

The source code for `send.c` is as follows:

```
send.c:
/*
 *      send.c
 *      X11 program for sending Key events
 *      to another window.
 */

#include "xbook.h"

#include  "sendev.xb"

#define MESSAGE "XSendEvent() Example"
#define PRESS_MESSAGE "Press mouse button in desired window."

/*
 *              Globals for send program
 */
int             RefreshFlag = False;
int             QuitFlag    = False;
GC              AppGC;
char            SendText[ BUFSIZE + 1 ];
```

```
main( argc, argv )

int             argc;
char            *argv[];

{               /* -- main */
                Display                 *display;
                int                     screen;
                Window                  window;
                int                     x, y, width, height;
                XFontStruct             *font;
                Pixmap                  icon;
                int                     font_height;
                unsigned long           black, white;

                /*
                 *      Set up X connection
                 */
                display= SetUpDisplay( argc, argv,
                                        &screen );

                black  = BlackPixel( display, screen );
                white  = WhitePixel( display, screen );

                /*
                 * Check size and location of window
                 */
                x       = 10;
                y       = 10;
                width   = 510;
                height  = 80;
                CheckGeometry( argc, argv,
                        DisplayWidth( display, screen ),
                        DisplayHeight( display, screen ),
                        &x, &y, &width, &height );

                /*
                 * Create Window
                 */
window = TopWindow( display, x, y, width, height,
                        sendev_bits, sendev_width, sendev_height,
                        &icon, &AppGC );

/*
 * Load font
 */
```

```
font = LoadFont( display, AppGC, argc, argv, "variable" );

font_height = font->ascent + font->descent;

/*
 * Store values for window manager
 */
SetNormalHints( display, window,
        x, y, width, height );

SetWMHints( display, window, icon );

NameWindow( display, window,
        "send", "send", "Send" );

SetICCCM( display, window,
        argc, argv );

/*
 * initializxe global for
 * string storage
 */
SendText[ 0 ] = '\0';

XFlush( display );

/*
 * Create buttons of user interface items
 */
MakeButtons( display, window,
        black, white, font->fid );

/*
 * Map windows */
MapWindow( display, window );

/*
 * Handle any events
 */
while( QuitFlag = = False )
        {
        EventLoop( display,
                window, AppGC, font,
                &width, &height );

        if ( RefreshFlag = = True )
```

```
                {
                Refresh( display, window, AppGC, font_height );

                RefreshFlag = False;
                }

        }

    /*
     * Shut down
     */
    XFreeFont( display, font );
    XFreePixmap( display, icon );

    CloseDisplay( display, window, AppGC );

    exit( 0 );

}   /* -- main */

SendData( display, window )

Display     *display;
Window      window;

{           /* -- function SendData */
            Window  send_window;

            send_window = FindSendWindow( display, window );

            if ( send_window != (Window) None )
                    {
                    SendString( display, send_window, SendText );
                    }

            RefreshFlag = True;

            XFlush( display );

            XClearWindow( display, window );

}           /* -- function SendData */

ClearData( display, window )

Display     *display;
```

```
Window      window;

{           /* -- function ClearData */

            SendText[ 0 ] = '\0';

            XClearWindow( display, window );

            RefreshFlag = True;

}           /* -- function ClearData */

EventLoop( display, window, gc, font, width, height )

Display         *display;
Window          window;
GC              gc;
XFontStruct     *font;
int             *width, *height;

/*
 *      EventLoop() handles generic X events, but passes
 *      most events on to specific functions to handle
 *      the particular event.
 *
 *
 */

{       /* -- function EventLoop */
        XEvent      event;
        KeySym      keysym;

        /*
         *      Block on input, awaiting
         *      an event from X.
         */
        NextEvent( display, False,
                *width, *height,
                &event,
                &keysym );

        if ( ButtonEvent( display, &event ) = = True )
                {
                return( True );
                }

        /*
         *      Decode the event and call
```

```
         *     a specific routine to
         *     handle it.
         */
        switch( event.type )
                {
                case ClientMessage:
                    if( IsDeleteWindow( display, &event ) = = True)
                        {
                        QuitFlag = True;
                        }
                    break;
                case Expose:
                    RefreshFlag = True;
                    break;

                case ConfigureNotify:
                    *width = event.xconfigure.width;
                    *height = event.xconfigure.height;
                    break;
                case KeyPress:
                    TextEdit( display, window,
                              gc, font,
                              5, 2 * BUTTON_HEIGHT,
                              keysym,
                              SendText, BUFSIZE );
                    break;
                }

        return( True );

}       /* -- function EventLoop */

QuitApplication( display, window )

Display     *display;
Window      window;

{       /* -- function QuitApplication */

        QuitFlag = True;

}       /* -- function QuitApplication */

MakeButtons( display, window, fore, back, font_id )

Display             *display;
```

```
Window              window;
unsigned long       fore, back;
Font                font_id;

{       /* -- function MakeButtons */
        int     QuitApplication();
        int     SendData();
        int     ClearData();
        int     x;

        x = 1;
        CreateButton( display, window,
            x, 2,
            fore, back, font_id,
            "Quit",
            QuitApplication );

        x = BUTTON_WIDTH + 5;
        CreateButton( display, window, x, 2,
            fore, back, font_id,
            "Send",
            SendData );

        x += BUTTON_WIDTH + 5;
        CreateButton( display, window, x, 2,
            fore, back, font_id,
            "Clear",
            ClearData );

}       /* -- function MakeButtons */

Refresh( display, window, gc, font_height )

Display     *display;
Window      window;
GC          gc;
int         font_height;

{           /* -- function Refresh */

            XDrawImageString( display, window, gc,
                ( 3 * ( BUTTON_WIDTH + 5 ) ) + 5,
                BUTTON_HEIGHT - 5,
                MESSAGE, strlen( MESSAGE ) );

            XDrawImageString( display, window, gc,
                5, ( 2 * BUTTON_HEIGHT ),
```

```
                    SendText, strlen( SendText ) );

            XFlush( display );

}       /* -- function Refresh */

Window FindSendWindow( display, window )

Display *display;
Window  window;

{       /* -- function FindSendWindow */
        int         screen;
        Window      rootwindow, send_window;
        Cursor      cursor;

    /*
     * Display message to user
     */
    XDrawImageString( display, window, AppGC,
            ( 3 * ( BUTTON_WIDTH + 5 ) ) + 5,
            BUTTON_HEIGHT - 5,
            PRESS_MESSAGE, strlen( PRESS_MESSAGE ) );

    XFlush( display );

    /*
     * Pick a window to send characters to
     */
    screen      = DefaultScreen( display );
    rootwindow      = RootWindow( display, screen );

    cursor = XCreateFontCursor( display, XC_gumby );

    send_window = PickWindow( display,
                              rootwindow,
                              cursor );

    XFreeCursor( display, cursor );

    return( send_window );

}   /* -- function FindSendWindow */

/*
 * end of file
 */
```

AN ICON FOR send

Figure 18-1 shows the send icon.

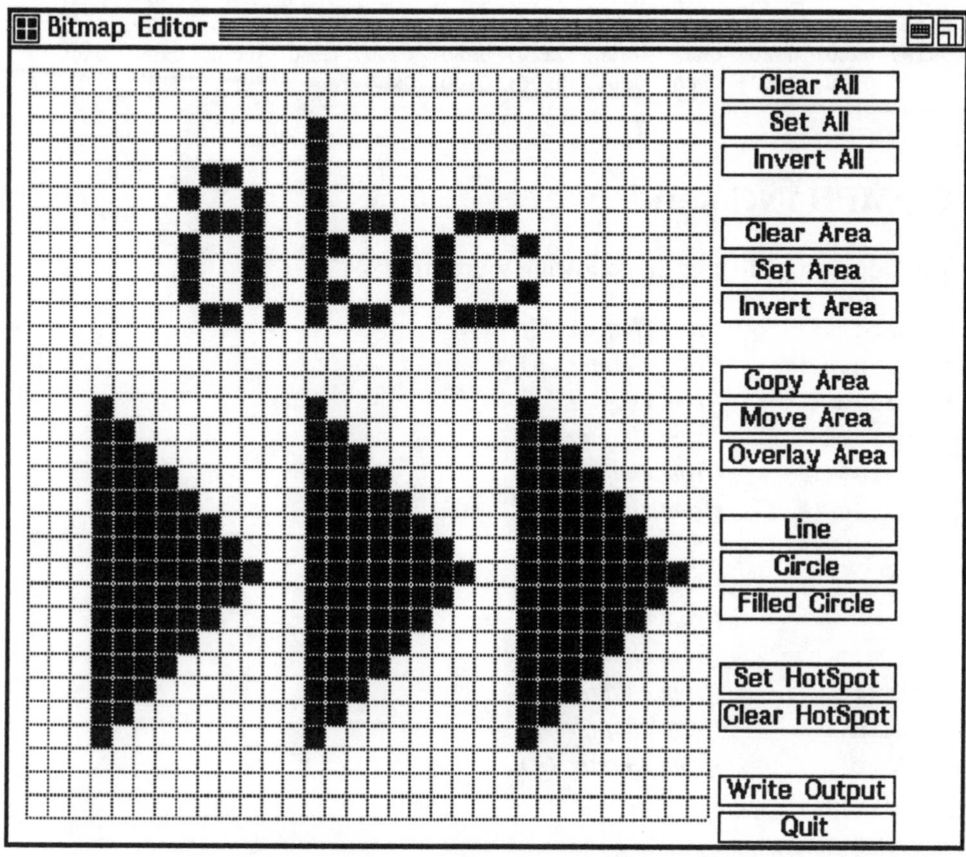

Figure 18-1. The Send Icon

The contents of the send icon are as follows:

```
sendev.xb:
#define sendev_width 32
#define sendev_height 32
static char sendev_bits[] = {
0x00, 0x00, 0x00, 0x00, 0x00, 0x00, 0x00, 0x00, 0x00, 0x20, 0x00, 0x00,
0x00, 0x20, 0x00, 0x00, 0x00, 0x23, 0x00, 0x00, 0x80, 0x24, 0x00, 0x00,
0x00, 0xa7, 0x71, 0x00, 0x80, 0x64, 0x8a, 0x00, 0x80, 0x24, 0x0a, 0x00,
```

```
0x80, 0x64, 0x8a, 0x00, 0x00, 0xab, 0x71, 0x00, 0x00, 0x00, 0x00, 0x00,
0x00, 0x00, 0x00, 0x00, 0x00, 0x00, 0x00, 0x00, 0x08, 0x20, 0x80, 0x00,
0x18, 0x60, 0x80, 0x01, 0x38, 0xe0, 0x80, 0x03, 0x78, 0xe0, 0x81, 0x07,
0xf8, 0xe0, 0x83, 0x0f, 0xf8, 0xe1, 0x87, 0x1f, 0xf8, 0xe3, 0x8f, 0x3f,
0xf8, 0xe7, 0x9f, 0x7f, 0xf8, 0xe3, 0x8f, 0x3f, 0xf8, 0xe1, 0x87, 0x1f,
0xf8, 0xe0, 0x83, 0x0f, 0x78, 0xe0, 0x81, 0x07, 0x38, 0xe0, 0x80, 0x03,
0x18, 0x60, 0x80, 0x01, 0x08, 0x20, 0x80, 0x00, 0x00, 0x00, 0x00, 0x00,
0x00, 0x00, 0x00, 0x00, 0x00, 0x00, 0x00, 0x00};
```

COMPILING send

The `send` program uses the following source files:

`atom.c`	*(from chapter 17)*
`button.c`	*(from chapter 16)*
`bytes.c`	*(from chapter 15)*
`cursor.c`	*(from chapter 7)*
`display.c`	*(from chapter 2)*
`error.c`	*(from chapter 17)*
`event.c`	*(from chapter 5)*
`font.c`	*(from chapter 8)*
`gc.c`	*(from chapter 4)*
`icccm.c`	*(from chapter 15)*
`pickwind.c`	*(from chapter 11)*
`pixmap.c`	*(from chapter 6)*
`prop.c`	*(from chapter 17)*
`send.c`	
`sendev.c`	
`subwind.c`	*(from chapter 11)*
`textedit.c`	*(from chapter 16)*
`topwind.c`	*(from chapter 9)*
`xstring.c`	*(from chapter 16)*
`window.c`	*(from chapter 3)*
`sendev.xb`	

On Unix-based systems, you can use the `Makefile` in appendix C, with:

```
make send
```

Or, you can compile with:

```
cc -o send atom.c button.c bytes.c cursor.c display.c error.c \
   event.c font.c gc.c icccm.c pickwind.c pixmap.c \
   prop.c send.c sendev.c subwind.c \
   textedit.c topwind.c xstring.c window.c -lX11
```

As you can tell, it's a lot easier to use the `Makefile`.

RUNNING send

`Send` needs no command-line parameters. You may specify a window geometry, a display name, and a font name, all in the usual manner:

```
-display display_name
-geometry geometry_spec
(e.g., 120x300+40+13)
-font font_name
```

When you run the `send` program, type a text string into the send window. Then, when you choose the `send` choice, the text string will be sent to a window using `KeyPress` events. You also need to choose the window using the `PickWindow()` function from chapter 11. `Clear` clears out the current text string and `Quit` quits the program. Figure 18-2 shows the `send` program with the ls -CF command.

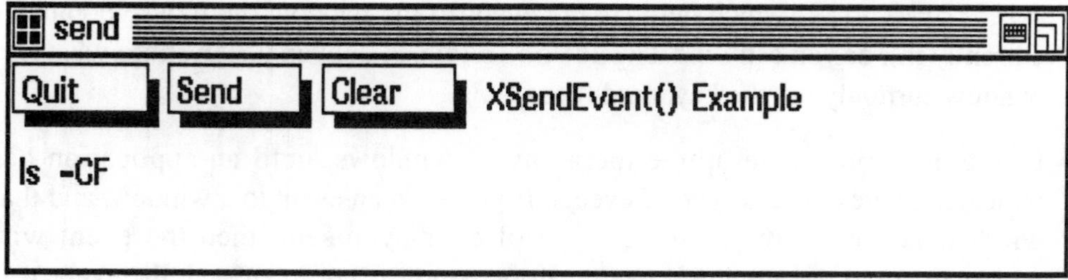

Figure 18-2. The send program with the command "ls -CF"

FUNCTIONS DEVELOPED IN THIS CHAPTER

SendKeyCode
SendKeysym
SendString

XLIB FUNCTIONS AND MACROS USED IN THIS CHAPTER

XSendEvent
XKeysymToKeycode

SUMMARY

- Communicating between programs can be achieved with the XSendEvent() function which sends an X11 event packet to the given send_to_window. It is up to you to choose the event type and fill in the XEvent structure. While XSendEvent() sends an X11 event packet to the given send_to_window, it does not necessarily send this packet to a given application program.
- The key to using XSendEvent() is figuring out which window to send the event to. This is not always easy. However, Xlib offers two easy ways around this. You can avoid the selection of a specific window ID if you are aiming for the "current" application instead of a particular application. To do this, you can send the constant PointerWindow (which delivers the event to the window the mouse pointer is currently in), or you can send InputFocus (which delivers the event to whatever window currently has the keyboard focus).
- Events may propagate up the hierarchy of windows, until an application has indicated interest in that type of events. If you send an event to a window, and that window is not interested in the type of event you sent, then the event will propagate up to the window's parent. If the parent is not interested, the event will continue to propagate up the window hierarchy until it finds an interested window on the root window. When you send an event using XSendEvent(), be sure to flesh out the entire event structure with good values for the particular type of event you want to send, or you may have problems.

- A special event type, `ClientMessage`, exists so applications may exchange private data. `ClientMessage` events can be handy for exchanging data between applications, but you have to get both applications to agree beforehand on how the data will be formatted.

- Even though few applications are willing to deal with `ClientMessage` events, most will accept `KeyPress` events since the keyboard is an integral part of most workstations. The `SendKeyCode()` function sends a `KeyPress` event to a given window on a given display. To keep up with the symmetry in X, `SendKeyCode()` also sends a `KeyRelease` event to better mimic the action of a real keyboard.

- A `KeyCode` is a number that usually refers to a position on the keyboard (some magic vendor-specific number). Since each vendor's keyboards are different, `KeyCodes` are inherently unportable. To make `SendKeyCode()` more portable, we layer the `SendKeysym()` function on top. Since `KeySyms` are X's portable key identifiers, `SendKeysym()` provides a much nicer interface to `SendKeyCode()`.

Chapter 19

Selections

Even among experienced X programmers there's some fear and loathing toward selections, so don't be afraid if the subtleties of selections are unclear at first. This stuff ain't simple.

Selections are X's means for providing an active cut-and-paste mechanism. They also provide a generalized query-reply interprocess communication (IPC) mechanism.

Unfortunately, most books on X don't explain selections. This is a shame, since the use of selections is one of the most powerful features of X. Just remember don't panic. You'll get the hang of it. Really.

SELECTIONS ARE YOUR FRIENDS

It took us a long time to be convinced that selections are really good. Just look at how simple it is to use the cut buffers and how difficult to use the selections. A little enhancement to the cut buffers could have gone a long way in providing most of the features of selections.

By far the most important information on selections is in the *Inter-Client Communications Conventions Manual*, the ICCCM. If you plan on developing X applications, you should grab a copy of the infamous ICCCM as soon as possible. If the ICCCM gives you a warm, fuzzy feeling when you're done reading it, you probably don't need to read the rest of this chapter. If you're still confused (as most people are), read on.

SELECTION BASICS: SELECTIONS AS QUERY-RESPONSE

It helps to think of each selection as an `atom`. As such, you need to convert the selection name, say "`UNCLE_FRAMROD`," to an `atom`, using `XInternAtom()`. Next, some program gets up and tells the X server, "I now own the `UNCLE_FRAMROD` selection, so there!" Usually, a program does this after a user clicks a mouse or in some way asks the program to select some data. Just to be sure (especially because of the "so there"), the program asks the server, "Who REALLY owns the `UNCLE_FRAMROD` selection?" The X server responds with the window ID of the selection owner—the program's window (we hope).

Now the program owns the `UNCLE_FRAMROD` selection. Other programs, if they know about the `UNCLE_FRAMROD` selection (we could call these `UNCLE_FRAMROD`-aware applications), may ask the `UNCLE_FRAMROD` owner (really a window, but an application sits behind the window) questions about the `UNCLE_FRAMROD` selection.

Depending on what the UNCLE_FRAMROD-aware applications previously agreed to, the most obvious question usually asks for the data associated with UNCLE_FRAMROD in a string format (the vast majority of user data is in a string format). This is called asking for the selection with a target type of XA_STRING (where XA_STRING is a predefined atom). Another program could ask, "How big is UNCLE_FRAMROD?," which normally would be translated into a request for the UNCLE_FRAMROD selection with a target of "LENGTH." Note that anything in quotes is a character string and probably needs to be passed to XInternAtom() to get an atom value for that string--some atoms are predefined, but most are not. You can guess that UNCLE_FRAMROD is not built into the Xlib.

The owner of the UNCLE_FRAMROD selection then converts the selection data into the proper target type, puts the data in a property on the asking program's window, and then sends a SelectionNotify event to the asking program. Figure 19-1 shows this process.

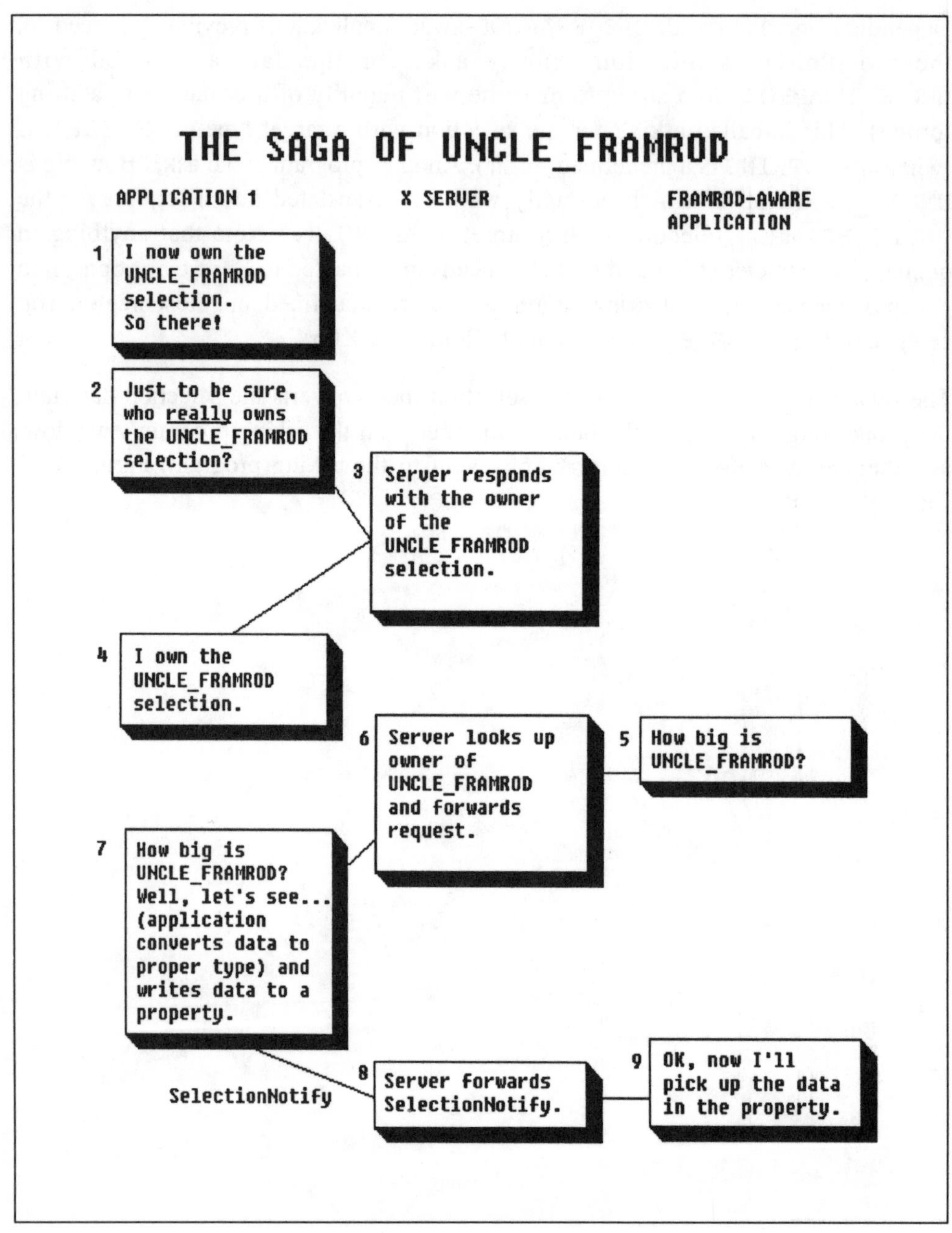

Figure 19-1. Selection Overview

The basic underlying concept of selections is that you ask the owner of a selection for "the data" and you ask the owner to put "the data" into the target type you want. This can lead to a form of twenty questions: How big is it? How long is it? What file is it in? What font is it displayed in? What color?

The idea, though, is that you can ask the selection owner to give you data in any target type you want, provided the owning program supports that data target type. We could call this formatting the data, but X selections use the term "format" to refer to the size of each basic element: 8, 16, or 32 bits. So, to avoid confusion we'll stick to target type to refer to the type of data you want.

For example, if the user selects some text with a mouse (hence the term "selection"), another application could ask the owning program for the selected text (you ask for the selection with a target type of `XA_STRING`). Another program, perhaps an editor, could ask the owning program for the name of the file in which the selected text is to be found, the line numbers where the selected text starts and ends, and a number of other things.

We've been assuming that the base type of the selected data is text. This, of course, isn't always so. The beauty of the selection mechanism is that it allows elements other than text to be cut and pasted. For example, a bitmap editor could allow users to cut and paste bitmaps between applications, and a color chooser could allow the user to select a color. Other applications could ask for a color from the owning application. The neat feature here is that, with "interoperable" applications, you can concentrate each application on what it does best. You no longer have to make each application into a be-all, end-all program. An Internet news reader doesn't have to have an electronic-mail program built in. The news reader and the mail program could communicate through selections. Isn't this fun? (Unfortunately, few applications support selections. This should get better, though.)

FINDING OUT HOW SELECTIONS WORK

Selections are still a bit confusing, right? To see how selections work, we've put together a program called "primary," which plays the game of twenty questions (we're exaggerating a bit, it's actually nine). Primary will ask the owner of the `PRIMARY` selection nine questions and display the answers in a window.

THE PRIMARY SELECTION

The main selection in the ICCCM for typical cut-and-paste operations is named "PRIMARY." It uses the built-in atom called XA_PRIMARY. PRIMARY is the selection used when a user selects some text in an xterm window, by far the most common use of cut and paste in X.

See section 2.6.1.1 in the ICCCM for more information on the PRIMARY selection.

Our primary program will either query the owner of the PRIMARY selection, or assert ownership of it and then answer the questions from other applications.

SELECTION OWNERSHIP

Each selection in use is owned by a window. This ownership is global to the display. The selection is just an atom, but an atom with an owner.

To find out who owns a given selection, call XGetSelectionOwner(). Note that a window owns a selection and the application that created the window usually owns that window.

```
Display    *display;
Atom       selection;
Window     owner_window;

owner_window = XGetSelectionOwner( display, selection );
```

The selection is an atom, so you'll usually need to call XInternAtom() to convert the name to an atom ID. The name "PRIMARY" is already built in as the XA_PRIMARY atom.

To assert ownership of a selection, call XSetSelectionOwner():

```
Display    *display;
Atom       selection;
Window     owner_window;
Time       timestamp;

XSetSelectionOwner( display, selection, owner_window, timestamp );
```

You should pass a valid timestamp to XSetSelectionOwner(), not the constant CurrentTime. You can also pass a owner_window of None, to make the selection owned by no one, but usually you should pass the ID of your application's top-level window. Note that XSetSelectionOwner() does not tell you if your call was successful.

The function AssertOwnership() handles the task of asserting ownership of a selection. It also calls XGetSelectionOwner() right after the call to XSetSelectionOwner() to see if the attempt was successful. The contents of AssertOwnership() are as follows:

```
AssertOwnership( display, window, selection, timestamp )

Display    *display;
Window     window;
Atom       selection;
Time       timestamp;

{   /* -- function AssertOwnership */
    Window  owner;

    if ( ( window = = (Window)None ) || ( selection = = (Atom) None ) )
        {
        return( False );
        }

    XSetSelectionOwner( display, selection, window, timestamp );

    /*
    * Now check if we made it.
    */
    owner = XGetSelectionOwner( display, selection );

    if ( owner != window )
                                            {
                                            return( False );
                                            }
    else
        {
        return( True );
        }

}       /* -- function AssertOwnership */
```

The OwnPrimary() function further hides some of the details of asserting ownership of the PRIMARY selection (the built-in atom XA_PRIMARY) and sets up a number of global variables if the attempt was successful. The contents of OwnPrimary() are as follows:

```
OwnPrimary( display, window, timestamp )

Display    *display;
Window     window;
Time       timestamp;

{   /* -- function OwnPrimary */
    int      status;

    PrimaryIsOurs    = False;

    status = AssertOwnership( display, window, XA_PRIMARY, timestamp );

    if ( status == True )
        {
        PrimaryOwnership = timestamp;

        PrimaryIsOurs = True;
        }

    return( status );

}       /* -- function OwnPrimary */
```

We need to keep track of the timestamp, since other applications can ask our application for the timestamp when it has ownership of the selection. The timestamps are supposed to help prevent the race conditions that can occur as many programs run essentially in parallel on a multitasking system, all competing for the same display.

SOURCE CODE FOR sel_own.c

The file sel_own.c has functions for checking and asserting the ownership of the PRIMARY selection. Its contents are as follows:

```
sel_own.c:
   /*
    * sel_own.c
    * X11 routines for asserting Primary selection
    * ownership.
    */

#include    "xbook.h"

/*
*   Globals for ownership of the primary selection
*/
Time    PrimaryOwnership = CurrentTime;
int     PrimaryIsOurs    = False;

LoseSelection()

{        /* -- function LoseSelection */

        PrimaryIsOurs = False;

}        /* -- function LoseSelection */

OwnPrimary( display, window, timestamp )

Display    *display;
Window     window;
Time       timestamp;

{   /* -- function OwnPrimary */
    int     status;

    PrimaryIsOurs     = False;

    status = AssertOwnership( display, window, XA_PRIMARY, timestamp );

    if ( status = = True )
            {
            PrimaryOwnership = timestamp;

            PrimaryIsOurs = True;
            }

 return( status );

 }       /* -- function OwnPrimary */
```

```
AssertOwnership( display, window, selection, timestamp )

Display    *display;
Window     window;
Atom       selection;
Time       timestamp;

{  /* -- function AssertOwnership */
    Window  owner;

    if ( ( window = = (Window)None ) || ( selection = = (Atom) None ) )
        {
        return( False );
        }

    XSetSelectionOwner( display, selection, window, timestamp );

    /*
     * Now check if we made it.
     */
    owner = XGetSelectionOwner( display, selection );

    if ( owner != window )
            {
            return
            ( False );
            }
    else
            {
            return( True );
            }

}        /* -- function AssertOwnership */

CheckIfPrimaryIsOurs( timestamp )

Time    timestamp;

{        /* -- function IsPrimaryOurs */

    if ( ( PrimaryIsOurs ) && ( timestamp >= PrimaryOwnership ) )
            {
            return( True );
            }
    else
            {
```

```
            PrimaryIsOurs = False;
            return( False );
            }

}       /* -- function IsPrimaryOurs */

IsPrimaryOurs()

{       /* -- function IsPrimaryOurs */

        return( PrimaryIsOurs );

}       /* -- function IsPrimaryOurs */

Time PrimaryTimeStamp()

{       /* -- function PrimaryTimeStamp */

return( PrimaryOwnership );

}       /* -- function PrimaryTimeStamp */

/*
 * end of file
 */
```

EXCHANGING SELECTION DATA

When you want data from a selection, the owner of the selection will, if all goes well, write that data to a property on one of your application windows. You must pick the window. You must also pick the property to place the data in (on your window) and the target type. The owner may not support the target type you want, so you have to watch for problems.

ASKING THE SELECTION OWNER FOR DATA

When users ask to paste data, they are essentially asking for the contents of a selection to be pasted. You need to ask the owner of the selection for data in a certain target type, depending on the context of the paste operation.

If you want some data from the owner of a selection, call `XConvertSelection()`:

```
Display *display;
Atom    selection_you_want;     /* -- e.g., XA_PRIMARY */
Atom    target;                 /* -- type of data */
Atom    property_to_place_data;
Window  window_to_place_data;
Time    timestamp;

    XConvertSelection( display,
        selection_you_want,
        target,
        property_to_place_data,
        window_to_place_data,
        timestamp );
```

You should pass a valid timestamp (not `CurrentTime`) when calling `XConvertSelection()`. Usually you'll get this timestamp from an X event where the user asked that data be pasted (such as a `ButtonPress` event).

If your application owns the selection, you should have the data already; therefore, you don't have to call `XConvertSelection()`.

ASKING FOR SELECTION DATA

`AskPrimaryData()` calls `XConvertSelection()` to ask for the contents of the `PRIMARY` selection, with a given target type. Its contents are as follows:

```
AskPrimaryData( display, window, property, target, timestamp )

Display     *display;
Window      window;
Atom        property;
Atom        target;
Time        timestamp;

{       /* -- function AskPrimaryData */

   XConvertSelection( display,
       XA_PRIMARY,
```

```
        target,
        property,
        window,
        timestamp );

    XFlush( display );

}       /* -- function AskPrimaryData */
```

SELECTION EVENTS

If everything goes well, the owner of the selection will get your request (generated by the call to XConvertSelection) and then send your program a SelectionNotify event. If things went wrong, you may get a SelectionNotify event with a property of None. If things really went wrong, you may get nothing at all (or an X error).

In addition to SelectionNotify, two other selection events are covered below, including SelectionRequest events and SelectionClear events.

SelectNotify EVENT

A SelectionNotify event looks like:

```
typedef struct
    {
    int             type;           /* -- SelectionNotify */
    unsigned long   serial;
    Bool            send_event;     /* -- Most likely True */
    Display         *display;
    Window          requestor;
    Atom            selection;      /* -- XA_PRIMARY, etc. */
    Atom            target;         /* -- type of data */
    Atom            property;
    Time            time;
    } XSelectionEvent;
```

Most of the fields in the XSelectionEvent structure are just the data values you passed to XConvertSelection(). The property field will be None if the owner of the selection failed to convert the data to the target type you wanted.

If everything went fine, however, your application should read the given property on the given window (the requester window, that is, your window). Whenever you read this property, be sure to pass a delete flag of True. This will to delete the property data after reading.

GRABBING SELECTION DATA

GetSelectionData() handles most errors from an incoming SelectionRequest event. It calls GetPropertyData() from sel_prop.c, covered later in this chapter. The contents of GetSelectionData() are as follows:

```
GetSelectionData( display, window, event )

Display             *display;
Window              window;
XSelectionEvent     *event;

{   /* -- function GetSelectionData */
    int      status;

    /*
    * Check for errors
    */
    if ( event->selection != XA_PRIMARY )
        {
        PropSetData( "Returned selection is not PRIMARY." );
        return( True
        );
        }

    if ( event->requestor != window )
        {
        PropSetData( "Requestor window returned != our window." );
        return( True );
        }

    if ( event->property  = = (Atom) None )
```

```
    {
    PropSetData( "Returned property is None." );
    return( True );
    }

if ( event->target = = (Atom) None )
    {
    PropSetData( "Returned target is None." );
    return( True );
    }

status = GetPropertyData( display,
    event->requestor,
    event->property,
    event->target );

return( status );

}       /* -- function GetSelectionData */
```

SelectionClear EVENT

A SelectionClear event is sent to your application when it loses the ownership of a selection. If you lose ownership of a selection, your application should no longer receive (or answer) SelectionRequest events until the next call to XSetSelectionOwner.

A SelectionClear event looks like:

```
typedef struct
    {
    int             type;           /* -- SelectionClear */
    unsigned long   serial;
    Bool            send_event;
    Display         *display;
    Window          window;         /* -- former owner */
    Atom            selection;      /* -- what was lost */
    Time            time;
    } XSelectionClearEvent;
```

When a SelectionClear event arrives, be sure to mark your selection as no longer valid. If your application highlighted the selected data, you should unhighlight the selected data as it is no longer considered selected. The whole idea is for the user to control what data is selected on the display. Your applications shouldn't fight the user, so don't play games like asserting ownership all the time (especially if you are using the PRIMARY selection).

SelectionRequest EVENT

The call to XConvertSelection() generates a SelectionRequest event that is sent to the owner of the selection. If your application owns the selection after calling XSetSelectionOwner(), you need to respond to these events (this will be covered a bit later in this chapter).

A SelectionRequest event looks like:

```
typedef struct
    {
    int             type;           /* -- SelectionRequest */
    unsigned long   serial;
    Bool            send_event;
    Display         *display;
    Window          owner;          /* -- who has it */
    Window          requestor;      /* -- who wants it */
    Atom            selection;      /* -- e.g., XA_PRIMARY */
    Atom            target;         /* -- data type */
    Atom            property;       /* -- Where to put data */
    Time            time;
    } XSelectionRequestEvent;
```

PROVIDING SELECTION DATA

When your application receives a SelectionRequest event, it should make an effort to translate the data of the selection into the asked-for target type. There are three required target types—TIMESTAMP, MULTIPLE, and TARGETS—and a host of common types your application should support.

PutSelectionData(), developed later in this section, answers a SelectionRequest event. First, PutSelectionData() checks the event fields. Then it checks if the target type is MULTIPLE. The MULTIPLE type is a special target type that allows a requester to ask for many types of data at once.

THE MULTIPLE TARGET TYPE

The MULTIPLE target type has the name of a property and a window ID. In that property lie many ATOM_PAIR items (which are each two atoms, or pairs of XA_ATOM types). In each ATOM_PAIR, the first item is a target type (one of many) and the second item is a property ID. Your application should then convert the selection data to the asked-for target type and write that data to the paired property ID (all on the same given window ID). Repeat this process for every ATOM_PAIR stored in the original property. The contents of PutSelectionData() are as follows:

```
PutSelectionData( display, window, event )

Display                 *display;
Window                  window;
XSelectionRequestEvent  *event;

{   /* -- function PutSelectionData */
    int     status;
    char    *data;
    int     i, number_items;
    Atom    target, property;

    /*
     * Do we own the selection?
     */
    if ( ( event->selection != XA_PRIMARY ) ||
           ( event->owner != window ) )
           {
           return;
           }

    status = CheckIfPrimaryIsOurs( event->time );

    /*
     * Send out the data
     */
```

```
if ( status = = True )
        {
        /*
         * Handle MULTIPLE targets
         */
        if ( CompareAtomWithName( display, event->target,
        "       MULTIPLE"== True )
                {
                /*
                 *Get ATOM_PAIR data
                 */
            target = XA_ATOM;
            status = GetWindowProperty( display,
                             event->requestor,
                             event->property,
                             &target,
                             &number_items,
                             &data );
            /*
             * Handle multiple properties and targets
             */
            if ( ( number_items > 0 ) && ( status == True ) )
                    {
                    while( ( i < number_items ) &&
                            ( status == True ) )
                            {
                            /*
                             * Each ATOM_PAIR contains
                             * a target and a property
                             */
                            target = Bytes2Long( &data[(i * 4)] );
                            i++;
                            property = Bytes2Long( &data[(i * 4)] );
                            i++;

                            /*
                             * Call PutPropertyData() for each one
                             */
                            status = PutPropertyData( display,
                                           window,
                                           event->requestor,
                                           property,
                                           target );
```

```
                    }

                XFree( data );
                }
            }
        else
            {
        status = PutPropertyData( display,
                    window,
                    event->requestor,
                    event->property,
                    event->target );
            }
        }

    /*
     * Notify the requestor window
     */
    if ( status = = True )
        {
        SendSelectNotify( display,
                event->requestor,
                event->selection,
                event->property,
                event->target,
                event->time );
        }
    else
        {
        SendSelectNotify( display,
                event->requestor,
                event->selection,
                (Atom) None,
                event->target,
                event->time );
        }

}       /* -- function PutSelectionData */
```

If `PutSelectionData()` is successful, it sends a `SelectionNotify` event to the asking window ID. Send `SelectNotify()` handles this task; its contents are as follows:

```
SendSelectNotify( display, window, selection, property, target, timestamp )

Display    *display;
Window     window;
```

```
Atom        selection, property, target;
Time        timestamp;

{           /* -- function SendSelectNotify */
            XSelectionEvent selectevent;
            /*
             * Set up return event.
             * We need to send an event
             * to the requesting window
             * when done placing the
             * data on the requestor
             * window.
             */
             selectevent.type          = SelectionNotify;
             selectevent.property      = property;
             selectevent.display       = display;
             selectevent.requestor     = window;
             selectevent.selection     = selection;
             selectevent.target        = target;
             selectevent.time          = timestamp;

            /*
             * Send an event to the
             * requestor window that the
             * data is now available
             */
             XSendEvent( display,
                   window,
                   False,
                   0L, /* -- empty event mask */
                   &selectevent );

}       /* -- function SendSelectNotify */
```

Note that we used an event mask of `zero` (nothing) and use a propagate flag of `False` after filling in the fields of the `SelectionNotify` event.

Figure 19-2 shows how data exchange with selections works, from the point of view of the application that asks for data.

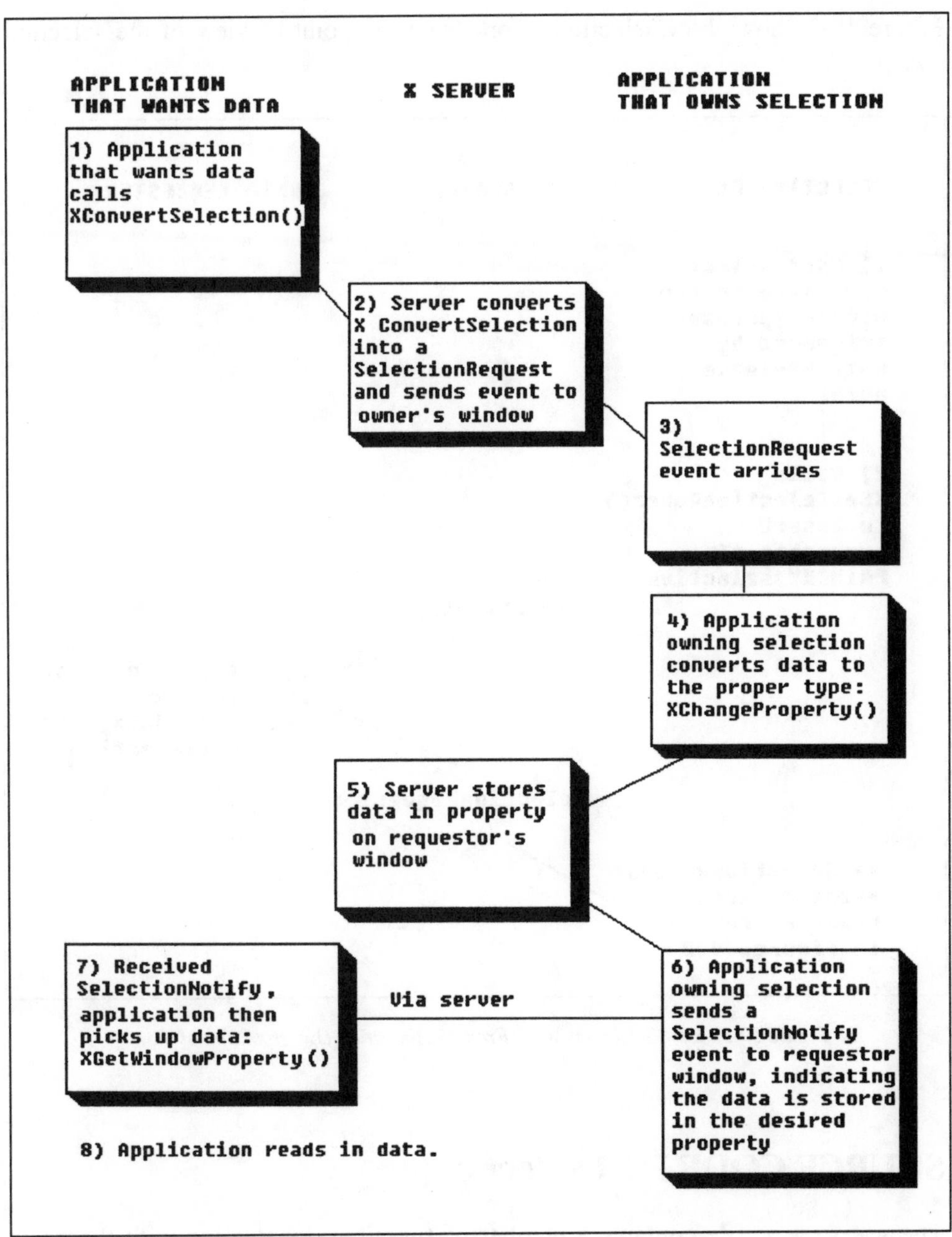

Figure 19-2. How Selections Work From the Data Requester's Point of View

Figure 19-3 shows how selections work from the point of view of the selection owner.

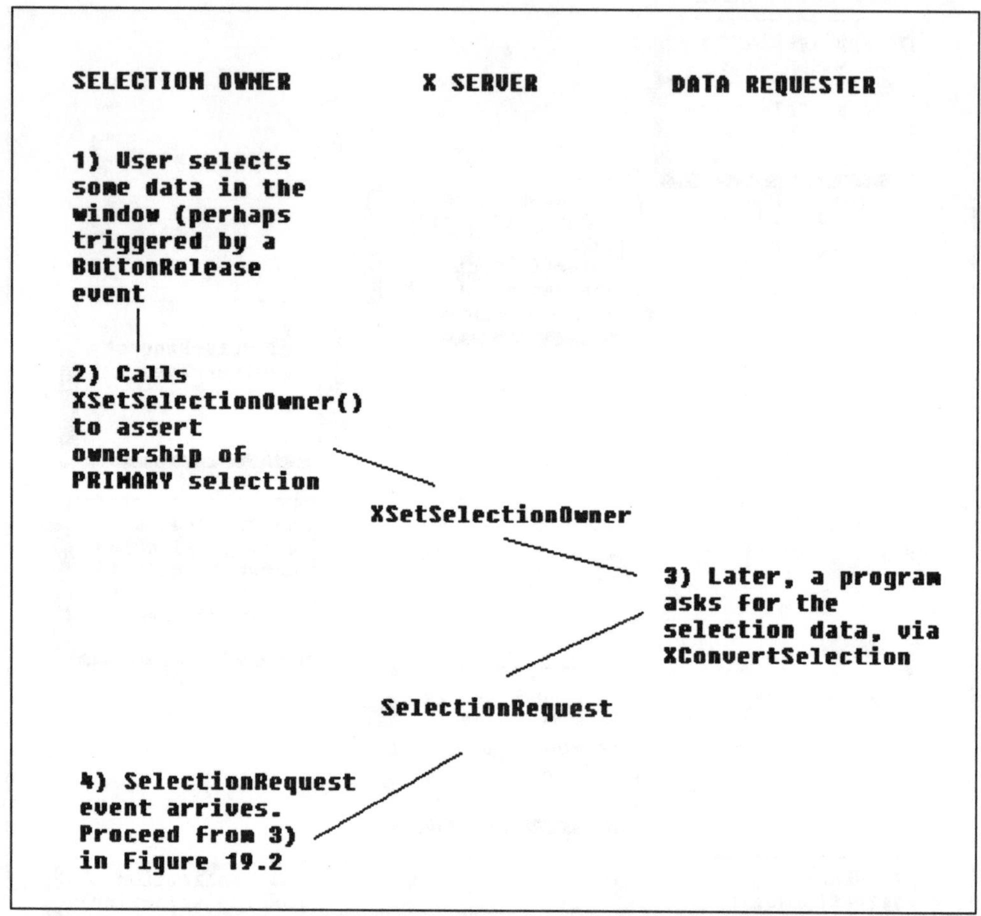

Figure 19-3. How Selections Work From the Selection Owner's Point of View

SOURCE CODE FOR select.c

The `select.c` file contains a number of functions for dealing with the basic selection events. Its contents are as follows:

```
select.c:
/*
 * select.c
 * X11 functions for handling Selections
 *
 */

#include   "xbook.h"

AskPrimaryData( display, window, property, target, timestamp )

Display    *display;
Window     window;
Atom       property;
Atom       target;
Time       timestamp;

{       /* -- function AskPrimaryData */

   XConvertSelection( display,
      XA_PRIMARY,
      target,
      property,
      window,
      timestamp );

   XFlush( display );

}       /* -- function AskPrimaryData */

GetSelectionData( display, window, event )

                                          Display              *display;
                                          Window               window;
                                          XSelectionEvent      *event;

{  /* -- function GetSelectionData */
   int     status;

   /*
    * Check for errors
    */
   if ( event->selection != XA_PRIMARY )
      {
      PropSetData( "Returned selection is not PRIMARY." );
      return( True );
      }
```

```
    if ( event->requestor != window )
            {
            PropSetData( "Requestor window returned != our window." );
            return( True );
            }

    if ( event->property  = = (Atom) None
            )
            { PropSetData( "Returned property is None." );
            return( True );
            }

    if ( event->target = = (Atom) None )
            {
            PropSetData( "Returned target is None." );
            return( True );
            }

    status = GetPropertyData( display,
            event->requestor,
            event->property,
            event->target );

    return( status );

}       /* -- function GetSelectionData */

PutSelectionData( display, window, event )

Display                 *display;
Window                  window;
XSelectionRequestEvent  *event;

{   /* -- function PutSelectionData */
    int     status;
    char    *data;
    int     i, number_items;
    Atom    target, property;

    /*
     * Do we own the selection?
     */
    if ( ( event->selection != XA_PRIMARY ) ||
            ( event->owner != window ) )
            {
            return;
            }
```

```
status = CheckIfPrimaryIsOurs( event->time );

/*
 * Send out the data
 */
if ( status = = True )
    {
    /*
     * Handle MULTIPLE targets
     */
if ( CompareAtomWithName( display, event->target,
        "MULTIPLE" ) = = True )
        {
        /*
         * Get ATOM_PAIR data
         */
        target = XA_ATOM;
        status = GetWindowProperty( display,
                    event->requestor,
                    event->property,
                    &target,
                    &number_items,
                    &data );
        /*
         * Handle multiple properties and targets
         */
        if ( ( number_items > 0 ) && ( status = = True ) )
        {
        while( ( i < number_items ) &&
                ( status  == True ))
                {
                /*
                 * Each ATOM_PAIR contains
                 * a target and a property
                 */
                target = Bytes2Long( &data[(i * 4)] );
                i++;
                property = Bytes2Long( &data[(i * 4)] );
                i++;

                /*
                 * Call PutPropertyData() for each one
                 */
                status = PutPropertyData( display,
                            window,
                            event->requestor,
                            property,
                            target );
```

```
            }

            XFree( data );
            }
            }
        else
            {
            status = PutPropertyData( display,
                    window,
                    event->requestor,
                    event->property,
                    event->target );
            }
        }

        /*
         * Notify the requestor window
         */
        if ( status == True )
            {
            SendSelectNotify( display,
                event->requestor,
                event->selection,
                event->property,
                event->target,
                event->time );
            }
        else
            {
        SendSelectNotify( display,
                event->requestor,
                event->selection,
                (Atom) None,
                event->target,
                event->time );
        }

}       /* -- function PutSelectionData */

SendSelectNotify( display, window, selection, property, target, timestamp )

Display     *display;
Window      window;
Atom        selection, property, target;
Time        timestamp;
```

```
{   /* -- function SendSelectNotify */
    XSelectionEvent selectevent;

    /*
     * Set up return event.
     * We need to send an event
     * to the requesting window
     * when done placing the
     * data on the requestor
     * window.
     */
    selectevent.type      = SelectionNotify;
    selectevent.property  = property;
    selectevent.display   = display;
    selectevent.requestor = window;
    selectevent.selection = selection;
    selectevent.target    = target;
    selectevent.time      = timestamp;

    /*
     * Send an event to the
     * requestor window that the
     * data is now available
     */
    XSendEvent( display,
        window,
        False,
        0L,     /* -- empty event mask */
        &selectevent );

}       /* -- function SendSelectNotify */

/*
 * end of file
 */
```

REQUIRED TARGETS

We've already covered the MULTIPLE target type. In addition to MULTIPLE, every X application should support the TIMESTAMP and TARGETS target selection types. Your application, if it owns a selection, must be able to respond to the MULTIPLE, TIMESTAMP and TARGETS queries.

THE TIMESTAMP TARGET

The TIMESTAMP target is the timestamp (in X server terms) of when your application became the given selection's owner. If you call XSetSelectionOwner() on the XA_PRIMARY selection, your application should be able to return the timestamp passed to XSetSelectionOwner().

The proper response to a TIMESTAMP request is to format the timestamp as a 32-bit integer (real type XA_INTEGER) and write that value into the requested property on the requested window.

THE TARGETS TARGET

It's hard for another application to guess what kind of data types your application supports. So, the ICCCM designers came up with the TARGETS target.

The TARGETS target is the list of data types (targets) your application supports. Since each target type is an atom, the TARGETS response is a list of atoms (atoms are 32-bit values). Your application should respond with the list of target types (atoms) that your application supports. The only ones your application must support are MULTIPLE, TIMESTAMP, and TARGETS (read more about this in section 2.6.2 of the ICCCM). It's a good idea to support more targets than this. See MakeTargets() later in this chapter for the list supported by the primary application.

COMMON TARGETS

The following chart lists some COMMON TARGET TYPES (See Section 2.6.3 in the ICCCM)

TEXT NAME	BASE TYPE	BUILT-IN	DESCRIPTION
BITMAP	BITMAP	XA_BITMAP	Bitmap ID (for sharing)
CHARACTER_POSITION	SPAN	XA_INTEGER	Two integers: start and end position of selection inbytes
CLIENT_WINDOW	WINDOW	XA_WINDOW	top-level window
FILE_NAME	TEXT (STRING)		Full name of a file (with path)

HOST_NAME	TEXT (STRING)		Name of host machine (WM_CLIENT_MACHINE)
LENGTH	INTEGER	XA_INTEGER	Number of bytes in selection
MULTIPLE	ATOM_PAIR	XA_ATOM	multiple requests (really paired list of atoms)
NAME	TEXT (STRING)		Name of application (WM_NAME)
PIXMAP	DRAWABLE	XA_PIXMAP	Pixmap ID (for sharing) (XA_DRAWABLE)
STRING	STRING	XA_STRING	ISO Latin-1 text (superset ofASCII)
TARGETS	ATOM	XA_ATOM	List of supported targets
TEXT	(really STRING)		Text in your preferred format (usually STRING)
USER	TEXT (STRING)		Name of user

Pass the text name to XInternAtom() to get the proper target type. When writing out data to a property and reading it in, use the base types. When asking for the data from a selection owner, use the specific type.

STRING AND TEXT TARGETS

If your application places text in a window, you should allow the user to select that text, as well as paste in the PRIMARY selection (as text). Any text drawn into a window should be selectable if you want to create well-behaved applications.

Text is easy and is probably the most common target type for selections. The only problem is what kind of text to use. The TEXT target type means for the selection owner to choose a text type and use that. Most users in the USA want the target type to be STRING (XA_STRING) for ISO Latin-1 text (essentially a superset of ASCII). Users in Saudi Arabia, on the other hand, may wish to have their text displayed in Arabic. The basic idea to replace the TEXT type with a textual format that makes sense for your application. Most will use XA_STRING.

CLIENT INFORMATION TARGETS

There's a host of client information targets for selections. Client information targets include the machine you are running on (HOST_NAME), what user is running this program (USER), the application's name (NAME), and so on.

When responding to SelectionRequests (if your application owns the PRIMARY selection):

- CLIENT_WINDOW should be the window ID of your application's top-level window.
- USER should be the name of the user (as shown in GetUserName in chapter 15).
- NAME should be the name of the application (stored in icccm.c, also in chapter 15).
- HOST_NAME should be the name of the machine your application is executing on (which may very well be different than the machine the X server is running on).

All these types are TEXT types. USA-based application writers should use a real target type of XA_STRING when writing or reading property data for these types.

I SAY TO_MA_TO, YOU SAY TOMATO

According to the ICCCM section 2.6.2, to ask for the name of the host machine an application is running on, use the target type HOST_NAME. In Release 4, most applications, like xterm and xclipboard, say they support the target HOSTNAME (without the "_" underscore) . Calling XInternAtom() with both names results in two different atom values (of course, they are different text strings), so they're not the same. What can you do? Support both. Someone will later tell you that you're all wrong, but what the hey—support what works and worry about it later.

SPANNING TARGETS

The CHARACTER_POSITION target type has a base type of SPAN. A SPAN is two integers (that is, two of the built-in atom XA_INTEGER). The CHARACTER_POSITION target type should be the start and end position of the selected data, in bytes.

The `LENGTH` target type should be the length of the selection (the number of bytes) stored as an `INTEGER`.

MANY ITEMS, ONE TYPE

With each type of target, you can usually store more than one item. For example, `SPAN` is really two `INTEGERS`. So, when you write out the property data, use a target type of `XA_INTEGER` and a number of items of 2 (with enough bytes of data filled in, of course). That way, the `TARGETS` target is really just an `XA_ATOM` type, with many `atoms` stored in the list. That's what the `number_items` variable is about in the calls `XGetWindowProperty()` and `XChangeProperty()`.

FUNCTIONS FOR DEALING WITH SELECTION PROPERTY DATA

When your application owns the `PRIMARY` selection, it needs to respond to `SelectionRequest` events. `GetTargetData()` is the main function used to collect the different types of data and prepare the raw data bytes, which will be later written to the requesting program's window.

The target types we support are:

`CHARACTER_POSITION`	
`CLIENT_WINDOW`	
`HOST_NAME`	*(re: ICCCM)*
`HOSTNAME`	*(re:* `xterm`)
`LENGTH`	
`MULTIPLE`	*(not covered in* `GetTargetData`)
`NAME`	
`STRING`	
`TARGETS`	
`TEXT`	
`TIMESTAMP`	
`USER`	

This is a fairly common set of targets, and some of the more interesting ones that `xterm` and `xclipboard` support. Since applications need to work together, we thought we'd focus on common target types.

```
GetTargetData( display, window, target, type, string, format )
Display     *display;
Window      window;
Atom        target;
Atom        type;
char        string[];
int         *format;

{       /* -- function GetTargetData */
        int             number_items = 0;

        if ( ( CompareAtomWithName( display, target, "TEXT" ) = = True ) ||
            ( target = = XA_STRING ))
            {
            (void) memcpy( string, PropertyData, PropertyLength);
            number_items = PropertyLength;
            }

        if ( ( CompareAtomWithName( display, target, "HOSTNAME" ) = = True ) ||
        ( CompareAtomWithName( display, target, "HOST_NAME" ) = = True ) )
            {
            GetHostName( string );

            number_items = strlen( string );
            }
        if ( CompareAtomWithName( display, target, "LENGTH" ) = = True )
            (
            {
            Long2Bytes( (long) PropertyLength, string );
            number_items = 1;
            }
        if ( CompareAtomWithName( display, target,
            "CHARACTER_POSITION" ) == True )
            {
            Long2Bytes( 0L, string );
            Long2Bytes( (long) PropertyLength, &string[ 4 ] );

            number_items = 2;
            }

        if ( CompareAtomWithName( display, target, "USER" ) = = True )
```

```
        GetUserName( string );

        number_items = strlen( string );
        }

if ( CompareAtomWithName( display, target, "CLIENT_WINDOW" ) = = True )
        {
        Long2Bytes( (long) window, string );

        number_items = 1;
        }

if ( CompareAtomWithName( display, target, "NAME" ) = = True      )
        {
        GetAppName( string
        );

        number_items = strlen( string );
        }

if ( CompareAtomWithName( display, target, "TARGETS" ) = = True )
        {
        number_items = MakeTargets( display, string );
        }

if ( CompareAtomWithName( display, target, "TIMESTAMP" ) = = True )
        {
        if ( IsPrimaryOurs() = = True )
        {
        Long2Bytes( (unsigned long) PrimaryTimeStamp(),
            string );

        number_items = 1;
        }
    }

*format = GetFormat( type );

return( number_items );

    /* -- function GetTargetData */
```

You'll notice that `GetTargetData()` often calls `CompareAtomWithName()`. The application should really cache the target `atom` IDs, but we wanted to make the names very visible and make the application display-independent. It's slower, but the X performance is rather good, so you hardly notice the speed difference (this code is designed for learning, after all).

SOURCE CODE FOR sel_prop.c

The `sel_prop.c` file contains a number of property-oriented functions for working with selections. The selected data is stored in the global character array `PropertyData` (with property length being the number of bytes in `PropertyData`). `Sel_prop.c` contains functions for placing selection data into a property, reading in selected data from a property. For display, all selection data is converted to strings (to make the data readable by humans). The contents of `sel_prop.c` are as follows:

```
sel_prop.c:
/*
 *  sel_prop.c
 *  X11 Property functions for use
 *  with selections.
 *
 */

#include  "xbook.h"

/*
 *  Global string data to store latest
 *  property/selection information
 */
char PropertyData[ (4 * FULL_LENGTH) + 1 ];
int PropertyLength = 0;

PropDisplayCurrent( display, window, gc, font_height, x, y )

Display     *display;
Window      window;
GC          gc;
int         font_height;
int         x, y;
```

```
/*
 * PropDisplayCurrent() displays the current
 * global PropertyData  in the given window,
 * starting at the given location.
 */

{       /* -- function PropDisplayCurrent */

        if ( PropertyLength > 0 )
                {
                DrawStrings( display, window, gc, font_height,
                    x, y, PropertyData, PropertyLength );
                }

}       /* -- function PropDisplayCurrent */

GetPropertyData( display, window, property, target )

Display    *display;
Window     window;
Atom       property;
Atom       target;

/*
 * GetPropertyData() gets the data from the given
 * property on the given window and converts that
 * data into a string, storing the string in the
 * Global PropertyData.
 */

{   /* -- function GetPropertyData */
    Atom             actual_target;
    unsigned long    number_items;
    int              status;
    int              length;
    char             string[ (4 * FULL_LENGTH) + 1 ];
    unsigned char    *data;

    actual_target = target;

    status = GetWindowProperty( display, window,
                property, &actual_target,
                &number_items, &data );
```

```
    if ( status = = False )
            {
            return( status );
            }

    /*
     * Convert Data to string
     */
    status = False;

    length = Property2String( display, actual_target,
       data, number_items, string );

    if ( length > 0 )
       {
       PropertyLength = length;

       (void)memcpy( PropertyData, string, length );

       status = True;
       }

    if ( data )
       {
       XFree( data );
       }

    return( status );

}       /* -- function GetPropertyData */

PropSetData( string )

char    string[];

/*
 * PropSetData() allows a program to set the
 * data in the global character string
 * PropertyData.
 */

{       /* -- function PropSetData */

        PropertyLength = strlen( string );
```

```
        (void) strcpy( PropertyData, string );

}       /* -- function PropSetData */

PropReturnData( string )

char    string[];

/*
 * PropReturnData() places a copy
 * of the global PropertyData into
 * string.
 */

{   /* -- function PropReturnData */
    int     length;

    length = PropertyLength;

    if ( length > BUFSIZE )
        {
        length = BUFSIZE;
        }

    if ( length < 0 )
        {
        length = 0;
        }

    (void) strncpy( string, PropertyData, length );

    string[ length ] = '\0';

}       /* -- function PropReturnData */

PutPropertyData( display, original_window, window, property, target )

Display    *display;
Window     original_window, window;
Atom       property;
Atom       target;

/*
 * PutPropertyData() places data in the given property
 * on the given window.  The data either comes from
 * the Global PropertyData or from various values
```

```
 *  stored with the program: original_window,
 *  user name, application name and so on.
 */

{   /* -- function PutPropertyData */
    Atom            new_target;
    int             status = False;
    char            string[ (4 * FULL_LENGTH) + 1 ];
    int             number_items;
    int             format;

if ( property = = (Atom) None )
        {
        return( status );
        }

new_target = ConvertTarget( display, target );

number_items = GetTargetData( display,
            original_window,
            target,
            new_target,
            string,
            &format );

if ( number_items > 0 )
    {
    status = AppendProperty( display,
            window,
            property,
            new_target,
            format, string,
            number_items );
    }

return( status );

}       /* -- function PutPropertyData */

GetTargetData( display, window, target, type, string, format )

Display     *display;
Window      window;
Atom        target;
Atom        type;
int         *format;
```

```
/*
 * GetTargetData() builds up raw data bytes for a given target
 * type, e.g., the window ID if the target type is the atom
 * for "CLIENT_WINDOW".  GetTargetData() returns the number of
 * ITEMS in the variable string, and also sets the proper
 * format (32 or 8 in our case).
 */

{   /* -- function GetTargetData */
    int             number_items = 0;

    if ( ( CompareAtomWithName( display, target, "TEXT" ) = = True ) ||
        ( target = = XA_STRING ) )
        {
        (void) memcpy( string, PropertyData, PropertyLength );
        number_items = PropertyLength;
        }

    if ( ( CompareAtomWithName( display, target, "HOSTNAME" ) = = True ) ||
    ( CompareAtomWithName( display, target, "HOST_NAME" ) = = True ) )
        {
        GetHostName( string );
        number_items = strlen( string );
        }
    if ( CompareAtomWithName( display, target, "LENGTH" ) = = True )
        {
        Long2Bytes( (long) PropertyLength, string );

        number_items = 1;
        }

    if ( CompareAtomWithName( display, target,
        "CHARACTER_POSITION" ) = = True )
        {
        Long2Bytes( 0L, string );
        Long2Bytes( (long) PropertyLength, &string[ 4 ] );

        number_items = 2;
        }

    if ( CompareAtomWithName( display, target, "USER" ) = = True )
        {
        GetUserName( string );

    number_items = strlen( string );
        }

    if ( CompareAtomWithName( display, target, "CLIENT_WINDOW" ) = = True )
```

```
        {
        Long2Bytes( (long) window, string );

        number_items = 1;
        }

    if ( CompareAtomWithName( display, target, "NAME" ) = = True )
        {
        GetAppName( string );

        number_items = strlen( string );
        }

if ( CompareAtomWithName( display, target, "TARGETS" ) = = True )
        {
        number_items = MakeTargets( display, string );
        }

if ( CompareAtomWithName( display, target, "TIMESTAMP" ) = = True )
        {
        Long2Bytes( (unsigned long) PrimaryTimeStamp(),
            string );

            number_items = 1;
            }
}

    *format = GetFormat( type );

    return( number_items );

}       /* -- function GetTargetData */

MakeTargets( display, data )

Display *display;
char    *data;

/*
 * MakeTargets() builds together the list of targets
 * our application supports.  Note that the ICCCM 1.0
 * has an atom titled "HOST_NAME" while Release 4
 * xterm (and other R4 apps) seem to use "HOSTNAME".
 * We support both.
 *
 * The list of targets is put into data as raw bytes.
 */
```

```
{   /* -- function MakeTargets */
    Atom     atoms[ 25 ];
    int      number_items;

    atoms[ 0 ] = XInternAtom( display, "TARGETS", False );
    atoms[ 1 ] = XA_STRING;
    atoms[ 2 ] = XInternAtom( display, "TEXT", False );
    atoms[ 3 ] = XInternAtom( display, "LENGTH", False );
    atoms[ 4 ] = XInternAtom( display, "HOSTNAME", False );
    atoms[ 5 ] = XInternAtom( display, "HOST_NAME", False );
    atoms[ 6 ] = XInternAtom( display, "NAME", False );
    atoms[ 7 ] = XInternAtom( display, "TIMESTAMP", False );
    atoms[ 8 ] = XInternAtom( display, "USER", False );
    atoms[ 9 ] = XInternAtom( display, "CLIENT_WINDOW", False );
    atoms[ 10] = XInternAtom( display, "MULTIPLE", False );

    number_items = 11;

    Atoms2Data( atoms, number_items, data );

    return( number_items );

}       /* -- function MakeTargets */

/*
 * end of file
 */
```

THE PRIMARY SELECTION

Just about every application wishing to use selections should support the PRIMARY selection. PRIMARY is the primary means for cut-and-paste operations between applications. From the user's point of view, selected text should be easily pasted into any other application. Figure 19-4 shows how selections work from the user's point of view.

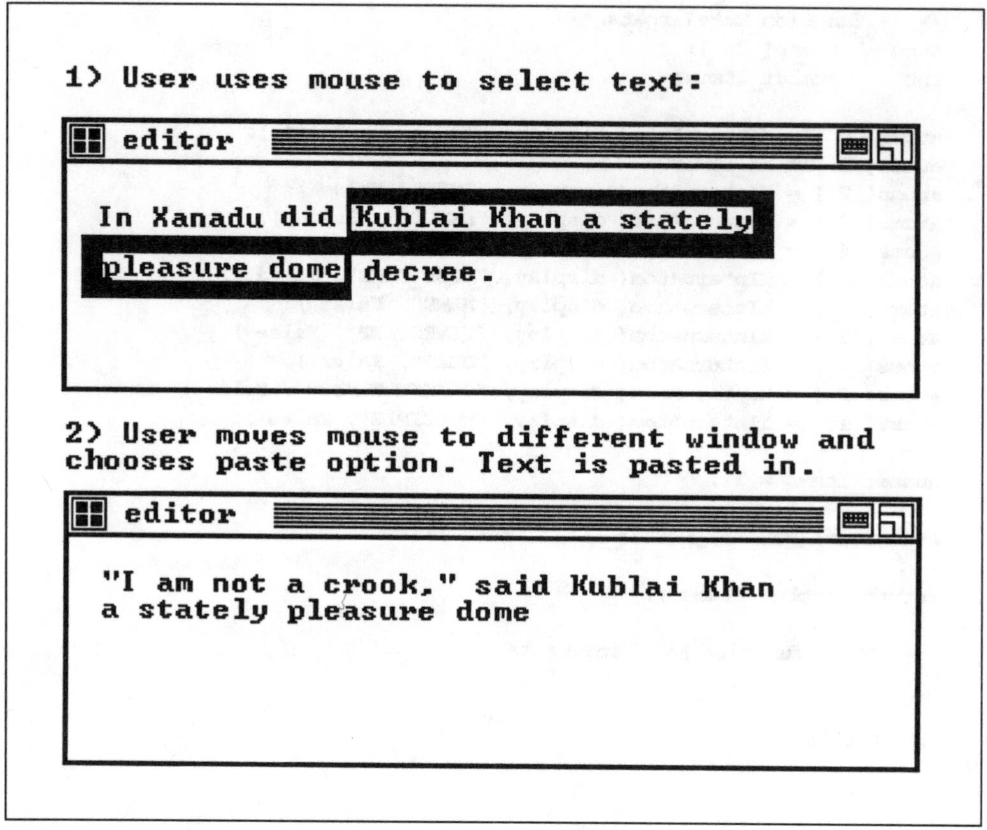

Figure 19-4. How Selections Work from the User's Point of View

SECONDARY SELECTIONS

As an aside, there is a `SECONDARY` (`XA_SECONDARY`) selection as well as a `PRIMARY` selection. `SECONDARY` exists mainly to allow a user to request that `PRIMARY` and `SECONDARY` be exchanged (allowing some form of backtracking or undoing). Don't worry so much about `SECONDARY`, though, `PRIMARY` is the primary concern.

THE primary PROGRAM

Selections are confusing, and if the concepts aren't crystal clear right now, don't worry. `Primary` is an application that examines the primary selection. The `primary` application was created to help show how data exchange with selections works, by exploring how selections are used by real X applications. `Primary` is based on a program we created when first learning about selections. The basic idea behind primary is this: select some text in an `xterm` window (or other text-based application you use) and then use `primary` to ask for the selected data. Ask for the `STRING` target and you should get the selected text. Ask for the `TARGETS` target and you should get a list of targets that the owning application (e.g., the `xterm`) supports.

Keep trying `primary` with different applications and different text selections. Play around a bit. The `primary` application shown in figure 19-5, more than anything else, should help visually describe how selections work.

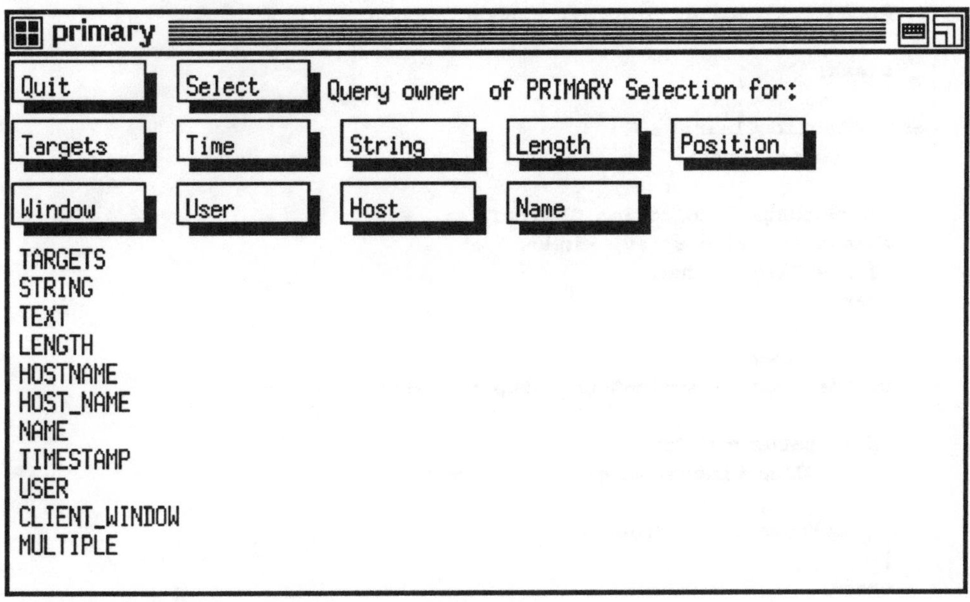

Figure 19-5. The primary Application

Primary will also select the text in the window, can then be pasted into other applications. Two primarys working together can show you how the sample application uses selections.

Source Code for primary.c

If you haven't guessed by now, the primary application looks a lot like the propsend and send applications. Primary does have special code to handle the selection events and many functions to handle all the buttons. These functions all look the same and ask the owner of the primary selection for a different target type. The Refresh() function also has special code to highlight the data if it has been selected (when you bonk on the "Select" push-button).

The selection event code contents are as follows:

```
...

    case SelectionRequest:
        PutSelectionData( display, window, &event );

        break;

    case SelectionClear:
        LoseSelection();

        PropSetData( "Selection Cleared" );
        XClearWindow( display, window );
        RefreshFlag = True;
        break;

    case SelectionNotify:
        status = GetSelectionData( display, window, &event );

        if ( status = = True )
            { XClearWindow( display, window );

            RefreshFlag = True;
        }
        break;
```

Fairly simple for such a complex topic, isn't it?

The source code for `primary.c` are as follows:

```
primary.c:
/*
 *
 * primary.c
 *
 * This program requests whoever owns the PRIMARY selection
 * to supply information about that selection.
 *
 */

#include  "xbook.h"

/*
 * Include Icon shape
 */
#include  "primary.xb"

/*
 * Top-level window Globals
 */
int RefreshFlag = False;
int QuitFlag    = False;

char    OwnerString[ BUFSIZE + 1 ];

main( argc, argv )

int     argc;
char    *argv[];

{   /* -- function main */
    Display          *display;
    int              screen;
    Window           window;
    GC               gc;
    int              x, y, width, height;
    XFontStruct      *font;
    Pixmap           icon;
    int              font_height;
    unsigned long    black, white;

    /*
     * Set up defaults
     */
    OwnerString[ 0 ] = '\0';
```

```
/*
 * Set up X connection
 */
display    = SetUpDisplay( argc, argv,
                        &screen );

black  = BlackPixel( display, screen );
white  = WhitePixel( display, screen );

/*
 * Check size and location of window
 */
x   = 10;
y   = 10;
width  = 510;
height = 320;
CheckGeometry( argc, argv,
   DisplayWidth( display, screen ),
   DisplayHeight( display, screen ),
   &x, &y, &width, &height );

window    = TopWindow( display, x, y, width, height,
               primary_bits, primary_width, primary_height,
               &icon, &gc );

/*
 * Load font
 */
font = LoadFont( display, gc, argc, argv, "variable" );

font_height = font->ascent + font->descent;

/*
 * Store values for window manager
 */
SetNormalHints( display, window,
   x, y, width, height );

SetWMHints( display, window, icon );

NameWindow( display, window,
   "primary", "primary", "Primary" );

SetICCCM( display, window,
   argc, argv );
```

```
    XFlush( display );

    /*
    * Create buttons of ruser interface items
    */
    MakeButtons( display, window,
        black, white, font->fid );

    /*
     * Map windows
     */
    MapWindow( display, window );

    /*
     * Handle any events
     */
    while( QuitFlag = = False )
        {
        EventLoop( display,
            window,
            &width, &height );

    if ( RefreshFlag = = True )
        {
        Refresh( display, window, gc,
            font_height, black, white );

    RefreshFlag = False; }

    }

    /*
     * Shut down
     */
    XFreeFont( display, font );
    XFreePixmap( display, icon );
    CloseDisplay( display, window, gc );

    exit( 0 );

}       /* -- function main */

EventLoop( display, window, width, height )

Display     *display;
Window      window;
int         *width, *height;
```

```
/*
 * EventLoop() handles generic X events, but passes
 * most events on to specific functions to handle
 * the particular event.
 *
 *
 */

{  /* -- function EventLoop */
   XEvent          event;
   KeySym          keysym;
   int             status;

   /*
    * Block on input, awaiting
    * an event from X.
    */
   NextEvent( display, False,
      *width,
      *height,
      &event,
      &keysym );

   if ( ButtonEvent( display, &event ) = = True )
      {
      return( True );
      }

   /*
    * Decode the event and call
    * a specific routine to
    * handle it.
    */
   switch( event.type )
      {
      case ClientMessage:
         if( IsDeleteWindow( display, &event ) = = True )
            {
            QuitFlag = True;
            }
         break;
      case Expose:
         RefreshFlag = True;
         break;
```

```
        case SelectionRequest:
            PutSelectionData( display, window, &event );
            break;

        case SelectionClear:
            LoseSelection();

            PropSetData( "Selection Cleared" );
            XClearWindow( display, window );
            RefreshFlag = True;
            break;

        case SelectionNotify:
            status = GetSelectionData( display, window, &event );

            if ( status = = True )
            {
            XClearWindow( display, window );

            RefreshFlag = True;
            }
            break;
        case ConfigureNotify:
            *width = event.xconfigure.width;
            *height = event.xconfigure.height;
            break;
        }

    return( True );

}       /* -- function EventLoop */

QuitApplication( display, window )

Display     *display;
Window      window;

{       /* -- function QuitApplication */

    QuitFlag = True;

}       /* -- function QuitApplication */

GrabSelection( display, window )

Display     *display;
```

```
Window     window;

{   /* -- function GrabSelection */
    int     status;
    Time    timestamp;

    timestamp = LastTimeStamp();

    status = OwnPrimary( display, window, timestamp );

    if ( status = = True )
        {
        RefreshFlag = True;
        }

}        /* -- function GrabSelection */

MakeButtons( display, window, fore, back, font_id )

Display        *display;
Window         window;
unsigned long  fore, back;
Font           font_id;

{   /* -- function MakeButtons */
    int     QuitApplication();
    int     GrabSelection(), AskTargets();
    int     AskStrings(), AskHost();
    int     AskUser(), AskName();
    int     AskTime(), AskLength(), AskPosition();
    int     AskWindow();
    int     x, y;

    CreateButton( display, window,
        1, 2,
        font_id,
        "Quit",
        QuitApplication );

    CreateButton( display, window, BUTTON_WIDTH + 11, 2,
        fore, back, font_id,
        "Select",
        GrabSelection );

    x = 1;
    y = 5 + BUTTON_HEIGHT;
```

```
CreateButton( display, window, x, y,
    fore, back, font_id,
    "Targets", AskTargets );

x += 10 + BUTTON_WIDTH;
CreateButton( display, window, x, y,
    fore, back, font_id,
    "Time", AskTime );

x += 10 + BUTTON_WIDTH;
CreateButton( display, window, x, y,
    fore, back, font_id,
    "String", AskStrings );

x += 10 + BUTTON_WIDTH;
CreateButton( display, window, x, y,
    fore, back, font_id,
    "Length", AskLength );

x. += 10 + BUTTON_WIDTH;
    CreateButton( display, window, x, y,
    fore, back, font_id,
    "Position", AskPosition );

/*
 * Second row
 */
x = 1;
y += BUTTON_HEIGHT + 5;
CreateButton( display, window
    fore, back,font_id
    "Window", AskWindow );

x += 10 + BUTTON_WIDTH;
CreateButton( display, window, x, y,
    fore, back, font_id,
    "User", AskUser );

x += 10 + BUTTON_WIDTH;
CreateButton( display, window, x, y,
    fore, back, font_id,
    "Host", AskHost );

x += 10 + BUTTON_WIDTH;
CreateButton( display, window, x, y,
    fore, back, font_id,
    "Name", AskName );
```

```
}       /* -- function MakeButtons */

Refresh( display, window, gc, font_height, fore, back )

Display         *display;
Window          window;
GC              gc;
int             font_height;
unsigned long   fore, back;

{   /* -- function Refresh */
    char    string[ BUFSIZE + 1 ];

    /*
     * Get selection owner
     */
    GetOwnerInfo( display, window );

    (void) sprintf( string, "Query owner %s of PRIMARY Selection for:",
        OwnerString );

    XDrawImageString( display, window, gc,
        ( 2 * ( BUTTON_WIDTH + 5 ) ) + 5,
        BUTTON_HEIGHT - 5,
         string, strlen( string ) );

    if ( IsPrimaryOurs() = = True )
        {
        SetGC( display, gc, back, fore );
        }

    PropDisplayCurrent( display, window, gc,
        font_height,
        5, 4 * BUTTON_HEIGHT );

    if ( IsPrimaryOurs() = = True )
        {
        SetGC( display, gc, fore, back );
        }

    /*
     * Display any selection data
     */
    XFlush( display );
```

```
}       /* -- function Refresh */

GetOwnerInfo( display, window )

Display    *display;
Window     window;

{   /* -- function GetOwnerInfo */
    Window  owner;

    owner = XGetSelectionOwner( display, XA_PRIMARY );

    if ( owner != (Window) None )
        {
        (void) sprintf( OwnerString, "(0x%lx) ", owner );
        }
    else
        {
        OwnerString[ 0 ] = '\0';

        /*
         * Clear owner area
         */
        XClearWindow( display, window );
        }

}       /* -- function GetOwnerInfo */

AskStrings( display, window )

Display    *display;
Window     window;

{   /* -- function AskStrings */
    Time     timestamp;
    Atom     atom;

    atom      = XInternAtom( display, PROP_NAME, False );

    timestamp = LastTimeStamp();

    AskPrimaryData( display,
        window,
        atom,
        XA_STRING,
        timestamp );
```

```
}        /* -- function AskStrings */

AskTargets( display, window )

Display    *display;
Window     window;

{   /* -- function AskTargets */
    Time      timestamp;
    Atom      xbook_atom;
    Atom      targets_atom;

    timestamp = LastTimeStamp();

    xbook_atom     = XInternAtom( display, PROP_NAME, False );
    targets_atom   = XInternAtom( display, "TARGETS", False );

    AskPrimaryData( display,
        window,
        xbook_atom
        targets_atom,
        timestamp );

}        /* -- function AskTargets */

AskHost( display, window )

Display    *display;
Window     window;

{   /* -- function AskHost */
    Time      timestamp;
    Atom      xbook_atom;
    Atom      hostname_atom;

    timestamp = LastTimeStamp();

    xbook_atom     = XInternAtom( display, PROP_NAME, False );
    hostname_atom = XInternAtom( display, "HOSTNAME", False );

    AskPrimaryData( display,
        window,
        xbook_atom,
        hostname_atom,
        timestamp );
```

```
}        /* -- function AskHost */

AskUser( display, window )

Display    *display;
Window     window;

{   /* -- function AskUser */
    Time      timestamp;
    Atom      xbook_atom;
    Atom      user_atom;

    timestamp = LastTimeStamp();

    xbook_atom     = XInternAtom( display, PROP_NAME, False );
    user_atom      = XInternAtom( display, "USER", False );

    AskPrimaryData( display,
        window,
        xbook_atom,
        user_atom,
        timestamp );

}        /* -- function AskUser */

AskName( display, window )

Display    *display;
Window     window;

{   /* -- function AskName */
    Time      timestamp;
    Atom      xbook_atom;
    Atom      name_atom;

    timestamp = LastTimeStamp();

    xbook_atom     = XInternAtom( display, PROP_NAME, False );
    name_atom      = XInternAtom( display, "NAME", False );

    AskPrimaryData( display,
        window,
        book_atom,
        name_atom,
        timestamp );
```

```
}       /* -- function AskName */

AskTime( display, window )

Display    *display;
Window     window;

{   /* -- function AskTime */
    Time      timestamp;
    Atom      xbook_atom;
    Atom      timestamp_atom;

    timestamp = LastTimeStamp();

    xbook_atom = XInternAtom( display, PROP_NAME, False );
    timestamp_atom = XInternAtom( display, "TIMESTAMP", False );

    AskPrimaryData( display,
        window,
        xbook_atom,
        timestamp_atom,
        timestamp );

}       /* -- function AskTime */

AskLength( display, window )

Display    *display;
Window     window;

{   /* -- function AskLength */
    Time      timestamp;
    Atom      xbook_atom;
    Atom      length_atom;

    timestamp = LastTimeStamp();

    xbook_atom     = XInternAtom( display, PROP_NAME, False );
    length_atom    = XInternAtom( display, "LENGTH", False );

    AskPrimaryData( display,
        window,
        xbook_atom,
        length_atom,
        timestamp );
```

```
}       /* -- function AskLength */

AskPosition( display, window )

Display    *display;
Window     window;

{   /* -- function AskPosition */
    Time      timestamp;
    Atom      xbook_atom;
    Atom      position_atom;

    timestamp = LastTimeStamp();

    xbook_atom    = XInternAtom( display, PROP_NAME, False );
    position_atom = XInternAtom( display,
                                  "CHARACTER_POSITION", False );

    AskPrimaryData( display,
        window,
        xbook_atom,
        position_atom,
        timestamp );

}       /* -- function AskPosition */

AskWindow( display, window )

Display    *display;
Window     window;

{   /* -- function AskWindow   */
    Time      timestamp;
    Atom      xbook_atom;
    Atom      window_atom;

    timestamp = LastTimeStamp();

    xbook_atom = XInternAtom( display, PROP_NAME, False );
    window_atom   = XInternAtom( display, "CLIENT_WINDOW", False );

    AskPrimaryData( display,
                    window,
                    xbook_atom,
                    window_atom,
                    timestamp );
```

```
}       /* -- function AskWindow   */

/*
 * end of file
 */
```

An Icon for primary

Figure 19-6 shows the `primary` icon.

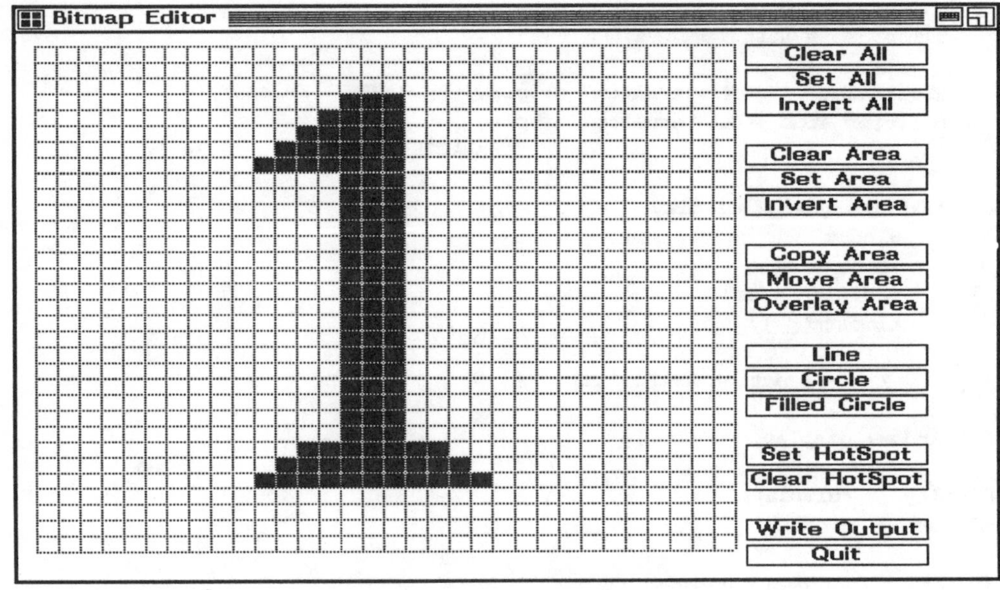

Figure 19-6. The Primary Icon

The code for the `primary` icon is as follows:

```
primary.xb:
#define primary_width 32
#define primary_height 32
static char primary_bits[] = {
   0x00, 0x00, 0x00, 0x00, 0x00, 0x00, 0x00, 0x00, 0x00, 0x00, 0x00, 0x00,
   0x00, 0xc0, 0x01, 0x00, 0x00, 0xe0, 0x01, 0x00, 0x00, 0xf0, 0x01, 0x00,
   0x00, 0xf8, 0x01, 0x00, 0x00, 0xfc, 0x01, 0x00, 0x00, 0xc0, 0x01, 0x00,
   0x00, 0xc0, 0x01, 0x00, 0x00, 0xc0, 0x01, 0x00, 0x00, 0xc0, 0x01, 0x00,
   0x00, 0xc0, 0x01, 0x00, 0x00, 0xc0, 0x01, 0x00, 0x00, 0xc0, 0x01, 0x00,
   0x00, 0xc0, 0x01, 0x00, 0x00, 0xc0, 0x01, 0x00, 0x00, 0xc0, 0x01, 0x00,
```

```
0x00, 0xc0, 0x01, 0x00, 0x00, 0xc0, 0x01, 0x00, 0x00, 0xc0, 0x01, 0x00,
0x00, 0xc0, 0x01, 0x00, 0x00, 0xc0, 0x01, 0x00, 0x00, 0xc0, 0x01, 0x00,
0x00, 0xc0, 0x01, 0x00, 0x00, 0xf0, 0x07, 0x00, 0x00, 0xf8, 0x0f, 0x00,
0x00, 0xfc, 0x1f, 0x00, 0x00, 0x00, 0x00, 0x00, 0x00, 0x00, 0x00, 0x00,
0x00, 0x00, 0x00, 0x00, 0x00, 0x00, 0x00, 0x00};
```

Compiling primary

The primary program uses the following source files:

`atom.c button.c`	*(from chapter 16)*
`bytes.c`	*(from chapter 15)*
`cursor.c`	*(from chapter 7)*
`display.c`	*(from chapter 2)*
`error.c event.c`	*(from chapter 5)*
`font.c`	*(from chapter 8)*
`gc.c`	*(from chapter 4)*
`icccm.c`	*(from chapter 15)*
`pixmap.c`	*(from chapter 6)*
`prop.c`	*(from chapter 17)*
`select.c`	
`sel_own.c`	
`sel_prop.c`	
`textedit.c`	*(from chapter 16)*
`topwind.c`	*(from chapter 9)*
`window.c`	*(from chapter 3)*
`xstring.c`	*(from chapter 16)*
`primary.xb`	

On Unix-based systems, you can use the `Makefile` in appendix C, with:

```
make primary
```

Or, you can compile with:

```
cc -o primary atom.c button.c bytes.c cursor.c display.c error.c \
   event.c font.c gc.c icccm.c pixmap.c prop.c primary.o \
   select.c sel_own.c sel_prop.c \
   textedit.c topwind.c xstring.c window.c -lX11
```

Running primary

Primary needs no command-line parameters. You may specify a window geometry, a display name and a font name, all in the usual manner :

```
-display   display_name
-geometry  geometry_spec
   (e.g., 120x300+40+13)
-font      font_name
```

Use the Quit push-button to quit. First, select some text in another application. Then ask for the text (String push-button). Ask for the window ID (use the winfo program to check on where the window ID is coming from) and the user name. Have fun. Primary should give you a good working knowledge of how selections work.

NOTE TO RELEASE 2 USERS

Early releases of the X Window System did not support selections very well, particularly Release 2 (remember, Releases 2 and 3 both predate the final version of the ICCCM 1.0). You may have some problems with selecting text in various applications. Don't worry. Just run two copies of primary and exchange data between them.

FUNCTIONS DEVELOPED IN THIS CHAPTER

AskPrimaryData
AssertOwnership
GetPropertyData
GetSelectionData
GetTargetData
OwnPrimary
PutPropertyData
PutSelectionData
SendSelectNotify

XLIB FUNCTIONS AND MACROS INTRODUCED IN THIS CHAPTER

XConvertSelection
XGetSelectionOwner
XSetSelectionOwner

SUMMARY

- Selections are X's means for providing a generalized query-reply interprocess communication (IPC) mechanism. Selections are powerful, but confusing; you'll earn your stripes as an advanced X programmer if you master them.

- Each selection is an `atom`. You need to convert the selection name to an `atom`, using `XInternAtom()`. After a program claims the selection, other programs, if they know about the selection, may ask the selection owner questions about the selection. These questions usually cover the data associated with a selection in a string format with a target type of `XA_STRING` (where `XA_STRING` is a predefined `atom`). The owner of the selection then converts the selection data into the proper target type, puts the data in a property on the asking program's window and then sends a `SelectionNotify` event to the asking program. Ideally, the selection owner provides data in any target type, provided the owning program supports that data target type.

- "`PRIMARY`" is the main selection in the ICCCM for typical cut-and-paste operations using the built-in `atom` called `XA_PRIMARY`. `PRIMARY` is the selection used when a user selects some text in an `xterm` window, probably by far the most common use of cut and paste in X.

- To find out who owns a given selection, call `XGetSelectionOwner()`. The selection is an `atom`, so you'll usually need to call `XInternAtom()` to convert the name to an `atom` ID. The function `AssertOwnership()` asserts ownership of a selection. It also calls `XGetSelectionOwner()` right after the call to `XSetSelectionOwner()` to see if the attempt was successful. The function `OwnPrimary()` further hides some of the details of asserting ownership of the `PRIMARY` selection and sets up a number of global variables if the attempt was successful.

- When you want data from a selection, the owner of the selection writes that data to a property on the application windows of your choice.You should pick the window, the property to place the data in (on your window), and the target type. If a user asks to paste data, this is essentially asking for the contents of a selection to be pasted. You need to ask the owner of the selection for data in a certain target type, depending on the context of the "paste" operation. If you want some data from the owner of a selection, call `XConvertSelection()`.

- `AskPrimaryData()` calls `XConvertSelection()` to ask for the contents of the `PRIMARY` selection, with a given target type.

- If everything goes well, the owner of the selection will get your request (generated by the call to `XConvertSelection`) and then send your program a `SelectionNotify` event. If things went wrong, you may get a `SelectionNotify` event with a property of `None`. If thing s really went wrong, you may get nothing at all (or an X error). In addition to `SelectionNotify`, two other selection events are covered, including `SelectionRequest` events and `SelectionClear` events. `GetSelectionData()` handles most errors from an incoming `SelectionRequest` event. A `SelectionClear` event is sent to your application when it loses the ownership of a selection. If you lose ownership of a selection, your application should no longer receive (or answer) `SelectionRequest` events until the next call to `XSetSelectionOwner`. The call to `XConvertSelection()` generates a `SelectionRequest` event that is sent to the owner of the selection.

- When your application receives a `SelectionRequest` event, it should make an effort to translate the data of the selection into the asked-for target type. There are three required target types `TIMESTAMP, MULTIPLE,` and `TARGET` your application *must* support, and a host of common types your application *should* support. `PutSelectionData()` answers a `SelectionRequest` event. The `MULTIPLE` type has the name of a property and a window ID. In that property lie many items of type `ATOM_PAIR` (really just two `atoms`, or pairs of `XA_ATOM` types). In each `ATOM_PAIR`, the first item is a target type (one of many) and the second item is a property ID. Your application should then convert the selection data to the asked-for target type and write that data to the paired property ID (all on the same given window ID). The `TIMESTAMP` target is the timestamp (in X server terms) of when your application became the given selection's owner. The `TARGETS` target is the list of data types (targets) your application supports. Since each target type is an atom, the TARGETS response is a list of atoms (atoms are 32-bit values).

- The CHARACTER_POSITION target type has a base type of SPAN. A SPAN is two integers (that is, two of the built-in atom XA_INTEGER).The CHARACTER_POSITION target type should be the start and end position of the selected data, in bytes. The LENGTH target type should be the length of the selection (the number of bytes) stored as an INTEGER.

- With each type of target, you can usually store more than one item. For example, SPAN is really two INTEGERS. So, when you write out the property data, use a target type of XA_INTEGER and a number of items of 2 (with enough bytes of data filled in, of course). That way, the TARGETS target is really just an XA_ATOM type, with many atoms stored in the list. That's what the number_items variable is about in the calls XGetWindowProperty() and XChangeProperty().

- When your application owns the PRIMARY selection, it needs to respond to SelectionRequest events. GetTargetData() is the main function used to collect the different types of data and prepare the raw data bytes, which will be later written to the requesting program's window.

- Just about every application that needs to use selections should support the PRIMARY selection. PRIMARY is the main means for cut-and-paste operations between applications. From the user's point of view, selected text should be easily pasted into any other application.

Section IV

Displaying X Programs Over a Network

Section IV covers programs that connect to multiple X servers and the issues you face when communicating this way. If you stay within the boundaries of good manners you'll be rewarded with well-behaved programs and won't face fatal X errors. If you're sloppy and greedy, your programs will crash and be most unhappy.

Two programs are introduced: `mchat`, a multiple machine chat-type program and `note`, a program that appends data to properties on multiple displays.

Chapter 20

A Multiple-Machine Chat Program

This short-and-sweet chapter introduces a sample program that connects to more than one X server. These multiple display connections are used for a small chat program. Setting up these multiple connections isn't complicated, but there are some pitfalls. We provide some tricks that keep track of the various values dependent on each server, and the problem of what happens if a server connection is lost.

MULTIPLE DISPLAY CONNECTIONS

The `XOpenDisplay()` Xlib function sets up a display connection to a given X server. `XOpenDisplay()` returns a pointer to a `Display` structure. You then use this pointer in just about every Xlib call. There's nothing to stop you from calling `XOpenDisplay()` two or three times and setting up multiple display connections in the process. You just have to keep track of the different display pointers and the separate windows, GCs, and whatnot.

Mchat, A MULTIPLE-MACHINE CHAT PROGRAM

`Mchat` is a multiple-machine chat program, opening display connections to a number of X servers. On each display, `mchat` puts up a top-level window. Users on a number of machines can then type into the `mchat` window on their display to communicate with the users on the other displays. Every letter typed is echoed to all `mchat` windows on all machines, making a sort of (very) primitive party line. Since only one program is running, any user on any machine can terminate `mchat` using the `Quit` push-button. Figure 20-1 shows the `mchat` program.

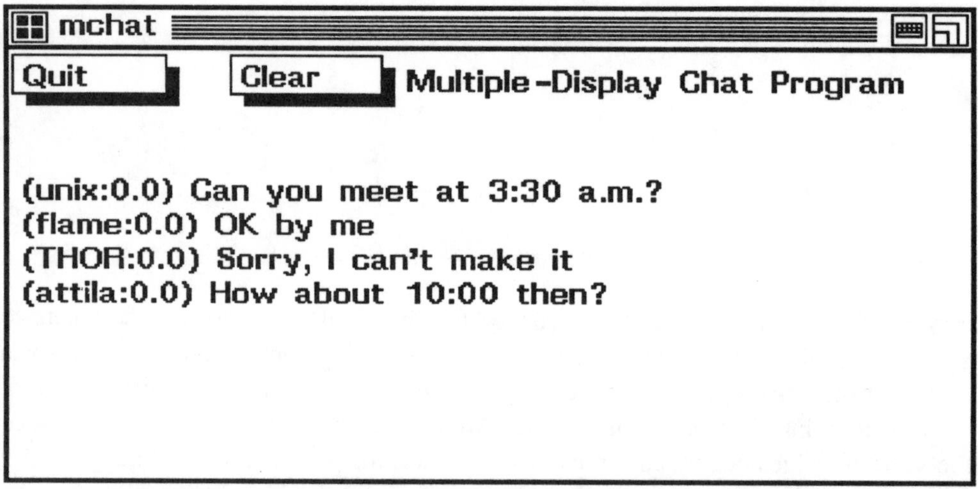

Figure 20-1. The mchat Program

The program itself is very simple, and so is the code. The main problems with multiple-display connections are keeping the various values dependent on each server straight and losing the server connection.

To keep each display connection apart, we've set up a global array of structures; one structure for each display connection.

The ChatStruct contains a display pointer, a top-level window, a graphics context, an icon pixmap, a display name, and character data. We use an array of ChatStruct, one for each display connected by mchat. We could dynamically allocate these structures, but we're trying to make this as easy as possible. The contents of ChatStruct are as follows:

```
#define MAX_SIZE  80    /* -- 80 chars per line */
#define MAX_HOSTS 30

typedef struct
    {
    Display     *display;
    Window      window;
    GC          gc;
    Pixmap      icon;
    XFontStruct    *font;
    char        name[ MAX_SIZE + 1 ];
    char        data[ MAX_SIZE + 1 ];
    } ChatStruct;

ChatStruct Chat[ MAX_HOSTS + 1 ];
int     number_hosts;
```

SETTING UP THE DISPLAYS TO TALK TO

SetUpHosts() sets up the connections to the multiple X servers. It takes the command-line parameters (argc and argv) and tries to connect to each host listed in the command-line.

The main loop in SetUpHosts() opens a display connection, creates a top-level window, and then sends all the necessary hints to the window manager. This code looks much like the code used to set up each of the example programs, only it is executed once for each host we want to talk to.

All command-line parameters (except for pairs that begin with a hyphen, like -font) are assumed to be display names. The contents of SetUpHosts() are as follows:

```
SetUpHosts( argc, argv )

int     argc;
char    *argv[];

{   /* -- function SetUpHosts */
    int                 screen;
    unsigned long       black, white;
    char                string[ BUFSIZE + 1 ];
    int                 counter, num_hosts;

    counter     = 1;
    num_hosts   = 0;

        while( ( counter < argc ) && ( num_hosts < MAX_HOSTS ) )
            {
            if ( argv[ counter ][ 0 ] = = '-' )
                {
                counter += 2;
                }
            else
                {
                (void) sprintf( string, "(%s) ", argv[ counter ] );
                (void) strcpy( Chat[ num_hosts ].name, string );

                Chat[ num_hosts ].data[ 0 ] = '\0';

                /*
                 * Set up X Connection
                 */
                Chat[ num_hosts ].display =
                    OpenDisplay( argv[ counter ], &screen );

                if ( Chat[ num_hosts ].display != (Display *) NULL )
                    {
                    black   =
                        BlackPixel( Chat[ num_hosts ].display,
                            screen );
                    white =
                        WhitePixel( Chat[ num_hosts ].display,
                            screen );

                    /*
                     * Create Windows
                     */
                    Chat[ num_hosts ].window =
```

```
            TopWindow( Chat[ num_hosts ].display,
                10, 10, 400, 200,
                mchat_bits,
                mchat_width, mchat_height,
                &Chat[ num_hosts ].icon,
                &Chat[ num_hosts ].gc );

    Chat[ num_hosts ].font =
        LoadFont( Chat[ num_hosts ].display,
                Chat[ num_hosts ].gc,
                argc, argv, "variable" );

    /*
     * Store values for window manager
     */
    SetNormalHints( Chat[ num_hosts ].display,
        Chat[ num_hosts ].window, 10, 10, 400, 200 );

SetWMHints( Chat[ num_hosts ].display,
    Chat[ num_hosts ].window,
    Chat[ num_hosts ].icon );

NameWindow( Chat[ num_hosts ].display,
    Chat[ num_hosts ].window,
        "mchat", "mchat", "MChat" );

SetICCCM( Chat[ num_hosts ].display,
    Chat[ num_hosts ].window,
    argc, argv );

/*
 * Create buttons for user interface items
 */
MakeButtons( Chat[ num_hosts ].display,
    Chat[ num_hosts ].window,
    black, white, Chat[ num_hosts ].font->fid );

MapWindow( Chat[ num_hosts ].display,
    Chat[ num_hosts ].window );

XFlush( Chat[ num_hosts ].display );

num_hosts++;
}
```

```
            counter++;
            }
        }

    return( num_hosts );

}   /* -- function SetUpHosts */
```

When SetUpHosts() finishes, we have set up display connections with a number of hosts. Each top-level window will look the same and start out in the same location (at least at program start) if the window manager lets them. Users can, of course, resize and move each window on each display.

We use the same function, though, to draw and refresh the contents of each window. Thus, all users on all displays see the same window and have the same interface. Mchat looks a lot like most of the programs in this book, though, except for all the looping.

BLOCKING AWAITING EVENTS

Mchat cannot block awaiting events from an X server, because events may never (or at least rarely) come from a given server, while events may be streaming in from other servers. Because of this, the mchat EventLoop() function calls CheckEvent() rather than NextEvent() like the rest of the programs in this book.

If a KeyPress event comes in, the effects of this event are echoed to every display connection. All the windows show the text being entered. The EventLoop() function itself is called in a loop for each display connection. It checks, in turn, for incoming events on every display.

The RefreshAllFlag and the RefreshFlag are globals:

```
int     host;

for( ; ; )      /* -- loop forever */
        {
        for( host = 0; host < number_hosts; host++ )
                {
```

```
            RefreshFlag = False;
            EventLoop( Chat[ host ].display, host );
            if ( RefreshAllFlag = = True )
                {
                RefreshAll();

                RefreshAllFlag = False;
                RefreshFlag = False;
                }

            if ( RefreshFlag = = True )
                {
                Refresh( Chat[ host ].display,
                    Chat[ host ].window,
                    host );

                RefreshFlag = False;
                }
            }
        }
```

SHUTTING DOWN ALL DISPLAY CONNECTIONS

The `QuitApplication()` function is a call-back function from the Quit push-button. It quits the whole application (not just the one connection), so any user can stop the program. Note that there is a quit button on every top-level window.

`QuitApplication()` has a loop (this is becoming familiar, isn't it?) that closes each display connection in turn. Its contents are as follows:

```
QuitApplication( display, window )

Display *display;
Window window;

{   /* -- function QuitApplication */
    int     host;

    /*
     * Clean up resources
     */
    for( host = 0; host < number_hosts; host++ )
```

```
        {
        XFreePixmap( Chat[ host ].display, Chat[ host ].icon );
        XFreeFont  ( Chat[ host ].display, Chat[ host ].font );

        CloseDisplay( Chat[ host ].display,
            Chat[ host ].window,
            Chat[ host ].gc );
        }

    exit( 0 );

}   /* -- function QuitApplication */
```

SOURCE CODE FOR mchat.c

The source code for `mchat.c` is as follows:

mchat.c:

```
/*
 *  mchat.c
 *  A multiple-display chat program--albeit very primitive!!
 *
 *  mchat opens display connections to a number of
 *  X servers. A user at each server can then
 *  entire in text, which is transmitted to
 *  all the servers mchat has connections with.
 *  This is a rather primitive "chat"-type program.
 *
 *  mchat needs a list of display names on the
 *  unix command line, e.g.,
 *  mchat display1 display2 ...
 *
 *  mchat will also take and window and font specification, e.g.,
 *  mchat display1 -font variable display2 -geometry geometry ...
 *
 */

#include  "xbook.h"

#include  "mchat.xb"

/*
 *  Structure to hold information for each display we
```

```
 * connect to.
 */ #define MAX_SIZE 80 /* -- 80 chars per line, punch cards strike again */

typedef struct
    {
    Display         *display;
    Window          window;
    GC              gc;
    Pixmap          icon;
    XFontStruct     *font;
    char            name[ MAX_SIZE + 1 ];
    char            data[ MAX_SIZE + 1 ];
    } ChatStruct;

/*
 * Arbitrary maximum number of hosts.  This is probably very
 * large for real usage.
 */
 #define MAX_HOSTS 30

ChatStruct      Chat[ MAX_HOSTS + 1 ];
int             number_hosts;
int             RefreshFlag    = False;
int             RefreshAllFlag = False;

#define   MESSAGE   "Multiple-Display Chat Program"

main( argc, argv )

int     argc;
char    *argv[];

{       /* -- main */
        int     host;

        /*
         * Set up the names
         * of hosts we want
         * to talk to
         */
        number_hosts = SetUpHosts( argc, argv );

        /*
         *     Must have at least one host
         */
        if ( number_hosts < 1 )
                {
```

```
            (void) fprintf( stderr,
                "Error: you must provide at least one host name\n" );
            exit( 1 );
            }

        /*
         * Handle events, QuitApplication() will exit
         */
        for( ; ; )
            {
            for( host = 0; host < number_hosts; host++ )
                {
                RefreshFlag = False;

                EventLoop( Chat[ host ].display, host );

                if ( RefreshAllFlag = = True )
                    {
                    RefreshAll();

                    RefreshAllFlag = False;
                    RefreshFlag = False;
                    }

                if ( RefreshFlag = = True )
                    {
                    Refresh( Chat[ host ].display,
                        Chat[ host ].window,
                        host );

                    RefreshFlag = False;
                    }
                }
        }

}   /* -- main */

EventLoop( display, host )

Display *display;
int         host;

/*
 * This EventLoop() is different from all the
 * other EventLoop() functions, in that this function
 * cannot block awaiting an event on any one connection,
```

```
 * because events may occur on any display at any time.
 *
 * This EventLoop() therefore calls CheckEvent()
 * (a non-blocking function) rather than NextEvent()
 * (a blocking function).
 *
 */

{   /* -- function EventLoop */
    XEvent  event;
    int     status, i, font_height;
    int     x, y;
    int     width = 100, height = 100;
    char    string[ BUFSIZE + 1 ];
    KeySym  keysym;

    status = CheckEvent( display,
            False,
            width, height,
            &event, &keysym );

    if ( status = = True )
        {
        if ( ButtonEvent( display, &event ) = = True )
            {
            return;
            }

    switch( event.type )
            {
            case Expose: RefreshFlag = True;
                break;
            case KeyPress:
                for( i = 0; i < number_hosts; i++ )
                        {
                        (void) strcpy( string,
                            Chat[ host ].data );

                        font_height =
                            Chat[ i ].font->ascent +
                            Chat[ i ].font->descent + 2;

                        y = 70 + ( host * font_height );

                        /*
                         * The same font name could have
```

```
                     * different widths on different
                     * X implementations.
                     */
                    x = 5 + XTextWidth( Chat[ i ].font,
                        Chat[ host ].name,
                        strlen( Chat[ host ].name ) );

                    /*
                     * We apply the edit function
                     * each time, very inefficient
                     */
                    TextEdit( Chat[ i ].display,
                        Chat[ i ].window,
                        Chat[ i ].gc,
                        Chat[ i ].font,
                        x, y,
                        keysym, string,
                        MAX_SIZE );
                    }

                (void) strcpy( Chat[ host ].data, string );
            break;
            }
        }

    XFlush( display );

}       /* -- function EventLoop */

SetUpHosts( argc, argv )

int     argc;
char    *argv[];

/*
 * All command-line parameters NOT associated
 * with -name data pairs ARE assumed to
 * be host (display) names to connect to.
 *
 */

{   /* -- function SetUpHosts */
    int             screen;
    unsigned long   black, white;
    char            string[ BUFSIZE + 1 ];
    int             counter, num_hosts;
```

```
counter = 1;
num_hosts = 0;

while( ( counter < argc ) && ( num_hosts < MAX_HOSTS ) )
    {
    if ( argv[ counter ][ 0 ] = = '-' )
        {
        counter += 2;
        }
    else
        {
        (void) sprintf( string, "(%s) ", argv[ counter ] );
        (void) strcpy( Chat[ num_hosts ].name, string );

        Chat[ num_hosts ].data[ 0 ] = '\0';

        /*
         * Set up X Connection
         */
        Chat[ num_hosts ].display =
           OpenDisplay( argv[ counter ], &screen );

        if ( Chat[ num_hosts ].display != (Display *) NULL )
           {
           black =
              BlackPixel( Chat[ num_hosts ].display,
                      screen );
           white =
              WhitePixel( Chat[ num_hosts ].display,
                      screen );

           /*
            * Create Windows
            */
           Chat[ num_hosts ].window =
              TopWindow( Chat[ num_hosts ].display,
                  10, 10, 400, 200,
                  mchat_bits,
                  mchat_width, mchat_height,
                  &Chat[ num_hosts ].icon,
                  &Chat[ num_hosts ].gc );

           Chat[ num_hosts ].font =
              LoadFont( Chat[ num_hosts ].display,
                  Chat[ num_hosts ].gc,
                  argc, argv, "variable" );
```

```
            /*
             * Store values for window manager
             */
            SetNormalHints( Chat[ num_hosts ].display,
                Chat[ num_hosts ].window,
                    10, 10, 400, 200 );

            SetWMHints( Chat[ num_hosts ].display,
                    Chat[ num_hosts ].window,
                    Chat[ num_hosts ].icon );

            NameWindow( Chat[ num_hosts ].display,
                    Chat[ num_hosts ].window,
                    "mchat", "mchat", "MChat" );

            SetICCCM( Chat[ num_hosts ].display,
                    Chat[ num_hosts ].window,
                    argc, argv );
            /*
             * Create buttons for user interface items
             */
            MakeButtons( Chat[ num_hosts ].display,
                Chat[ num_hosts ].window,
                black, white,
                Chat[ num_hosts ].font->fid );

            MapWindow( Chat[ num_hosts ].display,
                Chat[ num_hosts ].window );

            XFlush( Chat[ num_hosts ].display );

            num_hosts++;
            }

        counter++;
        }
    }

    return( num_hosts );

}   /* -- function SetUpHosts */

ClearData( display, window )

Display *display;
Window window;
```

```
/*
 * ClearData() clears the text associated with
 * one X display connection.
 */

{   /* -- function ClearData */
    int     host;

    host = FindHost( display, window );

    if ( host >= 0 )
        {
        /*
         * Wipe out data
         */
        Chat[ host ].data[ 0 ] = '\0';

        ClearAll();
        RefreshAllFlag = True;
        }

}   /* -- function ClearData */

QuitApplication( display, window )

Display     *display;
Window      window;

/*
 * QuitApplication() shuts down each X display
 * connection and then calls exit().
 */

{   /* -- function QuitApplication */
    int     host;

    /*
     * Clean up resources
     */
    for( host = 0; host < number_hosts; host++ )
        {
        XFreePixmap( Chat[ host ].display, Chat[ host ].icon );
        XFreeFont  ( Chat[ host ].display, Chat[ host ].font );

        CloseDisplay( Chat[ host ].display,
            Chat[ host ].window,
```

```
            Chat[ host ].gc );
        }

    exit( 0 );

}   /* -- function QuitApplication */

MakeButtons( display, window, fore, back, font_id )

Display        *display;
Window          window;
unsigned long   fore, back;
Font            font_id;

/*
 *  MakeButtons() makes the Quit and Clear Data
 *  push-buttons on one top-level window.
 *  MakeButtons() will be called once for each display
 *  connection.
 */

{   /* -- function MakeButtons */
    int     QuitApplication();
    int     SendData();
    int     ClearData();

    CreateButton( display, window,
            1, 2,
            fore, back, font_id,
            "Quit",
            QuitApplication );

    CreateButton( display, window,
            BUTTON_WIDTH + 22, 2,
            fore, back, font_id,
            "Clear",
            ClearData );

}   /* -- function MakeButtons */

Refresh( display, window, host )

Display     *display;
Window      window;
int         host;
```

```
/*
 * Refresh() refreshes the contents of one top-level window
 * on one display.  RefreshAll() handles all displays
 * that mchat is connected to.
 */

{   /* -- function Refresh */
    int     i;
    int     font_height;
    char    string[ BUFSIZE + 1 ];

    XDrawImageString( display, window,
            Chat[ host ].gc,
            ( 2 * ( BUTTON_WIDTH + 11 ) ) + 5,
            BUTTON_HEIGHT - 5,
            MESSAGE, strlen( MESSAGE ) );

    /*
     * Display host names and data
     */
    for( i = 0; i < number_hosts; i++ )
        {
        font_height = Chat[ host ].font->ascent +
                  Chat[ host ].font->descent + 2;

        for( i = 0; i < number_hosts; i++ )
            {
            (void) strcpy( string, Chat[ i ].name );
            (void) strcat( string, Chat[ i ].data );

            XDrawImageString( display, window,
                  Chat[ host ].gc,
                  5, 70 + ( i * font_height ),
                  string, strlen( string ) );
            }
        }

    XFlush( display );


}   /* -- function Refresh */

RefreshAll()

/*
 * RefreshAll() refreshes all of mchat's top-level windows.
 */
```

```
{   /* -- function RefreshAll */
    int     host;

    for( host = 0; host < number_hosts; host++ )
        {
        Refresh( Chat[ host ].display,
            Chat[ host ].window,
            host );
        }

}   /* -- function RefreshAll */

ClearAll()

/*
 *  ClearAll() clears all mchat top-level windows
 *  on all the displays mchat is connected to.
 */

{   /* -- function ClearAll */
    int     host;

    for( host = 0; host < number_hosts; host++ )
        {
        XClearWindow( Chat[ host ].display,
            Chat[ host ].window );
        }

}   /* -- function ClearAll */

FindHost( display, window )

Display *display;
Window window;

/*
 *  FindHost() finds a match in the global Chat data
 *  that matches the given display and window.
 */

{   /* -- function FindHost */
    int     host;

    for( host = 0; host < number_hosts; host++ )
        {
        if ( ( Chat[ host ].display = = display ) &&
```

```
                ( Chat[ host ].window = = window ) )
                {
                return( host );
                }
        }

    return( -1 );

}   /* -- function FindHost */

/*
 * end of file.
 */
```

AN ICON FOR mchat

Figure 20-2 shows the mchat icon.

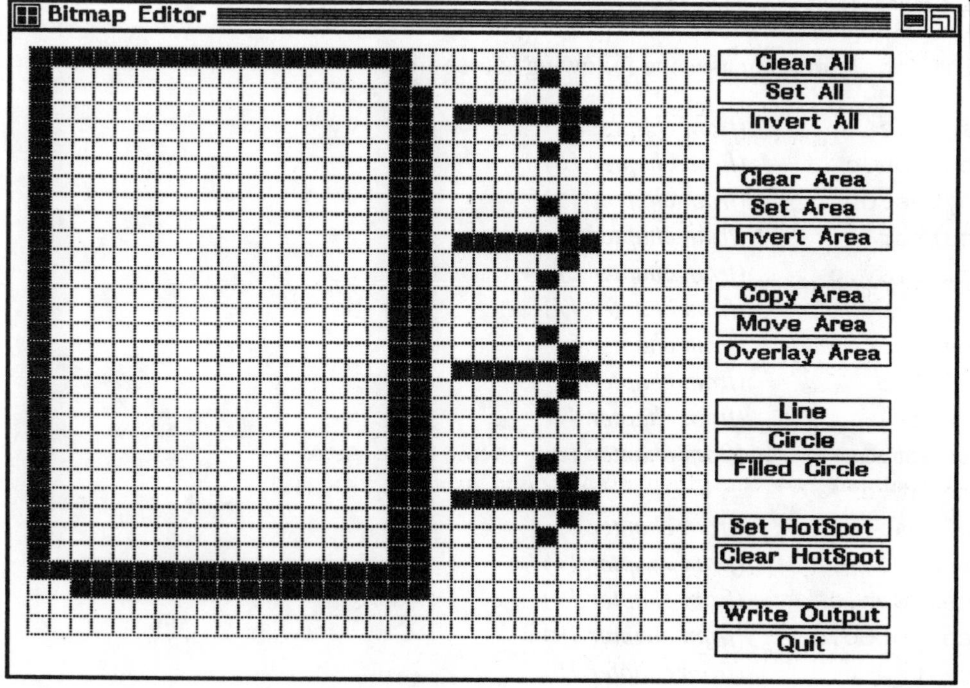

Figure 20-2. The mchat Icon

The code for the `mchat.xb` is as follows:

```
mchat.xb:
#define mchat_width 32
#define mchat_height 32
static char mchat_bits[] = {
0xff, 0xff, 0x03, 0x00, 0x01, 0x00, 0x02, 0x01, 0x01, 0x00, 0x06, 0x02,
0x01, 0x00, 0xf6, 0x07, 0x01, 0x00, 0x06, 0x02, 0x01, 0x00, 0x06, 0x01,
0x01, 0x00, 0x06, 0x00, 0x01, 0x00, 0x06, 0x00, 0x01, 0x00, 0x06, 0x01,
0x01, 0x00, 0x06, 0x02, 0x01, 0x00, 0xf6, 0x07, 0x01, 0x00, 0x06, 0x02,
0x01, 0x00, 0x06, 0x01, 0x01, 0x00, 0x06, 0x00, 0x01, 0x00, 0x06, 0x00,
0x01, 0x00, 0x06, 0x01, 0x01, 0x00, 0x06, 0x02, 0x01, 0x00, 0xf6, 0x07,
0x01, 0x00, 0x06, 0x02, 0x01, 0x00, 0x06, 0x01, 0x01, 0x00, 0x06, 0x00,
0x01, 0x00, 0x06, 0x00, 0x01, 0x00, 0x06, 0x01, 0x01, 0x00, 0x06, 0x02,
0x01, 0x00, 0xf6, 0x07, 0x01, 0x00, 0x06, 0x02, 0x01, 0x00, 0x06, 0x01,
0x01, 0x00, 0x06, 0x00, 0xff, 0xff, 0x07, 0x00, 0xfc, 0xff, 0x07, 0x00,
0x00, 0x00, 0x00, 0x00, 0x00, 0x00, 0x00, 0x00};
```

COMPILING mchat

The `mchat` program uses the following source files:

`atom.c`	*(from chapter 17)*
`button.c`	*(from chapter 16)*
`bytes.c`	*(from chapter 15)*
`cursor.c`	*(from chapter 7)*
`display.c`	*(from chapter 2)*
`error.c`	*(from chapter 17)*
`event.c`	*(from chapter 5)*
`font.c`	*(from chapter 8)*
`gc.c`	*(from chapter 4)*
`icccm.c`	*(from chapter 15)*
`mchat.c`	
`pixmap.c`	*(from chapter 6)*
`prop.c`	*(from chapter 17)*
`sel_own.c`	*(from chapter 19)*
`sel_prop.c`	*(from chapter 19)*
`textedit.c`	*(from chapter 16)*
`topwind.c`	*(from chapter 9)*

```
xstring.c       (from chapter 16)
window.c        (from chapter 3)
mchat.xb
```

On Unix-based systems, you can use the `Makefile` in appendix C, with:

```
make mchat
```

Or, you can compile with:

```
cc -o mchat atom.c button.c bytes.c cursor.c display.c error.c \
    event.c font.c gc.c icccm.c mchat.c pixmap.c prop.c \
    sel_own.c sel_prop.c \
    textedit.c topwind.c xstring.c window.c -lX11
```

RUNNING mchat

You must pass at least one display to `mchat`. Any command-line parameter is considered the name of a connectable display. You can also pass a window geometry and a font name, in the usual manner. Every parameter that doesn't start with a hyphen (-) (pair) is considered a display name.

```
    -geometry geometry_spec
        (e.g., 120x300+40+13)
    -font font_name
```

For example:

```
mchat flame:0.0 attila:0.0 THOR:0.0 -geometry 500x300+10+90
```

would start mchat at position (10, 90) with a window that is 500 pixels wide and 300 pixels high, on three displays: `flame`, `attila`, and `THOR`.

SUMMARY

- The `XOpenDisplay()` Xlib function sets up a display connection to a given X server. `XOpenDisplay()` returns a pointer to a Display structure. You then use this pointer in just about every Xlib call. There's nothing to stop you from calling `XOpenDisplay()` two or more times and setting up multiple display connections in the process.

- The `ChatStruct` contains a display pointer, a top-level window, a graphics context, an icon pixmap, a display name, and character data. `SetUpHosts()` sets up the connections to the multiple X servers. The main loop in `SetUpHosts()` opens a display connection, creates a top-level window and then sends all the necessary hints to the window manager.

- When `SetUpHosts()` finishes, we set up display connections with a number of hosts. Each top-level window will look the same and start out in the same location if the window manager lets it, at least at program start.

- `Mchat` cannot block awaiting events from an X server, because events rarely come from a given server while events are streaming in from other servers. If a `KeyPress` event comes in, the effects of this event are echoed to every display connection. All the windows show the text being entered. The `EventLoop()` function itself is called in a loop for each display connection. It checks, in turn, for incoming events on every display.

- The `QuitApplication()` function is a call-back function from the `Quit` push-button. It quits the whole application (not just the one connection), so any user can stop the program.

Chapter 21

Issues With Multiple-Display Connections

The worst problem facing any program making multiple connections is the IO error problem: if any server connection is lost, it generates a fatal X IO error. Even after calling `XSetIOErrorHandler()`, your error handler cannot return—if it does, Xlib will terminate your application. There's no real way around this, unless you edit the Xlib sources. Unfortunately, that's not an alternative for those with only the Xlib binary libraries.

Your only real option is to use the `setjmp()` and `longjmp()` Unix functions to save a jump environment and then jump to it (never returning from the IO error handler). Otherwise, someone could exit their X server (breaking all X display connections) and crash your program and all machines to which your application connected.

This is by far the worst problem for writing applications that span multiple displays. Fortunately, not many X applications span multiple displays, so few seem to feel the bite of this problem.

SHARING WINDOWS

To solve the IO error problem, developers are researching the concept of sharing windows across displays. The shared window concept is rather neat. The basic idea is that a window's contents are "shared" over multiple X servers. Each window looks the same to each user.

In addition, researchers are looking at ways to "pass the chalk" between the shared windows and create a conferencing system. Others have tried to distribute the problem, so that each user (each on a display) runs a single program. If any display connections go out, only one user—not all—will be cut off.

SOLVING THE IO PROBLEM

The IO problem forces you to answer an is the one-program-or-many question. Should a program, like `mchat` in chapter 20, span multiple displays, or should each user run a different program on each display, with the programs not communicating through X?

We've managed to avoid the question by using a hybrid method. Each program still opens multiple-display connections, but only for a short time. The data to be exchanged is then written to a property on each display's root window (this concept should be familiar by now). Once the data is written to the property, the display connection is shut down, to be opened again only with the next transmission.

This approach of opening a display (that is, a network) connection for each transmission is dreadfully inefficient and will only work if the transmissions are few and far between and not time dependent. Even so, the time to open a display connection, write a property to the root window of the display's default screen, and then close the connection is very short (shorter than we expected; X seems to have a pretty snappy performance in this regard).

This approach would not work for a real-time conferencing system (X on one display does not have real-time performance capabilities). The approach could work, though, for a notifying system or a calendar/scheduling system, such as a system that asks each user if a proposed meeting time is acceptable. We've created a program, called `note`, that uses this approach.

WRITING TO PROPERTIES ON MULTIPLE ROOT WINDOWS

The `NoteSend()` function (in `notesend.c`, developed in the next section) appends a given text message to the given property on the root window (of the default screen) of the given display.

All the parameters to `NoteSend()` are text strings, since the property `Atom` could be (and very likely is) different on each server.

This is how you call `NoteSend()`:

```
char    displayname[];
char    propname[];
char    message[];

NoteSend( displayname, propname, message );
```

SOURCE CODE FOR notesend.c

The source code for `notesend.c` is as follows:

```
notesend.c:
/*
 *      notesend.c
 *      Routine to send a "message" (or append to a property)
 *      to a given display.  With each message,
 *      a new display connection is established,
 *      and then shut down.  This minimizes the
 *      effect of errors on the program but dramatically
```

```
 *      increases the time needed to append data to
 *      the given property.
 *
 */

#include  "xbook.h"

NoteSend( displayname, propname, message )

char    displayname[];
char    propname[];
char    message[];

/*
 *      NoteSend() sends a text message to a given property
 *      on the root window of the given display.
 *
 */

{       /* -- function NoteSend */
        Display *display;
        int         screen;
        Window      rootwindow;
        Atom        property;

        /*
         * 1) Set up X Connection
         */
        display = OpenDisplay( displayname, &screen );

        if ( display != (Display *) NULL )
            {
            /*
             *      2) Send data to a root
             *      window property on
             *      the given display.
             *
             */
            rootwindow = RootWindow( display, screen );

            property   = XInternAtom( display, propname, False );

            if ( property != (Atom) None )
                {
                AppendProperty( display,
                    rootwindow,
```

```
                property,
                XA_STRING,
                8,
                message,
                strlen( message ) );
            }

        XFlush( display );

        /*
         * 3) Terminate connection
         */
        XCloseDisplay( display );
        }

}       /* -- function NoteSend */

/*
 * end of file.
 */
```

THE note PROGRAM

The `note` program uses the `NoteSend()` function to send the same text string to a list of display hosts. To see this text string, users must run a program on their display that will show the contents of the given property placed on the root window. It just so happens that we have a reminder program, shown in chapter 17, that does this task—what a coincidence!

Figure 21-1 shows text typed into the `note` program.

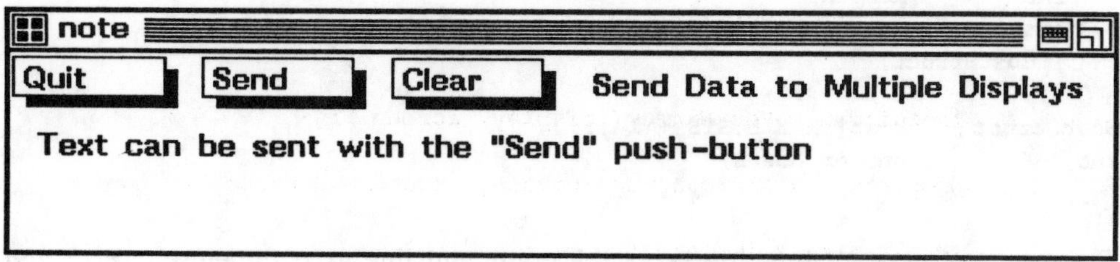

Figure 21-1. Text Typed into the note Program

Figure 21-2 shows text displayed in the Reminder program.

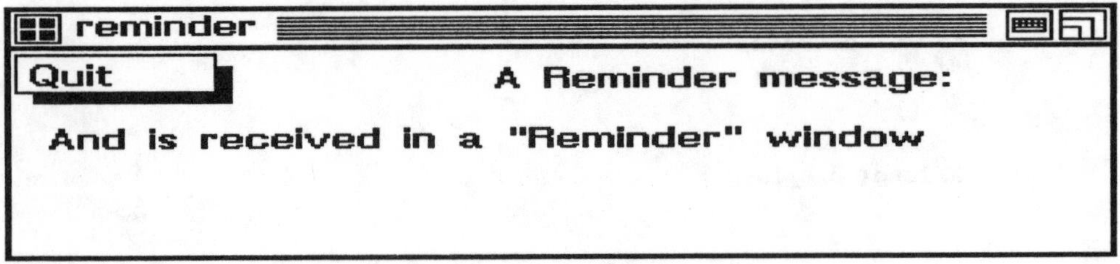

Figure 21-2. Is Displayed in the reminder Program

The first thing the note program does is set up display connections to a number of hosts.

Setting Up Hosts for the note Program

The SetUpHosts() function in note.c is a lot different from the one in mchat.c. While mchat maintains active connections to each display, note just maintains one active X connection, the display with its window. All other connections are briefly set up and then closed down.

Like mchat, we again have a structure for holding the information for each host, and a global array of these structures:

```
#define   MAX_HOSTS    30

typedef struct
    {
    int          length;
    char         name[ BUFSIZE + 1 ];
    } HostStruct;

HostStruct     Host[ MAX_HOSTS + 1 ];
int            number_hosts;
```

The SetUpHosts() function takes the command line as parameters (argc and argv) and returns the number of connectable hosts. Its contents are as follows:

```
SetUpHosts( argc, argv )

int     argc;
char    *argv[];

/*
 *      All command-line parameters NOT associated
 *      with -name data pairs ARE assumed to
 *      be host (display) names to connect to.
 *
 */

{       /* -- function SetUpHosts */
        int     counter, num_hosts, i;
        char    display_name[ BUFSIZE + 1 ];
        char    *display_check;

        display_name[ 0 ] = '\0';

        counter = 1;
        num_hosts = 0;

        while( ( counter < argc ) && ( num_hosts < MAX_HOSTS ) )
            {
            if ( argv[ counter ][ 0 ] = = '-' )
                {
                if ( strcmp( argv[ counter ], "-display" ) = = 0 )
                    { if ( ( counter + 1 ) < argc )
                        {
                        (void) strcpy( display_name,
                            argv[ counter + 1 ] );
                        }
                    }
                counter += 2;
                }
            else
                {
                (void) strcpy( Host[ num_hosts ].name,
                        argv[ counter ] );

                Host[ num_hosts ].length =
                    strlen( Host[ num_hosts ].name );

                num_hosts++;
```

```
                counter++;
                }
            }

        /*
         * We do not want to hook up again with our own
         * display, so check over list
         */
        display_check = XDisplayName( display_name );

        for( i = 0; i < num_hosts; i++ )
            {
            if( strcmp( Host[ i ].name, display_check ) == 0 )
                {
                Host[ i ].name[ 0 ] = '\0';
                Host[ i ].length = 0;
                }
            }

        return( num_hosts );

}       /* -- function SetUpHosts */
```

How note Works with the Reminder Program

The `note` program, of course, is only half the picture for appending data to the root window on multiple displays. The `reminder` program, from chapter 17, forms the other half. `Reminder` displays the contents of the "`__XBOOK`" property on the root window. `Note` writes to the "`__XBOOK`" property on a number of root windows (on a number of displays). On each display, you need to run the `reminder` program to see that the data was sent.

SOURCE CODE FOR note.c

The source code for `note.c` is as follows:

```
note.c:
/*
 *  note.c
 *  X11 program for sending text messages
```

```
 *  to a property on the root window
 *  of multiple displays
 */

#include "xbook.h"

/*
 * Icon bitmap for note program
 */
#include "note.xb"

#define   MESSAGE   "Send Data to Multiple Displays"

/*
 *  This GLOBAL array stores information
 *  about each host we want to talk to.
 *
 */

#define   MAX_HOSTS    30

typedef struct
    {
    int         length;
    char        name[ BUFSIZE + 1 ];
    } HostStruct;

HostStruct     Host[ MAX_HOSTS + 1 ];
int            number_hosts;

/*
 *     Top-level window Globals
 */
int     RefreshFlag = False;
int     QuitFlag    = False;

main( argc, argv )

int     argc;
char    *argv[];

{   /* -- main */
    Display            *display;
    int                screen;
    Window             window;
    GC                 gc;
```

```
int             x, y, width, height;
XFontStruct     *font;
Pixmap          icon;
int             font_height;
unsigned long   black, white;

/*
 *      Set up the names
 *      of hosts we want
 *      to talk to
 */
number_hosts = SetUpHosts( argc, argv );

if ( number_hosts < 1 )
        {
        (void) fprintf( stderr,
        "Error: You must specify some hosts\n" ); exit( 1 );
        }

/*
 * Set up X connection
 */
display= SetUpDisplay( argc, argv,
                &screen );

black      = BlackPixel( display, screen );
white      = WhitePixel( display, screen );

/*
 * Check size and location of window
 */
x    = 10;
y    = 10;
width   = 470;
height = 140;
CheckGeometry( argc, argv,
    DisplayWidth( display, screen ),
    DisplayHeight( display, screen ),
    &x, &y, &width, &height );

/*
 * Create Window
 */
window    = TopWindow( display, x, y, width, height,
                        note_bits, note_width, note_height,
                        &icon, &gc );
```

```
/*
 * Load font
 */
font = LoadFont( display, gc, argc, argv, "variable" );

font_height = font->ascent + font->descent;

/*
 * Store values for window manager
 */
SetNormalHints( display, window,
    x, y, width, height );

SetWMHints( display, window, icon );

NameWindow( display, window,
    "note", "note", "Note" );

SetICCCM( display, window,
    argc, argv );

PropSetData( " " );

XFlush( display );

/*
 * Create buttons of ruser interface items
 */
MakeButtons( display, window,
    black, white, font->fid );

/*
 * Map windows
 */
MapWindow( display, window );

/*
 * Handle any events
 */
while( QuitFlag = = False )
    {
    EventLoop( display,
        window, gc, font,
        &width, &height );

    if ( RefreshFlag = = True )
```

```
            {
            Refresh( display, window, gc, font_height );

            RefreshFlag = False;
            }

        }

    /*
     * Shut down
     */
    XFreeFont( display, font );
    XFreePixmap( display, icon );

    CloseDisplay( display, window, gc );

    exit( 0 );

}   /* -- main */

SendData( display, window )

Display *display;
Window window;

/*
 *  SendData() appends data to a property on the
 *  root window of each display we want
 *  to talk to.
 */

{   /* -- function SendData */
    int     i;
    char    TextData[ BUFSIZE + 1 ];
    Window  rootwindow;
    Atom    xbook_atom;

    PropReturnData( TextData );

    /*
     * Send out message
     */
    for( i = 0; i < number_hosts; i++ )
        {
        if ( Host[ i ].name[ 0 ] != '\0' )
            {
```

```
            NoteSend( Host[ i ].name,
                PROP_NAME,
                TextData );
            }
        else
            {
            rootwindow = RootWindow( display,
                    DefaultScreen( display ) );

            xbook_atom = XInternAtom( display,
                    PROP_NAME,
                    False );

            PutPropertyData( display,
                window,
                rootwindow,
                xbook_atom,
                XA_STRING );
            }

        }

}   /* -- function SendData */

ClearData( display, window )

Display    *display;
Window window;

{   /* -- function ClearData */

    PropSetData( " " );

    XClearWindow( display, window );

    RefreshFlag = True;

}   /* -- function ClearData */

EventLoop( display, window, gc, font, width, height )

Display         *display;
Window          window;
GC              gc;
XFontStruct     *font;
```

```
int             *width, *height;

/*
 *  EventLoop() handles generic X events, but passes
 *  most events on to specific functions to handle
 *  the particular event.
 *
 *
 */

{   /* -- function EventLoop */
    XEvent event;
    KeySym keysym;
    char   TextData[ BUFSIZE + 1 ];

    /*
     *     Block on input, awaiting
     *     an event from X.
     */
    NextEvent( display, False,
           *width, *height,
           &event,
           &keysym );

    if ( ButtonEvent( display, &event ) == True )
           {
           return( True );
           }

    /*
     * Decode the event and call
     * a specific routine to
     * handle it.
     */
    switch( event.type )
           {
           case ClientMessage:
               if( IsDeleteWindow( display, &event ) == True )
                   {
                   QuitFlag = True;
                   }
               break;
           case Expose:
               RefreshFlag = True;
               break;
```

```
        case ConfigureNotify:
            *width = event.xconfigure.width;
            *height    = event.xconfigure.height;
            break;
        case KeyPress:
            PropReturnData( TextData );

            TextEdit( display, window,
                gc, font,
                5, 2 * BUTTON_HEIGHT,
                keysym,
                TextData, BUFSIZE );

            PropSetData( TextData );
            break;
        }

    return( True );

}   /* -- function EventLoop */

QuitApplication( display, window )

Display *display;
Window     window;

{           /* -- function QuitApplication */

            QuitFlag = True;

}           /* -- function QuitApplication */

MakeButtons( display, window, fore, back, font_id )

Display    *display;
Window         window;
unsigned long  fore, back;
Font           font_id;

{   /* -- function MakeButtons */
    int     QuitApplication();
    int     SendData();
    int     ClearData();

CreateButton( display, window,
            1, 2,
```

```
                fore, back, font_id,
                "Quit", QuitApplication );

        CreateButton( display, window, BUTTON_WIDTH + 11, 2,
                fore, back, font_id,
                "Send",
                SendData );

        CreateButton( display, window,
                ( 2 *BUTTON_WIDTH ) + 22, 2,
                fore, back, font_id,
                "Clear",
                ClearData );

}   /* -- function MakeButtons */

Refresh( display, window, gc, font_height )

Display *display;
Window      window;
GC          gc;
int         font_height;

{   /* -- function Refresh */
    int     i;

    XDrawImageString( display, window, gc,
            ( 3 * ( BUTTON_WIDTH + 11 ) ) + 5,
            BUTTON_HEIGHT - 5,
            MESSAGE, strlen( MESSAGE ) );

    PropDisplayCurrent( display, window, gc,
            font_height,
            5, 2 * BUTTON_HEIGHT );

    /*
     * Display host names
     */
    for( i = 0; i < number_hosts; i++ )
            {
            XDrawImageString( display, window, gc,
                5, 100 + ( i * font_height ),
                Host[ i ].name,
                Host[ i ].length );
            }
```

```
    XFlush( display );

}   /* -- function Refresh */

SetUpHosts( argc, argv )

int     argc;
char    *argv[];

/*
 *      All command-line parameters NOT associated
 *      with -name data pairs ARE assumed to
 *      be host (display) names to connect to.
 *
 */

{   /* -- function SetUpHosts */
    int     counter, num_hosts, i;
    char    display_name[ BUFSIZE + 1 ];
    char    *display_check;

    display_name[ 0 ] = '\0';

    counter    = 1;
    num_hosts  = 0;

    while( ( counter < argc ) && ( num_hosts < MAX_HOSTS ) )
        {
        if ( argv[ counter ][ 0 ] = = '-' )
            {
            if ( strcmp( argv[ counter ], "-display" ) = = 0 )
                {
                 if ( ( counter + 1 ) < argc )
                    {
                    (void) strcpy( display_name,
                        argv[ counter + 1 ] );
                    }
                }
            counter += 2;
            }
        else
            {
            (void) strcpy( Host[ num_hosts ].name,
                    argv[ counter ] );

            Host[ num_hosts ].length =
```

```
                    strlen( Host[ num_hosts ].name );

                num_hosts++;

                counter++;
                }
        }

    /*
     * We do not want to hook up again with our own
     * display, so check over list */
    display_check = XDisplayName( display_name );

    for( i = 0; i < num_hosts; i++ )
        {
        if( strcmp( Host[ i ].name, display_check ) = = 0 )
            {
            Host[ i ].name[ 0 ] = '\0';
            Host[ i ].length = 0;
            }
        }

    return( num_hosts );

}   /* -- function SetUpHosts */

/*
 * end of file.
 */
```

An Icon for note

Figure 21-3 shows the `note` icon created by the bitmap editor.

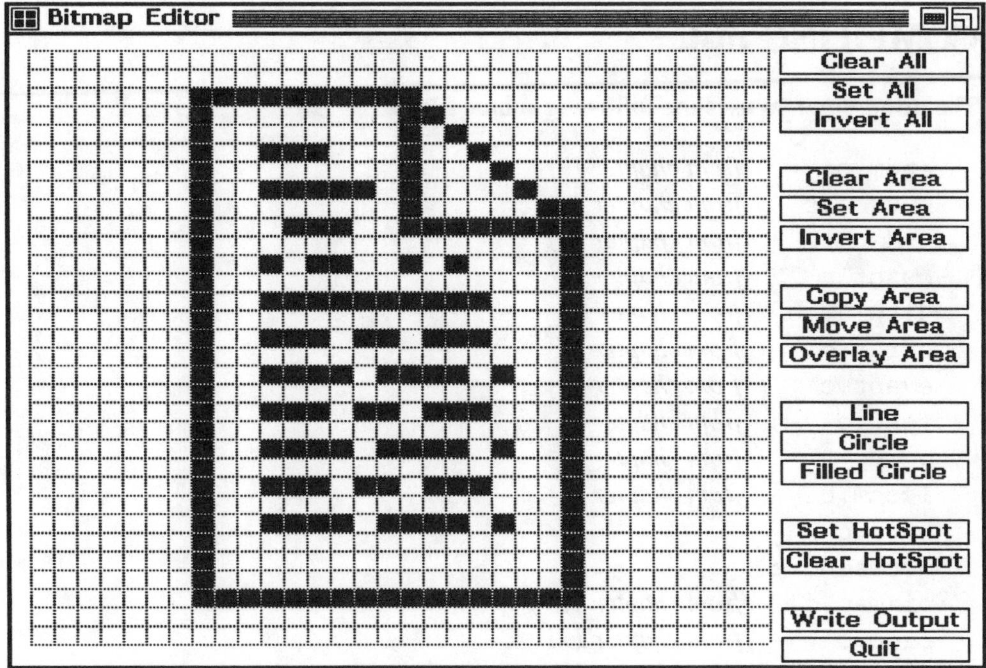

Figure 21-3. The note Icon

The contents of `note.xb` are as follows:

```
note.xb:
#define note_width 32
#define note_height 32
static char note_bits[] = {
0x00, 0x00, 0x00, 0x00, 0x00, 0x00, 0x00, 0x00, 0x80, 0xff, 0x01, 0x00,
0x80, 0x00, 0x03, 0x00, 0x80, 0x00, 0x05, 0x00, 0x80, 0x1c, 0x09, 0x00,
0x80, 0x00, 0x11, 0x00, 0x80, 0x7c, 0x21, 0x00, 0x80, 0x00, 0xc1, 0x00,
0x80, 0x38, 0xff, 0x00, 0x80, 0x00, 0x80, 0x00, 0x80, 0x34, 0x85, 0x00,
0x80, 0x00, 0x80, 0x00, 0x80, 0xfc, 0x8f, 0x00, 0x80, 0x00, 0x80, 0x00,
0x80, 0xdc, 0x8e, 0x00, 0x80, 0x00, 0x80, 0x00, 0x80, 0xbc, 0x97, 0x00,
0x80, 0x00, 0x80, 0x00, 0x80, 0xdc, 0x8e, 0x00, 0x80, 0x00, 0x80, 0x00,
0x80, 0xbc, 0x97, 0x00, 0x80, 0x00, 0x80, 0x00, 0x80, 0xdc, 0x8e, 0x00,
```

```
0x80, 0x00, 0x80, 0x00, 0x80, 0xbc, 0x97, 0x00, 0x80, 0x00, 0x80, 0x00,
0x80, 0x00, 0x80, 0x00, 0x80, 0x00, 0x80, 0x00, 0x80, 0xff, 0xff, 0x00,
0x00, 0x00, 0x00, 0x00, 0x00, 0x00, 0x00, 0x00};
```

COMPILING note

The `note` program uses the following source files:

`atom.c`	*(from chapter 17)*
`button.c`	*(from chapter 16)*
`bytes.c`	*(from chapter 15)*
`cusor c`	*(from chapter 7)*
`display.c`	*(from chapter 2)*
`error.c`	*(from chapter 17)*
`event.c`	*(from chapter 5)*
`font.c`	*(from chapter 8)*
`gc.c`	*(from chapter 4)*
`icccm.c`	*(from chapter 15)*
`note.c`	
`notesend.c`	
`pixmap.c`	*(from chapter 6)*
`prop.c`	*(from chapter 17)*
`sel_own.c`	*(from chapter 19)*
`sel_prop.c`	*(from chapter 19)*
`textedit.c`	*(from chapter 16)*
`topwind.c`	*(from chapter 9)*
`xstring.c`	*(from chapter 16)*
`window.c`	*(from chapter 3)*
`note.xb`	

On Unix-based systems, you can use the `Makefile` in appendix C, with:

```
make note
```

Or, you can compile with:

```
cc -o note atom.c button.c bytes.c cursor.c display.c error.c \
```

```
    event.c font.c gc.c icccm.c note.c notesend.c pixmap.c prop.c \
sel_own.c sel_prop.c textedit.c topwind.c xstring.c window.c -lX11
```

RUNNING note

Note needs command-line parameters for connectable hosts. You may also specify a display (for note's window), a window geometry and a font name, all in the usual manner:

```
-display display_name
-geometry geometry_spec
   (e.g., 120x300+40+13)
-font font_name
```

SUMMARY

- Setting up multiple connections can be tricky, and it's up to the programmer to avoid fatal IO errors. An alternative is the shared-window concept, where a window's contents are "shared" over multiple X servers.

- This chapter illustrated another approach to multiple display connections with the note application. This program still opens multiple-display connections. The data to be exchanged is then written to a property on each display's root window (this concept should be familiar by now). Once the data is written to the property, the display connection is shut down, to be opened again only with the next transmission.

- The NoteSend() function appends a given text message to the given property on the root window of the given display. All the parameters to NoteSend() are text strings since the property Atom could be (and very likely is) different on each server.

- The SetUpHosts() function in note.c is a lot different from the one in mchat.c. While mchat maintains active connections to each display, note just maintains one active X connection, to the display with its window. All other connections are briefly set up and then closed down.

Section V

Introducing X11 Release 4

As of this writing, Release 4 is the latest from the MIT X Consortium. Release 4 is the most professional X release to date, but it will probably take a year before most vendors have migrated to R4. In addition, many X users are still running Release 2 and 3 systems and probably will be for years to come.

Section 5 covers some of the major changes introduced in Release 4 to help programmers port over from Release 3 (and 2).

Release 4 solidifies the X library and offers hope that most applications will adopt the infamous ICCCM.

Section V

[illegible] Release 4

[illegible]

[illegible] Release 4 [illegible]

[illegible]

Chapter 22

Changes in Release 4

This chapter summarizes some of the changes introduced in the Release 4 Xlib. This book already covered many of the changes, in particular the window manager interface functions in chapter 3. This chapter briefly summarizes the changes and goes over a few important new functions.

ROUND WINDOWS

The best change in Release 4 is the SHAPE extension that introduces round (like oclock in the standard release) and other odd-shaped windows. This isn't in Xlib, but it's darn fun anyway. The SHAPE extension allows you to change a window's shape to be that of a region or a bitmap. The best part about the SHAPE extension is that to try it out you only need one function call—talk about simple.

Try out this code in any of the example programs used so far.:

```
...

#ifdef X11R4

#include  <X11/extensions/shape.h>

#include  "shape.xb"

#endif

    ...

    Display    *display;
    Window     window;
    int        x, y, width, height;
    Pixmap     icon;
    GC         gc;
    int        shape_kind;
    int        x_offset, y_offset;
    int        shape_op;

    ...

    /*
     * Look for the TopWindow() function call
     */
    window = TopWindow( display, x, y, width, height,
                shape_bits, shape_width, shape_height,
                &icon, &gc );

    /*
     * Put the shape stuff right after the TopWindow()
     * function call.
     */

#ifdef X11R4
    shape_kind = ShapeBounding;
    x_offset = 0;
    y_offset = 0;
    shape_op = ShapeSet;

    XShapeCombineMask( display, window,
```

```
        shape_kind,
        x_offset, y_offset,
        icon,
        shape_set );
#endif
    ...
```

This code makes the window's shape be that of a pixmap (in this case, the pixmap icon, stored in `shape.xb`). Note that when you link your program, you need to link in the extension library (`libXext.a` or add a `-lXext` to the compile command line) before you link in the Xlib library (-lX11). Figure 22-1 shows the shape icon.

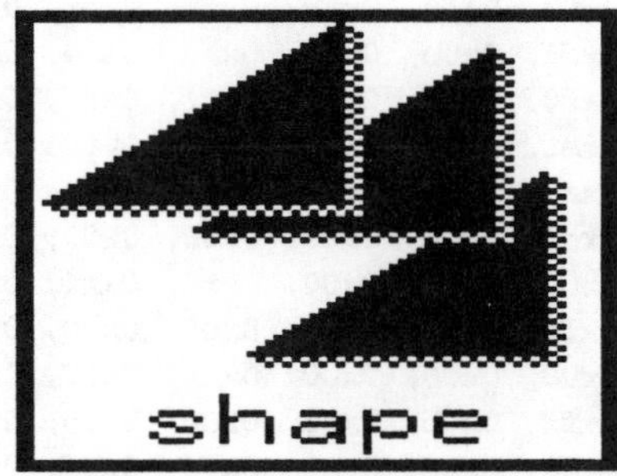

Figure 22-1. The Fun Shape Icon

For more fun and information on the `SHAPE` extension, see the document titled "X11 Nonrectangular Window Shape Extension" by Keith Packard of the MIT X Consortium (this document should come with the standard Release 4).

The following is the bitmap for `shape.xb`, included for completeness:

```
shape.xb:
#define shape_width 64
#define shape_height 64
static char shape_bits[] = {
0x00, 0x00, 0x0e, 0x00, 0x00, 0x00, 0x00, 0x00, 0x00, 0x00, 0x17, 0x00,
0x00, 0x00, 0x00, 0x00, 0x00, 0x80, 0x0f, 0x00, 0x00, 0x00, 0x00, 0x00,
0x00, 0xc0, 0x17, 0x00, 0x00, 0x00, 0x00, 0x00, 0x00, 0xe0, 0x0f, 0x00,
0x08, 0x00, 0x00, 0x00, 0x00, 0xf0, 0x17, 0x00, 0x1c, 0x00, 0x00, 0x00,
0x00, 0xf8, 0x0f, 0x00, 0x2e, 0x00, 0x00, 0x00, 0x00, 0xfc, 0x17, 0x00,
0x1f, 0x00, 0x00, 0x00, 0x00, 0xfe, 0x0f, 0x80, 0x2f, 0x00, 0x00, 0x00,
0x00, 0xff, 0x17, 0xc0, 0x1f, 0x00, 0x00, 0x00, 0x80, 0xff, 0x0f, 0xe0,
```

```
0x2f, 0x00, 0x00, 0x00, 0xc0, 0xff, 0x17, 0xf0, 0x1f, 0x00, 0x00, 0x00,
0xe0, 0xff, 0x0f, 0xf8, 0x2f, 0x00, 0x00, 0x00, 0xf0, 0xff, 0x17, 0xfc,
0x1f, 0x00, 0x00, 0x00, 0xf8, 0xff, 0x0f, 0xfe, 0x2f, 0x00, 0x00, 0x00,
0xfc, 0xff, 0x17, 0xff, 0x1f, 0x00, 0x00, 0x00, 0xfe, 0xff, 0x8f, 0xff,
0x2f, 0x00, 0x00, 0x00, 0xff, 0xff, 0xd7, 0xff, 0x1f, 0x00, 0x00, 0x80,
0xff, 0xff, 0xef, 0xff, 0x2f, 0x00, 0x00, 0xc0, 0xff, 0xff, 0xf7, 0xff,
0x1f, 0x00, 0x00, 0xe0, 0xff, 0xff, 0xef, 0xff, 0x2f, 0x00, 0x00, 0xf0,
0xff, 0xff, 0xf7, 0xff, 0x1f, 0x00, 0x00, 0xf8, 0xff, 0xff, 0xef, 0xff,
0x2f, 0x00, 0x00, 0xfc, 0xff, 0xff, 0xf7, 0xff, 0x1f, 0x00, 0x00, 0xfe,
0xff, 0xff, 0xef, 0xff, 0x2f, 0x00, 0x00, 0xff, 0xff, 0xff, 0xf7, 0xff,
0x1f, 0x00, 0x80, 0xff, 0xff, 0xff, 0xef, 0xff, 0x2f, 0x00, 0xc0, 0xff,
0xff, 0xff, 0xf7, 0xff, 0x1f, 0x02, 0xe0, 0xff, 0xff, 0xff, 0xef, 0xff,
0x2f, 0x07, 0xf0, 0xff, 0xff, 0xff, 0xf7, 0xff, 0x9f, 0x0b, 0xf8, 0xff,
0xff, 0xff, 0xef, 0xff, 0xef, 0x07, 0xfc, 0xff, 0xff, 0xff, 0xf7, 0xff,
0xdf, 0x0b, 0xfe, 0xff, 0xff, 0xff, 0xef, 0xff, 0xef, 0x07, 0x54, 0x55,
0x55, 0x55, 0xf5, 0xff, 0xdf, 0x0b, 0xa8, 0xaa, 0xaa, 0xaa, 0xea, 0xff,
0xef, 0x07, 0x00, 0x00, 0xf0, 0xff, 0xff, 0xff, 0xdf, 0x0b, 0x00, 0x00,
0xf8, 0xff, 0xff, 0xff, 0xef, 0x07, 0x00, 0x00, 0xfc, 0xff, 0xff, 0xff,
0xdf, 0x0b, 0x00, 0x00, 0xa8, 0xaa, 0xaa, 0xaa, 0xea, 0x07, 0x00, 0x00,
0x50, 0x55, 0x55, 0x55, 0xd5, 0x0b, 0x00, 0x00, 0x00, 0x00, 0x00, 0xf0,
0xff, 0x07, 0x00, 0x00, 0x00, 0x00, 0x00, 0xf8, 0xff, 0x0b, 0x00, 0x00,
0x00, 0x00, 0x00, 0xfc, 0xff, 0x07, 0x00, 0x00, 0x00, 0x00, 0x00, 0xfe,
0xff, 0x0b, 0x00, 0x00, 0x00, 0x00, 0x00, 0xff, 0xff, 0x07, 0x00, 0x00,
0x00, 0x00, 0x80, 0xff, 0xff, 0x0b, 0x00, 0x00, 0x00, 0x00, 0xc0, 0xff,
0xff, 0x07, 0x00, 0x00, 0x00, 0x00, 0xe0, 0xff, 0xff, 0x0b, 0x00, 0x00,
0x00, 0x00, 0xf0, 0xff, 0xff, 0x07, 0x00, 0x00, 0x00, 0x00, 0xf8, 0xff,
0xff, 0x0b, 0x00, 0x00, 0x00, 0x00, 0xfc, 0xff, 0xff, 0x07, 0x00, 0x00,
0x00, 0x00, 0xfe, 0xff, 0xff, 0x0b, 0x00, 0x00, 0x00, 0x00, 0xff, 0xff,
0xff, 0x07, 0x00, 0x00, 0x00, 0x80, 0xff, 0xff, 0xff, 0x0b, 0x00, 0x00,
0x00, 0xc0, 0xff, 0xff, 0xff, 0x07, 0x00, 0x00, 0x00, 0xe0, 0xff, 0xff,
0xff, 0x0b, 0x00, 0x00, 0x00, 0xf0, 0xff, 0xff, 0xff, 0x07, 0x00, 0x00,
0x00, 0xf8, 0xff, 0xff, 0xff, 0x0b, 0x00, 0x00, 0x00, 0xfc, 0xff, 0xff,
0xff, 0x07, 0x00, 0x00, 0x00, 0xfe, 0xff, 0xff, 0xff, 0x0b, 0x00, 0x00,
0x00, 0xff, 0xff, 0xff, 0xff, 0x07, 0x00, 0x00, 0x00, 0xaa, 0xaa, 0xaa,
0xaa, 0x0a, 0x00, 0x00, 0x00, 0x54, 0x55, 0x55, 0x55, 0x05};
```

NEW AND CHANGED XLIB FUNCTIONS

That's it for fun—now the functions that have changed since Release 3 will be reviewed. Many of these functions were covered in earlier chapters.

As with any changes, there's a dilemma: should you use the new functions and perhaps be incompatible with many X systems in existence, or should you use the old routines which will probably soon become obsolete as users convert to the new version. If you need to make applications that work now and work on a variety of platforms, this isn't an easy question.

The following chart shows the changed or new Xlib functions in Release 4.

Function Name	Described in Chapter	Source File
XAllocClassHints	chapter 3	window.c
XAllocIconSize	--	--
XAllocSizeHints	chapter 3	window.c
XAllocStandardColormap	--	--
XAllocWMHints	chapter 3	window.c
XFreeStringList	chapter 3	--
XGetCommand	chapter 3	--
XGetErrorDatabaseText	--	--
XGetGCValues	--	--
XGetRGBColormaps	--	--
XGetTextProperty	--	--
XGetWMClientMachine	chapter 15	--
XGetWMColormapWindows	--	--
XGetWMIconName	chapter 3	--
XGetWMName	chapter 3	--
XGetWMNormalHints	chapter 3	--
XGetWMProtocols	chapter 15	--
XGetWMSizeHints	chapter 3	--
XIconifyWindow	chapter 15	--
XKeysymToString	--	--
XListDepths	--	--
XListPixmapFormats	--	--
XOpenDisplay	chapter 2	display.c
XReconfigureWMWindow	--	--
XrmDestroyDatabase	--	--
XScreenNumberOfScreen	--	--
XSetErrorHandler	chapter 17	error.c
XSetIOErrorHandler	chapter 17	--
XSetRGBColormaps	--	--
XSetTextProperty	--	--

XSetWMClientMachine	chapter 15	--
XSetWMColormapWindows	--	--
XSetWMIconName	chapter 3	--
XSetWMName	chapter 3	--
XSetWMNormalHints	chapter	window.c
XSetWMProperties	-	--
XSetWMProtocols	chapter 15	icccm.c
XSetWMSizeHints	chapter 3	--
XStringListToTextProperty	chapter 3	--
XStringToKeysym	--	--
XTextPropertyToStringList	chapter 3	--
XWithdrawWindow	--	--
XWMGeometry	--	--

SOME NEW XLIB FUNCTIONS

We've already covered most of the important new functions; unfortunately, space precludes covering them all in depth. Among the more important ones we haven't covered include XGetCommand(), XGetGCValues(), XGetTextProperty(), XListDepths(), and XSetTextProperty().

XGetCommand

XGetCommand() is the opposite of XSetCommand(), introduced in chapter 3. XGetCommand() reads the WM_COMMAND property (see chapter 15) on the given window. XGetCommand() is useful when responding to WM_SAVE_YOURSELF messages or when nosing about other clients. Its contents are as follows:

```
Display*  display;
Window    window;
char      **argv;
int       argc;
int       status;

status = XGetCommand( display, window, &argv, &argc );

if ( status != 0 )
```

```
{
/* -- Success */

...

XFreeStringList( argv );
}
```

XGetGCValues

`XGetGCValues()` is a function that should have been around well before Release 4. It will retrieve values set in a graphics context and is, therefore, really handy to use with a routine that reverses the foreground and background colors of a graphics context or with any routine that needs to know what was set into a graphics context before. The contents of `XGetGCValues` are as follows:

```
Display          *display;
Window           window;
int              status;
XGCValues        gcvalues;
unsigned long    wanted_mask;  /* -- e.g., GCFunction | GCForeground */

/*
 * OR-together the GC flags for the fields you want
 * returned (filled in) in the gcvalues structure.
 */
status = XGetGCValues( display, gc, wanted_mask, &gcvalues );

if ( status != 0 )
    { /* -- success */

    ...

    }
```

With `XGetGCValues()`, you choose the fields of the `XGCValues` structure that should be filled in by the routine. This is a lot like the routines that set values into a GC, like `XCreateGC()` and `XChangeGC()`.

XGetTextProperty and XSetTextProperty

Text properties are a new structure to hold text—text that could be in various national formats (we're still allowed to have an ASCII bias, but we're supposed to tone it down a bit now). Unfortunately, it will be years before the majority of software is updated to work in an international environment. At least these issues are being addressed, though.

We've already covered the `XStringListToTextProperty()` and `XTextPropertyToStringList()` (see chapters 3 and 15), which convert text strings to text properties. `XGetTextProperty()` reads a given property on a given window and places that data into a text property. `XSetTextProperty()` does the opposite: it writes out a text property structure onto a window property. These are some "under-the-hood" routines for other functions like `XSetWMIconName()`.

The structure name, `XTextProperty`, isn't the best name, especially when used with `XSetTextProperty()` which sets a text property on a property. Properties are normally associated with windows and the terminology becomes a bit confusing when you also use a structure directly as well. Call `XTextProperty()`:

```
Display         *display;
Window          window;
Atom            property;   /* -- to write data to and read from */
XTextProperty   text_property;
int             status;

status = XGetTextProperty( display,
    window,             /* -- window with property */
    &text_property,     /* -- Data read */
    property );         /* -- property to read */

if ( status != 0 )
    {
    /* -- success */
    ...

    }

XSetTextProperty( display, window,   /* -- window to write to   */
    &text_property,    /* -- data to write out     */
    property );            /* -- property to write to */
```

Whenever you write data to a property (that is, a property on a window), you are in danger of sucking all the memory from the X server, generating an X error. To avoid this you need to set up an error handler before you write data to a property (see chapter 17).

XListDepths

XListDepths() returns an integer array of the bit-plane (that is, color-plane) depths available on a given screen. Since screens may support multiple depths, this can be handy. You can choose the depth of your choice, especially if your X vendor decided to make the default depth be some weird value like a 1 bit-plane default depth on a 8 bit-plane color system (it may be correct, but it still is weird). The contents of XListDepth() are as follows:

```
Display *  display;
int        screen;        /* -- Screen number */
int        number_items;
int        *the_depths;
int        i;

the_depths = XListDepths( display, screen, &number_items )

if ( the_depths != (int *) NULL )
    {
    /*
     * Success. the_depths now
     * holds an array of possible depths.
     */
    for( i = 0; i < number_items; i++ )
        {
        printf( "Depth %d is %d bit planes\n",
            i, the_depths[ i ] );
        }
    ...
    XFree( the_depths );
    }
```

OBSOLETE XLIB FUNCTIONS

Along with a host of neat new functions, Release 4 also made a number of routines obsolete. If possible, switch to the new routines, though you may need to support systems running at a level prior to Release 4.

Old Function	New Function
XGeometry	XWMGeometry
XGetNormalHints	XGetWMNormalHints
XGetSizeHints	XGetWMSizeHints
XGetStandardColormap	XGetRGBColormap
XSetNormalHints	XSetWMNormalHints
XSetSizeHints	XSetWMSizeHints
XSetStandardColormap	XSetRGBColormap
XSetStandardProperties	XSetWMProperties
XGetZoomHints	(None: Not in ICCCM 1.0)
XSetZoomHints	(None: Not in ICCCM 1.0)

XLIB FUNCTIONS AND MACROS INTRODUCED IN THIS CHAPTER

```
XGetCommand
XGetGCValues
XGetTextProperty
XListDepths
XSetTextProperty
XShapeCombineMask
```

It's often difficult to remember all the parameters and the order they go in, for example, X is perfectly consistent in always using `argv` before `argc` when referring to command-line parameters. Unfortunately, a good number of people programming C start their programs with:

```
main( argc, argv )
int         argc;
char    *argv[]; { ...
```

X usually places the list parameter, `argv`, first and then it places the count parameter, `argc`.

Appendices

Appendix A

Hardware and Software

Unfortunately, there are no shrink-wrapped X packages on the market containing the proper hardware or software setups for X. You can't simply throw a diskette in the drive and—voilà!—X appears on your screen.

The most common way that people acquire X is by purchasing a Unix system of some sort that comes bundled with X.

These people have the double duty of learning X and Unix at the same time. This isn't an insurmountable task by any stretch—but be warned that an inexperienced computer user will put in a lot of work before ever reaching the X level.

For those of us without a Cray or a DEC VAX in our office, learning and using X is a matter of obtaining a workstation or PC with the firepower to run X. There are three basic paths to an X system: get a Unix workstation, an X terminal, or software to turn a personal computer (Amiga, Macintosh, or PC) into an X terminal. If you go the X terminal route, you'll also need another computer on a network that can run X applications because X terminals just provide the X server—not the most interesting of applications.

If your budget allows, purchasing a workstation is the most simple solution. (Our personal budgets, alas, don't allow this, but our employers' budgets do.) Workstations from Data General, Hewlett-Packard, Motorola, DEC, and others all come bundled with X. Such a workstation (equipped with hard disk) will set you back about $15,000 at the low end, but it's an invaluable tool if you're a professional software developer, analyst, or designer.

Our experience shows that a workstation is beyond the reach of a good portion of potential users. A lower-priced (and, unfortunately, a lower-performing) alternative is to configure a PC to run X by turning it into an X terminal or running X under Unix. This can be a simple solution, but not every PC is equipped to run X.

First of all, you'll want to configure a PC as an X server. In theory, you can use an 80286, 80386, or 80486 system equipped with 640K of RAM, a monochrome display, a networking card, and X software. Theory, though, loses its luster when it comes to performance. Reality dictates that you need at least an 80386 or an 80486 with four megs of RAM, a mondo hard drive (80MB is good, 120MB better), and a large-screen color display. When running graphics-intensive programs on top of Unix, the more power the better. With hardware prices (particularly in the RAM and 80386 fields) dropping rapidly, you' re looking at a speed demon for under $10,000.

SOFTWARE

The software you choose dictates your ultimate hardware configuration. For the PC, there are two software routes: X server software running under DOS or Unix configurations that support X.

Truth is, we haven't played with the DOS X servers (like PC Xview from Graphic Software Systems or Locus's PC Xsight). In theory, you can run Xview or Xsight in 640K on an AT. This software essentially turns your DOS PC into an X terminal. You'll still need another computer on the network to run X applications.

On PCs, our experience has been with versions of Unix from Interactive Systems (386/ix) and Apple (A/UX 1.1). Other vendors supporting X under Unix for PCs are SCO (Unix and Open Desktop), Everex (Esix), IBM (AIX), and Intel. Since X draws some features (in part) from the operating system underneath it, it seems like a good idea to use the power of Unix if it's available.

If you're an Apple fan, A/UX 2.0 will run Macintosh applications and X applications (via MacX)—a big, big bonus. You'll need a high-end Macintosh to run it (the IIfx is a perfect, though disgustingly expensive, choice). In addition, White Pine Systems offers eXodus, which allows you to open X windows within the Macintosh operating system.

CPUS

We're experienced with PCs, workstations, and Macintoshes. Again, more is better—more megahertz and more RAM. The amount of RAM needed will depend on the software—some PC versions of Unix require a minimum of two megs, while others (like AIX) require four. Don't buy the minimum, however—buy as much RAM as your checkbook allows. Eight megabytes is a realistic minimum for a system that runs Unix and X. Sixteen megs is a lot better. Release 4 of the X Window System requires less RAM and provides much better performance. Unfortunately, few vendors have upgraded their X offerings to Release 4 as of this writing.

Using a 386 or a 486 as an X server also allows the users to run DOS applications. While we're not huge fans of DOS, there are some applications in DOS that don't have counterparts in the X world.

In addition, there's a version of X that runs under AmigaDOS from GfxBase. We can't recommend it or argue against it, but it's worth checking out.

MONITORS

Since X is a graphic windowing product, your monitor's resolution is important. Again, the more power the better.

You'll need a minimum of 640-by-480 resolution (VGA). This is probably the minimum usable for X. Better yet is Super VGA (800-by-600 or 1024-by-768) or 8514/A (1024-by-768). High-end monitors cost more—you'll need to pay extra for both the monitor and graphics card—but they can increase performance because part of the X server can be loaded onto the card's limited memory. Your CPU doesn't have to work as hard, which will speed up your system.

HARD DRIVES

There's only one rule to remember about hard drives: the bigger the better. An 80MB drive is the minimum—especially with Unix—while 120MB or 330MB is better. If you can afford that high-performance Wren drive, go for it.

NETWORKING CARD

Most DOS X implementations won't work without a networking card of some sort. What you choose will ultimately depend on your networking needs.

X TERMINALS

If you already have a networked workstation in your business, you may want to look at dedicated X terminals. Several vendors—such as DEC, Hewlett-Packard, IBM, NCD, and Princeton Graphics—sell X terminals. These terminals are usually built around a Motorola 680X0 and come equipped with one and two megabytes of RAM and the necessary networking equipment. Because X is graphics intensive, you' ll want as much RAM as you can afford on an X terminal. These terminals aren't cheap—they cost between $2,000 and $5,000 (and beyond)—but they can be a bargain when compared to X workstations. One benefit of X terminals over workstations is that X terminals are easier to administer. One drawback of X terminals is the increased load you place on a few hosts: since X terminals just run the X server software, you always need other computers to run the X applications.

Appendix B

Obtaining X

The good folks at MIT and Project Athena make it amazingly easy to obtain the X Window System. They also put very few strings on it; you don't need to license X or pay royalties, and developers are encouraged to use X as a development tool.

There are three ways to obtain the X Window System: directly from MIT, through Internet and UUCP, and from commercial consulting firms and vendors.

MIT SOFTWARE DISTRIBUTION CENTER

MIT sells X, along with printed manuals and X Window System: *C Library and Protocol Reference* (Gettys, Newman, and Scheifler). X comes on a set of four

1600bpi tapes in Unix tar format. The book and manuals sell for $125, while tapes, book, and manuals sell for $400. You can write to:

MIT Software Distribution Center
Technology Licensing Office
Room E32-300
77 Massachusetts Avenue
Cambridge, MA 02139

Or call the "X Ordering Hotline" at (617) 258-8330.

INTERNET

If you're on Internet or UUCP, you can retrieve the release from the following locations:

LOCATION	MACHINE NAME	INTERNET ADDRESS	ANONOYMOUS FTP DIRECTORY
1) Western US	gatekeeper.dec.com	16.1.0.2	pub/X11/R4
Central US	mordred.cs.purdue.edu	12 .10.2.2	pub/X11/R4
2) Central US	giza.cis.ohio-state.edu	28.146.8.62	pub/X.V11R4
Southeast US	uunet.uu.net	192.48.96.2	XR4
3) Northeast US	crl.dec.com	192.58.206.2	pub/X11/R4
4) UK Janet	src.doc.ic.ac.uk	129.31. 1.36	X.V11R
UK niftp	uk.ac.ic.doc.src		<XV11R4>*
5) Australia	munnari.oz.au	128.250.1.21	X.V11/R4

The FTP directories contain a `README` file with further instructions. Since we had the text handy, here's what's in the `README` file:

Here is a roadmap to the Release 4 sources:

`README`
`RELNOTES.PS` R4 release notes in Postscript
`RELNOTES.txt` R4 release notes in plain text

`RELNOTES.lpt`	R4 release notes in lpt format
`R4notice`	R4 announcement (also where to get X)
`ERRATA`	helpful hints
`tape-1/`	core software for the X Window System (required)
`tape-2/`	contrib clients and core doc (recommended)
`tape-3/`	contrib libraries and other toolkits (optional)
`tape-4/`	contrib Andrew, games, etc.

The split pieces are all 512K (524288 bytes) long (except for the last one in each directory) and must be transferred in image mode (use the ftp `"binary"` and `"mget"` commands). If you are doing an `"mget"` you'll probably want to restart ftp with the `"-i"` option to prevent it from asking you about every file.

Each directory contains a CHECKSUM file containing both BSD- and SYSV-style checksums (generated with the "sum" command) and a FILES .Z file containing a compressed listing of the files stored in that directory.

To extract the sources into another directory (for example, `/usr/local/src/R4/`), make sure you have LOTS of disk space and type the followin g in each of the directories you have copied over:

```
% cat *.?? | uncompress | (cd /usr/local/src/R4/; tar xvf -)
```

While you are waiting for it to finish, read the release notes.

THE COMMERCIAL WORLD

The following consulting firms can ship you any X release or document your heart desires:

Integrated Computer Solutions
163 Harvard Street
Cambridge, MA 02139
(617) 547-0510
info@ics.com
uunet!ics.com!info

O'Reilly and Associates
632 Petaluma Avenue
Sebastopol, CA 95472
(800) 338-6887

In addition, the following workstation and software vendors include the X Window System in their products:

AT&T, Apple, Bull, DEC, Data General, Everex, Hewlett-Packard, IBM, IXI Limited, Intel, Interactive Systems, Motorola, NCR, Open Software Foundation, SCO, Solbourne, Sony, Sun Microsystems, Visix, and many more every day.

Appendix C

A Unix Makefile for the Example Source Code

The `make` program is a Unix program designed to help maintain software development projects. The `Makefile` has been set up to compile and link the example programs in this book. If you normally use `Makefiles`, `make` can simplify the steps needed to compile and link the example programs.

In each chapter, the proper Unix commands for using make were described.

CUSTOMIZING THE Makefile FOR YOUR SYSTEM

We've tried to make this set-up as simple as possible, but with the plethora of systems many different installations are available. So, before you get going, be sure to check for the system-specific customizations.

The basic things you need to check in the `Makefile` are the C compiler and the Libraries variable.

THE C COMPILER

`CC` is a `make` variable set to the command needed to invoke the C compiler. For most Unix-based systems, this will be simply `cc`, plus the necessary flags.

For example, on X11 Release 2, on a Mac IIx:

```
CC=     cc -O -DmacII -DX11R2
```

We included the `Xos.h` file in `xbook.h` (which is, in turn, included in every example source file). Inside `Xos.h`, there are a few tricky `#ifdefs`, so you may need to look there.

You should define the system you are running under, as needed by the include file `<X11/Xos.h>`, and also define which version of X you are running (although only the presence—or lack of—X11R4 is important). We've used:

`-Dsun`	on Sun Microsystems computers
`-DmacII`	on Apple Mac IIx's
`-Di386`	on Interactive 386.ix on 386 PCs
`-Dhpux`	on Hewlett-Packard's HP-UX

If you use the GNU project C compiler, you might use `gcc` rather than `cc`. Depending on your version of GNU C, you may need to call `gcc` with certain options.

THE LIBRARIES VARIABLE

If your X Window System libraries are installing in `/usr/lib`, you should be able to link in the `libX11.a library` by setting `LIBRARIES` to:

```
LIBRARIES=      -lX11
```

(All of the code in this book uses the Xlib. We did not use any toolkits.)

If your Xlib library is not in `/usr/lib`, you will need to customize this.

Also, if you are running Interactive's 386/ix operating system for 386 machines and you installed the TCP/IP developer's system, you will probably need to also link in the inet library, after the X11 library:

```
LIBRARIES=      -lX11 -linet
```

You will notice this problem if you get a lot of link errors for unresolved externals. For example:

```
inet_addr
gethostbyname
bcopy
htons
socket
setsockopt
```

If you have problems with the `Makefile`, just skip it. Each program is described with the C modules it needs, so you can compile and link by hand. Since there are a rather small number of C source files, it isn't worth major hassles if you have problems with make.

COMPILING EVERYTHING

To compile all the example programs, try:

```
make all
```

This might take some time, as every program will be updated.

Makefile FOR THE EXAMPLE PROGRAMS

The contents of `Makefile` are as follows:

Makefile:

```
#
#   Makefile for Advanced X Window Applications Programming
#
```

```
#------------------- C Compiler and Operating System-----------------
#   You will need to configure a few things to compile the example
#   sources. First, set up the C compiler (usually cc or gcc)
#   and any flags needed. Most of the flags come from the include
#   file X11/Xos.h, and some of them include:
#   i386    for Interactive's 386/ix on 386 PCs
#   hpux    for Hewlett-Packard's HP-UX
#   macII   for Apple Macintoshes running A/UX
#   sun     for Sun Microsystem's SunOS workstations
#
#   You may need to look in Xos.h to find the proper flags for
#   your system. Usually, add a -Dsymbol to the CC variable
#   below, e.g., -Dhpux if you are running HP-UX.
#
#-------------------Version of X11 ----------------------------------
#   X has, as yet, no easy sure-fire way to tell if you are
#   compiling under a X11R4 or X11R3 or X11R2 system. In general,
#   we've been careful to include no difference in our sources
#   between X11R2 and X11R3. With Release 4, however, the Xlib
#   has undergone some major changes, especially in the official
#   means to communicate with window managers. If your are using
#   X11R4, be sure to add a define, e.g., -DX11R4.
#
#------------------ Examples -----------------------------------------
#       1) Sun SPARCStation-1 running X11R4, using standard C compiler
#CC=    cc -O -Dsun -DX11R4
#
#       2) Apple macintosh IIx running X11R2
#CC=    cc -O -DmacII -DX11R2
#
#       3) Interactive 386/ix running X11R3
#CC=    cc -O -Di386 -DX11R3
#       (Note: with Interactive, you may need to link in the inet library.)
#
#
CC=     cc -O -DmacII -DX11R2
#
#
#-------------- Libraries for Xlib ----------------------------------
#   Usually, you can just add a line -lX11 to link in the standard
#   X11 Xlib library. You should not need any other X libraries
#   to compile and link the example sources. If you are running
#   386/ix, however, you may need to link in the inet library, e.g.,
#   -linet. If you placed your Xlib library in a non-standard place,
#   you may need to have a -L<library-path> option. See your
#   C compiler manual for details.
```

```
#
#   Examples
#   1) Most every one.
#LIBRARIES=    -lX11
#
#   2) 386/ix
#LIBRARIES=    -lX11 -linet
#
#
LIBRARIES=     -lX11
#----------------------------------------------------------------
#
#   Part 1
#   Part 1 develops a set of modules to help Xlib
#   application devlopment. These modules will be
#   linked to any application that needs them.
#
#
XBOOK_OBJS=    cursor.c display.o event.o \
               gc.o pixmap.o topwind.o window.o
#
#
#   All to make all items
#
all:           gumby bitview colort dinfo hosts mchat note \
               primary propinfo propsend reminder send winfo wfind wpick
# Part 1
#
# Gumby Program from Part 1, Chapter 1
gumby:         gumby.c
               $(CC) -o gumby gumby.c $(LIBRARIES)
#
#
# Bitview Program from Part 1, Chapter 9
#
BIT_OBJS=      $(XBOOK_OBJS) bitmap.o bitview.o

bitview:       $(BIT_OBJS)
               $(CC) -o bitview $(BIT_OBJS) $(LIBRARIES)
#
# dinfo, Display Information program from Part 2, Chapter 10
#
DINFO_OBJS=    dinfo.o display.o

dinfo:         $(DINFO_OBJS)
               $(CC) -o dinfo $(DINFO_OBJS) $(LIBRARIES)
```

```
#
# winfo, program to list the windows on the display, from Part 2, Chapter 11
#
WINFO_OBJS=     display.o winfo.o wprint.o wsearch.o

winfo:          $(WINFO_OBJS)
                $(CC) -o winfo $(WINFO_OBJS) $(LIBRARIES)

#
# wfind, program to list the windows on the display, from Part 2, Chapter 11
#
WFIND_OBJS=     display.o wfind.o wprint.o wsearch.o

wfind:          $(WFIND_OBJS)
                $(CC) -o wfind $(WFIND_OBJS) $(LIBRARIES)

#
# wpick program to choose a window via the mouse, from Part 2, Chapter 11
#
# PICK_OBJS are the modules needed to pick a window with the mouse.
#
PICK_OBJS= pickwind.o subwind.o wprint.o

WPICK_OBJS=     $(PICK_OBJS) display.o wpick.o

wpick:          $(WPICK_OBJS)
                $(CC) -o wpick $(WPICK_OBJS) $(LIBRARIES)

#
# propinfo, Property Information program from Part 2, Chapter 12
#
PROPINFO_OBJS=$(PICK_OBJS) atom.o bytes.o display.o font.o \
                lsprop.o propinfo.o

propinfo:       $(PROPINFO_OBJS)
                $(CC) -o propinfo $(PROPINFO_OBJS) $(LIBRARIES)

#
#
# hosts, program to list allowed hosts, from Part 2, Chapter 13
#
HOST_OBJS=      display.o hosts.o lshosts.o

hosts:          $(HOST_OBJS)
                $(CC) -o hosts $(HOST_OBJS) $(LIBRARIES)
```

```
#
# ColorT (Color Table) Program From Part 2, Chapter 14
#
COLOR_OBJS=     color.o colort.o cursor.o display.o event.o gc.o font.o \
                topwind.o window.o

colort:     $(COLOR_OBJS)
                $(CC) -o colort $(COLOR_OBJS) $(LIBRARIES)

# propsend, A propgram to send data to a property on the root window,
# from Part 3, Chapter 17
#
# PROP_OBJS are common property-related object modules
#
PROP_OBJS=          atom.o bytes.o error.o icccm.o prop.o xstring.o

PROPSEND_OBJS= $(XBOOK_OBJS) $(PROP_OBJS) button.o font.o \
                    propsend.o textedit.o

propsend:       $(PROPSEND_OBJS)
                $(CC) -o propsend $(PROPSEND_OBJS) $(LIBRARIES)

#
# reminder, A program that notices property changes on the root window
# from Part 3, Chapter 17
#
REMINDER_OBJS=$(XBOOK_OBJS) $(PROP_OBJS) button.o font.o \
                reminder.o

reminder:       $(REMINDER_OBJS)
                $(CC) -o reminder $(REMINDER_OBJS) $(LIBRARIES)

#
# send, a KeyPress XEvent sender, from Part 3, Chapter 18
#
SEND_OBJS=      $(XBOOK_OBJS) $(PROP_OBJS) button.o font.o \
                pickwind.o send.o sendev.o subwind.o textedit.o

send:           $(SEND_OBJS)
                $(CC) -o send $(SEND_OBJS) $(LIBRARIES)

#
# primary, PRIMARY Selection viewer, from Part 3, Chapter 19
#
PROPERTY_OBJS=      atom.o bytes.o error.o icccm.o prop.o \
                    sel_own.o sel_prop.o xstring.o
```

```
PRIMARY_OBJS=       $(XBOOK_OBJS) button.o primary.o select.o font.o \
                    $(PROPERTY_OBJS)

primary:            $(PRIMARY_OBJS)
                    $(CC) -o primary $(PRIMARY_OBJS) $(LIBRARIES)

#
# mchat, multi-display chat program, from Part 4, Chapter 21
MCHAT_OBJS=     $(XBOOK_OBJS) $(PROP_OBJS) button.o font.o mchat.o \
                textedit.o

mchat:          $(MCHAT_OBJS)
                $(CC) -o mchat $(MCHAT_OBJS) $(LIBRARIES)

#
#
# note, a multi-display notifier, from Part 4, Chapter 22
#
NOTE_OBJS=      $(XBOOK_OBJS) $(PROPERTY_OBJS) button.o font.o note.o \
                notesend.o textedit.o

note:           $(NOTE_OBJS)
                $(CC) -o note $(NOTE_OBJS) $(LIBRARIES)

#
#   end of file
#
```

Appendix D

Utility Functions Created In This Book

At the end of each chapter the utility functions created in that particular chapter are listed. This appendix is designed to provide an overview of these functions and to serve as a reference for anyone who wants to adopt (or adapt) a utility function to fit a particular need.

CHAPTER 2

`CheckDisplayName()` is passed to the C command-line parameters: `argc` (the number of parameters) and `argv` (a list of parameter strings). It fills in a `display_name` string.

```
CheckDisplayName( argc, argv, display_name )

int         argc;
char        *argv[];
char        display_name[];
```

`CloseDisplay()` frees common resources and closes the display connection. It is usually called when a program is just about to exit.

```
CloseDisplay( display, window, gc )

Display     *display;
Window      window;
GC          gc;
```

`OpenDisplay()` takes a display name and opens a connection to an X server.

```
Display     *OpenDisplay( display_name, screen )

char        display_name[];
int         screen;
```

`SetUpDisplay()` acts like `OpenDisplay()`, but exits if an error occurs and checks the command-line parameters for a display name.

```
Display     *SetUpDisplay( argc, argv, screen )

int argc;
char        *argv[];
int         *screen;
```

`QuitX()` prints out an error message (to `stderr`) and then calls `XCloseDisplay()`. It then finally calls `exit()` to terminate the program. Use `QuitX()` if you detect an error and need to quickly exit the program.

```
QuitX( display, error_message, error_file )

Display     *display;
char        error_message[], error_file[];
```

CHAPTER 3

CheckGeometry() searches through the command-line parameters (argc, argv) for a geometry specification and then sets x, y, width, height accordingly. You should place default values in x, y, width, and height since CheckGeometry() won't write over a value unless it was set in a geometry specification.

```
CheckGeometry( argc, argv, screen_width, screen_height, x, y, width,
height )

int         argc;
char        *argv[];
int         screen_width, screen_height;
int         *x, *y, *width, *height;
```

CreateWindow() helps create a window and gets it to appear on the screen.

```
Window
CreateWindow(display,parent,x,y,width,height,border,fore,back,events)

Display          *display;
Window           parent;
int              x, y, width, height, border;
unsigned long    fore, back; /* color pixel values */
long             events;     /* desired event mask */
```

MapWindow() maps a window and any subwindows.

```
MapWindow( display, window )

Display     *display;
Window      window;
```

NameWindow() sets the window's name, icon name and class. It also depends on the symbol X11R4.

```
NameWindow( display, window, name, class_name, class_type )

Display     *display;
Window      window;
char        *name;
```

```
char        *class_name;
char        *class_type;
```

`SetNormalHints()` hides most of the incompatibilities in setting the `WM_NORMAL_HINTS` property. Be sure to define X11R4 if needed.

```
SetNormalHints( display, window, x, y, width, height )

Display     *display;
Window      window;
int         x, y, width, height;  /* size and location of the window */
```

`SetWMHints()` takes a display, a window and a pixmap to be used as an icon. It also isolates X11R4 incompatibilities.

```
SetWMHints( display, window, icon )

Display     *display;
Window      window;
Pixmap      icon;
```

CHAPTER 4

`MakeGC()` creates a graphics context.

```
GC MakeGC( display, drawable, fore, back )

Display             *display;
Drawable            drawable;
unsigned long       fore, back; /* color pixel values */
```

`SetGC()` sets both the foreground and the background colors of the display. This is a convenience routine, used mainly by code that wants to reverse video (sets the background to fore and the foreground to back).

```
SetGC( display, gc, fore, back )

Display             *display;
GC                  gc;
unsigned long       fore, back;
```

CHAPTER 5

CheckEvent() returns True for an interesting event and False if no interesting event has arrived.

```
CheckEvent( display, want_exposes, width, height, event, keysym )

Display    *display;
int        want_exposes;
int        width, height; /* -- Size of application's top-level window */
XEvent     *event;
KeySym     *keysym;
```

Key2KeySym() converts an X event (KeyPress or KeyRelease event) into a KeySym.

```
KeySym  Key2Keysym( keyevent )

XKeyEvent        *keyevent;
```

LastTimeStamp() returns the last-known timestamp for an event. Some event types do not come with a timestamp. It takes no parameters.

```
Time LastTimeStamp()
```

NextEvent() blocks until an "interesting" event has arrived from the X server.

```
NextEvent( display, want_exposes, width, height, event, keysym )

Display    *display;
int        want_exposes;
int        width, height; /* -- Size of application's top-level window */
XEvent     *event;
KeySym     *keysym;
```

ParseEvent() filters out MappingNotify events, among others. In addition, on KeyPress events ParseEvent() will translate the key code into a portable X KeySym, and return the KeySym value. Thus, ParseEvent() is a handy way to filter many X events so that your event loop just has to deal with interesting events.

```
ParseEvent( event, want_exposes, width, height, keysym )

XEvent      *event;
int         want_exposes;
int         width, height;
KeySym      *keysym;
```

CHAPTER 6

ClearPixmap() clears a pixmap with its background color. When done, ClearPixmap() resets the pixmap's GC to the proper foreground color.

```
ClearPixmap( display, pixmap, gc, fore, back, width, height )

Display            *display;
Pixmap             pixmap;
GC                 gc;
unsigned long      fore, back;
int                width,height;
```

CreatePixmap() creates a pixmap and a graphics context for the pixmap. It will terminate the program if the pixmap cannot be created , with a call to QuitX().

```
Pixmap CreatePixmap( display, window, width, height, depth, fore, back, gc )

Display            *display;
Window             window;
int                width, height, depth;
unsigned long      fore, back;
GC                 *gc;
```

LoadBitmap() creates a one-plane pixmap from an X bitmap file and then returns the pixmap, width, and height. If the given bitmap file cannot be loaded, this function calls QuitX(), which will terminate the program. You may want to recover from these errors instead.

```
Pixmap LoadBitmap( display, window, filename, width, height )

Display     *display;
Window      window;
```

```
char        filename[];              /* -- name of bitmap(1)-format file */
int         *width, *height;         /* -- returned size of the bitmap */
```

CHAPTER 7

MakeCursor() creates a cursor resource in the X server and then sets a given window to use that cursor.

```
Cursor      MakeCursor( display, window, which_cursor )

Display            *display;
Window             window;
unsigned int       which_cursor;
```

CHAPTER 8

CheckFontName() checks the command line for a font specification.

```
CheckFontName( argc, argv, fontname )

int         argc;
char        *argv[];
char        fontname[];
```

LoadFont() checks for a font name and tries to load it. Failing that, it loads a default font.

```
XFontStruct *LoadFont( display, gc, argc, argv, default_name )

Display     *display;
GC          gc;
int         argc;
char        *argv[];
char        default_name[];
```

CHAPTER 9

`TopWindow()` creates the top-level window, as well as a graphics context and an icon.

```
Window TopWindow( display, x, y, width, height,
          bitmap_data, bitmap_width, bitmap_height, icon, gc )

Display             *display;
int                 x, y, width, height;
char                *bitmap_data;
int                 bitmap_width, bitmap_height;
Pixmap              *icon;
GC                  *gc;
```

CHAPTER 10

`GetDisplayInfo()` sets up a display connection and then gets information about the given X display. This information is printed to `stdout`.

```
GetDisplayInfo( display_name )

char    *display_name;
```

`GetScreenInfo()` prints out information about a given screen on a given display.

```
GetScreenInfo( display, screen )

Display    *display;
int        screen;
```

`GetVisualInfo()` lists out the visuals available on a screen.

```
GetVisualInfo( display, screen )

Display    *display;
int        screen;
```

ListExtensions() lists out the names of the X server extensions available on a given display.

```
ListExtensions( display )

Display *display;
```

CHAPTER 11

PickWindow() grabs control of the mouse pointer and waits until the user presses a mouse button. Then, it searches through the window hierarchy to find the lowest window in the hierarchy that the mouse pointer is over. If no such window is found, PickWindow() returns the rootwindow.

```
Window PickWindow( display, rootwindow, cursor )

Display    *display;
Window     rootwindow;
Cursor     cursor;
```

FindSubWindow() finds the lowest-level window that contains the coordinates x and y (as passed in the event structure: event.xbutton.x and event.xbutton.y).

```
Window FindSubWindow( display, topwindow, window_to_check, x, y )

Display *display; Window topwindow, window_to_check; int x, y;
```

PrintWinInfo() prints out information about a particular window.

```
PrintWinInfo( display, window )

Display *display; Window window;
```

SearchWindowTree() returns a window ID (of type Window) or None if no matching window was found. SearchWindowTree() will call itself recursively to traverse depth-first down the window hierarchy.

```
Window SearchWindowTree( display, parent,
starting_window,level,compare_func)
```

```
Display     *display;
Window      parent;
Window      starting_window; /* -- Where we start */
int         level; /* -- How far down are we? */
Window      (*compare_func)(); /* -- is this the one? */
```

CHAPTER 12

`ListWProperties()` lists out the names of all properties associated with the given window on the given display. This information is printed to `stdout`.

```
ListWProperties( display, window, string )

Display     *display;
Window      window;
char        string[];
```

CHAPTER 13

`ListHosts()` calls the Xlib routine `XListHosts()` to get an array of structures, one for each host with access permission for the given X display.

```
ListHosts( display )

Display *display;
```

CHAPTER 14

`GetColor()` converts a color name to a pixel value. It is passed a default color used if no color cells are available in the colormap , or if the color database does not have the color you want.

```
unsigned long GetColor( display, name, colormap, default_color )

Display             *display;
char                name[];  /* -- name of color we want, like LimeGreen */
```

```
Colormap         colormap; /* -- Colormap to use */
unsigned long    default_color;  /* -- What to return on failure */
```

CHAPTER 15

`Bytes2Long()` converts four bytes on data into a long number.

```
unsigned long Bytes2Long( data )

char    *data;
```

`ConvertIntegers()` takes a stream of data bytes (data) and converts the data into 4-byte (32-bit) integers, and then converts the integers to text strings. If the format is `XA_WINDOW`, then the text strings will be in hex.

```
ConvertIntegers( data, number_items, string, format )

char        data[];
long        number_items;
char        string[];
Atom        format;
```

`GetHostName()` does the obvious.

```
GetHostName( name )

char    *name;
```

`GetUserName()` gets the current user name, if possible.

```
GetUserName( name )

char    *name;
```

`IsDeleteWindow()` checks if an incoming `ClientMessage` event is really a `WM_PROTOCOLS` request for deleting the window (`WM_DELETE_WINDOW`).

```
IsDeleteWindow( display, event )
```

```
Display                 *display;
XClientMessageEvent     *event;
```

`Long2Bytes()` converts the four bytes of a long integer into four straight bytes of data.

```
Long2Bytes( l, data )

long      l;
char      data[];
```

`SetICCCM()` sets properties associated with an application's top-level window for both a session manager and a window manager.

```
SetICCCM( display, window, argc, argv )

Display    *display;
Window     window; i
nt         argc;
char       *argv[];
```

`SetProtocols()` sets up the `WM_PROTOCOLS` for the given window on the given display.

```
SetProtocols( display, window )

Display    *display;
Window     window;
```

The `SetWMClientMachine()` function sets the `WM_CLIENT_MACHINE` property on a given window:

```
SetWMClientMachine( display, window )

Display    *display;
Window     window;
```

CHAPTER 16

ButtonEvent() is a function that traps events for push buttons. It examines an incoming event and determines if the event pertains to any push-buttons in use. If so, ButtonEvent() acts on the event and returns True. A return of True tells the main application event loop that ButtonEvent() handled the event. A return of False means that the event did not pertain to any push button.

```
ButtonEvent( display, event )

Display     *display;
XEvent      *event;
```

CreateButton() creates a push button and stores all the necessary information in the AppButtons array. Each button requires a GC and that a window be created.

```
CreateButton( display, window, x, y, fore, back, font_id, text, function )

Display           *display;
Window            window;           /* -- bounding window, e.g., parent */
int               x, y;
unsigned long     fore, back;
Font              font_id;
char              text[];
int               (*function)();
```

TextEdit() is a simple function that edits text strings. You pass TextEdit(), a KeySym that was generated by a KeyPress event. TextEdit() then handles delete (and backspace, too; both are treated the same here) or plain ASCII characters.

```
TextEdit( display, window, gc, font, x, y, keysym, data, max_size )

Display           *display;
Window            window;           /* -- Where to do the editing */
GC                gc;               /* -- How to draw the text */
XFontStruct       *font;            /* -- for checking widths of strings */
int               x, y;             /* -- Where the data string starts */
KeySym            keysym;           /* -- Key entered */
char              data[];           /* -- the current data string */
int               max_size;         /* -- The largest #bytes for data */
```

CHAPTER 17

`AppendProperty()` appends data to a property.

```
AppendProperty( display, window, property, target, format, data, number_items )

Display     *display;
Window      window;
Atom        property;
Atom        target;
int         format;
char        *data;
int         number_items;
```

`ErrorHandler()` does the obvious.

```
ErrorHandler( display, error_event )

Display             *display;
XErrorEvent         *error_event;


NoError()
```

`NoError()` returns `True` if the `GLOBAL ErrorFlag` does not store an X error. `NoError()` is usually combined with `ResetErrorFlag()` so that you can reset the `ErrorFlag` with `ResetErrorFlag()`, perform an X call that could generate an error, especially property-writing routines, and then call `NoError()` to check and see if an error occurred.

`ResetErrorFlag()` resets the error flag. (See `NoError()`.)

```
ResetErrorFlag();

/*
 * Append data to property
 */

...
```

```
    /*
     * Check if an error occurred
     */
    if ( NoError() )
        {
        /* A-OK */
        }
```

SetErrorHandler() overrides the default Xlib error handler with the function ErrorHandler().

```
SetErrorHandler()

/*
 * Note that in X11R4, XSetErrorHandler() returns
 * the previous error-handler function.  In Release
 * 3 and below, though, XSetErrorHandler() does not
 * return the previous handler.  So, to write portable
 * code, we ignore the previous error handler.
 */

{   /* -- function SetErrorHandler */
    int       ErrorHandler();

    (void) XSetErrorHandler( ErrorHandler );

}        /* -- function SetErrorHandler */
```

CHAPTER 18

SendKeyCode() sends a KeyPress event to a given window on a given display. To keep up with the symmetry in X, SendKeyCode() also sends a KeyRelease event, to better mimic the action of a real keyboard.

```
SendKeyCode( display, window, keycode, state )

Display     *display;
Window      window;
KeyCode     keycode;
int         state;
```

`SendKeysym()` checks if a given character is upper case (using a U.S. ASCII-based test) and sets the proper modifier state for the call to `SendKeyCode()`. Next, `SendKeysym()` calls `XKeysymToKeycode()` to translate the portable `KeySym` to a system-specific KeyCode.

```
SendKeysym( display, window, keysym )

Display    *display;
Window     window;
KeySym     keysym;
```

`SendString()` calls `SendKeysym()` for each character in the input string and adds a carriage return at the end.

```
SendString( display, window, string )

Display    *display;
Window     window;
char       string[];
```

CHAPTER 19

`AskPrimaryData()` calls `XConvertSelection()` to ask for the contents of the `PRIMARY` selection, with a given target type.

```
AskPrimaryData( display, window, property, target, timestamp )

Display    *display;
Window     window;
Atom       property;
Atom       target;
Time       timestamp;
```

`AssertOwnership()` asserts ownership of a selection and checks if the attempt was successful.

```
AssertOwnership( display, window, selection, timestamp )

Display    *display;
```

```
Window     window;
Atom       selection;
Time       timestamp;
```

`GetPropertyData()` gets the data from the given property on the given window and converts that data into a string, storing the string in the global `PropertyData`.

```
GetPropertyData( display, window, property, target )

Display    *display;
Window     window;
Atom       property;
Atom       target;
```

`GetSelectionData()` handles most errors from an incoming `SelectionRequest` event.

```
GetSelectionData( display, window, event )

Display           *display;
Window            window;
XSelectionEvent   *event;
```

`GetTargetData()` collects the different types of data and prepare the raw data bytes, which will be later written to the requesting program's window.

```
GetTargetData( display, window, target, type, string, format )

Display    *display;
Window     window;
Atom       target;
Atom       type;
char       string[];
int        *format;
```

`OwnPrimary()` hides some of the details of asserting ownership of the `PRIMARY` selection (the built-in atom `XA_PRIMARY`) and sets up a number of global variables if the attempt was successful.

```
OwnPrimary( display, window, timestamp )

Display    *display;
```

```
Window      window;
Time        timestamp;
```

PutPropertyData() places data in the given property on the given window. The data either comes from the global PropertyData or from various values stored with the program: for example, original_window, user name, and application name .

```
PutPropertyData( display, original_window, window, property, target )

Display     *display;
Window      original_window,
window;     Atom property;
Atom        target;
```

PutSelectionData() answers a SelectionRequest event. First, PutSelectionData() checks the event fields, then it checks if the target type is MULTIPLE. The MULTIPLE type is a special magic type that allows a requester to ask for many types of data at once.

```
PutSelectionData( display, window, event )

Display                  *display;
Window                   window;
XSelectionRequestEvent   *event;
```

SendSelectNotify() sets up a return event.

```
SendSelectNotify( display, window, selection, property, target, timestamp )

Display     *display;
Window      window;
Atom        selection, property, target;
Time        timestamp;
```

Appendix E

Release 4 Enhanced Color Data Base

One of the many complaints about Release 3 of the X Window System was that the colors named in the RGB (Red Green Blue) data base didn't match up with their names on many monitors. In Release 4, this data base has been dramatically improved—growing from 66 basic color entries to over 600. The colors look much better with the newer release. Most users won't need "peru," "gainsboro," four shades of maroon, or other new colors. But, the improvements are worth it and it's best to try to stick to the default color database names. Remember, colormap cells are a scarce resource on most systems. Leave the extra colormap entries for the medical imaging, finite element analysis, and other packages that really need colormap cells.

Many entries below are doubled. In addition, both "grey" and "gray" are generally accepted spellings. The numbers are the Red, Green, Blue (RGB) numeric values, and the names are names you can use with a call to `XLookupColor()`. See chapter 14 for more information on color in X.

Red Grn Blue	Color Name	Red Grn Blue	Color Name
220 220 220	gainsboro	161 161 161	gray63
240 255 240	honeydew	252 252 252	gray99
255 228 225	mistyrose	0 191 255	deep sky blue
112 128 144	slategrey	0 100 0	darkgreen
135 206 235	skyblue	189 183 107	dark khaki
176 196 222	light steel blue	245 222 179	wheat
224 255 255	lightcyan	255 140 0	dark orange
50 205 50	limegreen	255 127 80	coral
154 205 50	yellowgreen	147 112 219	medium purple
218 165 32	goldenrod	216 191 216	thistle
205 133 63	peru	205 179 139	navajowhite3
255 160 122	light salmon	255 250 205	lemonchiffon1
199 21 133	medium violet red	240 255 240	honeydew1
139 137 137	snow4	187 255 255	paleturquoise1
238 213 183	bisque2	238 180 34	goldenrod2
205 183 158	bisque3	238 197 145	burlywood2
240 255 255	azure1	139 90 43	tan4
131 111 255	slateblue1	238 118 33	chocolate2
71 60 139	slateblue4	139 35 35	brown4
135 206 255	skyblue1	255 52 179	maroon1
141 182 205	lightskyblue3	238 48 167	maroon2
102 139 139	paleturquoise4	191 62 255	darkorchid1
142 229 238	cadetblue2	171 130 255	mediumpurple1
69 139 116	aquamarine4	255 225 255	thistle1
0 238 118	springgreen2	238 210 238	thistle2
192 255 62	olivedrab1	205 181 205	thistle3
238 238 0	yellow2	41 41 41	gray16
205 155 29	goldenrod3	59 59 59	gray23
139 105 20	goldenrod4	64 64 64	grey25
255 211 155	burlywood1	69 69 69	gray27
205 133 0	orange3	89 89 89	gray35
205 79 57	tomato3	105 105 105	gray41
178 58 238	darkorchid2	112 112 112	grey44
85 26 139	purple4	115 115 115	gray45
159 121 238	mediumpurple2	135 135 135	grey53
66 66 66	gray26	189 189 189	gray74
84 84 84	gray33	0 0 128	navy blue
87 87 87	grey34	0 191 255	deepskyblue
94 94 94	gray37	0 250 154	medium spring green
112 112 112	gray44		

107	142	35	olive drab	46	139	87	seagreen
184	134	11	darkgoldenrod	124	252	0	lawngreen
188	143	143	rosybrown	0	255	0	green
139	69	19	saddle brown	255	255	224	lightyellow
178	34	34	firebrick	184	134	11	dark goldenrod
208	32	144	violetred	165	42	42	brown
255	250	250	snow1	238	130	238	violet
193	205	205	azure3	186	85	211	medium orchid
122	103	238	slateblue2	139	121	94	navajowhite4
105	89	205	slateblue3	255	255	240	ivory1
0	178	238	deepskyblue2	131	139	131	honeydew4
0	154	205	deepskyblue3	0	191	255	deepskyblue1
0	104	139	deepskyblue4	162	205	90	darkolivegreen3
83	134	139	cadetblue4	205	190	112	lightgoldenrod3
238	173	14	darkgoldenrod2	255	185	15	darkgoldenrod1
205	149	12	darkgoldenrod3	139	115	85	burlywood4
139	101	8	darkgoldenrod4	255	231	186	wheat1
255	106	106	indianred1	205	102	29	chocolate3
139	126	102	wheat4	139	69	19	chocolate4
255	165	79	tan1	238	169	184	pink2
255	48	48	firebrick1	139	71	137	orchid4
238	149	114	lightsalmon2	0	0	0	gray0
255	127	0	darkorange1	10	10	10	grey4
255	62	150	violetred1	13	13	13	grey5
238	58	140	violetred2	43	43	43	grey17
205	50	120	violetred3	74	74	74	gray29
26	26	26	gray10	77	77	77	grey30
33	33	33	gray13	117	117	117	grey46
82	82	82	gray32	120	120	120	gray47
92	92	92	gray36	120	120	120	grey47
156	156	156	grey61	122	122	122	grey48
166	166	166	gray65	140	140	140	grey55
194	194	194	grey76	143	143	143	grey56
201	201	201	grey79	145	145	145	grey57
214	214	214	gray84	217	217	217	grey85
237	237	237	gray93	224	224	224	grey88
255	255	255	grey100	253	245	230	oldlace
255	250	240	floralwhite	250	240	230	linen
255	250	205	lemon chiffon	230	230	250	lavender
119	136	153	light slate grey	255	228	225	misty rose
0	0	205	mediumblue	47	79	79	darkslategrey
30	144	255	dodger blue	105	105	105	dim grey
70	130	180	steelblue	119	136	153	lightslategrey
64	224	208	turquoise	0	0	128	navyblue
102	205	170	medium aquamarine	135	206	250	lightskyblue
46	139	87	sea green	0	206	209	dark turquoise

Red	Green	Blue	Name
0	206	209	**darkturquoise**
34	139	34	**forestgreen**
250	250	210	**light goldenrod yellow**
188	143	143	**rosy brown**
205	92	92	**indianred**
245	245	220	**beige**
255	20	147	**deeppink**
199	21	133	**mediumvioletred**
153	50	204	**dark orchid**
205	175	149	**peachpuff3**
139	131	134	**lavenderblush4**
0	0	139	**blue4**
16	78	139	**dodgerblue4**
122	139	139	**lightcyan4**
78	238	148	**seagreen2**
124	205	124	**palegreen3**
139	105	105	**rosybrown4**
205	85	85	**indianred3**
139	58	58	**indianred4**
205	112	84	**salmon3**
139	76	57	**salmon4**
205	129	98	**lightsalmon3**
139	87	66	**lightsalmon4**
238	64	0	**orangered2**
255	20	147	**deeppink1**
205	150	205	**plum3**
20	20	20	**gray8**
23	23	23	**gray9**
28	28	28	**gray11**
31	31	31	**gray12**
54	54	54	**grey21**
97	97	97	**gray38**
115	115	115	**grey45**
138	138	138	**grey54**
145	145	145	**gray57**
179	179	179	**gray70**
196	196	196	**grey77**
199	199	199	**grey78**
219	219	219	**gray86**
222	222	222	**gray87**
224	224	224	**gray88**
242	242	242	**gray95**
245	245	245	**gray96**
247	247	247	**gray97**
255	250	240	**floral white**

Red	Green	Blue	Name
250	235	215	**antique white**
240	248	255	**aliceblue**
211	211	211	**light gray**
30	144	255	**dodgerblue**
102	205	170	**mediumaquamarine**
0	100	0	**dark green**
240	230	140	**khaki**
238	221	130	**lightgoldenrod**
255	105	180	**hot pink**
255	182	193	**light pink**
139	131	120	**antiquewhite4**
92	172	238	**steelblue2**
0	197	205	**turquoise3**
82	139	139	**darkslategray4**
127	255	212	**aquamarine1**
180	238	180	**darkseagreen2**
155	205	155	**darkseagreen3**
84	255	159	**seagreen1**
0	139	69	**springgreen4**
139	139	122	**lightyellow4**
139	117	0	**gold4**
238	180	180	**rosybrown2**
238	99	99	**indianred2**
238	121	66	**sienna2**
238	59	59	**brown2**
139	10	80	**deeppink4**
255	0	255	**magenta1**
255	131	250	**orchid1**
3	3	3	**grey1**
48	48	48	**grey19**
107	107	107	**grey42**
130	130	130	**grey51**
156	156	156	**gray61**
217	217	217	**gray85**
219	219	219	**grey86**
222	222	222	**grey87**
240	240	240	**gray94**
240	240	240	**grey94**
247	247	247	**grey97**
255	255	255	**gray100**
255	228	196	**bisque**
245	255	250	**mint cream**
112	128	144	**slate grey**
119	136	153	**lightslategray**
106	90	205	**slateblue**
176	224	230	**powderblue**

32	178	170	light sea green	255	64	64	brown1
173	255	47	greenyellow	255	165	0	orange1
189	183	107	darkkhaki	238	154	0	orange2
160	82	45	sienna	205	102	0	darkorange3
238	229	222	seashell2	139	95	101	lightpink4
238	203	173	peachpuff2	205	0	205	magenta3
238	233	191	lemonchiffon2	139	0	139	magenta4
58	95	205	royalblue3	145	44	238	purple2
202	225	255	lightsteelblue1	125	38	205	purple3
188	210	238	lightsteelblue2	28	28	28	grey11
144	238	144	palegreen2	38	38	38	grey15
0	255	127	springgreen1	56	56	56	gray22
118	238	0	chartreuse2	87	87	87	gray34
255	0	0	red1	102	102	102	gray40
238	18	137	deeppink2	105	105	105	grey41
139	28	98	maroon4	127	127	127	grey50
46	46	46	grey18	148	148	148	gray58
64	64	64	gray25	204	204	204	gray80
110	110	110	gray43	204	204	204	grey80
150	150	150	gray59	242	242	242	grey95
171	171	171	grey67	245	245	245	grey96
181	181	181	grey71	255	250	205	lemonchiffon
245	245	245	whitesmoke	255	240	245	lavender blush
255	222	173	navajowhite	25	25	112	midnightblue
240	248	255	alice blue	72	61	139	darkslateblue
211	211	211	lightgrey	106	90	205	slate blue
100	149	237	cornflowerblue	224	255	255	light cyan
124	252	0	lawn green	95	158	160	cadet blue
107	142	35	olivedrab	60	179	113	mediumseagreen
210	105	30	chocolate	173	255	47	green yellow
176	48	96	maroon	50	205	50	lime green
255	0	255	magenta	210	180	140	tan
205	201	201	snow3	233	150	122	darksalmon
255	239	219	antiquewhite1	255	160	122	lightsalmon
255	228	196	bisque1	255	140	0	darkorange
255	222	173	navajowhite1	240	128	128	light coral
238	207	161	navajowhite2	255	69	0	orange red
99	184	255	steelblue1	255	0	0	red
164	211	238	lightskyblue2	255	20	147	deep pink
154	192	205	lightblue3	219	112	147	pale violet red
0	229	238	turquoise2	148	0	211	darkviolet
139	134	78	khaki4	238	233	233	snow2
205	205	180	lightyellow3	39	64	139	royalblue4
255	255	0	yellow1	24	116	205	dodgerblue3
238	216	174	wheat2	176	226	255	lightskyblue1
255	127	36	chocolate1	238	230	133	khaki2

139	129	76	lightgoldenrod4
139	71	38	sienna4
255	160	122	lightsalmon1
139	69	0	darkorange4
205	0	0	red3
139	0	0	red4
205	145	158	pink3
238	0	238	magenta2
209	95	238	mediumorchid2
3	3	3	gray1
18	18	18	grey7
33	33	33	grey13
79	79	79	gray31
89	89	89	grey35
130	130	130	gray51
140	140	140	gray55
173	173	173	grey68
176	176	176	grey69
186	186	186	grey73
189	189	189	grey74
191	191	191	grey75
207	207	207	gray81
229	229	229	gray90
253	245	230	old lace
255	218	185	peach puff
47	79	79	dark slate gray
192	192	192	grey
211	211	211	lightgray
0	0	128	navy
132	112	255	light slate blue
176	224	230	powder blue
85	107	47	dark olive green
250	250	210	light goldenrod yellow
255	215	0	gold
139	69	19	saddlebrown
255	182	193	lightpink
218	112	214	orchid
139	125	107	bisque4
255	248	220	cornsilk1
224	238	224	honeydew2
104	131	139	lightblue4
105	139	34	olivedrab4
205	198	115	khaki3
255	130	71	sienna1
205	51	51	brown3
238	0	0	red2
205	104	137	palevioletred3
154	50	205	darkorchid3
104	34	139	darkorchid4
137	104	205	mediumpurple3
93	71	139	mediumpurple4
20	20	20	grey8
26	26	26	grey10
36	36	36	grey14
51	51	51	gray20
54	54	54	gray21
66	66	66	grey26
110	110	110	grey43
133	133	133	grey52
135	135	135	gray53
184	184	184	grey72
191	191	191	gray75
209	209	209	grey82
212	212	212	grey83
214	214	214	grey84
255	235	205	blanched almond
255	218	185	peachpuff
255	228	181	moccasin
245	255	250	mintcream
255	240	245	lavenderblush
119	136	153	light slate gray
192	192	192	gray
100	149	237	cornflower blue
0	0	255	blue
85	107	47	darkolivegreen
152	251	152	palegreen
127	255	0	chartreuse
250	128	114	salmon
240	128	128	lightcoral
255	192	203	pink
208	32	144	violet red
255	240	245	lavenderblush1
238	224	229	lavenderblush2
205	193	197	lavenderblush3
255	228	225	mistyrose1
139	125	123	mistyrose4
131	139	139	azure4
126	192	238	skyblue2
180	205	205	lightcyan3
118	238	198	aquamarine2
179	238	58	olivedrab2

202	255	112	darkolivegreen1	238	118	0	darkorange2
205	133	63	tan3	255	114	86	coral1
255	99	71	tomato1	139	62	47	coral4
205	41	144	maroon3	255	181	197	pink1
205	105	201	orchid3	238	162	173	lightpink2
8	8	8	grey3	139	71	93	palevioletred4
38	38	38	gray15	238	122	233	orchid2
48	48	48	gray19	255	187	255	plum1
77	77	77	gray30	139	123	139	thistle4
94	94	94	grey37	5	5	5	grey2
97	97	97	grey38	18	18	18	gray7
99	99	99	grey39	23	23	23	grey9
127	127	127	gray50	41	41	41	grey16
138	138	138	gray54	43	43	43	gray17
158	158	158	grey62	71	71	71	grey28
168	168	168	gray66	74	74	74	grey29
207	207	207	grey81	92	92	92	grey36
212	212	212	gray83	122	122	122	gray48
235	235	235	gray92	196	196	196	gray77
250	235	215	antiquewhite	199	199	199	gray78
255	235	205	blanchedalmond	201	201	201	gray79
255	248	220	cornsilk	232	232	232	grey91
47	79	79	darkslategray	235	235	235	grey92
25	25	112	midnight blue	237	237	237	grey93
135	206	235	sky blue	72	61	139	dark slate blue
135	206	250	light sky blue	65	105	225	royalblue
70	130	180	steel blue	72	209	204	medium turquoise
143	188	143	darkseagreen	0	255	255	cyan
32	178	170	lightseagreen	95	158	160	cadetblue
154	205	50	yellow green	0	255	127	springgreen
238	232	170	palegoldenrod	205	92	92	indian red
255	69	0	orangered	255	105	180	hotpink
221	160	221	plum	186	85	211	mediumorchid
205	201	165	lemonchiffon3	205	192	176	antiquewhite3
238	238	224	ivory2	139	137	112	lemonchiffon4
0	0	205	blue3	238	213	210	mistyrose2
110	123	139	lightsteelblue4	0	0	238	blue2
0	139	139	cyan4	79	148	205	steelblue3
151	255	255	darkslategray1	108	166	205	skyblue3
141	238	238	darkslategray2	209	238	238	lightcyan2
121	205	205	darkslategray3	0	134	139	turquoise4
69	139	0	chartreuse4	193	255	193	darkseagreen1
154	205	50	olivedrab3	205	205	0	yellow3
110	139	61	darkolivegreen4	255	215	0	gold1
255	193	193	rosybrown1	205	173	0	gold3
238	130	98	salmon2	238	154	73	tan2

238	44	44	firebrick2	139	99	108	pink4
255	140	105	salmon1	255	174	185	lightpink1
139	90	0	orange4	238	174	238	plum2
139	102	139	plum4	122	55	139	mediumorchid4
15	15	15	gray6	5	5	5	gray2
15	15	15	grey6	10	10	10	gray4
36	36	36	gray14	51	51	51	grey20
46	46	46	gray18	61	61	61	grey24
99	99	99	gray39	79	79	79	grey31
143	143	143	gray56	125	125	125	grey49
229	229	229	grey90	148	148	148	grey58
255	255	240	ivory	161	161	161	grey63
255	245	238	seashell	171	171	171	gray67
47	79	79	dark slate grey	186	186	186	gray73
105	105	105	dim gray	227	227	227	grey89
211	211	211	light grey	252	252	252	grey99
123	104	238	medium slate blue	248	248	255	ghostwhite
173	216	230	lightblue	105	105	105	dimgrey
175	238	238	pale turquoise	112	128	144	slategray
175	238	238	paleturquoise	132	112	255	lightslateblue
60	179	113	medium sea green	65	105	225	royal blue
255	255	0	yellow	152	251	152	pale green
222	184	135	burlywood	34	139	34	forest green
244	164	96	sandybrown	205	197	191	seashell3
233	150	122	dark salmon	139	119	101	peachpuff4
255	165	0	orange	238	232	205	cornsilk2
148	0	211	dark violet	139	136	120	cornsilk4
160	32	240	purple	205	205	193	ivory3
238	223	204	antiquewhite2	193	205	193	honeydew3
139	139	131	ivory4	224	238	238	azure2
191	239	255	lightblue1	185	211	238	slategray2
178	223	238	lightblue2	159	182	205	slategray3
0	245	255	turquoise1	108	123	139	slategray4
67	205	128	seagreen3	122	197	205	cadetblue3
46	139	87	seagreen4	105	139	105	darkseagreen4
0	255	0	green1	84	139	84	palegreen4
0	139	0	green4	0	205	102	springgreen3
127	255	0	chartreuse1	255	246	143	khaki1
238	238	209	lightyellow2	238	220	130	lightgoldenrod2
139	139	0	yellow4	255	193	37	goldenrod1
238	201	0	gold2	205	38	38	firebrick3
238	106	80	coral2	139	26	26	firebrick4
205	91	69	coral3	205	55	0	orangered3
255	69	0	orangered1	180	82	205	mediumorchid3
205	16	118	deeppink3	155	48	255	purple1
255	110	180	hotpink1	8	8	8	gray3

R	G	B	Name	R	G	B	Name
31	31	31	grey12	71	71	71	gray28
56	56	56	grey22	107	107	107	gray42
82	82	82	grey32	117	117	117	gray46
125	125	125	gray49	133	133	133	gray52
153	153	153	gray60	150	150	150	grey59
153	153	153	grey60	158	158	158	gray62
163	163	163	gray64	184	184	184	gray72
179	179	179	grey70	250	250	250	grey98
181	181	181	gray71	255	250	250	snow
227	227	227	gray89	248	248	255	ghost white
250	250	250	gray98	245	245	245	white smoke
255	222	173	navajo white	123	104	238	mediumslateblue
255	255	255	white	0	0	205	medium blue
0	0	0	black	0	255	127	spring green
112	128	144	slate gray	255	255	224	light yellow
173	216	230	light blue	238	221	130	light goldenrod
72	209	204	mediumturquoise	138	43	226	blueviolet
143	188	143	dark sea green	139	134	130	seashell4
219	112	147	palevioletred	255	218	185	peachpuff1
153	50	204	darkorchid	0	0	255	blue1
138	43	226	blue violet	54	100	139	steelblue4
147	112	219	mediumpurple	96	123	139	lightskyblue4
255	245	238	seashell1	150	205	205	paleturquoise3
205	200	177	cornsilk3	0	255	255	cyan1
30	144	255	dodgerblue1	0	238	238	cyan2
28	134	238	dodgerblue2	154	255	154	palegreen1
198	226	255	slategray1	255	236	139	lightgoldenrod1
162	181	205	lightsteelblue3	205	155	155	rosybrown3
174	238	238	paleturquoise2	205	104	57	sienna3
152	245	255	cadetblue1	13	13	13	gray5
0	205	205	cyan3	102	102	102	grey40
102	205	170	aquamarine3	209	209	209	gray82
0	238	0	green2	232	232	232	gray91
0	205	0	green3	255	239	213	papaya whip
255	255	224	lightyellow1	255	239	213	papayawhip
205	170	125	burlywood3	240	255	255	azure
205	186	150	wheat3	105	105	105	dimgray
238	92	66	tomato2	176	196	222	lightsteelblue
139	54	38	tomato4	127	255	212	aquamarine
139	37	0	orangered4	0	250	154	mediumspringgreen
205	140	149	lightpink3	238	232	170	pale goldenrod
255	130	171	palevioletred1	244	164	96	sandy brown
238	121	159	palevioletred2	255	99	71	tomato
224	102	255	mediumorchid1	205	183	181	mistyrose3
59	59	59	grey23	72	118	255	royalblue1
61	61	61	gray24	67	110	238	royalblue2

```
 74 112 139        skyblue4
224 255 255        lightcyan1
102 205   0        chartreuse3
188 238 104        darkolivegreen2
238 106 167        hotpink2
205  96 144        hotpink3
139  58  98        hotpink4
139  34  82        violetred4
  0   0   0        grey0
 69  69  69        grey27
 84  84  84        grey33
163 163 163        grey64
166 166 166        grey65
168 168 168        grey66
173 173 173        gray68
176 176 176        gray69
194 194 194        gray76
```

Bibliography

The first source of information about X is, of course, the manuals and documentation that came with your implementation of X. If you have the MIT X Consortium version of X, you should have reams and reams of online documentation, including the infamous ICCCM. If your X system comes from a computer vendor, you should have a set of manuals tuned to the particular vendor's release, such as releases from Hewlett-Packard or Apple Computer. This isn't a complete listing of all X-related books; some were released just as this book went to press, while others (such as two further volumes in the O'Reilly X series) were pending. We found the books listed here useful, although not all are directly related to X or the X library.

Gosling, James, David S. H. Rosenthal, and Michelle Arden *The NeWS Book.* New York:Springer-Verlag, 1989. ISBN 0-387-96915-2 (USA); ISBN 3-540-96915-2.

Not really on X, but later chapters cover Sun's NeWS/X11 merger.

Hopgood, F. R. A., et. al., editors. *Methodology of Window Management* . Berlin, Germany (BRD): Springer-Verlag, 1986. ISBN 3-540-16116-3; ISBN 0-387-16116-3 (USA).

This covers a very interesting conference on window systems. You can see much of where X and Sun's NeWS both came from.

Johnson, Eric F. and Kevin Reichard. *X Window Applications Programming.* Portland, OR: MIS: Press, 1989. ISBN 1-55828-016-2.

You can call 1-800-MANUALS in the USA to order.

Jones, Oliver. *Introduction to the X Window System.* Englewood Cliffs, NJ: Prentice Hall, 1989. ISBN 0-13-499997-5

Nye, Adrian. *Xlib Programming Manual*, vol. 1, 2nd printing. Sebastopol, CA: O'Reilly & Associates, 1988. ISBN 0-937175-26-9.

Nye, Adrian, ed. *Xlib Reference Manual*, vol. 2, 2nd printing. Sebastopol, CA: O'Reilly & Associates, 1988. ISBN 0-937175-27-7.

Quercia, Valerie, and Tim O'Reilly. *X Window System User's Guide,* vol. 3, 2nd edition. Sebastopol, CA: O'Reilly & Associates, 1988. ISBN 0-937175-36-6

A user's, not a programmer's, guide.

Scheifler, Robert W. *X Protocol Reference Manual*, vol. 0. Seastopol, CA: O'Reilly & Associates, 1989. ISBN 0-937175-40-0.

Basically, part II of the X Bible.

Scheifler, Robert W., James Gettys, and Ron Newman. *X Window System: C Library and Protocol.* Bedford, MA: Digital Press, 1988. ISBN 1-55558-012-2.

This is the X bible. The Release 4 updated version is expected in 1990.

Young, Douglas A. *The X Window System programming and Applications with Xt: OSF/Motif Edition.*. Englewood Cliffs, NJ: Prentice Hall, 1990. ISBN 0-13-497074-8.

Based on the Motif toolkit, but it still covers some features of Xlib.

MAGAZINE ARTICLES

Surprisingly few magazine articles have been devoted to the X Window System. Some of the better ones include:

Special section on Unix networking, supplement to November 1989 issue of *Unix World* . Includes informative articles on X terminals and X books.

Munsey, Grant J. "Moving X Window to Your Environment." *Unix World,* May 1988.

Pountain, Dick. "The X Window System," *Byte,* January 1989.

Rosenthal, David. "Going for Baroque." *Unix Review,* vol. 6, no. 6.

Also, interested researchers may want to check out proceedings from the last four years of Usenix conferences. These contain several pieces on different aspects of the X Window System.

In addition, your X installation disk should contain several articles in the doc directory; including the "Going for Baroque" piece mentioned above.

Index

A

B

C

D

E

I

K

L

M

N

O

P

Q

R

S

X

Y

ORDER FORM

PROGRAM LISTINGS ON DISKETTE

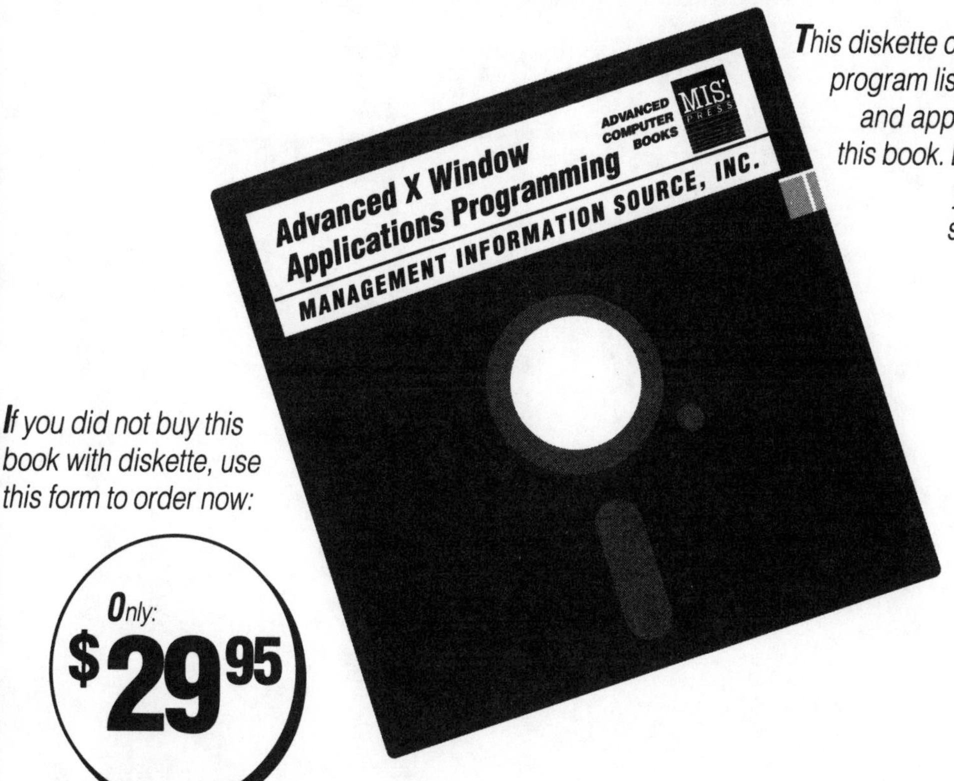

This diskette contains the complete program listings for all programs and applications contained in this book. By using this diskette, you will eliminate time spent typing in pages of program code.

If you did not buy this book with diskette, use this form to order now:

Only: $29.95

MANAGEMENT INFORMATION SOURCE, INC.
P.O. Box 5277 • Portland, OR 97208-5277
(503) 282-5215 FAX 222-7064

NAME(Please print or type) ____________________

Address ____________________

CITY ____________ STATE ______ ZIP ______

Call free
1-800-MANUALS

❑ Advanced X Window Applications Diskette only **$29.95**
Please add $2.00 for shipping and handling. (Foreign $6.00)

Check one:

❑ VISA ❑ MasterCard ❑ American Express

❑ Check enclosed $__________

ACCT. ____________________

EXP. DATE ____________________

SIGNATURE ____________________

MANAGEMENT INFORMATION SOURCE, INC.